1991

SARTRE
ALIVE

Edited by

Ronald Aronson

and

Adrian van den Hoven

〰 Wayne State University Press   Detroit

Copyright © 1991 by Wayne State University Press,
Detroit, Michigan 48202. All rights are reserved.
No part of this book may be reproduced without formal permission.
Manufactured in the United States of America.
95 94 93 92 91   5 4 3 2 1

Library of Congress Cataloging-in-Publication Data
Sartre alive / edited by Ronald Aronson and Adrian van den Hoven.
    p. cm.
    Includes bibliographical references and index.
    ISBN 0-8143-2176-3 (alk. paper).—ISBN 0-8143-2177-1 (pbk. :
alk. paper)
    1. Sartre, Jean Paul, 1905– —Criticism and interpretation.
    2. Philosophy, French—20th century. I. Aronson, Ronald, 1938–
    II. Van den Hoven, Adrian, 1939–
    PQ2637.A82Z834188   1991
    848'.91409—dc20   90-12500
                                                          CIP

The book was designed by Mary Krzewinski

CONTENTS

Contents

III. RETHINKING SARTRE: PHILOSOPHY, POLITICAL THOUGHT

IV. RETHINKING SARTRE: FICTION, BIOGRAPHY

V. SARTRE AND OTHERS

VI. A FAREWELL HOMAGE

CONTRIBUTORS

THOMAS ANDERSON is professor of philosophy at Marquette University. He is author of *The Foundation and Structure of Sartrean Ethics*, as well as numerous articles on Sartre and Gabriel Marcel. He is currently working on a book on Sartre's first and second ethics.

RONALD ARONSON is professor of humanities in Wayne State University's University Studies/Weekend College Program. He is author of *Jean-Paul Sartre: Philosophy in the World*, *The Dialectics of Disaster: A Preface to Hope*, *Sartre's Second Critique*, and *"Stay Out of Politics!" A Philosopher Views South Africa*.

HAZEL E. BARNES is Distinguished Professor of Philosophy Emerita at the University of Colorado at Boulder. She is translator of *Being and Nothingness* and *Search for a Method* and author of *Humanistic Existentialism: The Literature of Possibility*, *An Existentialist Ethics*, and *Sartre and Flaubert*.

ELIZABETH A. BOWMAN has taught French literature at Memphis State University and Middlebury College. She has written on Sartre's theater and unpublished ethics and is currently working on a book-length commentary on Sartre's unpublished dialectics of morals and history with Robert V. Stone.

MICHEL CONTAT is chair of the Sartre research group at the Institute of Modern Texts and Manuscripts (ITEM) of the French National Center of Scientific Research in Paris (CNRS). He is co-author of *The*

7

Works of Sartre, co-editor of the Pléiade edition of Sartre's writings and of *Sartre on Theatre,* and author as well of numerous essays of literary criticism.

GENEVIÈVE IDT teaches French literature at the University of Paris X-Nanterre. Author of *Le Mur de Jean-Paul Sartre: Techniques et contexte d'une provocation,* she was the secretary of the Groupe d'Etudes Sartriennes from its founding until 1989 and is now its president.

SONIA KRUKS teaches political science at Oberlin University. Her books include *The Political Philosophy of Merleau-Ponty* and *Situation and Human Existence.* She is also co-editor of *Promissory Notes: Women in the Transition to Socialism.*

MONIKA LANGER teaches philosophy at the University of Victoria, British Columbia. Her principal areas of interest include Continental philosophy, social and political issues, and philosophy of literature. She is author of *Merleau-Ponty's Phenomenology of Perception: A Guide and Commentary.*

ALAN LENNON taught philosophy for a number of years in the United States and Canada. He has also worked for the Canadian government, first with job creation programs and then as an immigration officer. He is currently on the staff of the Canada Employment and Immigration Union.

ADRIAN MIRVISH is professor of philosophy at California State University—Chico. He has published on Sartre's epistemology, ontology, and existential psychoanalysis.

PETER ROYLE is a professor of French at Trent University, Peterborough, Ontario. He is author of two books and numerous articles on Sartre and has published on a variety of topics in literary, political and philosophical journals. He is also the author of plays which have been performed in Canada and elsewhere.

WALTER SKAKOON teaches contemporary French literature and critical theory at the University of Windsor, Ontario. He is currently writing on the poetics of Sartre's biography, *Saint Genet.*

ROBERT V. STONE teaches at C.W. Post College of Long Island University. He is translator of Francis Jeanson, *Sartre and the Problem of Morality* and author of several articles on Sartre. With Elizabeth A. Bowman, he is writing a commentary on Sartre's unpublished dialectics of history and morals.

ADRIAN VAN DEN HOVEN is Head of the French Department at the University of Windsor. He is preparing a detailed study of *Nausea.* He is also editor of the *Canadian Journal of Netherlandic Studies.*

PIERRE VERSTRAETEN is professor of philosophy at the Free University of

8

Brussels. Author of *Violence et éthique,* he has also written numerous essays on Sartre, Lévi-Strauss, and Foucault.

KATHLEEN WIDER teaches philosophy at the University of Michigan—Dearborn. She has published other essays on Sartre, on the work of Thomas Nagel, and on female philosophers in ancient Greece. She is working on a book-length study of Sartre and Nagel on consciousness.

ROBERT WILCOCKS is professor of modern French literature at the University of Alberta. Editor of *Jean-Paul Sartre: A Bibliography of International Criticism,* he is currently working on two books: one, in English, on Freud's rhetoric of deception; one, in French, on Sartre's affective evolution.

PREFACE

Sartre alive: a decade after his death, Jean-Paul Sartre remains one of the freshest, most contemporary thinkers of the twentieth century. This collection includes an unpublished essay by Sartre, an interview with him appearing for the first time in English, an account of the making of the film *Sartre par lui-même* (*Sartre by Himself*), and other essays by some of the leading Sartre scholars in the world, including reflections on Sartre's unpublished and recently published works. It grew out of the second meeting of the Sartre Society of North America, held in two languages and two countries, at Detroit (Wayne State University) and Windsor, Ontario, Canada (the University of Windsor), in April 1987. We originally decided to gather some of the papers presented there because we were struck by their variety, vitality, and high quality. As the project got off the ground we received other equally fascinating contributions, and slowly a book took shape that developed its own raison d'être: to show the many ways in which Sartre's work and ideas are very much with us today. Whether in politics, philosophy, literature, or psychology—indeed, whatever the field—Jean-Paul Sartre remains alive and on people's minds today. We expect the reader to see how rich, radical, and contemporary Sartre's thought remains. Indeed, we make precisely this argument in our introductory essay, "Sartre Alive."

As this book took shape we were delighted to gain access to major pieces of Sartre's corpus unknown to the public at large. They show a sophisticated Sartre, more sensitive than has usually been thought to the close interaction of history and ethics. We present two of these in the first section, Discovering and Rediscovering Sartre. The first article is one of Sartre's rare analyses of American politics, a discussion of John F. Kennedy's 1960 victory in the West Virginia presidential primary. Ironically yet appropriately, this formed part of the notes for lectures Sartre was to give at Cornell University in April 1965 and which he canceled in protest against the American bombing of North Vietnam begun in February of that year. It appears here for the first time anywhere. We are also privileged to be able to present here the first account of notes for the Cornell lectures, entitled by Sartre *Morality and History*. This essay is by Robert Stone and Elizabeth Bowman, who are preparing a full-length study of these and other unpublished notes of Sartre's "dialectics of morals and history." This is followed by one of the most penetrating interviews ever held with Sartre, "I Am No Longer a Realist." It is a discussion with Belgian philosopher Pierre Verstraeten of the issues raised by Verstraeten's study of Sartre's theatre, *Violence et éthique*. It previously appeared in an obscure and short-lived Belgian journal, *Gulliver;* it becomes generally available for the first time in this, its first English translation.

The second section of this book is entitled Sartre's Continuing Political Relevance. One of the highlights of the Detroit/Windsor meeting was a charged discussion of the light Sartre might be able to shed on contemporary politics. Ronald Aronson reflected on the Israeli-Palestinian conflict, Alan Lennon on labor organizing, and Robert Stone on the nuclear threat to New York City. Each attempted to show how the radical—in the original meaning of "going to the root"—political and theoretical impulses of Sartre might illuminate the current situation. Because of the enthusiasm generated by that discussion and the widespread feeling that Sartre's thought has considerable applicability to today's problems, each of the discussants has here expanded his remarks into an article.

The third section, Rethinking Sartre: Philosophy, Political Thought, begins with an essay by the doyenne of American Sartre specialists, Hazel E. Barnes, a critical reexamination of the role of the ego in Sartre's thought. Professor Barnes originally presented this essay to the Sartre Society's 1988 meeting in Pittsburgh and graciously contributed it to this volume. Thomas Anderson shows how the posthumously published *Cahiers pour une morale* throws light on, and confirms, the ontology of *Being and Nothingness*. And Peter Royle clarifies the Sartrean conception of morality by an analysis of the phenomenon of evil. Pierre

Verstraeten's reconsideration of the ideas of *Violence et éthique* fifteen years later was one of the highlights of the Detroit/Windsor meeting. We present a revised version of it here as "The Revolutionary Hero Revisited."

Rethinking Sartre: Fiction, Biography, the fourth section, includes a new interpretation of the vision underlying *Nausea* by Adrian van den Hoven. Robert Wilcocks shows the striking parallels between the young and the adult Gustave Flaubert and Jean-Paul Sartre. And Walter Skakoon applies Northrop Frye's categories of Romance to Sartre's biography of Jean Genet.

The next section, Sartre and Others, shows how fruitfully Sartre may be related to other thinkers and modes of thought. Sonia Kruks shows how Sartre modified and enriched his thinking about freedom in relation to the work and thought of Simone de Beauvoir, usually considered his philosophical pupil and follower. Adrian Mirvish illuminates the phenomenon of bad faith by showing how Sartre's conception can be related to Gestalt psychology. And Kathleen Wider discusses the remarkable parallels between Sartre's and Ludwig Wittgenstein's views of the self.

We are pleased to be able to conclude with two contributions by leading French Sartre scholars, the first one published for the first time anywhere, the second appearing in English for the first time. Michel Contat, director of the Sartre group at the Centre National de la Recherche Scientifique in Paris, tells the director's story of the making of the film *Sartre by Himself.* A farewell homage concludes in the spirit of Sartre's enterprise: Geneviève Idt's study of the reception of, and her defense of, Simone de Beauvoir's *Adieux: A Farewell to Sartre.* It may seem ironic to conclude *Sartre Alive* with an essay that deals with all the gruesome details of his slow deterioration. In fact, Idt's article, which, as she told us, she put her heart and soul into, is a ringing defense of Simone de Beauvoir's graphic and unsettling description of Sartre's final years. In spite of everything, it reaffirms that Sartre lives on, in others.

We would like to thank the following people for their help and cooperation. Robert Stone and Elizabeth Bowman selected and made available their typescript of "Kennedy and West Virginia." Elizabeth Bowman translated it; Arlette Elkaïm-Sartre granted us permission to publish it here in English translation. Pierre Verstraeten provided us with his interview with Sartre; Basil Kingstone translated it. The editors translated "The Revolutionary Hero Revisited" with the assistance of Walter Skakoon. Kingstone also translated "Simone de Beauvoir's

Adieux," and the editors translated *"Sartre by Himself:* An Account, an Explanation, a Defense." The Sartre Society of North America, and especially its first chair, William L. McBride, encouraged this project from the beginning. McBride and Michel Contat read and provided helpful suggestions for our introduction and other essays. Joseph Culliton, dean of the Faculty of Arts, University of Windsor, provided financial assistance, as did the late Dean Lawrence Murphy, of the College of Lifelong Learning, Wayne State University. Yvette Bulmer, of the French Department, University of Windsor, typed and retyped many of the contributions, as did the staff of the Wayne State University Word Processing Center.

INTRODUCTION: SARTRE ALIVE

Ronald Aronson and Adrian van den Hoven

Sartre lives on, as he, perhaps unconsciously, predicted: "Even after death, our acts pursue us. We survive ourselves in them, even when they develop in opposite directions, in directions that we have not wanted."[1] Of course, there are those who would gladly bury him forever. At present, many scholars in France would prefer to study him only as an archeological curiosity, while others would dismiss him because "he has been wrong on so many issues" (they cite communism, the Soviet bloc, Cuba, Vietnam). Others again, both in France and elsewhere, continue to express the same virulence toward Sartre dead as his enemies did while he was alive. To one critic Sartre is reduced to the man who called Nabokov "déraciné"; to another he is the man who denounced Nazi collaborators after World War II while he himself did little to combat the Nazis during the Occupation. In North America, when the *New York Review of Books* got around to its own summing up, it did so through a philosophically and politically weightless attack on Sartre's entire career that dismissed everything he wrote in the forty years after *Nausea*.[2]

Still, people continue to read and study Sartre's well-known works. And a steady stream of posthumous writing continues to surprise us by its extent and variety, its richness and geniality. Sartre, who must have noticed that after their deaths writers' reputations take a nosedive, may have

15

planned it this way. His executor, Arlette Elkaïm-Sartre, Simone de Beauvoir, his disciples and friends, and others who would understand and present him have been faithfully releasing the works he held back until after his death, doing the summing up, relating the career of *Les Temps Modernes,* publishing biographies. And so Sartre's name, eclipsed during the last few years of his life, has returned to the public eye. Sartre thrives even after death, in some sense remaining in control of his reputation.

Rough spots and all, the posthumous works continue Sartre's project of reaching farther and deeper than most of us would dare. They return us to the incredible Sartrean energy we were first dazzled by, then grew accustomed to, and perhaps had once become irritated by: his insistence on tackling a dazzling variety of issues and genres, his determination to pass judgment on everything and everyone. These were traits we never ceased to be amazed by, that we found so admirable and yet obtrusive. And so, even after his death, our efforts to keep up with Sartre are exhausted by this man who always began anew. As if by design, the barrage of posthumous hostility is countered by Sartre's Freud screenplay, his ethics, his Mallarmé, his second *Critique,* his letters, his war journals. Both for and against, in biography and analysis, and, above all, in his own writings, once again we are brought face to face with the radical extravagance of Jean-Paul Sartre. Once again, in his vast, still-expanding oeuvre, in his phenomenal boundless energy, we are brought face to face with the Sartrean project. This project of recreating and presiding over the universe is so bold and presumptuous that in searching for a fitting description of it we are left with his own philosophical formulation: Sartre "is the being whose project is to be God."[3]

Sartre's Radical Extravagance

Sartre imposes himself on his century in extravagant ways, trying to become the measure of all things. Sartre wanted to be everywhere, to do everything, and to understand all. His teenage fantasy, not unusual in a bright young man attending elite schools, became an adult project. He sought, at various times and even simultaneously, to be a great writer, a great lover, a major political actor. He wanted to occupy center stage. His extravagance was not confined to his ambition. He praised others extravagantly, just as he blamed them extravagantly. Edmund Husserl "reinstated horror and charm to things. He has revived the world of artists and prophets: frightful, hostile, dangerous, with havens of grace and love."[4] Sartre showered enthusiasm on John Dos Passos and Albert Camus, on Albert Giacometti and, later on, the *gauchiste* leader Pierre

Victor (Benny Lévy). It is typical of Sartre to proclaim that they reinvented the novel, or sculpture, or politics.

Similarly, his extravagant criticism withered François Mauriac, whose career was temporarily checked by a few well-chosen words from Sartre ("God is not a novelist and neither is M. Mauriac").[5] Sartre's study of Baudelaire reeks of the same extravagant hostility (later Sartre himself called the book "a very inadequate, an extremely bad one").[6] Upon hearing about the attempted frame-up of Communist Party leader Jacques Duclos in the wake of the anti-NATO riots of 1952, Sartre violently rejected his class: "In the name of those principles which it had inculcated into me, in the name of its humanism and of its 'humanities,' in the name of liberty, equality, fraternity, I swore to the bourgeoisie a hatred which would only die with me."[7]

Sartre's antagonists lived in bad faith, were *salauds* and *cons*. "An anti-Communist is a dog. I couldn't see any way out of that one, and I never will."[8] He lacerated France for suppressing Indochina in the early 1950s, for brutally delaying Algerian independence in the late 1950s, for returning de Gaulle to power in 1958. During these years he more and more vehemently denounced colonialism along with all those who profited from and went along with it. Committed to freedom, he spread his vitriol on all sides: after the invasion of Czechoslovakia in 1968, he called for the overthrow of "the Thing" that was choking Eastern Europe; just a few months earlier he had declared his old friend Raymond Aron unfit to teach because of his opposition to the student uprising in Paris. As he grew older Sartre denounced elections as a "trap for fools"—"un piège à cons"—and rejected totally any left-wing intellectual who refused to put his or her body on the line against the system. Indeed, the *gauchiste* Sartre denounced any purely intellectual project, pleading for exemption for his biography of Flaubert only because he was too old to change his ways.

Sartre set out to conquer the world with his pen, and he more than succeeded. He published ten volumes of essays, four novels, a volume of stories, three works of psychological theory, two major works of philosophy, two short biographical sketches, one longer biography, one multivolume biography of nearly three thousand pages, one autobiography, a dozen plays and screenplays, plus a variety of occasional works. Add to this Sartre's posthumous writings. If the quantity is striking, even more remarkable is Sartre's willingness to attack all genres, comment on all subjects, claim authority in all fields: the nature of art, the nature of human reality, Freudian theory, Marxism, socialism, contemporary political questions, psychological questions, literary criticism, sculpture, painting.[9] They add up to a truly incredible outpouring of energy and brilliance.

Equally striking is Sartre's extravagant determination, once he decided to involve himself in the world, to tackle all pressing historical realities: fascism, the French paralysis before the Nazi menace, the Resistance, the Liberation, anti-Semitism, the Cold War, the problems of French communism, Algeria, the return to power of de Gaulle, neocolonialism, the meaning of Stalinism, the American war in Vietnam, the May 1968 uprising, the Israeli-Palestinian conflict, the Soviet invasion of Hungary, and, a dozen years later, of Czechoslovakia. Not only did Sartre relate to these as commentator, as writer, but he lived them as political activist, forming political organizations, speaking at rallies, circulating petitions.

Sartre's political trajectory is an unusual one. We see its roots in such an apolitical novel as *Nausea,* where he denounces the bourgeoisie as "swine." There he ridicules and parodies all conventional styles and attitudes (including the Self-Taught Man's socialist humanism), and his protagonist dreams about writing "a story . . . something that could never happen, an adventure."[10] Roquentin's literary anarchism hints that the behavior of the ruling class not only is intertwined with a systematic bad faith but is also part and parcel of its determination to remain at the top of the social hierarchy.

Sartre's first attempt at uncovering the anguish of man alone, also dating from the thirties, "The Wall," presents the protagonist being interrogated by the Falangists during the Spanish Civil War. Pablo Ibietta is taken "beyond death" and back again. Everything becomes a farce to him, including his participation on behalf of the Republic, and the consequences of his acts begin to ricochet in various tragic directions.

Sartre discovered his first real public (and thus activism) in a prisoner-of-war camp where, at Christmas 1940, he wrote and acted in a play of resistance, *Bariona.* This newfound spirit continues in his short-lived efforts under the Occupation to form a resistance group, then in writing plays and a few essays for Resistance publications. His activism rose to a peak in the late 1940s and the 1950s. And it continued unabated with the old man assuming financial and legal responsibility for New Left newspapers (including *Liberation*), indeed selling *La Cause du Peuple* on the streets of Paris. In his sixties, Sartre lent his name and his body to movement events, being smuggled into factories to speak to workers, giving his name and energy to a book-length statement of *gauchiste* philosophy, until he lost his powers.

As if all this were not enough, Sartre, along with Merleau-Ponty, founded a journal that successfully coalesced a political-intellectual trend. *Les Temps Modernes* won great respect at home and elsewhere as France's leading independent Left journal, publishing most of the important writers of the time. As one after another of its original editors departed, usually for political reasons, Sartre remained its editor-in-chief, gathering around him a close band of friends and former students.

Writer, activist, editor: it is not hyperbole to say that Sartre seeks to embrace everything. In this respect the conclusion of *The Words* is revelatory. There Sartre provides a definition of himself. He claims to be "a whole man, composed of all men and as good as all of them and not better than any."[11] This is typical language for a man who wants it all: he seeks to be all-powerful and all-inclusive, while at the same time remaining modestly immodestly modest. And so he thought and lived. Philosophically he absorbs Descartes, Husserl, and Heidegger, the ethics of Kant, Hegel's philosophy, Marxism as idea and reality. He travels to Brazil, Cuba, Africa, the Middle East, the Soviet Union, the United States. In rejecting the bourgeoisie and its institutions and honors, he seeks out its underside in the evil and blackness of Genet, his explorations of pederasty, violence, murder, and torture. At the same time this man who lives a highly privileged, dependent, and passive bourgeois way of life seeks fame and respectability, covets the Pléiade edition of his prose, enjoys honors such as the Nobel Prize even as he rejects them.

Sartre's limitless ambition appears clearly if we compare him with the authors he chooses to study. Baudelaire's achievement fades after publishing two volumes of poetry; Genet's work slowly peters out; Flaubert's greatness is embodied in a single masterpiece, *Madame Bovary*. Sartre rejects their limitations. And if we place him alongside the contemporaries with whom he broke—Camus, Aron, and Merleau-Ponty—this becomes even clearer. Each one had moments of radical politics, but each decisively rejected radical politics. Further, each *could* write about a broad range of topics and continued writing essays but also made a fundamental professional choice to limit himself. Each worked with greater stability, care, and solidity in his chosen area than Sartre did in any of his fields. However, Sartre moved in the political and historical world of Aron, *and* the philosophical world of Merleau-Ponty, *and* the literary world of Camus. And at the very least Sartre equaled their effect in their chosen areas. *Being and Nothingness* had greater impact than anything written by Merleau-Ponty, *Nausea* and *No Exit* certainly no less an impact than anything written by Camus, Sartre's political essays a greater impact than anything written by Aron.

In fact, Sartre strikes one as constantly matching himself against

19

others so that he may go them one better. Sartre seeks to be the intersecting point of his era.

Blind Spots

Sartre's blind spots are not any less extravagant. If we use the term *blind spot* literally, it is because Sartre does so himself in the *War Diaries*. There he draws interesting parallels between himself and Kaiser Wilhelm II. Upon accession to power, Wilhelm had to staff his government with men of his grandfather's generation; hence in his youth he was surrounded by Bismarck and his contemporaries. The Kaiser also suffers from a congenital disability: an atrophied arm.

This disability becomes the Kaiser's *way of being*. Sartre explicitly establishes the connection and the behavior that flows from this "signifying situation":[12]

> My own manner of being my dead eye is certainly my way of wanting to be loved through intellectual seduction; of refusing an easy abandon that would not become me and also of regretfully refusing to view films in 3-D or look through stereoscopes. I *am* that man with the blank eye only when I'm it freely. And I am it insofar as I choose myself beyond that blank eye.[13]

Is Sartre's determination to be a great writer part of the "clever seduction"? Another, connected, aspect of that choice, as well as perhaps being a response to his ugliness, was clearly to live in total disregard of his own body: the for-itself in permanent opposition to the in-itself, the nonphysical sexual being, the writer who, consuming tobacco, drugs, and alcohol, used himself up well before he died.

Beginning with such a negativity at his core, Sartre the writer was characterized by extravagant negativities as well, as his critics have always delighted in pointing out. Sartre will leap with dizzying speed through the twentieth century, run up many blind alleys, and stumble over several major obstacles, all of his own making: his writing is often sloppy and unfinished, careless and unsystematic. *Being and Nothingness,* his most famous work of philosophy, is undermined by an inability to remain on the same plane of thought, an insistence on confusing ontology, epistemology, and everyday experience.[14] Later, his absorption of Marxism is fundamentally crippled by his underlying ontological individualism.[15] His major works are all unfinished: *The Roads to Freedom,* the ethics that was to complete *Being and Nothingness, Critique of Dialectical Reason,* his autobiography, his biography of Flaubert. Accordingly, we never know what Sartre was going to conclude, because the conclusions are missing.

The list of shortcomings could go on and the analysis of Sartre's weaknesses applied to work after work. Perhaps his most significant blind spot appears as Sartre enmeshes himself in a variety of contradictions. For example, he often denounces beforehand what he will embrace later. After lacerating all forms of humanism in *Nausea,* he claims it for existentialism after World War II. After denouncing posthumous glory in *Situations* II, he will eagerly look forward to the publication of his own *Pléiade* edition in later life. After dismissing historical materialism in *The Transcendance of the Ego,* he will embrace it as the "philosophy of our time" in *Search for a Method.* The man who never marries or has offspring goes bourgeois society one better and creates around him a tight circle of devoted friends known as "la famille." He denounces the "star system" after having become so privileged that his words are snapped up and printed virtually uncorrected. He rejects his reputation and the bourgeois honors that go with it, but he deliberately cultivates a new coterie of high-placed friends in the Third World.

The old man is equally at home with young Maoists and with the remains of Gustave Flaubert. Perhaps it is no contradiction that the man who never held a regular job after the age of forty fiercely denounces exploitation under capitalism, but it is striking that he became the century's outstanding incarnation of the bourgeois intellectual, all the while coveting, manipulating, and enjoying his reputation. This extravagant man is, in short, a living contradiction. He is comfortable with all roles, even after he denounces them. The contradiction is perhaps best summed up in Sartre's receiving yet rejecting the Nobel Prize.

Sartre's Project

How do we explain these extravagances and contradictions? Let us assume, with Sartre, that we are speaking of a single, coherent project. Each attempt to capture Sartre's project pushes us beyond it, into a deeper layer. Yes, he sought to be a writer, a great writer. As a writer he seeks to absorb, think, and say everything. And then to act on the world. In fact, we can see him seeking to remake the world in thought and writing, and then in action. But this extravagant ambition should be no surprise, given the quintessential human project of being God, as Sartre himself described it. We would suggest that Sartre's philosophical description of the human goal, after all, leads us to Sartre's personal goal, "the in-itself-for-itself, consciousness become substance, substance

21

become the cause of itself, the Man-God."[16] Or, in language drawn from *What is Literature?* he seeks to "make that unique and absolute object which is the universe come into being in an unconditioned movement."[17] Sartre seeks to appropriate and recreate the world, but "as if it had its source in human freedom"[18]—his own.

In sum, then, is Sartre an absolute creator of the universe, through words? One day, when a sufficiently ambitious biographer appears who will write the Sartrean biography of Sartre, the ultimate sources of this project and its full meaning will be explored. That biographer will note that the project continues well past Sartre's first formulation in *Being and Nothingness:* famous author, creator of work after work, future Nobel Prize-winner, Sartre in the 1950s undertakes to reconcile existentialism and Marxism. More, he seeks in the *Critique of Dialectical Reason* to understand the meaning of human history from its origin in the action of separate individuals.

Sartre lived a conventional enough life, and even his excesses—drinking, taking drugs, smoking, chasing women—were conventional excesses. He totally avoided becoming a society idol, a Kissinger or Capote, basking in his fame and hobnobbing with the rich and famous. Instead, to the very end of his active career, Sartre continued in his attempt to do the impossible. What did he pursue if not the "true novel" about Gustave Flaubert? Interviewed in 1971, Sartre denied that his ambition was to be God. He went on to declare that the "most important project in the *Flaubert* is to show that fundamentally everything can be communicated, that without being God, but simply as a man like any other, one can manage to understand another man perfectly, if one has access to all the necessary elements."[19]

The future Sartrean biographer of Sartre will not lack for personal and historical sources of his ambitions: Sartre's blind spot, his lack of a real father to shape himself against, his early immersion in the smug but illusory world of the late-nineteenth and early-twentieth-century French petite bourgeoisie. The irrational ambitions of a Hitler or a Stalin are fueled by their origin in an ultimately impossible situation rather than by the self-confidence Marx attributes to the bourgeoisie at the height of its power which "creates a world in its own image." Similarly, Sartre, equally a child of impotence, describes the project of being God: it arises from a fundamental split at the heart of being between consciousness and existence. As such, it springs from, and collapses into, its own impossibility. "But the idea of God is contradictory and we lose ourselves in vain. Man is a useless passion."[20] We find a similar attitude demonstrated in Sartre's early literary works. "The Wall" and *No Exit* can be viewed as reflecting an archetypical pattern of Sartre's psyche—an anguished, tortured, and eternally frustrated consciousness. Sartre's then, is a characteristic twentieth-century project, predestined to fail, outrageously ambitious, an astounding mingling of impotence and power.

Radical and Moralist

The scope of Sartre's project is enough to provoke discomfort, if not hostility, but two of its major features must be stressed if we are to grasp the full extent of the bitterness against him. The great heritage of Sartre is that he was a moralist and a political radical. Indeed, he is the great moralist of the twentieth century, condemning budding fascists, bourgeois humanists, Nazi sympathizers, anti-Semites, racists—the manufacturers of every form of excuse, the accomplices of every form of evil. Above all, he exposed to all of us, as no one else has done, that every possible action involves our own choice. Before judging or acting he did not wait to see whether or not he would resolve the unfinished questions keeping *Being and Nothingness* from containing an adequate moral philosophy—issues such as the incompatibility between a universal and objective ethics and Sartre's attack on such universality and objectivity. After all, *Being and Nothingness* already contains an ethics denouncing bad faith, and work after work contrasts authenticity with bad faith, opposes accepting contingency with striving for being, treating humans as humans with treating them as objects. If he never completed an ethics, his theater was a powerful and cumulative reflection on one ethical dilemma after another.

Sartre's works, ring, above all, with moral passion: against any and all forms of dishonesty, the evasion of contingency and freedom, false respect for propriety and convention. And this moral passion becomes a moral-political one as he denounces the American intervention in Vietnam, the use of torture in Algeria, colonialism, the distortions of anti-communism, the Communist Party liners who can justify anything.

It is important to note that Sartre remained radical while his former friends looked elsewhere. What does it mean that Sartre kept alive a commitment to a Left which others found increasingly untenable? Some of Sartre's most interesting works deal precisely with the questions separating him from Camus, Aron, and Merleau-Ponty. He sought to keep his radical hopes alive by grounding them in the real world. The commitment of a Paul Nizan, Sartre's closest childhood friend become novelist and Communist militant, might be the stuff of discussions of revolutionary purity, or heroism, or tragedy. Sartre, in contrast, showed a special kind of courage, braving not death (except once or twice) but ridicule. He struggled to keep commitment alive and strengthened it, over another forty years, in ordinary times as well as heroic. The evolving commitments of Camus, Merleau-Ponty, and Aron all had their integrity: Camus was devoted to the individual besieged on all sides in the modern world, especially by its political processes; Merleau-Ponty to intellectual clarity and the force of criticism; Aron to the realities of power and political responsibility. But these commitments reflected renunciation as well, a losing of heart. Sartre, in contrast, refused to yield to renunciation, by connecting these kinds of commitments with a deeper one: to those oppressed by power and exploiting by privilege, to those abused for racial or religious reasons. His primary allegiance became to the wretched of the earth, to the masses, to the suffering, to all of those whom social and political structures had designated as unfit and inferior. Unlike the more "realistic" Camus, Merleau-Ponty, or Aron, Sartre's major impulse was solidarity. In the film *Sartre by Himself,* we see the old man, speaking in the shadow of the Montparnasse Tower, in the Paris of today, asserting that only a revolution can save France. This is the same man we also see standing in a small truck, smuggled into a factory, advising the latest generation of Nizans.

"The Most Hated Man in France"

As the Cold War overcame Europe, Sartre refused to side with the West and equally refused to join the Communist Party; instead this socialist en route to becoming a Marxist insisted on finding, and keeping to, his own way. He continued to demand and denounce. In the early 1950s Sartre became, in André Gorz's words, "the most hated man in France."[21] His brief alignment with the PCF, still denounced thirty years later and ten years after his death, provoked a rage even greater than usual. That he sought to understand Stalinism rather than denounce it still provokes befuddled anger, even today, even after his own ringing attack on the invasion of Czechoslovakia.[22]

But the underlying reasons, then and now, lie elsewhere. In John Gerassi's words, Sartre had become and remained the "hated conscience of his century."[23] A citizen of France, a man of the West, he insisted on confronting both with their own image. Perhaps he did not denounce and analyze every injustice (and his critics would delight in showing this), but he never stopped denouncing and analyzing injustices; perhaps he did not politically act against every evil, but he never stopped acting against evils; perhaps *Les Temps Modernes* did not explore every major social problem, but it never stopped exploring major social problems. Sartre can be faulted for many things, but he remained a moralist, committed to the oppressed, totally involved in the world, unassuming about his fame, courageous, driven by massive, extravagant energy.

Every new study provides Sartre's many enemies with an opportunity to assail him. Admittedly, he makes a perfect target. His womanizing, drinking, pill popping, violent statements, opinionated views—all part of his radical extravagance—provide his critics with excuses for dismissing him. One critic, for example, dismisses all of Sartre's writings after *Nausea* as a "brilliantly confused mass of words which, moreover, runs counter to some of the essential Absurdist insights contained in *La Nausée*"—which, of course, allows this writer's analysis to concentrate on Sartre's scandalous behavior toward Simone de Beauvoir and to dismiss his political commitment as a "resounding and tragic failure."[24] Another presents the graduate student's revenge, a rapid tour through a few of this "poseur's" basic concepts, reduced to ashes in a single summary sentence: "Sartre's philosophical writing ultimately leaves the impression that he was more obstinate than philosophical, a magisterial sloganizer and mass marketer of philosophical observations than a careful or responsible arguer of them."[25] Freed from Sartre's work, this critic then delightedly borrows from the biographies to demonstrate how "the sense of being in the presence of a brilliant PR campaign—not just an intellectual career—takes hold."[26] And so there appears a new, entrepreneurial essence of Sartre: the clever huckster, exploiter of public susceptibilities and ripe social conditions.

Sartre's Exemplary Failures

Scoring points against a man who exposed most of his life to the public gaze is not difficult, and it is easier yet in a hostile political-moral-intellectual climate. For our part, we are more interested in understanding Sartre and in asking whether his work continues to be vital and relevant for today. Are his works, or can they be, useful for posing and answering our own questions?

As do the recent critics, we accept the need to dwell on Sartre's failures. We have already indicated that Sartre never completed major projects; not only was his Flaubert unfinished but so were his ethics, *Critique of Dialectical Reason,* and *Roads to Freedom*—virtually all of his major projects of the 1940s, 1950s, 1960s, and 1970s. As we have suggested, the projects represent efforts to do the impossible, to recon-

25

cile the irreconcilable. Yet let us not make a cult out of success. As Russell Jacoby has suggested, political failure automatically reduces the stature of those whose projects are judged "incorrect" by those who, having won, have the power to condemn them.[27]

Sartre's works are scarcely imaginable without the same all-encompassing ambition that drove him and doomed him to fail. He asserted himself against common-sense limits merely in moving out of philosophy to write fiction, in writing for the theater, in demanding that literature become political, in becoming politically active. And he continued, thematically, in trying to reconcile morality with political commitment, in trying to reconcile existentialism and Marxism. But are these impossible, any of them, all of them? Exactly where are the limits he should not have crossed? Sartre attempts to remake every genre and every discipline to which he is attracted, whether it be the novel, theater, biography, psychology, or Marxism. In retrospect, we can see that a certain project *was* impossible. But Sartre had the boundless energy and (nearly) blind courage to try; his failures, consequently, are as exemplary as his successes.

In trying to do virtually everything that one could possibly do with words, and to join this with action, Sartre was also trying to overcome the fragmentation that is so widely accepted and yet insupportable. He was trying to live as a whole—to act, to think, to judge, to create. Moreover, he was trying to live as one who is responsible for his world. As the second *Critique* and *Cahiers pour une morale* suggest, the evolution of history has both created world history and left us without purely private, personal histories of our own. There are no corners where we can hide: we are all in and of the larger world, world citizens, and whatever happens in that world matters to us just as what we do potentially matters to it.

In short, if Sartre's failures reveal his own personal weaknesses, such as incredible ambition and overweening self-confidence, and his conceptual weaknesses, such as an unshakable commitment to a dualistic individualism, the problems they contain and seek to overcome are the central problems of the age itself. This is what we mean by speaking of exemplary failures. Sartre, for example, never reconciled the social with the individual. His brilliant studies of the social basis of individual behavior—as in the third volume of *The Family Idiot*—make use of an understanding of sociality that Sartre was unable to theorize and that, indeed, he consistently argued against. Characteristically, the Sartre ontologically committed to the priority of individual consciousness was unable to understand sociality as an equally primary plane of being.[28]

But how are we to treat this shortcoming of Sartre's thought? Certainly it is a sign that he never fully grasped Marxism's understanding of the social dimension. But what then of Sartre's project of founding Marxism or his intention to reinsert the person back into it? Does Sartre's failure give us reason to dismiss his other insights, such as that into the nature of the practico-inert or the deviation of praxis by its products? Or do we assert an ontologically unclarified Marxism to be right and Sartre wrong? Above all, if Sartre trips himself up because of his own commitments, where do we find the correct answer to the question of relations between social structures and human subjects?

It turns out that Sartre's inability to reconcile existentialism and Marxism is a historical, not "merely" theoretical, problem. His failed effort is worth much more to us than any premature "success" that would have short-circuited the genuine, historical solution. First, it shows us the inability of any traditional individualistically oriented perspective to explain the social, just as any traditional socially oriented perspective cannot explain the individual. Second, Sartre leaves us not with a false solution paying homage to an orthodoxy but with an incomplete *Critique* and an unwritten ethics, both testifying to the enormous gap between individual subject and general social, historical, or ethical structure. If today we can sketch possible paths to a solution,[29] we can sketch them only. It is in reality, in our experience and our world, that individual and society are fundamentally at odds and will remain at odds unless the conflict is historically and socially resolved. History gave Sartre no reason to overcome his "ideological interest" in his individualist starting point.

But isn't the effort to connect two such impossibles typical of the Sartrean enterprise? Certainly it may be considered idiosyncratic, but the situation also drives us to the task. In assessing Sartre's heritage, we must learn to appreciate not only his extravagance, his built-in weaknesses, and limitations, but also the limitations imposed on him by the historical situation. For example, the project to be God and its inevitable shipwreck—man is a useless passion—ontologize both a specific individual and historical project and its failure. In sifting through what Sartre has left us, it is as wrong to reject his entire project as it is to embrace it uncritically. Conversely, it is as wrong to make all of his failures reflections of our historical situation as it is to make all of them exemplary. It is as wrong to try to succeed everywhere he failed as it is to walk away.

First, then, a tenet of Sartrean criticism: understand him in his own terms, and see the larger social and historical forces operating within

27

him and motivating him. If his failures suggest our projects, they do so without the specific coloration given by his drives and limitations (which, if truth be told, are also social and historical in origin but confuse the issues and paths to their solution because of their idiosyncratic and limiting character). In short, we must filter out what is worthwhile and applicable in Sartre's project, rather than trying to carry out everything he attempted and failed at. Appreciating his outrageous quest to be God, we must separate it from what Sartre shares with us, the effort to understand and change the world.

In the end, Sartre will serve us to the extent that we displace him with ourselves. In his studies of them, Genet and Flaubert eventually give way to Sartre, indeed in some sense are replaced by Sartre. His error is to not be as explicit and conscious about this as he might be, to use them for his own purposes even when he pretends to be talking about them. We at least can make clear that we become Sartrean for our own reasons.

To Be Sartrean

Everything we have said should explain why there are almost no Sartreans today. His was a movement of one person, a single, coherent, unique project. To become a Sartrean, it would seem on the face of it, is to become the man himself: his "Flaubert, c'est moi" would be replaced by our "I am Sartre." Yet we insist that his heritage ought to be generalized and made widespread. Key themes, tools, and aspects of his spirit deserve a clear, definite existence beyond their specific ties to this man and his works. If it makes little sense to try to be *a* Sartrean, then, it makes considerable sense to absorb these aspects of the Sartrean project. In this sense, we issue a call to be Sartrean. We propose to disentangle a heritage from *this individual.* We would like to take up those of Sartre's projects still remaining relevant and integrate them with our own; we would like to absorb his tools and spirit, to use them alongside our own.

What can we learn? First, we must abandon any reticence about entering into Sartre, just as he entered into Genet or Flaubert. He has given us instructions: to feast off him as he feasted off others. Let him disappear, as we extract from him what remains usable today and tomorrow. Annie Cohen-Solal is too enthusiastically respectful while being ultimately uncomprehending: nowhere does she get near enough to Sartre to treat him as he would have treated himself. Her biography lacks the hard work to *grasp* him. Ronald Hayman has gone farther, seeking

28

to understand and take the measure of Sartre. But his project unfolds at enormous distance from the Sartrean enterprise, ultimately deeply hostile to it. John Gerassi's work is more Sartrean in spirit: he attempts to present Sartre as Sartre saw himself and, above all, wanted to be seen. We seek to *use* Sartre, to detach the usable essence from the man himself, to give him new life by burying him.

Using Sartre: Making Ourselves

Sartre, by his own example, invites harsh treatment. In this specific sense, today's critics are being more Sartrean than many Sartre scholars. But even if we appreciate their irreverence, they insist on giving us only his flaws, Sartre without the substance, his extravagance as egomania without the content. They will not feast on Sartre, because they see nothing nourishing. What is the content that needs paying attention to? What would be the basis for being Sartrean today? We would begin with certain major themes or concerns worthy of being dusted off and brought into the present: that individuals determine themselves, that human beings are the source of all social and ideological forces and "realities," the theme of responsibility and complicity, and a preoccupation with the problem of individual morality and politics.

First, theoretically, as all the world knows, Sartre begins with the individual. Leaving aside the problematic issues, indicated above, of Sartre's prioritization of the individual and the need to clarify the relationship between individual and society, Sartre's richest line of thought lies in exploring human action. Aristotle's *Nichomachean Ethics* and *Poetics* had made much of human action more than two thousand years ago. But only Sartre treats choice and action as the core of what it means to be human and as permeated with history. First and foremost, then, is Sartre's emphasis that we act to make ourselves, beyond all determinism.

At the beginning this is an abstract, almost rhetorical position— "The slave in chains is free to break them" and "Whatever the circumstances and wherever the site, a man is always free to choose to be a traitor or not." But it takes on added force as Sartre places the individual in history and society and then understands the individual psychologically. Then freedom slowly evolves, taking on all the weight of the world until it becomes "the slow movement which makes of a totally conditioned social being someone who does not render back completely what his conditioning has given him."[30]

Human beings interiorize their conditioning, their history, their shaping experiences, their biological limitations, and reexteriorize them

29

as projects within which all of these determinations are given meanings. In short, action remains decisive. In this sense one must avoid the tendency to see humans as if they were stones, passively shaped from the outside. "There is no non-human situation."[31] Even neurotic and apparently self-destructive projects may be understood as being invented by the subject "in order to be able to live an unlivable situation."[32] No matter what, then, we make ourselves.

The individual human being is at the center of philosophy, of politics, of Sartre's theater and fiction, of the biographies. To understand human beings, then, means to understand what they make themselves to be, rational or not, beneficial or not, and why. It means studying how people create and choose to become themselves. This is the sense in which a person can be understood "perfectly" without the interpreter being God. Sartre means that we can grasp the interior praxis-process of choosing and creating oneself, warts and all, based as it is on the situation in which one finds oneself and how one responds to that situation. Sartre refuses all reductionism about such projects. Specifically, he rejects the reductionism (of some Marxists or Freudians) that neglects that humans make themselves. Indeed, this reductionism ignores that dialectical step that, in Marx, makes possible revolutionary social change and, in Freud, makes possible psychoanalysis. Making ourselves and our situations is the only possible basis for *remaking* them.

Even so, it is possible to become nonhuman. But only as a human project, underpinned by human subjectivity, as an interiorization of one's conditioning and its reexteriorization into a goal deemed worthy of being pursued. In this sense all definition becomes self-definition, all slavery must be accepted. The need to assert being human has never disappeared, will never disappear, can never disappear.

We have been talking about the Sartrean theme of themes. There are others that must be included, which we will briefly sketch. The second is that Sartre's entire career explores the "objective" world of events, social norms, forces, classes, and objects. These may well become powers over us, dominating, even shaping our possibilities. But they are all human, each and every one, created by people in the first instance and then constantly reanimated by people insofar as they continue in existence. Practico-inertia is a material product of praxis, and its passive power appears only in and through further praxis. The trends of history become what they are only through being interiorized and reexteriorized by every generation, indeed by every individual of every generation. Thus does subjectivity constitute each and every objectivity, even those that crush us.

Third, the Sartre who begins with a hopelessly free individual and then plunges that individual into the world of political action explores in depth the implications of engagement. Especially in his plays Sartre asks, again and again, How is it possible to be committed to a better world and be effective in changing this one? How can this individual, motivated by values and goals, keep them as the guiding force of real politics in the real world? How can one avoid becoming apparatchik or terrorist? Sartre explores how one can avoid both opportunism—the cynical abandonment of all values in the face of the demands of reality—and dogmatism—holding to those values against, and in violation of, reality.

Fourth, Sartre explores the meaning of responsibility and complicity in the contemporary world. Responsible for ourselves and the world, we are counted morally and politically, whether we are passive or active, silent or vocal. Anyone who tolerated anti-Semitism before World War II was responsible for its consequences; the same is true for Nazism, the war in Algeria, and racism and colonialism in general. Sartre shows specifically how Flaubert and his generation became responsible for the massacres of 1848. He develops a sophisticated sense of responsibility which can be the basis of an analysis of complicity today anywhere people are oppressed.

Living Our History

These are some components of the heritage we would choose to wrest from the ashes and keep with us today, for our purposes. Sartre gives us one of the twentieth century's strongest, most coherent, and most persuasive visions of what it means to be human. Sartre's vision slowly developed in a total and radical engagement with the world, from the point of view of seeking to build a better one. Sartre himself lived the words of his introduction to the first issue of *Les Temps Modernes:*

> Since the writer has no means to escape, we want him to embrace his time tightly, it is his unique chance; it made itself for him and he is made for it. One regrets Balzac's indifference to the 1848 Revolution, Flaubert's frightened incomprehension of the Commune. One regrets it for *them.* There is something there that they missed forever. We do not want to miss anything in our time. There may be some more beautiful, but this one is our own.[33]

After all is said and done, one does not regret Sartre's indifference or lament that he missed his time forever. In engaging with it so deeply, in fact, he changed himself. Shall we speak of choice? He could have

31

courted safety by remaining an interesting, even important writer who might today anger no one and be left in the past, sifted through by the loving hands of a few specialists. Instead, the extravagance that drove him to become the "hated conscience of his century" makes him, even after death, a provocative, irritating, always vital guide into some of the thickets of the present.

Notes

1. Michel Contat and Michel Rybalka, *Les Ecrits de Sartre* (Paris, 1970), 256.

2. John Weightman, "Summing Up Sartre," *New York Review of Books,* August 13, 1987. See also Jankélévitch, "Le Mal de la bivalence," *Libération,* June 10, 1985, 34–35, and "Sartre jugé par Jankélévitch," *Le Monde,* June 11, 1985. Other posthumous attacks include those by Clément Rosset, "Questions sur Sartre," *Le Débat,* no. 35, May 1985; Richard Bernstein, "Revisionists and Storytellers—Is It Passé to be Engagé?" *New York Times Book Review,* January 5, 1986; Carlin Romano, "Sartre Imitates Life," *Village Voice Literary Supplement,* November 1987.

3. *Being and Nothingness,* trans. by Hazel E. Barnes (New York, 1956), 566.

4. "Une idée fondamentale de la phénoménologie de Husserl: l'intentionnalité," *Situations* I (Paris, 1947), 31.

5. "François Mauriac et la liberté," *Situations* I (Paris, 1947), 52.

6. "The Itinerary of a Thought," *Between Marxism and Existentialism* (London, 1983), 42.

7. "Merleau-Ponty," *Situations,* trans. by Benita Eisler (New York, 1966), 198.

8. Ibid., translation changed.

9. Science and poetry are notable exceptions. Sartre self-consciously leaves poetry outside his embrace and explains why in an essay attempting to show his domination of it (*What Is Literature?* trans. by Bernard Frechtman [New York, 1949]). In the Sartrean scheme of things, science would seem to fall within the *human* sciences with which he is concerned and to be controlled by them. Moreover, in the *War Diaries* he suggests that his partial blindness disqualifies him from a scientific career (trans. by Quintin Hoare [London, 1984], 305–6).

10. *Nausea,* trans. by Lloyd Alexander (New York, 1964), 237.

11. *The Words,* trans. by Bernard Frechtman (New York, 1964), 255.

12. *War Diaries,* 311.

13. Ibid., 371.

14. See Ronald Aronson, *Jean-Paul Sartre—Philosophy in the World* (London, 1980), 71–88.

15. See Ibid., 243–92.

16. *Being and Nothingness,* 575.

17. *What Is Literature?* 54.

18. Ibid., 51.

19. "On the *Idiot of the Family,*" *Life/Situations,* trans. by Paul Auster and Lydia Davis (New York, 1977) 123.

20. *Being and Nothingness,* 202.

21. *Sartre by Himself,* transcript of the film directed by Alexandre Astruc and Michel Contat, trans. by Richard Seaver (New York, 1978), 61.

22. It is visible in Paul Berman's discussion of the Jankélévitch controversy and (without having read it) of *Critique* II. See "Moral Insomnia," *Village Voice,* December 17, 1985.

23. See John Gerassi, *Jean-Paul Sartre: Hated Conscience of His Century* I: *Protestant or Protester* (Chicago, 1989).

24. Weightman, "Summing up Sartre," 45.

25. Romano, "Sartre Imitates Life," 16.

26. Ibid., 17.

27. See Russell Jacoby, *Dialectic of Defeat* (Cambridge, 1981).

28. See Ronald Aronson, *Sartre's Second Critique* (Chicago, 1987), 219–43.

29. See Ibid.

30. "The Itinerary of a Thought," 35.

31. *Being and Nothingness,* 554.

32. Sartre's foreword to R. D. Laing and David Cooper, *Reason and Violence* (London, 1964), 7.

33. "Introduction to *Les Temps Modernes,*" in Eugen Weber, *Paths to the Present* (New York, 1960), 433–34.

I

DISCOVERING
AND
REDISCOVERING
SARTRE

1

KENNEDY AND WEST VIRGINIA

Jean-Paul Sartre

Translator's Introduction: The following extract is from Sartre's *Morality and History,* a series of lectures Sartre intended to present at Cornell University in April 1965, but canceled in protest against the American escalation of the war in Vietnam. Robert V. Stone and I introduce these lectures as a whole in the next chapter of this volume. While the passage presented here has a compelling argument running throughout, its rhetorical surface—especially at the start—has an unpolished first-draft quality which I have not tried to smooth over. The extract occupies most of the second half of the work's second chapter, entitled "The Specificity of the Moral Experience." Sartre's description there of presidential candidate John Kennedy's use of the value of tolerance in the 1960 West Virginia primary is part of the chapter's phenomenology of the normative domain. Sartre offers this description as an example of how the normative can have a specific effectiveness in political campaigns, and superficially in history generally. He argues that the normative not only is ideological and superstructural, as official Marxism holds, but can itself produce historical events.

Perhaps in part a result of his extensive travels in the United States in 1945–1946,[1] Sartre shows a good grasp of U.S. political life, though perhaps overestimating Americans' knowledge of if not their respect for the Constitution. Throughout this discussion, he refers to "Wisconsin" when it is obvious that he is describing the primary in West Virginia. Accordingly, I have changed "Wisconsin" to "West Virginia" in each occurrence, leaving all else unchanged. The Wisconsin primary was held on April 6, 1960. Kennedy, with 56 percent, defeated Humphrey. In a state almost 33 percent Catholic,[2] his victory was not considered substantial. However (and this may have been the origin of Sartre's confusion), Wisconsin was the first state in which Kennedy's Catholicism became an issue: several Protestant ministers warned that a Catholic could not distinguish his public duties from his religious beliefs.[3] The West Virginia primary came a month later, on May 10, 1960. It was in a speech on April 21, 1960, that Kennedy himself first overtly tackled the Catholic "issue" head-on, promising to respect all religious beliefs and challenging voters to elect the best person regardless of religion. He won by 61 percent in a state where less than 6 percent of the population was Catholic. Kennedy's aide Theodore Sorensen had encouraged him to press the Catholic issue, arguing that Kennedy himself was a victim of religious bigotry.[4] Sartre's analysis underlining the religious issue was fairly common at that time. His source is almost certainly Theodore H. White's *The Making of the President 1960*, chapter four, "The Art of the Primary: Wisconsin and West Virginia."[5] Nonetheless, Kennedy's win in West Virginia was decisive; it was henceforth assumed he would be the Democratic candidate against Nixon in the 1960 election.

The parallels between Kennedy, a Catholic, and Jesse Jackson, a black running in the 1988 Democratic primaries, seem obvious. Jackson could have argued, as Sartre suggests in this section of his *Morality and History* of a black candidate: "I am a citizen and I am eligible, will you not vote for me because I am black?" But where Sartre relates that Kennedy said, "Never in my childhood would I have thought that a man would be excluded from the presidency because of his *religion*," it would have been highly implausible for Jackson to say, "Never in my childhood would I have thought that a man would be excluded from the presidency because of his *race*." This is because racism's ability to keep blacks from the real levers of power is clear to almost all blacks before they reach their teens. It is evident to most adult white voters—to whom such a statement would also be addressed. The differences between Kennedy and Jackson are instructive: the wealthy Kennedy ran a largely self-financed, liberal campaign calling for a strong defense but with many hints at new benefits for the underprivileged. Jackson, whose own roots are among the underprivileged, ran a small contributor–financed class campaign for empowerment of the excluded in pursuit of economic justice. A civil rights activist questioning the justice of the existing distribution of privilege, Jackson has been anathema to the ruling class. Kennedy, a member of that class, was certainly acceptable to it.

I wish to thank Arlette Elkaïm-Sartre, not only for her permission to bring out the translation of this extract in this volume but also for her careful verification and correction of the typescript against Sartre's manuscript. All the notes to the text are mine.

Elizabeth A. Bowman

Here we have a real and measurable event (due to its being an election) which happened recently and which—without our leaving the surface of ethical experience—will show us both the practical effectiveness of ethos[6] and the curious dialectic of the political and the normative. When Kennedy ran in the West Virginia primary, the majority of voters voted for him with the formal intention of carrying out a *moral behavior.* It is important to insist here on the originality of this process. Frequently, in fact, especially in local elections, a personality's (true or false) integrity, firmness, courage, and (true or false) purity can contribute to his victory. The normative element is certainly undeniable: voters vote for the good to the extent that the candidate incarnates it in their eyes. But regardless of the fact that good and evil are here determined—even without the public knowing it—within the framework of a certain politics (which simply refers us to the ethical dimension of a public action and to the manipulation of ethos by the politician), this determination makes it impossible to appreciate the vote's normative meaning without clarifying the profound relationships between the norm and interests. We must also recognize that the voter's behavior is only partially moral: voting for "the good man" is no doubt voting for the Good, but it is to expect from him especially *that he do the good for us,* that he put his virtues, his integrity, his generosity, his devotion in the service of our interests. We do not yet have the instruments needed to untangle this web. To do so, it would be necessary to know in advance the fundamental characteristics of the normative and what one calls interest. On the other hand, the West Virginia voters did not—or did not only—choose Kennedy because they judged him a good man, but they chose him *above all* in order to act themselves as good persons. Here ethos motivates the political choice.

We know how things happened. In a state with a Protestant majority, one had to choose between two Democrats, one of whom was Kennedy. West Virginia is a *threatened* state. Its wealth was formerly in

39

mining; it was one of the largest suppliers of coal for the entire United States. In recent decades, the largest national industries chose other combustibles—oil, gas—that were more convenient or less costly. There resulted a devalorization of the principal resource of West Virginia, a massive drop in production, and chronic underemployment. When Kennedy and Humphrey ran against each other, one might have expected the voters, in exchange for their votes, to ask the candidates to propose an economic and technical program, to ask: if you are president of the United States what will you do for West Virginia? Looking closer, what we have here in effect are citizens conditioned by a certain past (the considerable development of the mining industry to supply the national demand) and who are put into danger by the present conjuncture. The rigidity of this conjuncture, i.e. of the practico-inert structures (an immense industrial mechanism with the social and demographic consequences that one can imagine having been put into place during the first half-century), does not permit the West Virginians to adapt to the present situation. They cannot act on the diminution of demand because it conditions the mining state *from the outside*. Because West Virginia is ruined by the American nation—taken as a practical ensemble acting upon its means of production—aid for West Virginia becomes a national problem and therefore relies upon the competency of the future federal government. Such an undertaking should be historical and technical. Historical because it would permit West Virginia to rearrange its inherited structures without breaking them, which means that it would struggle in the name of a future objective against the fatalities of the past. This undertaking would be technical because the possibilities of action would be determined and a plan arrived at (for example, building new industries) in light of the national whole and the international conjuncture, risks of failure, and, as far as possible, future consequences would be calculated for West Virginia considered in relation to the probable evolution of national production, and inversely. No departure from the domain of facts is necessary. This restructuring, if it must take place, will be based on actual facts, the given situation of West Virginia, in order to modify those facts by producing others whose factual consequences in turn this restructuring will try by exact methods to foresee for decades to come. Voters' demands, if indeed voters thought they had to show them, might well be based on profound values—a matter we cannot yet decide—but *in fact* such demands would appear as bargaining: I scratch your back, you scratch mine.

For Kennedy, though, the West Virginia primary has a test value. The problem for him is not just to obtain a favorable vote by making concrete proposals, but rather to determine, based on the results, whether Protestant voters can vote for a Catholic. The primaries influence the decisions of the Democratic Convention. It will decide whether the religious obstacle is determining. In a way one could almost say that a victory obtained in West Virginia due to the presentation of a plan of help would be less significant[7] since the vote's meaning would be unclear. The ideal would be that the voter decide *solely on the religious question*. Several factors will work in Kennedy's favor. First, a candidate for the presidency does not normally run in the primaries with a precise program, and above all he does not support local demands like a senator or a member of Congress. Because it is the American nation in its entirety that he aspires to incarnate, he speaks of the *social whole*. At this level, for Humphrey as well as for Kennedy, the problems of West Virginia are not formulated in and of themselves: they must find their solution within a general political position which serves the interests of everyone and which is indicated in the form of an orientation and not of a true program. However, under the rubric "Democrat," very diverse interests with diverse political options are united. One can say that the candidates, regardless of their individual differences (ethnic origin, social milieu, financial means, etc.), do not yet oppose each other very distinctly on the general orientation of domestic politics. Humphrey, without a personal fortune, is perhaps closer to the interests of the masses, but the very rich Kennedy wants to raise the general standard of living and fight against poverty. There is not a single person in West Virginia who would submit to them an emergency plan and ask them to declare themselves for or against it. Everything remains vague. The influence on votes of the candidates' individual traits remains very ambiguous. For example, the extreme youth of Kennedy can have an effect for or against him according to the age, sex, and profession of the voters. His immense fortune serves him indirectly by putting at his disposal practically unlimited means and puts him at a considerable advantage vis-à-vis his opponent. But it cannot exercise any direct influence on the election: one will not vote for him *because of his wealth*. For all of these reasons, the religious factor will be more easily emphasized. It can decide between the contenders. Consequently, Kennedy takes the bull by the horns. Catholics have the reputation of being intolerant. He solemnly commits himself, if elected, to respect religious freedom—in other words, quite simply, the Constitution. In each of his important speeches, he puts the voters' feet to the fire: will they refuse him their vote for the sole reason that he is Catholic? He adds—I quote from memory—"Never would I have thought in my adolescence that one

41

could exclude a man from the presidency because of his religious opinions. . . ."[8] The deal is in the bag: instead of *proposing* economic and technical projects which tend to reduce underemployment in West Virginia, he *imposes* a normative option on the voter. The choice that the voters will make is ethical and not *religious*. The problem is to know if the voters—regardless of their religion—will accord the same rights to the faithful of all churches. Faith is by essence intolerant: how can one believe the relativity of the absolute? Tolerance was at first a historical compromise (regardless of what was then the ethical dimension) between men who wanted national unity in spite of the multiplicity of religious beliefs. From this compromise was born the Constitution. But when one solicits the people of West Virginia, it is not in the name of the Constitution. The Constitution does not forbid a Protestant from *preferring* another Protestant; it only guarantees the eligibility of Catholics. Kennedy runs and all the voters *recognize* his eligibility. Thus the question he poses to voters goes well beyond the institution. In this respect it is specific. Everything happens as if Kennedy said: "You must elect me *because* I am Catholic and you are Protestant; you must, against all your prejudices, your habits, your religious preferences, show by your vote this capital value: *tolerance*."

This summary makes us quickly leave the terrain of the conditional. Political bargaining was expressed in these terms: I give you my vote on the *condition* that . . . etc. . . And the program of economic aid itself was undertaken on the basis of *present conditions* (practico-inert, development of the economic whole, conjuncture, disposition *of others*—for example, producers and consumers of *other states*). One can even theoretically envision a national and international situation such that the ensemble of conditions needed to undertake the recovery of West Virginia were not brought together. However, by calling on the voters to vote for Kennedy, Kennedy himself manifested an unconditional exigency. To be more precise, he did not demand of the voter that the voter vote for Kennedy, but rather that his vote not be conditioned by any outside determination (prejudices, religious narrowness: particular traits which are only the *image* of the past). "If you elect Humphrey, then your past, to the extent that it conditions your present, *must be nothing* in your choice; you must keep in mind only the public good (that of the United States and of West Virginia). In other words, *the future alone* should determine your choice."

We see the trap. In the absence of any precise program, how does one determine if, by opting for Humphrey, one has nothing else in view but the future of the United States? A Protestant cannot be sure of breaking with his past conditionings except by voting for the Catholic Kennedy. The rub is to have only the public good in mind. Tolerance is both an ethical means of achieving it (by ridding oneself of conditionings) and a consequence of its realization (a better integration of citizens within the community, which is linked to the growth of the nation, will save human relationships from all presuppositions). But as the public good remains undetermined in this case, tolerance becomes both the means to it and its incarnation. Voting for Kennedy is *in any case* to improve relations between Catholics and Protestants; it is to assume and go beyond the contradiction between internal intolerance which characterizes religion and social tolerance which characterizes democratic persons.

The trap functions all the better because Humphrey cannot fight on this terrain. Protestant, he cannot demand the votes of Protestants in the name of tolerance; Democrat, he cannot demand them in the name of religious intolerance. In a word, Humphrey remains on the terrain of facts while his adversary, making his handicap into the source of an unconditioned exigency, has raised himself to the terrain of the norm. Kennedy obliges the Protestant voters to choose between two conceptions of the human: according to your vote, man is either the product of previous circumstances or he is capable of affirming himself as his own product regardless of circumstances. The freedom of bourgeois democracies—completely formal though it is—is suffocated in the United States by the evolution of capitalism and the development of an economy of monopolies. Kennedy gives the exercise of a civic right—voting—all its value by demanding that it be for the West Virginians the opportunity of reaffirming their freedom. This freedom is certainly not the concrete possibility of living better and overcoming alienations—whose fundamental link with ethics we will have to study—but instead manifests itself as normative through the demand that the citizens pull himself free of the clutches of the past.

And this is not all: an *exemplary* behavior is asked of the voter. In fact, the primaries precede the national election; inhabitants of other states decipher the primaries, seeing in them signs, indications, a prefiguration of their own decision. When the state of West Virginia votes, it must know that all the states of America have their eyes on it. By choosing Kennedy, it invites all Americans to place tolerance above everything as the ethical rule of human relationships. By choosing Humphrey, it runs the risk of being blamed in the name of the virtue it failed to demonstrate and that other states will perhaps demonstrate later. The pressure of the ethical is too strong. Mandated to act as good people before an immense public, the Protestant voters of West Virginia vote for Kennedy. What kind of moral exigency did they obey? Certain of them no doubt (and we will return to this determination) were tempted by the Good. In other words, they were tempted—given this singular opportunity and in spite of all their historical conditionings and their social ills—by the formal possibility of producing themselves freely. But the statement made at the time by an older voter shows that others were inclined toward the Catholic candidate because of the ethical horror of scandal, that is by a coercive morality that bases its commands on the axiological judgment of others: "We are already unhappy enough," she said, "without being accused of bigotry." This singular sentence establishes a qualitative homogeneity between a lived situation and a moral fault. But we should not see in this the reduction of the norm to fact. On the contrary, it is unhappiness which is elevated to the level of the ethical as a *negative value*. This woman repeats what the Greek tragedies have said a hundred times: "The unhappy are the object of scandal; it is all the more necessary for them to behave as good people." Between these two attitudes—temptation and coercion—there is room for an infinite play of subjective determinations. But the subjective experience of the norm does not concern us for the moment.

Instead, it is important to study more closely the efficacy of the moral norm. At first sight, one might take ethos to be a ruse of politics. Kennedy made tolerance a means for his political undertaking, that is his electoral campaign. Yet we must note right away that we have no proof of his cynicism. On the contrary, everything leads us to believe his sincerity. His class and his economic power have helped him appreciate formal democracy. For him, this formalism is not visible and democracy becomes concrete because the institutions favor it. No doubt, he is attached to the Constitution because it protects his interests, but we don't yet know whether this attachment itself might have an ethical dimension. What is certain in any case is that, to the extent he is convinced that the real functioning of democracy serves the American citizen taken in his universality, he experiences as an ethical scandal the possibility that his religious convictions make him a second-class citizen—someone to whom it is a priori forbidden to aspire to the presidency. The absolute certainty of not being elected tends to suppress his eligibility, to take away a right from the entire Catholic community of which he is a member. And certainly, the majority of Americans have no chance of being elected, regardless of the nineteenth-century myth that "each of us can be president." This myth remains alive for many in spite of social upheavals. Kennedy would no doubt say that there are unfavorable but material circumstances—work conditions, living standards, culture, traits of character—which de facto

44

take away from his co-citizens the possibility that they conserve *by right*. Here, on the contrary, the scandal stems from an American possessing all the factual conditions which make his election possible, seeing himself deprived in advance of his *eligibility* because of a certain ethical, yet negative, disposition of the Protestant electorate (fanaticism, bigotry, churchliness, anti-Catholic prejudice, etc.). At this level the problem takes on its moral dimension: Americans are not worthy of the Constitution they made since they reject unity founded on the equality of rights; in the person of Kennedy, they oppose the integration of the Catholic minority into the social whole. It seems that the Catholic community has accepted this incomplete integration as a state of fact because, from the Declaration of Independence until the moment when Kennedy entered the lists, there has only been *one* Catholic candidate for the presidency of the United States.[9] His unglorious failure confirmed the other Catholics in their resigned pessimism.

Under these conditions, Kennedy's candidacy takes on the aspect of an ethical invention. It is the affirmation of a moral optimism: it is morally impossible that American voters put religious sectarianism above national interests. The inverted result is: it is *unconditionally possible* that a Catholic be president. I am speaking here of *moral invention* to the extent that this ethical optimism appears as a novelty among Catholic Americans and affirms itself as a human exigency without finding justification or help in historical traditions. Of course, the reasons for Kennedy's candidacy are many, the principal ones being social and political. This candidacy itself also has a history. The idea of going head to head with the electorate in order to provide the social whole with the opportunity to bring about the total integration of all its members did not come to just any Catholic, nor even at first to the candidate himself, but to the collective interiority of the powerful Kennedy family. Historically this family is pushed to demand political power by the formidable economic power that it possesses. At the start the religious problem was secondary. And at this moment, there is even within the family the quasi-certainty that it possesses the means to break the resistance of certain electoral groups, thereby affirming the predominance of fact over norms. But when the enormous undertaking is launched, the reality of the religious problem becomes evident; the Kennedy billions will not suffice to conquer the negative will of the voters *on this point*. The invention here consists in transforming a handicap into a normative exigency. Invention is put in the service of political ambition, but it cannot itself be political. Political cynicism—which could be expressed by this maxim: "I'm going to throw them the tolerance punch"—cannot

45

really be founded on any calculation of chances. Chances will instead be figured *according to* the West Virginia elections. No one would base a political campaign on the probability that ethical tolerance might win over religious intolerance precisely because it is the voter himself who will measure and judge on this point. No one can predict an act that is based on previous and present conditions and yet that one also demands be unconditional. In such a case, the only possible foresight is *ethical* inasmuch as such foresight posits the future as unforeseeable, the possibility of tolerance as unconditional, and confidence in humans as the norm of all undertakings.

Thus one can consider that in West Virginia Kennedy invents the idea of addressing himself to the ethos of its voters to the exact extent that he produces himself—for example, in his speeches—as *ethical agent.* A politician can in any number of cases imitate ethical attitudes in order to elicit the same from his co-citizens or militants of his party. But, in that case, the collective ethos is so well known that he can foresee the reactions of the social group. In the typical case that we have chosen, analysis shows that imitation of the prevailing ethos did not pay off due to the uncertainty of the candidate's situation. The political undertaking, regardless of its reasons and its objectives, is forced to undergo the normative moment. The ethical can here become the clever maneuver of the political on the condition of living the ethical in its purity. The most awkward error would have been to slide into the religious question, and to confront it by trying to skirt it, or, above all, to give the impression that one feared posing it. Kennedy's supreme political cleverness was to temporarily, but totally and sincerely, renounce politics and to transform himself internally for others and for himself into a *man of exigency.*

Even if we suppose that the West Virginia campaign was only a clever maneuver, and that the Kennedy team counted on the moral reaction of the voter as a fact, it would not be less true that it put *ethical effectiveness* in the service of politics. In other words, even if one admits that there was manipulation, that a trap was built into which the inhabitant of West Virginia plunged head-first, it was still necessary that the West Virginian go beyond the ethico-religious contradiction by a normative choice. That means that the West Virginia voter had put values into a hierarchical order, that he placed tolerance on top, that he refused all conditionings, and that he took it upon himself to affirm his freedom by recognizing the (religious) freedom of others. And he did so in full and lucid consciousness of providing an example to the free voters of other states. But his intention went even further. By voting for the candidate who appealed to his freedom, he intended to put into power the man of freedom. In other words, the West Virginian did not choose the political Kennedy, about whom he knew nothing, but the one whom he had seen with his own eyes make himself into an ethical agent by his very demands. In short, West Virginia required that the future president put ethical action in the place of politics. In a way, by doing so, the West Virginia voter only produced himself as an American: it is a trait of puritanism in the United States to live politics ethically. In short, he became what he was: in effect, as we will see, the *ethical paradox* comes from the moral agent *realizing what he is* in the very moment when he rips himself from being in order to produce himself in freedom. But if he becomes what he is, his tearing himself from being is nonetheless a reality. In this sense the Protestant voter defines by his vote a type of human relationship that Power is now to facilitate: that among human beings, reciprocity must be unconditional; one must always be able to eliminate the practico-inert from human relationships; the unity of the social whole must always be founded on a rigorous equality not only of rights but of one's initial chances.

In truth this normative ensemble remains formal: he who votes for a Catholic would certainly not vote for a black. Yet were it conceivable that a black was a candidate, would he not use the same language as Kennedy? Couldn't he say, and even more strongly: I am a citizen and am eligible, will you not vote for me because I am black? There is thus at the interior of the norm an inner limit, a sort of interiorized exteriority, that the voter can perceive or not, depending on the case. In fact, by voting for Kennedy, the voter believes he is advancing universal humanity, and this positive intention covers up his racial particularism according to which the absence of blacks from the ballot means that all whites are humans and all humans are white. And yet this ethics of human relationships and of unconditional reciprocity does not lead him to denounce the reification and alienation of which he is both victim and accomplice. In a way one can even say that his vote contributes to justifying reification and alienation ethically: they are not, he seems to say, so radical or profound that I cannot, given the opportunity, produce myself freely outside their reach. Yet in this moment of ethical freedom, there is no doubt that he denounces the rigorous conditions of his daily life because he summarily suspends all conditionings in this singular opportunity. In this behavior there is therefore something like an idealistic contestation of the social regime: contestation, because he tears himself away from these conditionings by an act; idealistic, because he affirms the regime in the same action which denies it. He proceeds as if human relationships can always make themselves transparent and free at the price of a forever possible moral effort—without any need to change the social order which distorts and destroys those same relationships.

In any case, this idealistic contestation is effective. Kennedy wins, not Humphrey. And, regardless of what one might say, the election is the measurable result of a relationship of ethical reciprocity between the candidate and the electorate. The vote's national consequences are more difficult to determine: other factors intervene, in particular, the confrontation of the Democratic and Republican parties. But there remains, undeniably, the exemplary value of an initial choosing: without this primary, the Democratic Convention would not have had confidence in Kennedy. This victory allowed the Democrats to evaluate *politically* the chances of this Catholic. It no doubt inclined Protestant Democrats of other states to "vote tolerant" (in the sense that one counsels to "buy French"). In short, ethos reveals itself as a practical conduct which regulates itself on norms and can have a historical effectiveness. In this same example we will also see the limits of this effectiveness. But *we must emphasize* that these limits (grasped in the factual result) are in truth born from the normative limits of the intention. It is at this moment of our research that we have blindly stumbled up against the *ethical paradox*. And we do not know—to cite but one example—if ethical idealism is an essential limit within the norm (if every norm in the very movement of its self-affirmation also posits its own limits, that is, decides about its means, and, consequently, prescribes for itself limits to its real effectiveness) or if certain circumstances oblige it to interiorize its *exterior* borders. In short, to consider *the result,* which presents itself as both consequence and as mystification (at least in appearance) of the ethical option: we cannot decide if all ethical behavior is a deliberate choice of the mystified condition, or if West Virginia's decision is the result of a *certain ethics* defined by a historical mystification (one that is localizable and dated) which is exercised on that ethics from the outside through conditionings from the social whole.

By voting for the ethical man, the electorate of the state voted for *Kennedy.* We must understand: no one can a priori deny a candidate the possibility of acting *ethically,* that is, doing acts characterized by their ethical effectiveness. One can do so all the less because Kennedy manifested himself as a normative agent (to his profit, it is true) by demanding tolerance from an unknown ensemble of co-citizens. As for the rest, taking for example his subsequent decisions on the black problem, is not the racial integrationist policy that he initiated already indicated in the normative appeal that he addressed to West Virginia? In a sense this policy goes beyond and confirms their vote: by integrating *all* minorities into the social whole, it is likely, as I have already said, that many of them understood "all white minorities." But Kennedy, refusing to distinguish American citizens according to their skin, dissolves the limit of interiorized exteriority which characterizes the ethical response of certain people. By presenting laws on integration to Congress, Kennedy unveils for his first voters the ethical truth of their earlier decision: it went *that far,* as far as anti-racism, even if they did not see it. The contradiction between the inert limit of interiority which determines the national choice, and the going-beyond of this limit in the name of that very choice (a going-beyond which contains, we will see later, other equally rigorous and even deeper limits), this contradiction was marked, we know, by a wavering of public opinion: at the moment of his death (for this reason and for others), Kennedy was losing speed.

But Kennedy is neither initially nor above all a normative exigency: he is a man of a class, a milieu, a family. He represents interests, a certain will to power; he also is defined by a certain political group which represents a faction in the heart of the Democratic Party. This political group, by producing itself, produced him, and inversely the candidate by expressing that group tends to reproduce it and to make it more precise. We do not yet know the profound relationship of ethics with these historical determinations. But, at the superficial level where we still are, we see clearly that this ethical behavior implemented political structures which condition a certain number of undertakings whose goal is to rearrange certain givens of the national whole in order to preserve these givens from any profound transformation. In short, the political position of Kennedy and his supporters aims at furnishing American capitalism with the means *to change in order to stay the same.* Kennedy will find himself, however, confronted with these same social forces, and, if he is to achieve any of his initial projects, he will have to come to terms with them: the ethical man disappears within political compromise. In the meantime, he inherits policies begun by previous governments (for example, the expedition against Cuba) which he must allow to develop to their conclusion even if it means learning lessons from them *without disavowing them.* And above all, regardless of what he does, he expresses a society structured by its economic and social history. He must, regardless of the superficial rearrangements that he makes, take on at a deep level and promote the great options of American imperialism (his position on aid to Latin America, regardless of what his personal intentions were, is a transparent disguise for a ferocious exploitation). In international politics, he wishes no doubt for *détente,* but he puts into place, perhaps without knowing it, the conditions for a resumption of the Cold War when he gets the United States bogged down in its *colonial-ist* politics in South Vietnam. In short, by bringing to power an *ethical agent,* the West Virginia voters voted for the tacit continuation of the same politics (despite superficial rearrangements). Since 1945 this political orientation has not changed because the deep structures of American society demanded it and because one cannot renounce, for example, imperialism without breaking these structures at the price of a total upheaval.

The mystification seems obvious: the moral option is suppressed and uncovers a political option. But was there mystification? The choice to determine oneself based only on ethics (and an ethics whose norms are specifically American): does this not presuppose a political abstention or, what amounts to the same thing, a *laissez-faire* which is advantageous to the reigning political order? And tolerance as a civic virtue of Americans, apart from what might otherwise be the universality of its value: is it not itself a permanent norm, conditioned by the diversity of groups which constitute the nation, and is it not therefore *conservative?* We will note, for example, that during a revolutionary period it is *intolerance* that becomes normative: at the moment when a society rearranges its profound structures (and singularly its relations of production) any opponent, as Merleau-Ponty says, becomes a traitor. Tolerance is therefore the norm of a stable regime, one that seeks to maintain itself at the expense of the continually greater integration sought by the groups within it.

That's true. But the consequence that we should draw from it is not the negation of normative specificity. Rather the consequence is simply a moral pluralism founded upon a profound linking—our goal is to bring it to light—of ethical action and historical praxis. We must note that the Protestants of West Virginia, by voting for Kennedy, not only confirmed their adherence to the "American way of life," but they also put aside the solution to their problems. It is in this choice that we see the sometimes painful refusal of the *conditional.* This refusal is facilitated by the *fact* that neither Humphrey nor the local politicians nor the unions had an emergency program to propose. The West Virginian's choice remains nonetheless a normative one. And, in a sense, this normative option opens out onto the confirmation of a political position. But, in another sense, one cannot call it mystified because it wants no end other than its own practical existence. At this level, the difference between ethics and politics—to which we will return at length—is that politics must assume even the unforeseen consequences of its action. The ethical person, however, refuses a priori the nonethical consequences of the action, as

50

in the maxim: "Do what you must and let the chips fall where they may." Solicited to choose tolerance, the Protestants of West Virginia made themselves *tolerant*. This means that in their action they rejected both previous conditionings of their praxis and subsequent consequences of their moral action. Of course, West Virginians' choice of tolerance itself had a *meaning* (antiracism, etc.) which goes beyond them and of which they are not conscious at the moment of acting. But these normative consequences can *be learned* progressively and are not immediately at issue. The problem is limited: the proposed moral act consists of going beyond religious intolerance while conserving the integrity of faith. The result of this unconditional exigency is limited but absolute: it is the election of *a Catholic* (and not Kennedy) by a Protestant majority. "Let the chips fall where they may" means either: it matters little that this Catholic is Kennedy since we accept in advance all the consequences of our choice; or, though it comes down to the same thing, we brush aside the consequences, assuming them politically but not ethically. If this champion of tolerance revealed himself in spite of his promises to be an intolerant president, too bad. The ethical absolute—that is, the moment when the historical agent denies his conditionings—is realized in the precise moment when the voter votes. The ethical result, to the extent that it holds ethical interests for the community, lasts no longer than the tabulation of the votes. The television says: "Kennedy wins," and the listener understands: "Tolerance triumphed in West Virginia." Or, if you prefer, "We have proved by putting our interests aside that relationships of reciprocity are always *possible.*" Such is the ethical intention reduced to its essence. Such is its effectiveness. Such is the rigorously limited objective that it proposes by rejecting any resulting consequences if they do not stem from the norm. On the ethical option, the agent pretends to produce himself by objectifying himself in a result rigorously identical to the end originally proposed. By thus refusing to consider the consequences, his undertaking simultaneously rejects all compromises. The ethical paradox reappears here in a new form because the moral agent can say, by pushing his maxims to the limit, both: "I *vote ethics* because I accept the regime and the politics which flows from it," and "Let West Virginia perish rather than the freedom to obey norms."

The analysis of this example, without giving us access to the fundamental questions, permits us to state that the norm, far from being reduced to some comfortable formulation of demagogic propaganda, had a specific efficacy, however limited its extent may have been. In other words, the norm produces *facts*. These facts, immediately reabsorbed by the infinite conditioning of the universe, have themselves qua facts unforeseen and perhaps fearful consequences. But the agent *recognizes* them only to the extent that they manifest his *normative objectivation*. In this sense we must recognize both that history makes itself—often, always? it remains to be seen—against the ethical and that ethics is a specific factor of history—at what level? to what extent? Our task is to decide about this.

Notes

1. Annie Cohen-Solal, *Sartre: A Life* (New York, 1987), 238, 277.
2. Harold Faber, ed., *The Kennedy Years* (New York, 1964), 71.
3. Ibid., 74.
4. David Burner and Thomas R. West, *The Torch Is Passed* (New York, 1984), 84.
5. Theodore H. White, *The Making of the President 1960,* (New York, 1962).
6. *Ethos,* a term Sartre does not define here, appears to refer to the body of moral beliefs and practices that are actually in force in a given community. Later, in his work on Flaubert, Sartre subsumes ethos in the notion of the "subjective neurosis" of a historical epoch.
7. Kennedy's opponent, Hubert H. Humphrey, campaigned as a liberal New Dealer on economic and social issues, producing somewhat more of a plan for West Virginia's economic recovery than Sartre indicates. However, this fact may only reinforce Sartre's basic argument. Kennedy promised to build an interstate highway in West Virginia, but he called for a more active economy in the depressed coal-mining state. Burner and West, *The Torch Is Passed,* 83.
8. Cf. White's citation of Kennedy: "I refuse to believe that I was denied the right to be president on the day I was baptized." *The Making of the President 1960,* p. 107.
9. Alfred E. Smith ran against Herbert Hoover in 1928.

2

SARTRE'S *MORALITY AND HISTORY:*

A First Look at the Notes for the Unpublished 1965 Cornell Lectures

Robert V. Stone and Elizabeth A. Bowman

"The politics of violence practiced in Vietnam by the U.S. government with the approval of the majority of the American people constitutes for me a major obstacle to my coming to the U.S. Deeply regret being obliged to break the commitment made. Beg you to believe in my high esteem for Cornell and for you." Signed: Jean-Paul Sartre.[1] With this short cable, received three weeks before his scheduled visit to the United States, after almost three years of negotiations and after months of preparation at Cornell University, Sartre gave up not only the prestigious Messenger Lectures in Cornell's centennial year, but a well-publicized opportunity both to expound his highly developed views on ethics and to denounce the recent escalation of the U.S. war in Vietnam.

Sartre had been scheduled to give a series of five lectures between April 7 and 14, 1965, with the title *Morality and History.*[2] Professor Jean-Jacques Demorest, Sartre's main host and representative of the Department of Romance Studies, had begun sending feelers in 1962. By the fall of 1963, the project was well advanced, and in the spring of 1964, about a year before the scheduled lectures, Sartre accepted, after which a formal invitation was sent by Dr. Perkins, then president of Cornell.[3] Plans were afoot to meet Sartre and Simone de Beauvoir at Kennedy Airport and escort them to Ithaca in the Cornell airplane.[4] The largest of

Cornell's auditoriums was to be used for the first three lectures on April 7, 8, and 9; the second largest was reserved for the last two. Sartre was to speak in French (he never mastered English). Every seat was to be wired for simultaneous translation.

Then, in the two months before Sartre was to come to the United States, President Lyndon Johnson ordered the first (and heavy) bombing of North Vietnam in February and the first deployment of U.S. combat troops on March 8—the two escalations that put the United States on a full war footing in Vietnam.[5] Although at the time the civil rights movement was at its height—the "Mississippi Freedom Summer" had taken place the previous year—the then-nascent antiwar movement was too small, Sartre thought, to be hurt by his absence. So he canceled. Explaining this to *Le Nouvel Observateur,* Sartre likened his visit to Faulkner visiting France at the height of the Algerian War after the bloody bombing of Sakiet. Had Faulkner protested in that context, he would no doubt have been politely heard, but his protest would have been resented and useless. Fearing such treatment by the U.S. press, Sartre reluctantly concluded that cancellation—though it might unfortunately disappoint some of his friends at Cornell—was the best form of protest available to him.

> Certain newspapers would have published extracts from my lectures— ten lines here, twenty lines there—and that would have been it. It wouldn't have troubled the surface of American political life. On the other hand, they might also say that Sartre, "Nobel prize-winner" in quotation marks, had come to the United States for calm discussions of American policy in Vietnam among people who respect each other. I did not want the latter.[6]

Sartre's position was criticized by Professor D. I. Grossvogel of Cornell's Department of Romance Studies, who happened to be in Paris at the time. Contending that "governments will play their games" in any case, Grossvogel chided Sartre for choosing to say no before millions of French over "shedding a ray of light on ethics" for a few students whose very attendance at his lectures would be a form of *engagement.*[7] As for his claim that his trip might light an "ethical glimmer" in one American eye, Sartre replied: "Well no: an indirect approach is not enough to start this glimmer; the students must be shown American society in its truth. That is Mr. Grossvogel's concern—though he seems too prudent to recognize it—and not mine."[8]

Having studied these notes, we find sections such as "Kennedy and the West Virginia Primary of 1960,"[9] that analyze American political life very directly. For the most part, however, Sartre's approach is indeed indirect. It shows a remarkable sensitivity to his audience, which would have been composed for the most part of daughters and sons from among the most affluent American families. Though these young people would likely have had ambiguous feelings about the trajectories plotted for them by their life situations, they would also have had few resources for conceiving alternatives. Yet at no point does Sartre play the role of conscience that Grossvogel seemed to wish to assign him. Far from aiming, in the manner of a sermon, at lighting "an ethical glimmer" in his audience, *Morality and History* shows Sartre's concern to question philosophically the ethical as such, to reveal it in the historical contexts in which it arises, to push the ambiguity in his listeners to its limit, and to enable them to freely explore on their own the historical outcomes of their own ethical choices.

In short, Sartre was not striking a political pose to conceal philosophical bankruptcy. We have found in *Morality and History* material for a dozen lectures, even if, in the end, they break off without completion—perhaps because of the cancellation. They hold the greatest interest for Sartre specialists but also for any students of ethics and the social sciences who are concerned to understand moral phenomena in relation to living history. Where does this work fall chronologically in Sartre's career? It comes after he stopped working on *Critique of Dialectical Reason*[10] but before he turned all his efforts toward bringing out his large work on Flaubert.[11] In this period Sartre worked on the second of the "two"[12] theories about ethics that he claimed to have written. From perhaps as early as November 1962 until mid-1965 Sartre engaged in an extended writing project on morality and history. Up to now we have been content to follow the practice of Sartre's bibliographers in calling this overall effort Sartre's "dialectical ethics."[13] However, it turns out that this phrase may not have been Sartre's.[14] It is moreover misleading inasmuch as calling these writings an ethics of any kind implies Sartre is advancing a new normative theory of the right and the good as such—which we will show he is *not* doing. His actual undertaking during these years—which aims *toward* "the dialectics of ethics and history" (a phrase from *Morality and History* that we prefer as a title for this overall project)—produced three writings, only fragments of which have thus far been published. The chronological order of these three writings (in our best guess) is: (1) 589 typed pages of unorganized preparatory notes on ethics, obviously from Sartre to Sartre, which could have been written over several years;[15] (2) 139 typed pages of organized notes which we call *Notes for the 1964 Rome Lecture,* drafted on the occasion of the lecture Sartre gave in May 1964 at the Gramsci Institute in Rome, and which are already in very close to publishable form;[16] and, finally, (3) 120 typed pages of the Cornell lecture notes, *Morality and History,* which are also close to publishable in their present form.

Sartre had sought in vain for at least twenty years to write on ethics in a manner that pleased him. This gives these three writings a pivotal position. Both chronologically and philosophically they occupy a central place in Sartre's writing career. They examine moral phenomena in terms of "praxis," "totalization," and the "practico-inert"—all concepts that Sartre had developed five years earlier in his philosophy of history, *Critique of Dialectical Reason.* However, they also reach back to and extend analyses of "value," "sincerity," and "being-in-and-for-itself" that he had offered in 1943 in his phenomenological ontology *Being and Nothingness.*[17] Finally, they go beyond these works to forge a large new set of conceptual tools: "invention," "ethical radicalism," "unconditional possibility," and "pure future," among many others.

Referring to his entire career, Sartre told an interviewer in 1978, "I have not ceased being a moral philosopher."[18] To the extent that all of Sartre's considerable philosophical resources converge in these three works to provide his most developed written views on morality anywhere, they might even be called the missing center of Sartre's project as a philosopher. They were certainly much more satisfactory to him than either his lecture on humanism[19] or the notes he made on ethics after finishing *Being and Nothingness.*[20] In 1969, referring to this second attack on the ethical problem in the mid-1960s, Sartre told his bibliographers, Michel Contat and Michel Rybalka, that his book on ethics was "entirely composed in his mind, and that the only remaining problems he foresaw were problems of writing it up."[21] He had ample notes to do so. We hope that two of these works—*Morality and History* and the *Notes for the 1964 Rome Lecture*—will be published soon (the 589 pages will require work), since they afford a new and powerful understanding of morality and its relation to history.

Starting with Sartre's extremely brief introduction to the text—one short paragraph outlining the five tasks ahead—we will give a summary review, with little comment, of only the largest steps in the argument of *Morality and History,* a text of 192 manuscript pages. We will conclude by briefly discussing which of the initial five tasks have and have not been undertaken; the relation of *Morality and History* to *Notes for the 1964 Rome Lecture,* which may be called its earlier companion text; and, very briefly, the contemporary pertinence of certain points. We embark on our summary with the caution that it includes many interpretations and selections on our part. It reflects a certain act of reading for which we assume responsibility. Therefore, our summary might aid in grasping Sartre's own text when, after its publication, the reader is finally able to consult it, but it cannot substitute for Sartre's text.

Introduction

The brief introduction to *Morality and History* indicates that Sartre conceived it as applying his "progressive-regressive" method to understanding moral phenomena. This method starts with what is lived immediately in order to grasp it critically. Its first move is to "regressively" uncover intelligible structures of praxis and of human groupings which have been brought together in, and condition, that lived present. One then proceeds to "progressively" reunite these same structures in the present in order to grasp their interplay within living history.[22] In the case of *Morality and History* Sartre sets himself five tasks regarding moral phenomena: (1) to describe and fix ethical conducts and structures with their specific characteristics; (2) to ascertain, really as an extension of (1), whether ethics possesses its own efficacy in the evolution of a practical ensemble; (3) to elucidate the foundations of ethical conducts and their internal laws; (4) to carry out, through rigorous mediations, a progressive synthesis of the various foundational structures in an enriched account of the contemporary practical agent; and (5) to grasp the moral problem as it is manifested to this agent. The first two tasks are phenomenological preliminaries that acquaint us with the domain under investigation. The third is the "regressive" side of the method proper. The last two are the "progressive" side.

The Specificity of the Ethical Experience

Following the brief but dense introduction, the body of the text begins, under the number II and the title above, with a phenomenology of our experience of the ethical in everyday life. This first phenomenological step is "pre-ontological." The *essence* of the ethical will be investigated in the next chapter when Sartre initiates the "regressive" analysis as such. The phenomenology brings out two characters of the ethical in everyday life: first, that the ethical is an extremely *pervasive* structure of everyday experience and, secondly, that it is or can be *effective* historically by itself.

Sartre begins by describing his experience of *L'Aurore,* a conservative French newspaper. An article reports that outdated nerve gas is to be removed from an armory for immersion in the ocean in concrete containers. Sartre notes that this is largely a technical operation; there are alternative methods whose consequences could be discussed. But he remarks that instead of being given such a practical analysis, we are straightaway placed in the ethical domain by the article's headline which commands: "The ocean floor *must not* serve as a public garbage can." In the same issue, an editorial invites readers to vote in the coming elections. It points out the preferability of giving up immediate pleasures, such as the weekend in the country (elections in France being held on Sundays) for the long-term objective of barring the Communists' route to power. Again, however, the editorial's headline, instead of advising or suggesting, commands: "You *must* vote!" Evidently, what this paper disapproves of it treats as moral scandal; what it approves of it treats as civic duty. In both cases, however, it speaks in imperatives. On the whole, Sartre remarks, the paper presents itself as a daily moral guide, a sort of Old Testament update.

This is not just because *L'Aurore*'s writers know that ethical language influences opinion but because its readers prefer to be addressed as moral agents seeking to learn their duties rather than merely as practical agents with interests. Even before purchasing it, they are ready for the paper's "rudimentary" concept of the ethical.

Imperatives surround us, Sartre points out: "post no bills"; "no smoking"; "entry prohibited"; "silence." Each mortgages an aspect of our futures. Imperatives can masquerade as suggestions, pleas, and even as facts, as in the French version of the multilingual railroad car sign: "It is dangerous to lean out the window." The German version of this message—"Nicht hinauslehnen"—is the only one that makes explicit the imperative: "Do not lean out the window."

Just because there are many such imperatives, it does not follow that they are "hypothetical" in Kant's sense. Sartre maintains an ongoing dialogue with Kant in this work, to which we can only make the briefest references. An imperative if hypothetical if it is still binding only on condition of being the object of the agent's own inclination; it is categorical, or universal and necessary, if it is binding in abstraction from all inclination. Sartre takes the directions on a medicine bottle as an example of the ubiquity of categorical imperatives. If such directions presented themselves as hypothetical, they would have to read something like: "If you want to stop suffering, then take two to six capsules." Instead, however, they are strictly categorical: "Dosage . . . from two to six per day," they say. But this is only proper. Having purchased the medicine, when I read the directions I am already suffering and wanting the suffering to cease. Since the well-being I seek is the condition for any subsequent choices, I grasp the directions as rigorously categorical and not as hypothetical. Directions for use generally, typically of the ethical, show explicitly how matter worked by others acquires a specific character that imposes its thinglike rigidity on our present action in the form of imperatives. More subtle is the way workers are compelled to live among categorical imperatives. "Just as categorical is the machine's order to its servant in the milieu of the industrial complex to which he belongs. For it is not true that one can tell a worker: 'If you want to earn your living, etc. . .' Because he does want to, he has always wanted to; it was his future anterior, it is his present, it will be his future." This is because of the "destiny" the existing system imposes on him, and which he must accept. Machines will speak to the workers who serve them, Sartre holds, in a mute but categorical imperative, an imperative that the worker may indeed hate, but which "constitutes nonetheless an ethical determination of his experience."[23]

The Left press also uses imperatives: "Everyone to the polls!" says *L'Humanité,* the French Communist Party daily. But although this resembles *L'Aurore*'s "You must vote!" *L'Aurore* dissimulates the *origin* of its imperative, which lies in the interests of the paper's owners.[24] *L'Humanité,* on the other hand, makes itself a "third" or "medium" by which the working class becomes a self-conscious group.[25] Once formed, the fused group gives itself imperatives. But since the Communist paper, like the conservative one, is addressing the *serialized* masses of its readers, Sartre remarks:

> Meanwhile it suffices to compare [the headline in *L'Humanité*] "Everyone to the polls" to such an imperative as "Everyone get armed" or "Everyone to the Bastille"—which really do show the group projecting a *common* operation—in order to understand the very slight trickery [of *L'Humanité*]: it attempts to elicit the group in fusion by presenting it with a serial operation (each one votes alone) under the aspect of a group operation.[26]

The official Left is also prone to dressing up values and imperatives as facts: Nizan left the party; therefore, he was always a traitor.[27]

The press accumulates, systematizes, and reflects popular ethics and puts it to the service of political ends. But it is difficult for the press to divert such thinking from its own trajectory because of the social momentum of accepted norms. To live in any community, Sartre holds, is both to experience normative pressure and to make one's neighbors feel it.

So far we have seen that norms are widespread prereflexive social structures that usually appear in their imperative form. Clearly ethics is

59

a historical phenomenon. Can the normative also have historical *effects* in its own right? The second half of the second chapter attempts to refute the opinion of structuralists and "scientific" socialists that ethics is a historically ineffective by-product of society's superstructure. To show that ethics can in turn result in genuine historical determinations, Sartre examines the Democratic Party primary elections in the United States of four years earlier, when John F. Kennedy and Hubert H. Humphrey faced off in West Virginia.

As we have seen, Sartre holds that this election was novel, because instead of voting for good *policies,* or for someone who will *do* the electors some good, or even for a good *person*—all frequent normative elements in political life—West Virginians voted for Kennedy in order to *be* good *themselves,* that is, to display a moral virtue in themselves. Their political choice had a purely ethical motive.

Sartre stresses that West Virginia was suffering from chronic unemployment at the time (and today we note that it still is) because the nation's industries had moved from coal—extensively mined in West Virginia—to petroleum combustibles. West Virginians would have been entitled to demand an economic rehabilitation plan of the future president. The only notable difference between the two Democrats was religion: Kennedy was Catholic, Humphrey Protestant. A Catholic had never been elected president. For his part, Kennedy knew that his defeat in a typically Protestant state, if he did not mention religion, would demonstrate his ineligibility. Thus, instead of proposing a solution to West Virginia's unemployment problem, he addressed the question of religion and imposed on the people of the state the normative task of proving his eligibility by showing the virtue of religious tolerance at the polls. He challenged them to break with their conditioned pasts and to determine themselves with regard to a tolerant future which, because normatively required, is "unconditionally possible." Even if for Kennedy this was a "political ruse," it still shows the "historical effectiveness" of morality. The Protestants of West Virginia cannot demonstrate their break with all past conditionings, including the material needs of their state, by voting for Humphrey, who, as a Protestant, cannot ask for their votes in the name of tolerance. The morality that Kennedy imposes coercively invokes fear of moral disapproval by other states, but, since he wins, transforming his handicap into a "moral invention," it is proven effective.

Having shown the efficacy of ethics, Sartre underlines the limits to this effectiveness. In voting their tolerance, West Virginians also voted for a man of a certain class and party who represents definite interests, with the result that a norm is obeyed while the structures of capitalism, which give rise to their own problems, remain untouched. The absolute but evanescent ethical act of voting, with its intentionally limited aim of demonstrating virtue, indicates the enmiring of the West Virginia electorate in what Sartre calls "the paradox of ethics"—which he treats at length in Chapter V. In "voting tolerant" they realize themselves *as what they are*—namely, puritanical Americans who live politics ethically—at the very moment when they believe they are breaking away from their being in order to freely produce themselves. Is this the result of a certain *American* version of the ethical, or is *all* ethical conduct as such a choice of a mystified condition? To answer these questions, Sartre says, we must first define just what a norm is. Meanwhile, this phenomenology of the everyday ethical has shown both that ethics is "a specific factor of history" and that history makes itself "against the ethical."

Of the Essence of the Ethical Normative

The first half of Sartre's third chapter continues the phenomenology of the ethical by surveying the forms that ethical norms take in daily life. The second half, after mentioning what norms have in common, shows through examples the dialectical relations among norms as they are lived.

Norms aim at regulating *human relationships*. Those that seem to bear exclusively on matter do so only insofar as matter mediates human relations. Property, for example, though it is an absolute right in bourgeois society, is nevertheless limited by respect for human work. Sartre insists that even a completely individualistic ethics also defines human relationships, though in this case such relationships are modeled on those between mutually exclusive atoms, that is, as individuals in *a certain relation* to each other. Sartre then gives an inventory of the ways in which the ethical determines human relations: institutions, mores, values, goods, examples, and the ideal.

Institutions—such as the state, language, and property—rule our conduct by imperatives. "Nobody can ignore the law" is an interdiction based on an institution that sets out our duties to and rights against others.

Mores are acts required by custom that carry only the sanction of social disapproval. Mores and institutions sometimes forbid the same thing—murder, for example. On the other hand—Sartre takes the exam-ple of tax laws—the same institution can engender quite different mores. Those in the dominant class who can successfully hide income feel by

61

custom entitled to do so, while state employees, salaried workers, and wage workers in general who cannot hide income tell all to the tax collector and demand that cheaters stop cheating. Here the institution—the tax laws—engenders different mores depending on social class. Neither mores nor institutions alone suffice as a basis for grasping a given society; for that to be possible, they must be taken together in their normative relations to each other. This is because mores and institutions are not radically heterogeneous, both being parts of

> a social whole [which] is organized as the permanent and differential totalization of human relationships in direct link with the struggle against scarcity, that is, with the mode of production. The instrument or the machine, by appearing in a practico-inert field, prefigures the *optima* human relationships, those which will permit, taking into consideration the traditional structures and the conjecture, its *maxima* utilization. Inversely human relationships define and maintain the means of production. Based on this maintenance—according to historical and morphological determinations of the whole—these relationships will be customary or instituted.

In a given national whole the same agent belongs to several different communities at work, at home, at church, and so on. While each such community has its own norms for integrating one and the same agent, these norms are not usually juxtaposed but occur at different dialectical levels. When it does occur, ethical conflict in the same agent is therefore not by chance. Mores—norms unaccompanied by obligation—also include values, goods, examples, and the ideal.

Values in general are examined by Sartre through the value of sincerity, which is held particularly by the middle class of bourgeois society. The account draws together much of what Sartre said on these topics in *Being and Nothingness* but also goes beyond it and deepens it by placing it in the context of society and history. Sincerity is never commanded. It is a being beyond being. Sartre notes the contrast between sincerity and truthfulness, the former being a value, the latter being the object of the imperative "You must not lie."[28] Thus one can tell the truth sincerely or not. Sincerity is a relation to others through oneself: the speaker, in addition to giving the facts, also conveys the *meaning* they hold for him, while aiding the listener to grasp that meaning. Sincerity aims at deepening oneself, even at inventing oneself, as in psychoanalytic self-discovery, which is possible only on condition of self-renunciation. Sincerity may come to us as an imperative, as when a friend might urge a male friend, "Be sincere with yourself, you know . . . that you no longer love your wife." In this case, however, the friend must remain at the level of facts as he sees them, while in sincerity it is their meaning *for me* that is in question. Of course, as Sartre stressed in *Being and Nothingness,* sincerity can itself be undertaken in bad faith.[29] Thus the male friend, to avoid admitting the truth—for example, that he really has ceased to love his wife—might meditate sincerely on the deeper meaning of the word *love.* But, in general, whereas imperatives like "Tell the truth" are intrusions in human relations, values like sincerity aim at deepening them. This is because "sincerity is always reciprocal, which is to say that human relationships are a reciprocity of deepening." Sincerity is at once both a permanent scandal—insofar as one exposes to others the meaning of one's experiences—and a transcending of that scandal—insofar as the project of sincerity also calls for aiding others to grasp that meaning.

Values are norms, Sartre holds, because they propose an end of conduct which, by rearranging both conduct and the givens, can be unconditionally and immediately produced qua autonomous acts: "Thus value is given both as our unconditional and immediate possibility and as the indefinitely receding limit of an action which ceaselessly transforms itself by itself in order to produce itself as *autonomy.*" Autonomy here is not the end, but, because it is the means for realizing values, values are normative. The axiological judgment "This man is sincere" expresses the ethical paradox because it establishes a relation between the agent and an infinite end and at the same time confers on him "an *ethical being.*" The sincere man is motivated by the possibility of coinciding with himself as being-in-itself. Sincerity maintains noncoincidence, but it does so in order that one's actions might coincide with one's "self"— which Sartre defines as "a worked matter."[30] These apparently contrary pursuits of the sincere person are also typical of value in general, which is "being-in-and-for-itself" inasmuch as value gives intentional activity the inert determination of things. Thus: "The opaque heart of value is revealed here as a future exteriority which *comes to man* through the practical interiority of his future and proposes itself to him as the unsurpassable and unconditionally possible result of his creative freedom."

While values give themselves as ends, *goods* give themselves as the unconditional means for realizing either imperatives or values. Life in the biological sense can be either an imperative, a value, or a good, depending on the social class of the agent. For the unfavored, life is a fundamental exigency, an imperative. For the middle class, it is a value to be produced and reproduced. For the privileged, it is a good that is automatically preserved by the labor of others and, as such, is a means for realizing other supposedly more worthy norms.

63

Exemplary conducts are dated and situated acts that seem to be entirely conditioned but in effect deny conditionings and realize an imperative or value of the past or future. Against the ethical pessimism Kant expressed in leaving open the possibility that no one may ever have acted morally, exemplary behaviors encourage us by showing that what must be done can indeed be done because it has in fact already been done. Such conducts manifest the contradictory union of freedom with ethical being that is implicit in all axiological judgment.

The ideal presents itself to the social totality as the intention of uniting norms in a synthetic movement toward an end which would take them into itself.

The "nomenclature" of norms ends at this point.

Norms can show themselves in various ways: they can impose, propose, insinuate, and institute themselves. What do norms have in common? First, they pose determinate ends, that is, conducts that are rigorously defined, and, second, they pose these ends as unconditionally possible. But how can an enterprise present itself as *unconditionally possible* in a historical world in which our action seems conditioned at the least by the state of the practical field, our place in the social totality, our past, and the available means?

An "unconditionally possible" enterprise is not one that "brings together all the means necessary for its success," for such an action would *necessarily* succeed, whereas *one can fail to bring about* what is posed as unconditionally possible. Rather, "unconditionally possible" means "whatever the conditions." The unconditionally possible can remain "an objective but nonrealized possible. However, if it must be permanently a possible—even if it never turns into being—its possibility must be a permanent structure of human behaviors or, in any case, of some of them."

To illustrate, but also to ramify this point, Sartre turns to a case involving lying, the same one whose meaning he had pondered in the *Notes for the 1964 Rome Lecture,*[31] though now it is treated in much greater detail. A group of *lycéennes,* high school women, are asked in a polling questionnaire: "Do you lie?" Ninety percent answer yes. But to the question "Should lying be condemned?" ninety-five percent again answer yes. Sartre insists that the *lycéennes* are not saying the norm against lying applies only to others; it is themselves that they also condemn. How, then, should the *lycéennes'* contradictory answers be understood?

To answer, Sartre develops a series of further examples (not all of which we will summarize) to show how norms, and especially, *relations among norms,* are actually lived.

First, Sartre develops the hypothesis that the *lycéennes* are engaging in "moral casuistry." This, he explains, is the pretense of preserving a norm in general while permitting all the exceptions one wishes in particular circumstances—on the sole condition that these circumstances be rigorously defined. The Jesuits' "softening" of the imperative against usury (in the sixteenth century) is his example of how unlimited numbers of exceptions to a norm can be reconciled with its strict maintenance. Later he will say whether this hypothesis is confirmed or not.

Meanwhile, Sartre adds yet another hypothesis: perhaps the *lycéennes* are experiencing moral conflict. Sartre avoids a Marxian confinement of morality to "superstructures" by insisting that norms are at *all* social levels, deep norms linked by mediations to surface ones. Ethical conflict in the same agent—for example, the contradiction resulting from choosing a surface group over and against one's deepest memberships—is not accidental because there *are* contradictions between groups and between their norms. These conflicts occur in the unitary movement implied in each agent's reproduction of his singularity.

To probe this hypothesis of moral conflict, Sartre describes at length a young couple whose portrait would likely have resonated with his audience of young men and women at Cornell. He gives this context for the couple: they live in a Puritanical society; the wife is ill with a death-dealing cancer; the husband alone knows the truth that she will die within a year; and the overall normative perspective of the couple is conditioned by what Sartre calls "moral comfort," which is a form of inauthenticity. Normally this couple finds it *easy* to tell the truth to each other, which Sartre understands as follows: "This means: when the practical field and its practico-inert structure favor the realization of the unconditionally possible, the latter conserves its normative appearance but becomes a conditioned unconditional: there remains an exigency which must be realized regardless of the historical conditions, but which, from the outside and by their interiorization, the historical conditions happen precisely to prefigure." A deep conflict of norms is afoot in the case at hand, between the imperative of truthfulness and the value of life as fully lived. However, moral comfort consists here in the fact that circumstances cause this conflict to remain unfelt by the couple. The separation of communities to which we belong and the consequent separation of the norms integrating these communities usually allow such moral comfort. However, the upsurge of the risk of ruining his wife's life with the disclosure of her coming death breeches these separations and upsets moral comfort, forcing a nonhabitual choice on the husband. He asks himself: Should I tell her the truth, namely, that she is ill with leukemia and will die in a year's time?

Since this couple has up to now preferred the socially dominant imperative of truthfulness as a means of preserving itself, eschewing the more radical value of sincerity for this purpose, the husband, paradoxically, now chooses to lie. But the paradox recedes somewhat when we consider that the point of lying here, as with telling the truth in the normal case, is still to conserve the existing array of social structures, which of course include his own conjugal family. Lying now becomes his new imperative. Truthfulness in this critical situation would require him to invent a new model of relationship with his wife—a relationship up to now conditioned by Puritan prudery, lack of sincerity, and "inequality between the sexes." The husband lies now because he lacks the resources for such invention in himself or in his (typically dominant) class. The couple's possibility of surpassing the given reality is therefore rejected in favor of its "wise" preservation of itself as previously conditioned by the social whole: "We find again the reactionary presupposition of all wisdom: that in a given society, defined starting with its means of production by the institutions that rule human relationships, human life is ethically livable, or, if you prefer, that humanity is always possible."[32]

The knowledge of his wife's certain and approaching death introduces the husband to what is for him a new norm—that of dominated classes, namely, that nobody should be reduced to despair. He is thereby also introduced to moral conflict. Of course, as Sartre notes, the same social whole from whose lower ranks this norm comes also daily reduces many to despair. But the husband learns that his own wife's up-to-then "moderate" and "dignified" life free of despair is no longer possible, except *on the condition* that he lie to her. Lying effectively keeps her from facing in her own life the truth that haunts both their society and the particular couple that these two persons have chosen to institute based on that society. Of course, this means that truthfulness is henceforth understood by the husband to be historically conditioned. Historical conditions had up to then made it normal and easy to follow the dominant unconditional norm of truthfulness; now, with the threat of death, these same conditions require either renouncing the norm as such or explicitly violating it. The husband chooses the latter. There are two results. First, the husband's moral comfort and "ethical optimism" are shattered as he sees that realizing all norms is *not* unconditionally possible. Second, instead of "deepening" the norm of avoiding despair which originates in unfavored classes (a deepening that would at best be very hard for him precisely because of this norm's alien, unfamiliar origins), this norm is "transformed" by his conduct into "the fascist ethic." Sartre is pointing, by this harsh characterization, to the husband's theft of his wife's control over her future and to his systematic treatment of her as an object—both of which are implicit in his persistent, moral upholding of the imperative to lie.

What does this example have in common with the lying *lycéennes?* The two hypotheses Sartre entertains for understanding the *lycéennes* can also be considered in the case of the lying husband: are the *lycéennes* and the husband engaging in casuistry and/or experiencing moral conflict? Sartre remarks that both the husband and the *lycéennes* lie in contravention of the dominant ethic, and at the same time they want the lie to be universally condemned. Sartre now concludes that the hypothesis of casuistry is disconfirmed since there is no casuistical "softening" of the imperative of truthfulness for either the husband or the *lycéennes.* The *lycéennes* and the husband both judge their conduct as being morally wrong. As for the hypothesis of moral conflict, the husband at least certainly experiences it. For him the lie was a practical way out of this conflict; it avoided the difficult task of self-invention.

What, then, does Sartre conclude from this typically Sartrean "example" that itself defines the concepts it is to exemplify? Sartre draws two conclusions. First, "It is not in casuistry that one finds the possibility of 'humanizing' the norm but in the extension and the deepening of practice, that is to say, in *ethos* grasped as the unfolding totalization of life." Second, this "practice"—that is, breaking the impasse by lying in order to save his wife from despair—opposes the human as undertaking to the "man of repetition" who is maintained by obedience to imperatives, in this case, the imperative of telling the truth. This opposition between creative and repetitive praxis cannot itself be understood without distinguishing what is unconditionally possible, that is, ethical action, from what is historically possible, that is, historical action. This distinction is treated in Sartre's next chapter.

In general, the third chapter recalls to us the footnote in *Saint Genet* according to which ethics is "impossible." The next chapter shows, as the footnote goes on to say, that ethics is also "inevitable."[33]

Of Unconditional Possibility as Structure of the Norm

In the fourth chapter Sartre attempts to determine the character of the ethical "moment" as such within history. This is a preliminary to "establishing the foundations of a dialectics of the ethical and the histori-cal." This task is sketched and only partially initiated in *Morality and History*. In this chapter Sartre shows not only that the unconditionally possible, as a structure of ethical action, is characteristic of a sector of human activity called "ethical" but that this structure is founded on what Sartre calls "the moment of invention," which is present in all historical praxis as such.

Historical or conditioned action can engender unconditional action typical of the ethical because historical action already has a dialectical structure. First, ends and means are not separate but instead recipro-cally determine each other within historical action, which Sartre some-times refers to as "action" *simpliciter:* "But as indeed action tempo-ralizes itself we must understand the whole as an unfolding totalization. In this sense the objective to be attained by an action is presented in the course of the undertaking as the totalization of means used to attain it." The end of an action is already partially present as the internally linked or totalized parts of the action itself. Even aborted actions are compre-hensible only as incomplete parts of a whole in progress. As a result, from the practical viewpoint of agency, it is the future that conditions the present, illuminating the latter as a field of possible tools available for the realization of that future. The desire for something absent, some-thing that will constitute a *future* satisfaction, reveals action in the *pres-ent* as the conversion of an "impossibility" (say, hunger as the felt impos-sibility of eating) into something unconditionally possible, that is, into the satisfaction of the hunger through eating food. As the French say, "larks do not fall roasted into the mouth," meaning that I must first catch and cook the lark, that is, I *must* act, if my needs are to be met. But, in a novel twist of Kant's insight, this imperative to act also implies that I *can* meet my needs provided I undertake a project of doing so (though it is not guaranteed that I *will*). It is therefore praxis which "destructures" the impossibility that confronts me in the present (e.g., the absence of food around me) and "restructures" this same field as so many possibilities, that is, as means for getting food. Sartre calls this double process *invention*—a necessary moment of praxis that is specifi-cally ethical. Invention is that moment of historical praxis generally that can lend to any particular project its aspect of unconditional possibility. Of course, given the encounter with matter and the practico-inert, the project may also fail.

Invention is that moment in all human action that reveals the "uten-sility" of things, that is, their relative susceptibility to rearrangement in new hierarchies chosen according to *my* end, hierarchies that were not originally given before the invention–moment of praxis: "Invention as a fundamental moment of praxis qualifies all work as the transformation of the impossible into the possible by the modification of present conditions of possibility based on the goal to be realized." Thus it is in praxis that the future conditions the past through the present *instead of* (as in positivist metaphysics) the past making use of the present in order to condition the future. Thus: "far from envisaging the present—given as delimiting the possibilities for the realization of an end, the end defines the action as the invention of these possibilities by destructuration and restructuration of this given."

Again, to say that there is an unconditioned moment of praxis is not to say that praxis always succeeds. Impossibility can "reappear" *within* invention in the form of obstacles. Sartre refers to Gestalt experiments with monkeys that rearrange boxes in their cages in order climb up and grasp a banana suspended from the ceiling. The monkeys discover a gap between their highest reach and the banana because the pile of boxes is not tall enough. Even though this failure was foreseen and planned by the experimenters, that plan is not a univocal conditioning in exteriority of the future by a past since the gap could not have been discovered at all by the monkeys prior to the moment of invention. This shows that invention reveals *to itself* its conditionings and limits through restructuration of the field. Historical action, which embraces ethical action, can fail if circumstances change. Indeed such action can produce "counter-finalities"—inversion of the human into an inhuman future—but it can do so only on condition that something is first *undertaken*. We have discovered the root of Kant's "you must therefore you can," which, in terms of historical action, translates into "if I *must* do *x* then *I will find the means*." All human action has such an ethical moment—invention—even if the result—historical praxis—contradicts the act.

Sartre makes clear that so far we have only seen that norms are *possible*. We have described freedom prior to its alienation. No particular normative system can be deduced from the description of historical praxis up to this point. In short, we are still engaged in the regressive analysis of the essential structures of norms, and in particular of the unconditional possibility of doing the actions they enjoin.

Usually, Sartre remarks at this point, we undertake actions with *several* ends or values in view, all of which we attempt to realize at the least cost. So, to isolate and describe unconditional possibility in its purity, Sartre turns to those very rare cases when a single imperative must be maintained by the agent at all costs. He analyzes the cases of three victims of torture—Fucik,[34] Alleg,[35] and Brossolette[36]—who in two different ways maintained the imperative of silence, keeping the secrets of their clandestine organizations. Of Sartre's many approaches to the question of torture—literary and philosophical[37]—this is certainly the most philosophically systematic and, in our view, the most profound.

The torturers presume to use Fucik and Alleg, but by depriving their suffering of the negative moral value it otherwise possesses almost universally, Fucik and Alleg use their torturers for *their* end, which is silence. They do so without pursuing death as a means to silence. Brossolette, on the other hand, fearing he may talk after his first "session," seeks death, restructuring his practical field in order to bring about his own death as a good, that is, as an unconditional means to silence.

What Sartre calls "ethical radicalism" does not consist in choosing life or death but rather in making of one's contingent existence the means needed to realize an unconditioned end by integrating that very existence into praxis itself:

> At this level, the true meaning of unconditionality is revealed: it is the possibility in me of producing myself as an autonomy which affirms itself by dominating external circumstances instead of being dominated by them; or, if you prefer, it is the possibility of producing myself as a pure subject of interiority by subordinating my life to the success of the undertaking as if it was my end which had elicited my facticity in the historical world as its unique means of realizing itself.

So profoundly does the imperative of silence grip these three torture victims that one might say from the point of view of praxis that they are made or born in order to keep silent. Even one's character is modifiable in this perspective. If my past conditions me to lie habitually, then this past becomes, in the light of the pure future, *what it must have been* in order for me now to realize the imperative of truthfulness.

"Will I be able to hold out?" the Resistance militant ponders prior to arrest. Prediction is impossible: "I know that of the percentage of those who did talk, 100 percent held silence as the unconditioned norm. At this level the historical agent, for his part, will make history by giving it the meaning he wants to give it only by transforming himself into an ethical agent." How shall we understand a Resistance militant who says that he might not be able to hold out under torture yet also unhesitatingly condemns those who talk, just as the *lycéennes* lie and yet condemn lying? Both, Sartre says, wish to preserve the unconditional possibility of a conduct that excludes conditioning in order to conform itself to norms, as in Kant's "you must therefore you can." As Sartre had said in the *Notes for the 1964 Rome Lecture,* the *lycéennes* do not intend by their condemnation of lying to renounce the practice; rather, they simply want the option, the freedom, to tell the truth because "if lying is allowed [unopposed], it becomes reality and truth is only a deceptive illusion [*une apparence mensongère*]."

The content of norms aside, their very existence denounces our status as subhumans, which Sartre describes as our empirical inability, "revocable but never revoked," to surpass our "historical condition as subjects-objects" and become a "subject of interiority," that is, an autonomous project with an internal relation of end to means:

> Ethics envisaged as a determination of activity appears at first as an essential but provisional moment of all praxis: indeed praxis tears itself away from the given—that is, from present conditions—by transcending it toward a nonbeing from which praxis returns to the given in order to invent its own conditions of possibility. In this moment of *invention,* praxis posits its goal as unconditional, that is, as a future nonbeing which creates, from the heart of the future, the means for its realization.

There are particular ends, Sartre says, which give themselves as realizable solely through "pure praxis," that is, through praxis "defined" by its ethical moment, and which constitute this moment "as action itself in its full flowering." These ends are visible "through all historical ends as their true meaning." Thus Resistance-praxis, not the particular politics of the Resistance, implies as its end "the human." Though this end is left undefined, it is characterized in this case, according to Sartre, by transforming myself through integration of my fundamental contingency, taken as a means, into the enterprise of the Resistance as a historical undertaking. This is the only glimpse we are given in *Morality and History* of the optimistic universe of revolutionary praxis that is treated in *Notes for the 1964 Rome Lecture.*

At the level at which the inquiry has taken place up to now, ethical victory can be accompanied by historical failure. An obvious example would be the feudal knight who dies saying "All is lost except honor." Here ethics is the residue after history has broken the undertaking. One wants to succeed, but when one fails, the ethical end substitutes for the historical one. But here the contradiction between the ethical and the historical has been "emphasized in order to show the necessity of establishing the foundations of a dialectics of ethics and history."

Sartre says that this analysis shows that ethics is possible. Now he poses the question of "the structure of ends which demand to be attained by the realization of this possibility."

71

The Paradox of Ethos

The fifth chapter,[38] though short and obviously incomplete, initiates this topic. It begins by remarking that the ends of action are inseparable from its structure and from the process of making oneself a subject of interiority—Kant to the contrary notwithstanding. One cannot even attempt to make oneself such a subject by treating others as subjects in the abstract. Rather, one makes oneself a subject of interiority only by aiming at some precise end, for example, to tell the truth, to honor one's parents, to realize the value of sincerity, and so on.

Social ensembles have ambiguous attitudes toward ethical action. They both esteem and mistrust ethical agents inasmuch as the latter take the entire practical field—including the established social order—as unconditional means for realizing their ends. In general, social ensembles recognize themselves more in norms viewed as definite *tasks* for which people are the means than in the people who accomplish these tasks by realizing the unconditional—such people being unreliable in maintaining the status quo. But Sartre says this ambiguity in "popular thought"[39] actually reflects "a knot of contradictions" in "the very structure of ethos." He proceeds to describe the following four aspects of this paradox of ethos.

1. While the ends of action, which may also be characterized as "normative maxims" (examples would be to defend honor, to defend one's right not to die of hunger, etc.), vary enormously in history and in existing societies, the ethical radicalism required for attaining these ends is invariant: "Thus historically variable ends are attained from one end of history to another by the same type of action. In its ethical structure, the act of Harmodenes and Aristogiton, who sacrificed their lives to kill a tyrant, does not differ from the act of two Vietnamese who sacrificed their lives to blow up the U.S. embassy in Saigon."

2. Normative ensembles, even in historical societies where change is irreversible, tend to stabilize into repetitive forms. Like the present juridical system, such forms sustain the distribution of social power against change. Consequently, what is given as unconditionally possible for ethical radicalism may well be, paradoxically, the maintenance of existing relations of domination. Dominated groups then constitute themselves paradoxically as both ethical demands and as the radical negation of all ethics as such. Such groups are greeted either with casuistry or with rejection. Yet despite such efforts at exclusion, history moves on irreversibly. This fact was experienced more intimately by virtually all Resistance militants, for example, than by any of their reac-

tionary Nazi adversaries, insofar as facing the possibility of torture meant facing the absolute inability to "take back" any information that might be yielded to the Nazis. Sartre contends that as a result of this encounter with the irreversibility of historical time, Resistance groups of all political persuasions tended toward "progressivism."

3. Or, to put the paradox yet another way, even though the norms discussed up to now give themselves as suprahistorical, untranscendable, and unrealizable—sincerity, for example, as a value, can only be attempted, never attained—these "normative objects" also have an "internal inertia" that causes them to be constantly transcended by history. Feudal honor, a "good" that one can conserve but never possess, being tied to a certain mode of production which disappears with the rise of the new bourgeois class, simply becomes outdated and forgotten, dying qua good without a fight.

4. While unconditionality implies the novelty of a pure future, this novelty can be employed to preserve a dead past, and the pure future can be filled with repetition. "There is unconditionality," Sartre says, "when the pure future is subjected to an inert and repetitive past." The truth of this paradoxical formulation may even be evident to those agents who live it. Typically this includes those who know historical changes are eliminating their group and its normative ensemble yet who unconditionally maintain that group and its ethics in opposition to history. In short, in addition to being unconditional, norms are what Sartre calls "social facts." It is possible both to feel obligated by a norm and yet to describe it as a social fact, as would an anthropologist. Thus one might both be obliged to realize a certain marriage form as an unconditional possibility and yet also accurately report the same form as a social fact to a foreigner or a social scientist, as in "We marry in such and such a manner." The ethically radical act that realizes a norm is therefore in contrast with the fact that all societies view their normative systems as inert facts that protect the established order.

Having outlined these four aspects of the ethical paradox, Sartre briefly discusses conscientious objection to war and various responses to it, among which he considers the Kantian question "What if everyone did as you are doing?" The discussion is an interesting non sequitur. The chapter ends without conclusion.

The sixth and last chapter in the text is titled "Paradox and Marxist Structuralism."[40] It contains this single sentence: "A certain Marxist tendency tends to reduce the paradox by making normative and axiological ensembles into ideal but real structures of society."

As if one had raised the needle off the record in the middle of a song, as in Sartre's novel *Nausea,* the text stops at this point.[41] Just as the last sentence prefigures the writing's next phase, historical time seems to win out over ethical time.

Conclusion

In concluding, we would like to warn against one possible misunderstanding: to attribute to Sartre a Kantian idealism that would identify the mere undertaking of a conduct with its success, provided only that it is moral in intent. The ethical moment—unconditional possibility—is a moment of *historical* praxis. Sartre calls it the moment of invention. This is its foundational structure "prior to" alienation, which we take to indicate a logical rather than a chronological priority. But since invention is subsumed within history, it is of course subject to obstacles, to interruption, or to deviation into a "counterfinality"—such that one does not recognize one's action in the result. Thus it is possible for a project both to be undertaken as unconditionally possible and to *fail,* for the question of success or failure depends on history. On the other hand, within a historical totalization, once praxis is undertaken its ethical moment represents both freedom tearing itself unconditionally from being *and* the possibility of the free alienation of that freedom. It is also possible for failure to be "built into" the ethical project itself, because of a mistaken relation to the normative. The married couple enters a morass of alienation and failure in attempting to live according to a norm—a project whose a priori impossibility Sartre maintained throughout his *oeuvre.* But, contrary to many misreadings of Sartre's early remarks on ethics, failure is no more necessary than success.[42] The example of the Resistance militants shows how, through an "ethical radicalism" that makes one's contingent facticity itself into a means to an end, ethical praxis can be subsumed in a successful historical totalization. Thus merely because a conduct has a moral intent does not, either historically or a priori, guarantee its success or its failure.

How many of the introduction's original five tasks did Sartre actually undertake in *Morality and History* before suspending the effort? In Chapter II the phenomenology of the ethical and the demonstration of its historical effectiveness—tasks one and two—were obviously not only undertaken but finished. Task three, the regressive analysis of the essence of the ethical, begins with Chapter III's "nomenclature" displaying the various types of norms and extends through the lengthy analysis of unconditional possibility in Chapter IV. However, Chapter V, with its analysis of the paradox of ethos, continues the regressive task of laying out the foundations of ethical experience, paradoxical though they may be. And the glimpse we are given of Chapter VI suggests that even if Sartre had been able to finish this chapter, he would not have completed the regressive side of his analysis of moral phenomena. Consequently, as in the case of the first volume of the *Critique of Dialectical Reason*—the only volume published by Sartre himself—we must conclude that Sartre did not get as far as the progressive task of showing how normative structures interact within living history. In this case, the point of the progressive synthesis would have been to show how the ethical problem presents itself to his listeners, as of 1965—a question on which Sartre's views would have been most interesting. We surmise that the working out of the progressive synthesis was abandoned when Sartre decided not to go to Cornell.

What is the relation of *Notes for the 1964 Rome Lecture* to *Morality and History?* The optimistic morality of revolutionary praxis sketched a year earlier is curiously understated in the later writing, which is a more systematic if less complete work, dwelling on alienated forms of moral phenomena. It is helpful to keep in mind that the audience of the *Notes for the 1964 Rome Lecture* was mainly intellectuals of the Italian Communist Party (the speakers were mostly non-Italians). The audience of *Morality and History* was to be upper- and middle-class whites at Cornell University. In a sense the difference, no doubt itself carefully chosen by Sartre (who received large numbers of invitations to speak during that period), could be said to be between the working class and the ruling class at their respective points of self-consciousness. Given Sartre's warm relations with the Italian Communist Party, the least Stalinized of any of the mass-based Western parties, it would be natural for him to feel more at ease, and perhaps more philosophically expansive, with the Rome audience. It is even possible that he planned *both* lectures *before starting on the first,* since he had known of Cornell's interest for at least a year before May 1964 and even accepted Cornell's invitation the previous year at least a month before he was due to speak in Rome.

In any case, we believe, though we cannot provide the full argument here, that the fundamental ideas in *Morality and History* are the start of a detailed working out of some of the ideas sketched in the first half of the *Notes for the 1964 Rome Lecture. Morality and History* as a whole is "regressive" in method, developing what the *Notes for the 1964 Rome Lecture* had argued in summary form in the first two of its four chapters, namely, that morality "exists at the very level of what is called the infrastructure."[43] Chapter II of the *Notes for the 1964 Rome Lecture* develops the two-sidedness of values,[44] a point made more elegantly in

75

Morality and History but which had not been fully treated in that latter work even as it breaks off after Chapter VI. Only in *Notes for the 1964 Rome Lecture,* starting in Chapter III, does Sartre proceed to the progressive synthesis of moral phenomena—task four in the introduction to *Morality and History.* His analysis in this chapter on the Algerian Revolution, taken as a case of Third World struggles for self-determination, reunites the formal structures of norms in the historical present. And finally, Chapter IV of *Notes for the 1964 Rome Lecture,* which treats contemporary revolutionary praxis as the only "moral" form of praxis, prefigures a possible fulfillment of the fifth and last task that had been planned for Cornell, namely, to pose the moral problem as it presents itself to the contemporary practical agent.

Both sets of notes are, we believe, two aspects of a single project—to understand moral phenomena historically—and they yield a single conception of the human future. The *Notes for the 1964 Rome Lecture* sketch this ambitious project in its "optimistic" aspect, an amplitude perhaps determined in part by its audience of fellow leftists. *Morality and History* provides the project's darker and also more analytical aspects, perhaps in part because of *its* audience of heirs to the dominant power's privileged classes. In the paradoxes and dialectical oppositions they uncover, both works recall Sartre's description in *Saint Genet,* quoted above, of the tension in morality caused by its being both "impossible" and "inevitable." And yet, keeping in mind Sartre's account of history as we study these two sets of notes, we can perhaps now describe this tension in a less dichotomous manner, one that would allow us to envision its resolution. History for Sartre is always history as modified by scarcity. The ethical is therefore what mediates human relationships *within the struggle against scarcity.* In this context, norms legitimate the coding of groups for exclusion from production and consumption. But then this perspective also leaves open the possibility that norms will tend to be dissolved in praxis itself, along with other forms of the practico-inert, in proportion as a postscarcity society is attained. If and when such an end is approximated, freedom, understood as autonomous praxis, can gradually replace coincidence with norms as the goal of human conduct. The transitions from ethical radicalism through the paradox of ethos to human praxis as autonomy—which in turn implies struggle against all oppressions—are made gradually in these two works. Together they constitute "the culminating point" of Sartre's thinking on ethics[45] in their heroic effort to demonstrate that autonomy is a human possibility within history.

Not only *Notes for the 1964 Rome Lecture* but also the 589 pages of soliscript and *Morality and History* itself give many indications for projecting the ways in which the "dialectics of ethics and history" might be developed had Sartre continued this project. The incomplete text of *Morality and History* exemplifies what Sartre says within it, namely, that even actions that are stopped while in progress—in this case the writing of these very lectures—can be understood based not on their past but on the future toward which they aim. That which totalizes the means—namely, the end—is present in the parts of the act as their meaning, even when that end is not achieved.

It is uncanny to read this subversive and "indirect" text, hidden for twenty-three years, today. As the Reagan epoch and the ascendancy of the Christian right wane in the United States and evidence of renewed political activism grows, we may very well be at the threshold of an era of massive challenges to established social structures, like the one that actually followed Sartre's two sets of lectures. Two points that Sartre makes in *Morality and History* speak directly to our present situation.

First, Sartre argues that the domain of the moral, as uncovered so far, may be all that is left to the ethical agent after history has "broken" his project. In Sartre's example, "All is lost except honor" is the cry of the feudal knight as he dies. We have heard similar cries from Oliver North before the congressional committee investigating the Iran-contra scandal, and from mass-audience TV preachers before their congregations. These contemporaries treat the ethical domain containing their good intentions as a kind of cosmic consolation prize for being marginalized by history. Knowing that history has excluded them and their norms, they choose nonetheless to make a "last stand." (Of course, Sartre is also pointing out that the ethical *can be* part of a successful historical project, as the example of the Resistance militants shows.)

Second, as do many of Sartre's texts, *Morality and History* presents us with a choice. Sartre defined freedom in 1969 as "the small movement which makes of a totally conditioned social being someone who does not render back completely what his conditioning has given him."[46] Like the students Sartre was to address in 1965, we too have destinies laid out by our historical situations and interiorized as our "self." What do we make of this "self," this "worked matter" that amounts to a future destiny within us? We can fulfill it, assume it, choosing to repeat existing structures—and, in effect, to fail—like the lying husband. Or we can invent, and succeed historically, as did the Resistance militants. That is the choice we think Sartre is presenting his readers in this work. Sartre's couple is evidence that rendering back completely to the dominant morality its prior conditioning of us leads to bogging down in alienation, self-oppression, and oppression of others. Sartre is opening the possibility of an alternative, a novel future.

And that, after all, seems to be Sartre's urging in *Morality and History:* we are to radically restructure the given practical field toward human ends, rather than allow the inertia of that field to align our "self" and our praxis toward *its* inhuman counterfinalities.

Notes

We thank Arlette Elkaïm-Sartre for her generous authorization and correction of quotes from these unpublished writings and John Gerassi for granting us initial access to them.

1. Cable to Dr. James A. Perkins, president of Cornell University, received March 17, 1965. Reported in the *New York Times,* March 18, 1965, 4; reprinted in *Cornell Alumni News,* 67, no. 9 (April 1965), 25.

2. Since this title appeared in French as *Morale et histoire* (only in the first edition of the *New York Times* article cited above), we assume it is the one Sartre gave to his hosts. We thank Cornell University archivist Elaine Engst for finding this "first edition." The French title is translated in the *Cornell Alumni News* 67, no. 8 (March 1965), 23, as *Ethics and History.* However, since *Morality and History* is the correct translation of the French that is given, we shall refer to these lecture notes by the latter title. Sartre said in *Le Nouvel Observateur* (April 8, 1965) that his general topic would be "Flaubert or Kant"— the interview was reprinted in *Situations* VIII (Paris, 1972), 25. Much later, in 1978, Sartre said "Recherches pour une morale" was the title of his Cornell lectures ("Sartre," interview by Michel Sicard, *Obliques,* no. 18–19, 1979, 14). We use the title we believe Sartre gave his hosts *prior* to the time of the scheduled lectures, that is, when he still intended to present them.

3. We thank Professor Carol Greenhouse, current chair of Cornell's University Lectures Committee, for making extensive portions of the committee's files available to us. We are also grateful to Professors Jean-Jacques Demorest, Alain Seznec, and Edward Morris for their cooperation in pinning down the details of "the Sartre disaster," as the nonevent was called in the *Cornell Alumni News* of April 1965 and in the minutes of the first committee meeting after the cancellation. Cornell University Press was considering publishing Sartre's lectures, according to Professor Seznec.

4. By the fall of 1964, Professor Alain Seznec of the Department of Romance Studies had also conveyed Cornell's welcome of Simone de Beauvoir, a factor that apparently figured in confirming Sartre's willingness to come.

5. Sartre had reason to note the new aspect the conflict had assumed, starting in February 1965. On February 6, the Vietcong attacked Pleiku, a U.S. Army base, causing high casualties. The United States immediately retaliated by bombing North Vietnam. February 10 saw another Vietcong attack, to which the United States also retaliated. But defense became offense. By March 2, the United States had decided to begin regular and sustained bombing against North Vietnam. This policy was code-named "Rolling Thunder." On March 8, the first United States combat troops landed in South Vietnam, in addition to the United States advisors. In all, thirty-five hundred Marines went in at Danang. March 19 marked the beginning of the United States offensive. Astoundingly,

North Vietnam did not surrender. Tito of Yugoslavia, de Gaulle of France, the Chinese, and the UN all had negotiation plans proposed to the White House. The American response was the slowly ascending tempo of Rolling Thunder. The United States sent in eighteen thousand to twenty thousand "support forces." Source: Guenter Lewy, *America in Vietnam* (New York, 1978).

6. Sartre, "Il n'y a plus de dialogue possible," *Situations* VIII (Paris, 1972), 13–14. In 1964 Sartre had been awarded, and had declined, the Nobel Prize for Literature.

7. D. I. Grossvogel, "Un Américain écrit à Sartre," *Situations* VIII, 21–22. The article identifies Grossvogel as "a member of the group which invited J.-P. Sartre." However, while Grossvogel might well have helped with the arrangements as a member of the Romance Studies Department, he was not at the time a member of the University Lectures Committee which administered the Messenger Lectures and had invited Sartre. Significantly, the debate with Grossvogel over *Morality and History* opens Sartre's volume of selections of recent occasional pieces, *Situations* VIII.

8. Sartre, "Sartre répond," *Situations* VIII, 25. As it happens, Grossvogel is having the last word in this matter: he taught a course on Sartre at Cornell in the spring of 1988. When we approached Grossvogel, he communicated to us through his secretary that he had researched the Sartre affair of 1965 and found no records whatsoever available at Cornell.

9. See chapter 1 of this volume.

10. Jean-Paul Sartre, *Critique of Dialectical Reason*, Vol. I: *Theory of Practical Ensembles*, trans. by Alan Sheridan-Smith, ed. by Jonathan Rée (London, 1976); and Vol. II: *L'Intelligibilité de l'histoire*, text established by Arlette Elkaïm-Sartre (Paris, 1985). We henceforth cite the first volume of this work as *CDR*.

11. Jean-Paul Sartre, *L'Idiot de la famille*, Vols. I and II (Paris, 1970), and Vol. III (Paris, 1972).

12. *Sartre by Himself,* film directed by Alexandre Astruc and Michel Contat, trans. by Richard Seaver (New York, 1978), 81.

13. Michel Contat and Michel Rybalka, *The Writings of Jean-Paul Sartre*, Vol. I, trans. by Richard C. McLeary (Evanston, Ill., 1974), 449. We refer to this work henceforth as *Writings*.

14. This fact came out in conversations in March 1988 with Michel Contat, who finds evidence that Sartre continued to work on *Morality and History* after the cancellation. We are also mindful of the risk of overlooking the "co-implicative" character of "the ethical and the political and the historical" for Sartre after 1945, as has been pointed out by William L. McBride in "The Evolution of Sartre's Conception of Morals," *Phenomenological Inquiry* (October 1987), 31.

15. In *Obliques*, no. 18–19 (1979), 347, Contat and Rybalka refer to "[Notes sur la Morale] environ 600 feuillets de notes prises en 1964–65 sur la morale dialectique en vue de conférences que Sartre devait donner aux Etats-Unis en 1965." To our present knowledge, there exist 589 pages of this "soliscript" (Michel Contat's apt neologism) written, we believe, in preparation for, yet separate from, both the *Notes for the 1964 Rome Lecture* and *Morality and History*.

16. For a summary of the *Notes for the 1964 Rome Lecture,* see our "Dialectical Ethics: A First Look at Sartre's Unpublished *1964 Rome Lecture Notes*," *Social Text,* no. 13–14 (Winter–Spring 1986), 195–215; and for a discussion of one of the central arguments in the *Notes for the 1964 Rome Lecture,* see our "Making the Human in Sartre's Dialectical Ethics," in *The Future of Continental Philosophy and the Politics of Difference,* ed. by Hugh J. Silverman, (Buffalo, N.Y., 1989). The primary fragments of "the dialectics

of ethics and history" so far published are "Determinism and Freedom," in Contat and Rybalka, Vol. II, 241–52; this extract is typescript pp. 6–18 and pp. 23–28 of the 139 typescript pages of the *Notes for the 1964 Rome Lecture*. For a discussion of this short extract, see Gerhard Seel, "Wie hatte Sartres Moralphilosophie Ausgesehen?" in *Sartre, Ein Kongress,* ed. by Traugott König (Frankfurt, 1988), 276–93. Selected phrases from the *Notes for the 1964 Rome Lecture* are also in Francis Jeanson, *Sartre* (Paris, 1966), 137–38. The original manuscript of *Notes for the 1964 Rome Lecture* is available for consultation at the Bibliothèque Nationale in Paris.

17. *Being and Nothingness: An Essay in Phenomenological Ontology,* trans. by Hazel E. Barnes (New York, 1956).

18. Interview with Sicard, 14.

19. "Existentialism Is a Humanism," in *Existentialism from Dostoevsky to Sartre,* ed. by Walter Kaufmann (Cleveland, 1956). See Sartre's cautions against taking this work as representative of his thinking on ethics in Astruc and Contat, *Sartre by Himself,* 74–75.

20. One of several notebooks from this period up to 1950 has been published as *Cahiers pour une morale* (Paris, 1983). Sartre later renounced this effort as "a failed attempt" in the interview with Sicard, 14. See also *Sartre by Himself,* 77–78, 80–81; and also these same works for Sartre's contrasting expressions of satisfaction with his later work on ethics of the mid-1960s. We should also mention the so-called third ethics that Sartre is said to have composed after his blinding stroke of 1973 in taped conversations with Benny Lévy. So far this effort, which Sartre and Lévy called "Pouvoir et liberté," has resulted in a set of interviews and a book by Lévy: "L'Espoir, maintenant . . . ,"*Le Nouvel Observateur,* nos. 800, 801, 802 (March 10, 17, 24, 1980); *Le Nom de l'homme: dialogue avec Sartre* (Lagrasse, 1984). The book contains only small fragments attributed to Sartre. For Lévy's more recent comments on Sartre and ethics, see Stuart L. Charmé, "From Maoism to the Talmud (with Sartre Along the Way): An Interview with Benny Lévy," *Commentary* 78, no. 6 (December 1984), 48–53.

21. Contat and Rybalka, *Writings,* 449.

22. See "The Progressive-Regressive Method," in *Search for a Method,* trans. by Hazel E. Barnes (New York, 1963).

23. This analysis of categorical and hypothetical imperatives deepens the one offered in *CDR,* 187, 190.

24. Sartre's play satirizing right-wing journalism—*Nekrassov* (1955)—dramatizes this idea (in *The Devil and the Good Lord and Two Other Plays,* trans. by Sylvia Leeson and George Leeson [New York, 1960]). See also the account of "interest" in *CDR,* esp. 190, 197–219.

25. For an account of what he calls Sartre's "mediating third," see Thomas R. Flynn, *Sartre and Marxist Existentialism: The Test Case of Collective Responsibility* (Chicago, 1984), 113–19.

26. For Sartre's account of the series, see *CDR,* esp. 255–58; and for the group in fusion, see 357–58, 366–67, 389, 401.

27. Paul Nizan was a close friend of Sartre's who joined, then quit, the French Communist Party.

28. This account builds on the account of value in the lengthy footnote in *CDR,* 247n.

29. *Being and Nothingness,* 58–67. Indeed sincerity as something aimed at "in present immanence" (65) is *usually* "a phenomenon of bad faith" (63). Sartre leaves open the possibility of a sincerity in good faith that "bears on the past" (65).

30. Some thirty years earlier Sartre had called the self "an object *for consciousness*"

instead of a subject of consciousness, in *The Transcendence of the Ego*, trans. by Forrest Williams and Robert Kirkpatrick (New York, 1957), 42. Here, using tools developed in *CDR*, he tells us what *kind* of object the "self" is.

31. See our "Dialectical Ethics," referred to above in note 16.

32. For a discussion of "inauthentic" and "authentic" ways of pursuing humanity as an end of conduct, see our "Making the Human in Sartre's Dialectical Ethics," referred to above in Note 16.

33. "[W]hat is involved here is not a Nietzschean 'beyond' Good and Evil, but rather a Hegelian 'Aufhebung.' The abstract separation of these two concepts expresses simply the alienation of man. The fact remains that, in the historical situation, this synthesis cannot be achieved. Thus any morality which does not explicitly profess that it is *impossible today* contributes to the mystification and alienation of men. The moral 'problem' arises from the fact that morality is *for us* inevitable and at the same time impossible. Action must give itself ethical norms in this climate of unsurpassable impossibility." *Saint Genet: Actor and Martyr*, trans. by Bernard Frechtman (New York, 1963), 186n. This translation is ours.

34. Julius Fucik, a Czech Communist in the Czech resistance, was tortured to death by the Germans during World War II. He wrote an account of Communist militants in a Czech prison being tortured to death which was published after the war under the title *Notes from the Gallows* (New York, 1948) (*Ecrits sous la potence* is the French title, published in Paris by Seghers, 1948). Sartre wrote a commentary on Fucik's book which was originally published in *Les Lettres françaises*, June 17–24, 1954, and republished in Contat and Rybalka, *Writings*, II, 212–16.

35. Henri Alleg, an Algerian Communist, tortured by the French during the Algerian revolution, wrote an account of his torture entitled *The Question*, to which Sartre wrote the preface, "A Victory," trans. anonymous (New York, 1958). For the history of the publication of Sartre's preface, which involved seizure and censure by the French government, see Contat and Rybalka, *Writings*, II, 345–46.

36. Pierre Brossolette was a militant in the French Socialist Party and was tortured by the Gestapo during World War II. He jumped out of a window to his death in the course of his torture.

37. See, for example, Sartre's introductions to the books of Fucik and Alleg, but also "The Victors" (1946), trans. by Lionel Abel, in *Three Plays* (New York, 1949); and *The Condemned of Altona* (1960), trans. by Sylvia Leeson and George Leeson (New York, 1961).

38. Sartre numbers this chapter III, but since it starts on the same manuscript page as the last lines of Chapter IV and continues the overall discussion in terms of content, we are certain it should be numbered V.

39. Here the English *popular* is the rough translation of the French *populaire*, meaning "coming from all social classes *except* the ruling class."

40. Sartre numbers this chapter IV, but, again, since it continues on the same page as the last lines of Chapter V, we are certain it should be numbered VI.

41. *Nausea*, trans. by Lloyd Alexander (New York, 1964), 34.

42. Francis Jeanson has effectively laid this misunderstanding to rest regarding Sartre's early remarks on ethics. See his *Sartre and the Problem of Morality*, trans. by Robert V. Stone (Bloomington, Ind., 1980).

43. *Sartre by Himself*, 79. This statement from 1972 is made in a discussion of Sartre's attraction to and involvement with the Maoists in the wake of May 1968. He states: "That is why I find myself in a previous milieu [our translation] and at the same time

it proves a point—and this applies not only to the French Maoists but also to those from whom they take their inspiration, namely the Chinese—it proves in fact that when you get involved in politics, you should consider not that morality is a simple superstructure, but rather that it exists at the very level of what is called infrastructure. And that is something I've always believed." It is significant that Sartre's description of the Maoists' conception of morality—in his *Life/Situations: Essays Written and Spoken,* trans. by Paul Auster and Lydia Davis (New York, 1977)—was worked out in detail in his earlier writings on the dialectics of ethics and history of the mid-1960s. Having read these works, we suggest Sartre's interest in the French Maoists came not from being influenced *by them* but from their spontaneous enactment of *his own* thoughts as developed earlier.

44. This work has been published as "Determinism and Freedom" by Contat and Rybalka, see above, note 16

45. This apt phrase was used by Simone de Beauvoir to refer to the *Notes for the 1964 Rome Lecture,* in a personal letter to Robert V. Stone of February 21, 1986. However, we think it also applies to both of these writings, taken together.

46. Sartre, "Itinerary of a Thought," trans. by John Matthews, in *Between Existentialism and Marxism* (New York, 1974), 35.

3

"I Am No Longer a Realist": An Interview with Jean-Paul Sartre

Pierre Verstraeten

In 1972 the Belgian philosopher Pierre Verstraeten published a study of Sartre's theater called *Violence et éthique*. An interview between Sartre and Verstraeten produced the following discussion of the conditions that make a revolutionary commitment possible.[1] This discussion was first published in French in *Gulliver*, no. 1 (1972). The notes following the text are editors' notes.

SARTRE: I've read your book. What you do in the first part is examine the problem of violence in my plays. You have given a very good account of what is at stake in them. I completely agree with you, especially on the meaning of the evolution that you detect up to *The Condemned of Altona*. It's the problem of becoming, of taking up revolutionary positions when you are a bourgeois, of siding with the working class. But obviously that is not the real problem. The real problem is how ordinary people find themselves in a situation which is intolerable if they do not change it, their relationship with a situation which calls for a revolutionary development. That problem I did not tackle; it was not my subject, not my wish, I wanted to do something else.

VERSTRAETEN: Yes. But beside this thematic analysis, I tried to insert its meaning into the very movement of historical totalization, both as this

83

movement operates *in* your plays and as you yourself create it, and fit yourself into it, *by means of* these plays. To this end I tried to show how this renegade activity of the members of the middle class has fulfilled a specific dialectical and historical function in view of the impasses which the official revolutionary movements had run into, notably by taking over from the workers' movements, which are silent on this, the question of the meaning and authenticity of the revolution's demands.

SARTRE: That was the problem at the time, and still is today, though in a different form: the intellectual has to stop being satisfied with certain of his attitudes. To communicate with the people, he must stop being the unhappy consciousness and wanting to exemplify the contradiction between the universal and the particular. I have never stopped thinking about the problem of the relations of the intellectual and the proletariat, even in my lectures in Japan and my recent interview with *L'Idiot.*[2] When Goetz, at the penultimate stage of his journey, wants to be an ordinary soldier and obey like everybody else, to be just anybody, and I make him become a general, that is still the reflex of a classic intellectual. Today I do not see why he has to be a general, nor why anybody would especially want him in the ranks of the revolutionaries; but when I wrote the play, that is how I wanted it, that is how I thought. It seemed to me that history was blocked, and the intellectual, having a larger vision—in other words being in more direct contact with the universal—seemed to me necessary to get it going again. But now I no longer think this is quite the case. Those were problems of "realism," as you wrote: the privileged lucidity of one individual which enabled him to define the best revolutionary action, or gauge better than others which kind of politics would do the least harm. That was the period when I was a realist.

But the essential originality of your book, to my mind, lies in the second part and to some extent in the third. The first is an excellent thematic and descriptive study, but it does not go beyond what I put in my plays. In the second part, on the other hand, you start talking about important things, and especially about what you understand by "grace." It seems to me that you partly take up the theological import of that idea. You have the impression that "grace" exists, or at least it seems so to the reader. To be sure, you do not make it come down from Heaven, but there is a certain state which you call "grace"!

VERSTRAETEN: Indeed, that was what seemed to me to remain problematic after I had elucidated the meaning of your plays: the condition of the possibility of attaining a dialectical vision—in other words the possibility for the bourgeois to take up revolutionary positions. Because

84

this crossover, or this alignment, itself dialectically required by history to ensure its "dialecticity," even though it defines a possibility for every-body, is by no means assumed by everybody. And yet this phenomenon seems to me to correspond to a process that is sufficiently general to raise the question of its intelligibility. Even though they occupy a similar position and are marked by the same contradiction between the formal universality of its claims and the concrete particularity of its interests, not all bourgeois are swept up by the demand of revolutionary necessity. Why do they not all make this journey, which I think you have given us the genesis of, and thus its criterion of authenticity? Why do not all those who are in a position to travel this path do so? How is it that some people assume their contradictory fate with a sufficient radicalism, to the point where they adopt the positions of the working class, knowing that only this alliance will resolve their contradiction? If the intellectual is a bastard, why do not all those who are bastards exploit that proud passion—whose progress you have described in *Saint Genet*—which would lead them, by assuming the wrong that society has done them, to take up revolutionary positions?

This initiative—which is both original and proposed as a liberating destiny to any bourgeois and to the oppressed masses—has been called the *heroic dimension* of your favorite heroes; but it seems to me nothing more than an ad hoc qualification! What is the dialectical status of this "pride" if the dialectical totality of history is not to disappear into the contingency of a character trait, in other words of a purely psychological indulgence?

SARTRE: Don't you think that it is in the interest of those who go along with society in general to remain bourgeois? Look at M. Leprince Ringuet, he is doing very well! No doubt if there were another society, they would give him more to do, since he is a scientist, but it would not be the same; from the word go he is on the bourgeoisie's side, he is a bourgeois.

VERSTRAETEN: But all the same, since we can observe somebody changing sides, don't we have the right to wonder why some people are led to break the personal bonds of their privileges and others are not, why certain links seem forged forever and others do not, and why some people manage to settle the contradiction between the particularity of their interests and the universality of their ideology?

SARTRE: Some are content with this contradiction and others really suffer from it. And the reasons vary from case to case. For example, in my case, there is no doubt about it, I wrote about it already in *What Is Literature?* As a writer, I need *all* the public; not just the bourgeois, nor even, as now some petit bourgeois elements and the occasional worker thanks to paperback editions, but *all* the public. And since you cannot have the bourgeois and the workers at the same time, it means I had to make a choice. So it is my profession which led me to aim for universality!

VERSTRAETEN: But in that case surely every writer should have the same position as you, the same ambition, the same demands?

SARTRE: No, because a lot of writers think the only valid public is the bourgeois public, since it is a fact that right now workers do not read much. And when they do, they read bourgeois books. Factory libraries have found that the books most in demand were the same ones most in demand among the bourgeois. So these writers see the problem differently; they think the real public is the bourgeois public, and that at most there will be a slight effect on the other classes, that some workers will read them, perhaps some peasants too; but in any case the essential, in their eyes, is the bourgeois public. For example, when Queneau writes his books, he criticizes language in a learned manner which people without a bourgeois culture cannot appreciate. He sets the bourgeois some bourgeois problems, namely, a certain use of language, certain limits, and so on; certainly there has been more work done in that direction since, the question has been explored more deeply; but all the same, if his subject is language, and that is up to him, then by taking up that problem he automatically defines his public, since he can only interest people who are sufficiently educated.

VERSTRAETEN: Agreed, but the question remains: why did Queneau not have the same ambition as you in defining the extent of his public; why did he choose a kind of literary problem which at once limited the universal ambition that literature should have imposed on him?

SARTRE: Now there you would have to do an analysis, to find out why he chose that.

VERSTRAETEN: That is the whole point. Is there an order of analytical choice or an unconscious tendency to emerge into culture within childhood and from then on, which already has the meaning of universality which would then reappear in adult life as a more or less radical commitment to universality?

SARTRE: I would say that he came into literature with surrealism and subsequently with the idea of examining what language can do, what one can do with language, one's own possibilities, what narration is, the creation of different forms. It did not lead him to the essential public, but that is because he did not really see literature as communication between the writer and the public. So in Queneau's life there was a first period when he was a surrealist, then he wrote books to find out what narration was, what

86

language in narration was, and so he limited himself to a very small readership. And his contradiction is that after he agreed to join the Académie Goncourt, which brought him into contact with a wider public, he won a wider public as a writer only because of a misunderstanding. Everybody thought *Zazie dans le métro* was a joke, when in fact it was another of his very deep studies of a narration, of what one can do in the framework of a narration. Apart from that book, he has remained a writer such as Mallarmé was in the nineteenth century, a writer who finds the limits of his public in his subject matter, in the subject which is his own, namely language. On the other hand, he really needed to be more widely read, but this need took the form of his agreeing to join the Académie Goncourt. This contradiction is Queneau's, but all the same it might be the deep contradiction of any intellectual; but it was not understood in its intellectual form, in an intellectual and political form. The contradiction is objectively there, it is active, but it is not assumed as such.

VERSTRAETEN: So you think that what defines access to intellectual status is always particular circumstances, a concrete situation which, at a given moment, favors an uncoupling from the privileged exercise of culture?

SARTRE: Of course, because if they were workers, we could talk about the economic situation and general conditions which make them revolutionaries, if they are, and in that case their individuality is always a class individuality. There are facts affecting the whole class which condition the fact that a worker is a revolutionary or not. But when we are talking about renegades from a class which is nonrevolutionary as a matter of principle, which is against revolution because it gets all its power and strength from capital, which is exactly what the revolutionary class wants to overthrow, then to understand the crossover you have to look at particular conditions in each case.

VERSTRAETEN: And yet this crossover by the bourgeois intelligentsia from its own class to the revolutionary forces is such a generalized phenomenon that it seems to me it ought to have a less circumstantial mode of intelligibility, one that could grasp the meaning of its future universality. As far as that goes, the same problem arises among the working class. The working class is not always automatically revolutionary at every level and at every moment of the development of its consciousness and of historical conditions. But whatever the objective reasons for this delay, the difficulties to be overcome, there are always emergencies, radicalisms, particular cases—leaders—who preserve the meaning and possibility of revolution. Besides, you yourself have shown that spontaneous revolutionary consciousness in the working class is an

87

illusion; you have pointed out the forces of inertia, competition, antagonism, and growing passivity that affect it and crush its revolutionary potential. So each time we face the problem of who is going to take responsibility for the objective wrong done to him and to the oppressed class, bring it to consciousness—to his own first and then to other people's—by his action and his initiatives, by his ability to assume this objective wrong and reveal it and give it a revolutionary and subversive meaning. In this sense the problem that arises in the case of the bourgeois, the "theoretician of practical knowledge," the future "intellectual," already arises for the working class itself, which is not a priori a single solid mass oriented and directed toward violent revolution.

SARTRE: But it is toward reformism!

VERSTRAETEN: But what defines the really positive and progressive moment for your heroes, those whose political itinerary is fascinating and instructive, those whose revolutionary model you could not help but investigate right up to their defeat, is *not* reformism! Besides, the working class has always been *both* reformist and revolutionary, either one after the other or one in conflict with the other.

SARTRE: But it has taken time! And that is why I fail to see why you need to fall back on the idea of "grace." You know how I conceive of the intellectual now; well, I had to wait sixty-seven years and witness May 1968 in order to get there. The fact is that one can be perfectly content to be the classic intellectual, in other words an unhappy consciousness whose mind is at ease because he is unhappy and torn between the absolute and the relative, the universal and the particular, believing that as a lucid witness he is contributing to the movement of radicalization.

VERSTRAETEN: But that, precisely, is "grace": the absorbed radicalism which permits the revolutionary moment to grow deeper. It does so because of the unambiguous readiness to always be ready to call into question what has been acquired, in other words, to constantly revolutionize the positions gained. That is what it is, yet it cannot be that because we are not Christian. So we need a law by which to understand the possibility of that continuous radicalism, which remains anthropological.

SARTRE: But I know lots of intellectuals of that type who will go no farther. It is a very tenable position. Wrong, but very tenable. The proof is that the majority of intellectuals are still classical intellectuals. Personally I had to go through a long evolution before I realized I was not even a revolutionary such as Nizan was before the Second World War; it dawned on me bit by bit. But at the very beginning, in any case . . . You may wonder where it comes from? Well, there *were* reasons for me to protest, so right from the beginning I was against the bourgeois . . .

There's a nineteenth-century literary tradition behind it. Take Flaubert, for example. He is against the bourgeois, but what does that mean? He says, "I call bourgeois everybody who thinks basely." That is useless, it is psychological, a bourgeois is not like that, but no matter, it is a start. At least he realized that that layer of society was not for him. After that, to be sure, he went no farther. Why not? That is the question you ask me in your third part, because you say I believe in a genesis by which, if one starts out wrong and perseveres proudly enough in that wrongness, it will all come out right, in other words in a revolutionary manner! So why does Flaubert stop even though, as you point out, I grant him all the negative structures that should favor a revolutionary "redemption"?

To answer that you have to situate him in his period. Believe me, in those days radicalism did not go very far. If you look at Leroux or George Sand, the way they talk to the workers is awful, they are really lightweight reformers. Now, neither George Sand nor Leroux was antibourgeois like Flaubert; he was *radically* so. But then, if you are against the bourgeois you must be somewhere. And he could not be with the workers, the proletariat was not developed enough, it had not really become aware of itself; it staged riots but it was not allowed to have a real revolution such as happened in 1848. So it remained far behind the social evolution. But oddly enough, Flaubert's relationship with the workers remained ambiguous. He did indeed say that the Communards were mad dogs, but he did not hate them so much as the democratic bourgeoisie.

All I am trying to say is that he undoubtedly had negative radicalism, but he could not find a social group to belong to, so that in the end he was quite unhappy. He was completely pessimistic, and he would not have been if he had found a group (but there was none at the time) to say to him, "Yes, you are right, but look at the positive side of your rejection of the bourgeoisie," or whose real action would have had both objective and probably also causal affinities with his own negativism. In my case, on the other hand, the class struggle took a much more pronounced form than in the nineteenth century. My protesting state of mind before the war led me to become much more intensely radical, to side with people who are protesting, in the name of something they want. And I do not see why I have to have received some sort of "grace." It is an interesting problem, though, because in a sense it is the problem of freedom!

VERSTRAETEN: And yet I cannot help thinking that what must correspond to the problem of the persistence of your commitment is the passion for protest which makes you constantly deepen your opposition to bourgeois society. Frantz has no revolutionary situation, either, to get him out of the sequestration in which he has subjectively conquered the nothingness of a certain freedom. But this historical lack does not destroy the order of existential passion which inspires him and which defines most of your heroes, giving them a fate of liberation, a sort of conditioning by and for freedom.

SARTRE: Yes, but how can we understand that? If it is really a superior possibility which allows certain people to see more clearly and join the revolution, then that "grace" can only come from God! How can we tolerate the future of man coming from elsewhere and not from himself?

VERSTRAETEN: Perhaps it is because I use psychoanalysis more radically than you do to explain this situation. You constantly refer to it as the foundation of your understanding of Flaubert, but in a paradoxical manner: you think it contains the law of his conditioning. *I* use it to bring to light the problematics of an emergence to freedom. This seems to me more compatible with a philosophy of freedom. Because you do believe in a genesis of freedom. To be sure, freedom is ontological, but it does have a birth. What is worse, there is a problem of the ontology of that freedom, it is the problem which means that you *have to write* that ontology, and you did, in *Being and Nothingness*. Is that not proof that freedom has been lost, or at least that it is not yet completely aware of itself, that there is a sort of freedom in-itself which hasn't yet become for-itself?

SARTRE: Right, there is a liberation of freedom!

VERSTRAETEN: Exactly. So there are normative rules of freedom in regard to itself. Now it seemed to me that all through your itinerary, your analysis and research and the applications you made of it to writers, characters, and political events, you show the effort to tear freedom away from a certain alienation, an effort that should allow it to find itself. And it is from this point of view, it seems to me, that bit by bit you have understood that socialism was a decisive element in the possibility of ensuring a universalization and a reconciliation of freedom with itself—of the being of man, as free, with himself. What poses a problem for me is what makes possible the lifting of "original sin"—to continue with the translation into theological terms—which caused the fall of freedom, its loss of itself, or rather which caused it to always seem at first lost to itself, which made freedom, even though it is really always there—ontologically it is the very being of humanity—seem to need to win itself back. To be sure, in the first part of your work there is a sort of immanence of the loss of freedom, because freedom is so anguishing for itself that it refuses to consider itself—

SARTRE: Yes, and what is more, I went farther, because since then I have shown that it was scarcity.

VERSTRAETEN: Yes, that is the second stage. It seems to me that you felt obliged to assign a historical and concrete role to something that was still too connected with a sort of original sin.

SARTRE: You're right, I will not talk in terms of "sin," but I remember what Aron said about *Being and Nothingness:* "They all choose, but they all choose badly!" Why do they? Today I would answer: because freedom is in situation. There is a history of man which is the history of scarcity. Given that, we can understand the alienation of freedom.

VERSTRAETEN: So you admit that initially one could be dissatisfied with the need for a fall from freedom, one could be dissatisfied with the description insofar as it had no other mode of intelligibility than the idea of an original sin, the idea of a sort of fated fall relative to itself, and that it was to eliminate this sort of religiosity that you have reinterpreted philosophically the concept of scarcity?

SARTRE: Indeed, there have been two arguments which made me feel *Being and Nothingness* was incomplete. One was Aron's argument, and the other was a remark of Beauvoir's that one is not free in every situation. Thus I produced Heinrich in *The Devil and the Good Lord* to indicate that there are situations where, whatever one chooses, one chooses badly. He can choose the church or he can choose the poor, but in one case he causes the slaughter of church people, which he cannot like because after all he is a priest only because there is a church, and in the other case he causes the slaughter of the poor, which he cannot like either because he is really the poor people's priest. So whatever he does he is damned—to use the language of his time. And that is why he goes mad. There are circumstances that condition one to be unable to choose anything good! So in that case, you would no doubt say that Heinrich does not have grace and Goetz does?

VERSTRAETEN: Yes, he is a bastard of inferior quality, I mean in what must be postulated as more or less radical in his mode of accession to the symbolic universe of culture and ideology. But I only say Goetz has grace because it seems to me that you yourself grant it to him. And this is the second stage. Now that scarcity has defined the need for the loss of freedom relative to itself, we have to know how that loss is to be made good. And here again, the theological schema seems to fit perfectly. For it seems to me that throughout your work, your judgments, the stands you take, even your praxis, you do postulate the possibility of eliminating the effects of that scarcity, of what caused the loss of freedom, and the possibility of finding freedom again. It seems to me as if there were a possible assumption of man, a way of understanding his relationship to himself and to others in the framework of scarcity, which will lead him either to confirm his alienation or get beyond it. If there seems to be no way out for Heinrich, are there not others who, being in an analogous situation—because, I mean, Goetz is also in an impossible situation—by plunging headlong into that situation break out of the apparent dead end? You know the double function I think Heinrich has in *The Devil and the Good Lord.* His "tragic nature" allows him both to denounce Goetz's Manichean illusion and to mark the dead end of a freedom that does not assume its contradiction radically enough. He is at the same time ahead of the first Goetz, since good and evil are equivalent for him, but he remains behind the revolutionary Goetz, because unlike him he does not take up the theological challenge of an impossible and tragic world.

SARTRE: The reason is that Heinrich was brought up by the church, in other words he is "good," and when you are good you are lost! Whereas Goetz has no ties; he is a bastard, he killed his brother solely as a result of events. So when he has explored as much as he has, he can only be a radical; the only possibility left to him is the revolutionary one.

VERSTRAETEN: But it is this ceaseless exploratory search that is the sign of his "grace," of a certain passion for existence. Its key must be in his early childhood, because it would be just as easy to imagine him remaining the jester of the nobility, in other words going on doing harm for the pleasure he gets out of it, as he does at the beginning of the play. Why doesn't he remain the submissive tolerated bastard he could be?

SARTRE: Everybody is different. It depends on the choice you have made and the childhood you had.

VERSTRAETEN: But what defines this choice, or rather the *content* of this choice, this radical assumption of a certain fate of being a bastard which invests an individual at the outset, and which at the end of his experience leads him to turn its negative against the society that produced him? It's the same with Genet. What defines the initial radicalism of his "will" to be a thief, in other words to become one so as to free himself from it? How do you pick up your fallen freedom, how do you tear off the masks by which it hides its own powers from itself?

SARTRE: Indeed, the others do not do that, and yet any thief should be able to do what Genet did, and say "I am the thief." If he does not, it is because society was too strong after all, it alienated him too powerfully. In Genet's case, he did have breathing space, he most certainly had some culture, which his lovers gave him—he quotes some of them. He was teaching French in Prague at a time he told us he was in prison; a private teacher, but still a teacher. The prison was sheer invention; he was teaching French. So he is a much more complex character than the one I showed, but I knew that.

So if we look at Genet's works, indeed, they suppose a "grace," which he must have gotten from having the worst possible situation. Except it is not true. In fact, if he went on to construct everything he constructed, it is thanks to a bunch of pederasts who gave him a culture. A pederastic culture, remember. When he chose to be a pederast, because he was a thief, he chose protest, but he did not know what it would lead to, namely, to radical protest. It is perfectly clear: he wanted to be the absolute opposition, and thus not just to be a thief, which he did not especially want to be, but to be a pederast, in other words to accept the externalization. At that moment he finds a culture, constructs his universe, and opposes himself to the others.

VERSTRAETEN: And doesn't he thus reach the most advanced forms of practical participation, those that have the best chance of bringing about a fate of freedom? It's a freedom that shows itself in retrospect as the meaning of truth in its becoming, and thus as the retrospective "transfiguration" of his history, the real illusion of his having been "chosen" to live it.

SARTRE: Does he see it as that? It's very complicated.

VERSTRAETEN: In other words, if I understand rightly why you hesitate, you would not accept the formal schema thanks to which one should be able to succeed in circumscribing a sort of "evolutionary law" of freedom, the guarantee of its coming about. And indeed I tried to mark and assume its problematic nature, precisely so as not to run the risk of seeing its intelligibility ascribed entirely to the magic effect of a "grace," the law of what makes freedom choose itself rather than choose to forget itself. Because let me make clear that for me, falling back on a "historical grace" would fulfill, in the field of revolutionary problematics, much more of a function of interrogation and suspicion than of absolution! You would abandon, or rather deny, the very principle of this schema, making every apparent exemplarity of your heroes, whether they be real or imaginary, into the effect of a sort of "circumstantiality," an effect of situation. But this surely runs the risk of making suspect the very outcome of the process or experience, because freedom would be conditioned by something other than itself, namely, by circumstances. Doesn't this cast suspicion on the meaning and content of the revolutionary objective that this experience is supposed to reach?

SARTRE: One can always suspect it, in fact I still dispute it! For

93

example, I have chosen something at this very moment [an alliance with Maoists]; I have chosen in a certain way, but I am not sure it is the right way. Freedom is all the time! It is there, and when it fails, this means it has alienated itself all over again!

VERSTRAETEN: In that case, why not speak instead of processes, different multiple processes which meet and confront each other, each endowed with an impact of meanings, not always compatible with each other, most often competing? For example, revolutionary processes and reactionary processes, respectively defining relationships of strength, some of which bank on appealing to the other as to the same, as to the *alter ego,* while others count on the effects of inertia and favor dispersion and the centripetal individualism of people, and so on?

SARTRE: Because if you talk to me about processes I do not know what that means. How do you link one moment in the process to the next one? Since we do not talk in terms of determinism but of conditioning, since we suppose one can get beyond the process, that there is a way of getting beyond what is toward what is not, I must put myself on the level of freedom, which anyway is itself a form of what we have to call dialectics. Otherwise I do not see how I could "interpret" the moments of the process.

Whether it is an individual or a group of individuals who define a process at a given moment, if I am to understand why, at some later moment, they did *something else,* I must needs go to the element of freedom, of tearing oneself away from being. And I can only observe that we do it all the time. If I take out a cigarette, I am tearing myself away from being; if I speak to you, I am tearing myself away from being.

VERSTRAETEN: But don't you also know, or at least haven't you also told us, that the feeling of being torn away from being must become aware of itself? Isn't it the feeling of becoming aware of this tearing away that defines a revolutionary political orientation, or at least an accomplishment carried out in view and in function of an assumption of freedom?

SARTRE: But those are truths for me! It isn't grace which gives me that, which invests me with that belief; or if you like, "grace" *is* the truth, at any rate the truth for me! Because if that tearing away must be put at the foundation of the human being, then you have to seize it by the throat, according to what it means. For example, smoking a cigarette means tearing oneself away from being because the cigarette is not in me. There is no way to pass from being to action, that mixture of being and nonbeing, of contingency and necessity. To understand that passage, you have to pass to freedom which, as I said in *Being and Nothingness,* will fall back into an alienation. If I freely take a cigarette, I am going to find myself led to smoke more than I intended, so I have alienated myself.

VERSTRAETEN: But aren't there two ways to understand that tearing away? There is the understanding that, it seems to me, you have always proposed, and which all the same is responsible for the political impact of your work and your influence, namely, that there is a finality to this being-torn-away from circumstances which is none other than the tearing away itself; it is just the exacerbation of the acute awareness of its power. Then there is the understanding defended by all those who would be ready, even within the existentialist tradition, to admit that there is the moment of awareness as a being-torn-away from the contingency of being, but that then there is always necessarily a falling back, and that we could only be witness to a phenomenology without end, a becoming with no teleology, a totality that is constantly detotalized, but never a movement of totalization.

SARTRE: Ah! One or the other! Socialism or barbarism. Barbarism in this case being freedom with no term of reconciliation, yet without rejecting any chance for freedom. But that is a moral philosophy! I wrote one, too, for the Italians especially; it is there, but incomplete, not good enough.[3] But at bottom, what I would say is that I know what I must tear myself away from, but I do not quite know what for. Or to put it another way, the thing that is the least well founded in me is optimism, the reality of the future. I have this optimism but I cannot find a basis for it. And that's the heart of the matter.

VERSTRAETEN: Isn't this also where you run the risk of being accused, as you often have been, of being above all a moralist? In fact, isn't this where theology sneaks in the back door? If you are a moralist who can't find a basis for the status of hope in his moral system, it means you have a certain faith; and in those conditions, what supports that faith? That is the risk I tried to exorcise when I dared to describe this situation in terms of faith, or fervor, in other words as a "grace" granted to certain people capable of being invested with it. Because it seemed to me that you sometimes granted certain characters you felt were privileged, certain heroes, the features of an experience that makes their story, their evolution, into a sort of way of the cross, a sort of visible transfiguration, whose end (definable as pure freedom or revolution) would be a witnessing of faith!

SARTRE: No, because I refuse theological status. What I am sure of is that a certain present action is the only possible one; you have to get into politics, into radical politics. But by doing that, can you obtain a result in a certain number of years? To believe this would really be faith, which I know nothing about!

VERSTRAETEN: No, *this* is not faith. Faith is the previous stage; it is what tells you that in a given situation, which is completely determining and explainable, you must radically contest. You don't measure the "fervor" of the revolutionary initiative at the level of the result, but in the postulation that tells you if there is to be any chance of achieving the goal you're pursuing, you must take on a critical, contesting and active responsibility. Not even Marx, I think, would have defined the quality of the revolutionary act by just its effect. But it is the intensity of that quality that supports faith, faith in the effectiveness of an action that must be undertaken—come what may, if possible the revolution! Now if that is where conviction sneaks in, before you are even sure of the outcome, how does it get beyond the fideist status of its commitment? On the other hand, if you abandon the order of proof attached to that conviction, do you still have the right to make it an ideological instrument for uniting the masses?

SARTRE: All I need to know is my reasons for rejecting this society. It is possible to demonstrate that it is badly organized and immoral, that bourgeois society is unacceptable as is, so clearly it has to be changed. I can show that capitalist society is an evil, that it is not made for man but for profits. From that I can show the sum of the particular evils that result, and consequently I can say that this society must be radically rejected. From the moment you decide to change it, you must do it radically. Because if it were possible to change it by reform, that would be very nice: if the bourgeois came and assured us they were going to legally abolish all the privileges of their society, that would be very nice. But since by their nature they are bound to oppose us with force, we have no choice but violence. Given that, I am not the only one who is going to reject it; everybody is.

And so, I will not say the only faith, but the only attempt I can support, the only one the intellectual can pursue, is to try to win all the working class over to this radicalization. For that you have to come to them as one of them, to get off your horse, as Mao Zedong says. You have to come toward the people like one of the people, and not like a classic intellectual, on horseback.

VERSTRAETEN: So society is radically intolerable because it sets profit as its goal and not man as his own goal. In these conditions, can one question oneself about the status of the goal given to man, which authorizes us to reject this society which does not consider him as his goal?

SARTRE: Well, but man *is* his own goal! From the moment there are people, they are their own goal; that is communication.

VERSTRAETEN: So it is contract, agreement, communication as the ruler of every rule, the law as the condition of possibility of agreement and communication between people, culture as aware of itself in the self-responsibility of all men to define its content?

SARTRE: It is the law, though less so. I like the idea of law less. It is culture insofar as culture does not and cannot exist. It is not available to everybody who is supposed to define it, and never will be. The history of paperback books shows it: the public that *can* read keeps growing, but we do not reach those who *cannot.* So we have to completely overturn culture and start over. I am not saying we will not use the previous culture, but in any case we will go in a different direction, in a different way, with different projects, it will be a different culture.

VERSTRAETEN: But that is just what I think I meant in my search for a dialectical basis for moral philosophy. Namely, that the kind of hope that despite everything makes you act, judge, form judgments about society, and so on, is not supported by a faith come down from Heaven, but by the will to recognize that man is a being of culture, and that the very content of man's being of culture is universality as a regulated and above all self-regulatable relationship of communication, or human communication made more and more transparent to itself.

SARTRE: But I do not use the word *culture,* because I am not yet quite sure what culture is. It is a serious problem at the moment. Freedom, at bottom, is culture emerging from nature, but without it being possible to see what it represents. We can only know what we do not want. And that is the central point of your book. It is interesting, but that is your way of internalizing my work by raising a problematics that you would like to perceive as latent in it, whereas it seems to me that it does not arise. For me, the principle of communication motivates my whole project even though it remains hidden from itself, or rather without my feeling authorized to say what's what about this principle. Yet at the same time I know enough about it to know what I am in revolt against. Which is a negative definition. You would tend to circumscribe more positively the motivations of revolutionary action. And certainly, unless you are an intellectual with nothing to lose and everything to gain, if you are a revolutionary you have to be optimistic. For example, if the guys who carried out the kidnapping are caught, and if they did not have the conviction that it would work, and that if it did not work this time it would work in another five or ten years, they would not even have tried, and that would mean they did not even have a revolutionary frame of mind.[4] In fact we can be sure that if they are caught today they will get five years in prison, but that they will still think they did right, that society was against them, but that one day it will be overthrown.

The only thing is, if you believe that, you have a nonexistent future conditioning your freedom, and I cannot believe this. I do think the future conditions the present, but you know how: as a possibility of going beyond it, not as a completed and determined reflexive term of that possibility. The idea that that freedom it at bottom itself conditioned, since it would be "in order to do that," seems to me a limit imposed on its understanding. Whereas you've always tended to think the future has a conditioning force with respect to present freedom. But for me that would not *be* freedom. And it is this belief, which is your belief, that leads you now to denounce its eventual illusion!

And at this point other criticisms arise, those which no doubt motivate your stress on finality, at the risk of falling into the finalist trap that you then have to denounce. We have not talked about those criticisms, but I remember them well. They boil down to this: "At this point, if you take freedom out of the conditioning that it would be for itself as its own future, you can do anything. If you do not have something that can be seen in the future as a goal to reach, then you can reach anything, General Pétain just as much as a Nazi horde." This criticism exists. And indeed, I say both that freedom must have no goal in front of it and that despite this we must do whatever tearing away is involved in achieving freedom, against everything that prevents it from achieving itself; but having said that, we must do it now! One cannot just do anything; we must act immediately and in action, and yet without knowing exactly in the name of what. It is hard, but this is the present situation. This is the *fact* of my praxis and my thought. To define its *right,* we would need other philosophical foundations, as indeed you say!

VERSTRAETEN: Indeed. But isn't it in this way that you can avoid a certain structuralist criticism, with which I have a more ambivalent relationship? It denounces *any kind* of determination of action by the future, in the name of what has been called the eruption of desire onto the stage of history; in other words the end of acting in concert. You would avoid it by not exposing your flank through the idea of a finality assigned to freedom, but at the same time you would denounce it by rejecting the sheer neglect of desire. In this sense, I questioned the status of eventual finality assigned to freedom in your work. I also denounced the risk of limitation, of a shadow cast over freedom itself, namely, that one cannot with impunity propose to master the cultural order that freedom makes possible without putting it at risk. I did both in order to forestall and avoid the risk of a certain possible interpretation of your thought, a risk inherent in the political temptation in your plays: this "optimistically realistic" stage you, after all, passed through, and which rather gives the reader the feeling that it is still active today in the battles you fight!

SARTRE: Yes, finality is as impossible for freedom as is the pure violence of desire.

Notes

1. Sartre's political attitudes and actions during this period, including his reformulation of the role of the radical intellectual, have been discussed by Ronald Aronson, *Jean-Paul Sartre: Philosophy in the World* (London, 1980), 303–24.

2. The Japanese lectures are "Plaidoyer pour les intellectuels," *Situations* VIII (Paris, 1972); trans. by John Matthews as "A Plea for Intellectuals," in *Between Existentialism and Marxism* (London, 1974). The interview with *L'Idiot* is reprinted as "L'Ami du peuple," *Situations* VIII.

3. This is the Rome lecture, mentioned above in "Sartre's *Morality and History*," chapter 2 herein.

4. Sartre is referring to the kidnapping of Renault's personnel director, Robert Nogrette, by two members of the Nouvelle Résistance Populaire in retaliation for the killing of Maoist Pierre Overney during a period of agitation at Renault's Billancourt plant. The kidnappers quickly released their captive. See Simone de Beauvoir, *Adieux: A Farewell to Sartre* (New York, 1984), 28.

II

SARTRE'S CONTINUING POLITICAL RELEVANCE

4

DECIPHERING THE
ISRAELI-PALESTINIAN CONFLICT

Ronald Aronson

What is Sartre's political heritage today, a decade after his death? What are we to take from this life which, after the first years of adulthood, was so constantly preoccupied with the issues of his times? How are we to use the fruits of half a lifetime during which Sartre devoted himself to political activity, political essays, political theater, political philosophy? Rejecting Sartre's political vitality, denying it, and ignoring it are much the fashion today, but this tries to recast the man himself. It would be truer to Sartre to go against the fashion and suggest that even today he has a greater deal to offer to those who remain alive to the issues he struggled with, issues that, in any case, have not been resolved.

Several Sartrean themes are especially important today. Sartre's writings remain a basis for all contemporary discussions of responsibility and complicity. Second, Sartre tells us much about how individuals make themselves, especially by interiorizing their political and social situation and reexteriorizing it as their project. Further, Sartre's interpretation of Stalinism shows how a liberatory project, under life-and-death pressure, can become other than it started out to be, even as it remains true to fundamental aspects of its original mission. In this discussion Sartre describes the relationship between praxis and the process it becomes, showing how action *and* consciousness become deviated as a result.

Elsewhere he leaves us hints for understanding, as praxis, the social madnesses that have dominated so much of twentieth-century life. And he gives us tools for developing an appreciation of progress in the modern world, based on an understanding that all forces are, in the final analysis, human actions.

Sartre offers insights and tools enough, I am suggesting, to warrant serious study by those committed not only to understanding the world but also to changing it. He remains alive, politically, even in this world dominated by those most antithetical to his spirit.

My own relationship to his thought may help illuminate this. After years of close study I thought that it was time to move on to other political and theoretical tasks. In bidding farewell I stressed Sartre's weaknesses. Above all, his was not really a social thought: his radical impulse was useful in understanding individuals, but he never explored how to apply his work to social issues because Sartre's starting points, the cogito (in its early incarnation), then individual praxis (in its later version), were nonsocial.[1] In spite of the marvelous analyses in the third volume of *The Family Idiot,* theoretically Sartre never sees the social layer as anything but derivative. He rejects that it is in some sense as primary as the individual, and that it indeed makes the individual possible.[2] And so he does not accomplish the passage from Descartes to Marx in spirit any more than in fact: his main interest, beginning to end, is not understanding social structures but explaining how they affect individuals.

Rooted in and reflecting on political engagement, I went on to ask a social and historical question: How is hope possible as we near the end of the twentieth century? Exploring this, to my surprise, required leaning at least as much on Sartre as on a more obvious inspiration, my teacher Herbert Marcuse. This is because Sartre, more than any other thinker, insists that human praxis is at the origin of what is most terrifying about this century. The main impulse of his thought is to deconstruct all of the forces, weights, and demons of our century into their source, human action. We live spellbound by our own creations, and Sartre seeks to break the spell.

Sartre is particularly important at two key historical points in such explorations. First, he helps us to clarify the nagging issue of responsibility for the Nazis' "final solution to the Jewish problem." An early statement, in *The Emotions,* characterizes the unchanging core of Sartre's thought: "For human reality, to exist is always to assume its being; that is, to be responsible for it instead of receiving it from outside like a stone."[3] He enables us to insist on the full responsibility, each in his or her own way, of all those who made the Holocaust possible, from Hitler

104

right down to the Jews overseas who failed to press their governments to intervene. This question is urgent because it is as alive in the present as in the past. Today, for example, we must ask who has been responsible for making it possible to perpetuate apartheid. And similarly, the answer extends from those anti-apartheid whites in South Africa passively acquiescing in their government's policies to Americans who have allowed their government to support the South African state's interventions in Angola.[4]

Second, Sartre helps us to understand the various social irrationalities that have made this century so brutal—as in Nazism, Stalinism, and the American war in Vietnam—as being the deliberate choice of leading social groups faced with extremely difficult situations. Sartre describes neurosis as the path chosen by the organism "in order to be able to live an unlivable situation."[5] We might add that social classes and ruling groups, as well as such individuals as the German industrialist's son Frantz in *The Condemned of Altona,* choose irrational and self-destructive courses when all other paths are blocked. Freely and creatively, we might say without irony, they embark on suicidal and genocidal fantasy projects when an impossible reality permits no other way. We continue to create ourselves, even in situations allowing no exit.

Each of these lines of thought builds upon and departs from Sartre. The first attempts to combine his stress on total responsibility with a recognition of the many and different roles people play on various spirals of responsibility, from those who give the orders, to those who carry out the evil acts, to those who simply go along (and thus make them possible). The second line of thought seeks the logic of the irrational, taking even blatantly self-destructive behavior as intentionally chosen and self-determined, rather than being somehow imposed on individuals and social forces from the outside. The inspiration and starting point of both lines of thought, however, is Sartrean.

Becoming aware of this led me to return to Sartre more systematically, to study his second *Critique* as a possible source for further insights and tools for exploring our current situation. In this unfinished work, especially in the study of Stalinism that takes up half the book, Sartre provides sustained explorations that illuminate how human projects become deviated from their goals by the very act of trying to realize them. The effort to safeguard the Bolshevik Revolution resulted in the introduction of a series of policies and a subsequent set of structures that in turn deviated the Revolution. And yet, at the end, this massive practico-inert praxis-process, carried so far from its original goals, remains human to its core, and susceptible to change.

105

Sartre leaves unanswered the driving questions of the second *Critique:* Does history have a shape? How do separate individual actions coalesce, even in conflict, to cause the larger reality we know as human history? Is there progress, and in what sense? But the failure, duly registered and understood, should not blind us to the accomplishment. Sartre expands his, and our, sense of the relationship of human practice to its demonic results.

Returning to study the idea and reality of progress with Sartre in mind provokes a new awareness of the need for a "Sartrean moment" in any understanding of progress today. In other words, scientific and technological progress has been considered as an autonomous force, moving without human control, or even understanding, while dominating our world and prospects. Sometimes even social and political progress has been seen in this way. A Sartrean moment would insist that what we call progress is no more than a praxis-process, human activity building on itself and its products, deliberately allowed to get out of control, renewed and reanimated at each moment by the human praxis driving it forward. Such an understanding would have to include, as above, a decidedly un-Sartrean element: in this case, appreciating the social and political side of progress means stressing that a *positive* practico-inert has been deposited by human struggles for greater dignity. Such practico-inert results as higher levels of human social morality and more humane social relations, embodied in legislation protecting civil rights, become in turn the starting point in relation to which each future generation shapes itself and defines its projects.

Progress, deviation, interiorization, and reexteriorization, responsibility, social madness—these are some of the politically important themes that come directly from or can be illuminated by Sartre's work. Sartre has left us a significant heritage for understanding and clarifying our situation. I hope to demonstrate the vitality of some of these themes by using them to explore a single contemporary issue, the Israeli-Palestinian conflict. Sartre is useful both in developing an overall approach to the conflict and in clarifying one of its most perplexing aspects: the mutual denial of Israelis and Palestinians.

An early and strong supporter of Israel, Sartre later became progressively more concerned with the Palestinian cause. As the Palestinian issue became more prominent, Sartre adopted a characteristic approach. Above all, because of his deep and instinctive identification with the oppressed, he rejected taking sides with one people or the other. Having written one of the most powerful dissections of anti-Semitism in 1944, Sartre was not about to forget the Jewish past. Yet, having gone on to become one of the most forceful enemies of colonialism and champions of the Third World in the 1960s, neither could he ignore the Palestinian present, especially after 1967 when the West Bank and Gaza came under Israeli rule. We know that those on one side of the issue easily forget the past victimization of Jews and its still-powerful force today; those on the other let this become justification for the present victimization of Palestinians. Being consistent, Sartre insisted on listening to both sides and on attempting to be an agent for a solution that both peoples could live with. In a world where being pro-Israeli has come to mean being anti-Palestinian, and where being pro-Palestinian has usually led to equating Zionism with racism *tout court* and to denying Jewish rights to national self-determination, Sartre's response of being pro-Israeli *and* pro-Palestinian still can help us to approach the conflict. Starting from this general approach, we can build an understanding using some of the themes I sketched above.

Specifically, on each side a process of dehumanization and demonization has set in that has made it virtually impossible to glimpse an end to the conflict. Listening to a typical defender of Israel would give us one side of this; listening to a typical Palestinian spokesperson would give us the other. Each side makes a forceful case which, taken by itself, seems compelling—until we hear the other side. Listening to both we might then begin to notice the selective readings of the history, the skewed presentation of rights and wrongs, the refusal on one side to even think the concept of "dispossession," on the other to even consider the category of "terrorism." Each side has appeared, to itself and its supporters, as wholly right, the other wholly wrong. All conflicts are like this, of course, but the Israeli-Palestinian conflict has taken this demonization to its logical conclusion. Above all, each side has rejected not only the justice of the other but its very existence as a "side." Each side has denied the other.

As a psychological phenomenon, denial is common and easily understood. We may begin there in order to grasp its political meaning. Denial, after all, is the refusal to acknowledge the existence of an important aspect of reality. Like our other psychic "states" described by Sartre in his early psychological writings, denial is an act, not something that we undergo passively or mechanically. In other words, denial is a praxis carried out in a certain situation, for certain reasons, in order to achieve certain ends.

And the reasons? In *The Emotions* and *Psychology of Imagination,* Sartre himself explored specific forms of psychological denial, projects of escaping from a difficult world into feelings or fantasies. His plays

107

furnish examples of people who are enmeshed in denial for the simple reason that they are unwilling or unable to face reality. I have mentioned Frantz in *The Condemned of Altona:* we might equally think of the circle of denial in *No Exit* or the people of Thebes in *The Flies.* On the other hand, Sartre's most optimistic plays, *Kean* and *The Devil and the Good Lord,* show us the opposite: characters who overcome denial and decide to live with and in reality.

But denial is not solely a psychological phenomenon. Golda Meir's famous remark that "there are no Palestinians" was a classic example of political denial. So was the Palestinian refusal to call terrorism by its proper name. Denial does not merely appear in statements and interpretations, however, but above all in actions having far-reaching consequences. The reality of terror by the Palestine Liberation Organization was such an example on one side, as was the Israeli root-and-branch destruction of Palestinian villages after 1949 on the other. As I have suggested, the Israeli-Palestinian conflict is suffused with denial. It begins at the beginning, with the Zionist slogan "A land without people for a people without land." The claim, by Israelis and their apologists, that the Palestine coveted by Zionism was scantily populated flies in the face of a population density in pre–World War I Palestine already equal to the postfrontier United States.[6] The current Palestinian view of historic Jewish settlement in Palestine, describing it as "settler-colonialism," is equally an act of denial. Correct as far as it goes, this characterization omits both the project of Jewish national liberation that motivated the Second Aliyah, the movement of the great Zionist leaders, and the desperate effort to find shelter, after 1922 in Poland and 1933 in Germany, by Jews menaced by anti-Semitism and then annihilation. Without the equally decisive motivations of national liberation and shelter, Israel would never have come into being; omitting their centrality caricatures Zionism beyond recognition.

Virtually the entire history could be told, on both sides, in terms of this mutually reinforcing practice of denial. Of course, *denial* has problematic connotations. When it becomes political, denial—of other people or decisive aspects of their reality—tends to be violent or to provoke violence.[7] Zionists consistently and successfully prevailed on the British to reject Palestinian demands for democratic self-determination in Palestine, until a cartographically grotesque, majority Jewish state could be gerrymandered in 1947 on slightly over half of Palestine; Palestinians consistently and unsuccessfully fought any expansion of a Jewish presence that they recognized as threatening their own claim to sovereignty. The conflicts of 1929, 1936–39, and 1947–49 were the results.

Second, psychological denial implies pathology, or at least danger: the denied reality, after all, becomes part of a situation that on principle can no longer be grasped adequately and appropriately. Sooner or later the day of reckoning will come. Israelis, dimly aware of a "demographic" threat—the number of young Palestinian children in Eretz Israel/ Palestine now exceeds the number of young Jewish children, and a Palestinian majority is now within sight—may have rendered themselves incapable of dealing with it; Palestinians know that most of the West Bank has now been expropriated by Israel but have not been able to effectively combat the creeping annexation. While the Intifada, one of the great mass uprisings of the twentieth century, has led to decisive shifts towards accommodation among Palestinians, they have not been able to soften Israeli rejectionism. In spite of all contrary evidence, Jews still pretend to themselves that Palestinians will be satisfied with less than the Jews themselves fought so hard to achieve—national self-determination. Indeed, the term *transfer*—a grim euphemism for *expulsion*—has become a legitimate term in Israeli political discourse. In spite of the Intifada and the PLO's breakthrough steps of November 15, 1988—declaration of the state of Palestine, recognition of Israel, disavowal of terrorism—the Israeli reshaping of the remaining 22 percent of Palestine beyond the Green Line—the West Bank and Gaza—continues.

Dangerous or not, the various practices of denial were originally selected for a reason, namely, that the alternative, full recognition of the threatening reality, would have created greater problems. Denial has become a central feature of the Israeli-Palestinian conflict, to the point of becoming constitutive of Israeli and Palestinian identity, only because for each side acknowledging reality was politically impossible. Can one imagine the Zionist project without the pretense that the land was empty, that the people living on it were just "Arabs" and not Palestinians (in other words, had no political claims to sovereignty there, on that land)? Admitting the reality would have delegitimized the project itself, of "returning" to "our" home. In other words, the Israeli identity could not have come into being, morally or politically, without systematically ignoring this other people's very existence as a people. Otherwise, seen as having the very same rights that Jews claimed for themselves, and thus fully entitled to political power in their own homeland, their presence would have fatally demoralized the Zionist project. To continue dismissing the PLO as a "terrorist organization" is to ignore that the PLO's objectives and tactics have changed rather significantly. But this only continues the practice installed at the heart of Zionism from the beginning, of denying the Palestinian claim to national self-determination.

109

Similarly, the Palestinians could not acknowledge the profound Jewish attachment to the same land, because it might have meant conceding some right to Jewish settlement. And they could not accept a Jewish need for shelter as having validity because immigration threatened their claim to sovereignty. Just as the Israeli sensibility took shape refusing to see the Palestinians as full, equal persons, so did the Palestinian sensibility take shape in rejecting Zionist claims, in seeing them as no more than colonial settlers. Only recently in Palestine, their very presence was illegitimate. Each denial is understandable and was perhaps the only possible route that could have been taken.

To speak of Israeli and Palestinian identities is not to suggest phenomena that are primarily psychological. These identities are in reality practico-inert structures, with their own political substance, organizational forms, and supporting ideologies. One such form is the Jewish National Fund, which owns land "in perpetuity" for the Jewish people in Israel *and* the diaspora, and so excludes many of those born on that very land. The PLO's resort to and acceptance of terrorism, and its self-construction as an apparatus for "armed struggle," to take another example, meant attacks on the only targets available for attack: innocent civilians. Such attacks appeared to be the only path open to a displaced people in the wake of total Arab defeat. They were cheered in the villages and the camps and the Palestinian diaspora, and were widely credited for dissolving the despair and passivity that settled over the community after the War of June 1967.[8]

Once willed, these forms of denial became congealed in organizational structures which came to perpetuate themselves, recruit their staffs, and produce their own self-justifications. "On their own," they have tended to perpetuate the same blindness, in no matter what situation. In other words, the praxes of denial have yielded their practico-inert deposits. More: these deposits served to deviate each project from its original goals. Israel exists, and it no longer needs to deny the Palestinians in order to create, justify, or defend itself. It no longer needs to assert Jewish sovereignty against Palestinian demands, to make Palestinian land over into Jewish land, to take control of large enough spaces to house the waiting refugees. Nevertheless, the Israeli nonrecognition of Palestinians continues dangerously beyond the situation that gave rise to it, thereby ensuring continual conflict, which may one day destroy Israel. Nonrecognition has ceased to be functional even in Israeli terms.

On the other hand, the Palestinians have been slowly, painfully, moving away from denial, moving beyond rejectionism and glorification of the "armed struggle" to a greater and greater acceptance of the reality of their situation. The decisive steps in this have been the popular uprising in the West Bank and Gaza, and the consequent breakthrough of November 15, 1988. To regard armed attacks on civilians—terrorism—as equivalent to attacks on military personnel and installations—"the armed struggle"—was to deny the very nature of the PLO struggle, as well as to fatally misconceive the nature of the enemy and Jewish psychology. To speak only of "the Zionist entity" and not indicate acceptance of Israel was to refuse to play the only card that could change that situation. If this denial once provided the moral and political cement necessary to make possible the self-creation of the Palestinian identity, it seems no longer necessary given the conditions created by the struggle against the Israeli occupation. The original drafts of this article insisted on a rigorous parallelism between Israeli and Palestinian denial, but in 1990 this is no longer possible. The Palestinians have broken through decisively; the Israelis have not.

Why? Why have the Palestinians been able to move decisively to free themselves from their denial, while the Israelis seem unwilling to face reality? Sartre can help us to understand the tendency for each side in the struggle to become blinded to its original goals by the structures created during the struggle. In each case a deviation of praxis by its results has taken place. For several years a growing international consensus has insisted that, if it is to be secure and flourishing, the Jewish state demands accommodation with the Palestinians; in fact, its stability demands a Palestinian state.[9] On the other hand, Palestinian self-determination and flourishing in a Palestinian state is possible, in the real world of today, only with its full acceptance by Israel. If in each case there have been a number of political and social obstacles to mutual recognition, studying them reveals a praxis-process in which each side became deviated from its own original and deepest goals in the very praxis of pursuing them.

Until 1988 it might have been argued that each side lost track of its most basic needs and came to develop an institutionalized stake in fundamentally rejecting the other. Until the Intifada and the Palestinian breakthrough it seemed to many that a deviation had become mutually determining and reinforcing; Israelis would not allow the "terrorists" to rule an independent state alongside Israel, and the Palestinians, already displaced and occupied, would not acquiesce to the point of giving Israel the necessary assurances to make it budge. It seemed that because the Israelis would not recognize the Palestinians, the Palestinians would not recognize the Israelis, and that because the Palestinians would not recognize the Israelis, the Israelis would not recognize the Palestinians. Right-wing Jewish fundamentalists on the West Bank, their blind arrogance in some sense a product of Israeli military superiority, formed a physical human obstacle to Palestinian sovereignty. Similarly, it seemed, second- and third-generation Palestinian populations of Syrian, Jordanian, and Lebanese refugee camps—indeed, the entire Palestinian diaspora— nourished on forty years of dreams of returning home to their vanished villages, seemed to form the social basis of Palestinian rejectionism.

Inertia on each side seemed locked in place by a reciprocal inertia on the other side, confirming and justifying each side's unwillingness. "Ein Breira" is the famous formula of Israeli self-justification: there is no choice. It seemed that to understand the situation we were thrown back from relying on such mature Sartrean texts as *Critique of Dialectical Reason* to the most depressing (and widely criticized) area of his early thought, the description of the inevitable and intractable self-other conflict of *Being and Nothingness*. But in a series of remarkable moves in the fall of 1988, Yassir Arafat and the PLO committed themselves, for the first time, to formal acceptance of a two-state solution to the Israeli-Palestinian conflict; to living in peace alongside Israel on the basis of United Nations resolutions 242 and 338; to negotiate with Israel in the context of an international conference; and they rejected "terrorism in all of its forms." To argue, as most Israeli political figures and commentators did, that Arafat did not dot every *i* and cross every *t*—did not go "far enough"—was to ignore the fact that his declarations continued a long-term Palestinian trend towards moderation, realism and reconciliation.

Why is it that the Palestinians have been able to move further toward shedding the blindness so central to their self-constitution than have the Israelis? At the end of his major study of deviation in *Critique* II, Sartre speculated that the deviated Bolshevik revolution might one day return to its original goals. In the final pages of *Critique* II, Sartre stresses that human needs lay at the origin of the dialectic; they remain at the origin of the structures humans create no matter how far these structures stray from their original goals. Need may compel praxis to return to its original purposes. What does this suggest about a path out of the Israeli-Palestinian conflict?

In fact, *need* is behind the new moderation of the Palestine Liberation Organization. To question whether the new positions are sincere is disingenuous, in addition to being self-serving; it implies that the only acceptable changes are those that arise, unmotivated, from the goodness of the heart. In fact, need is always behind political shifts, be they major or minor. A combination of forces, internal and external, has been at work on the PLO, pushing it away from rejectionism and toward acceptance of Israel. One of the greatest of these has been the continuing

Israeli transformation of the West Bank and Gaza, aided, ironically, by the Palestinian laborers who built the dwellings for the growing numbers of the most nationalist of Israelis. Refusal to recognize the reality, indeed, the permanence of Israel, continuing to take refuge in fantasies about its destruction and a "secular, democratic State" in all of Palestine, meant risking losing forever what remains of Palestine.

But it was the Intifada that tipped the scales. Those who took their fate into their own hands were the Palestinians of the West Bank and Gaza—who already live side by side with Israel, who already know its real, palpable presence in their daily lives, who largely live in their own homes and villages and seek to free *these* from occupation. In other words, *these* Palestinians tipped the scales towards recognition—by their self-activity and their needs, as well as their moderation and self-control. *They* made possible the declaration of the state of Palestine and the recognition of Israel. A PLO remaining rejectionist, refusing to negotiate on their behalf, refusing to see the opportunity their struggle presented as well as its urgency, would not long remain their leadership. *Need,* then, has been bringing about the end of Palestinian denial, in a double sense: the need of those under Israeli occupation, the need of their leadership.

Conversely, Israeli intransigence persists because at the present time there is no compelling need to face, and accept, the reality of Palestinian national aspirations. This is so even though the Intifada has permanently changed the status quo. Certainly it imposes moral, political and financial costs on Israel. It impedes the normalization of the Israeli economy, continues the sense of siege, of international isolation, of militarization, under which Israelis have lived from the beginning. But that is just the point: all of these consequences of continued nonrecognition of Palestinian national aspirations are only continuations of the familiar results of an "Arab problem" that has existed from the beginning. Israelis have always lived under a sense of isolation and siege: "ein breira"—there is no alternative. This is as true of traditional Labor Zionists as it is Israelis of Middle Eastern origin. Furthermore, the new religious nationalists and the Jabotinskyite revisionists alike have strong ideological reasons for accepting the situation—their mission is to control *all* of Eretz Israel. Moreover, even if refusing to face reality and continuing to deny the Palestinians may have costs, Jews are skeptical about achieving normalization in any event, and do not hesitate to point to a twentieth-century experience that confirms this skepticism. American Jews, Israel's main pillar of support, in spite of their impressive integration into American life see in Israel's besieged and outcast status a confirmation of their own past as well as their inner fears and feelings. They will not break with Israel on this issue.

What then could make Israelis *need* to abandon their denial and accept the idea of Palestinian national self-determination? The only possible source of such pressure would be a shift in the social, political, and economic landscape so severe that the costs of continuing Israeli policy would be felt to be unbearable. The PLO's softening is not enough: Israelis must not only *see* a change but also *feel* the need to give up their "PLO—terrorist" equation. The threat of a serious drop in American aid, for example, might force Israel to face material and political consequences of continued denial, consequences which its privileged status as the largest single recipient of American aid has spared it. A clear converging of United States and Soviet policy might announce such a change. Or a massive new financial burden might require a drastic shift of priorities, such as the strains imposed by a new wave of immigration from the USSR. Certainly, continuing Palestinian moderation will aid any changes in Israel in the long run; in the short run, however, opposition to a Palestinian state has lost none of its strength, and the Israeli Right has only grown.

In spite of the dramatic changes made by the Palestinians, the situation remains stuck. Sartre reminds us, however, that the most congealed and reified situations, the most routinized dances of death, remain inescapably human. "There is no non-human situation."[10] Even if we are able to see and explain why no other course was chosen than this one, we are still able to see and explain, *and act on behalf of,* the prospects for choosing a different path. As I said at the outset, central to the political heritage Sartre leaves us is his stress on not waiting on trends or forces to justify our action, or to be validated, afterwards, but on acting to create such trends or forces.

Sartre's most eloquent message to us in this respect is not his initially tentative, then ringing, reaffirmation of the dialectic at the end of *Critique* II, but his own life. To accept practico-inertia as final is to pretend to turn oneself into a human thing, the consummate form of bad faith, a wholly determined being. Sartre himself acted, again and again, sometimes foolishly, sometimes heroically, to change this or that impossible, intractable situation.

"For human reality, to exist is always to assume its being; that is, to be responsible for it instead of receiving it from outside like a stone." Surveying the Israeli-Palestinian conflict we can see such efforts to break the passivity engendered by the mutually reinforcing stalemate. A mass peace movement, equivalent to the American anti-Vietnam war movement at its peak, sprang up in Israel within a few weeks of the invasion of Lebanon in 1982. Palestinian youth in Gaza and the West Bank heroically rose up against the occupation in late 1987, transforming Palestinian consciousness. The PLO has officially accepted a two-state solution. When least expected, when the situation seems the most stuck, humans who refuse to accept their passivity have created these deeply important, but not yet decisive, moments. Perhaps then it is worth stressing the long-term developments that have taken place on both sides: the PLO's official statements of November 15, 1988, culminated a trend of several years in which it has clearly become less rejectionist, more realistic; although their government is not disposed to a resolution, a sizeable minority of Israelis accept and argue for the need for negotiating with the PLO to achieve a Palestinian state. Indeed, this position has had representation in the cabinet. All of this is not yet enough, but it will continue. Perhaps each people's original goals, Jewish and Palestinian self-determination, can still be rediscovered at the core of what has become a congealed, reified conflict? Perhaps, just perhaps.

Other explorations of the Israeli-Palestinian conflict inspired by Sartre are certainly possible, and other aspects of the situation demand illuminating. In this sketch of a Sartrean approach to the situation, I have tried to show its usefulness *and* to describe one of the central and most puzzling aspects of the conflict.

I began with Sartre, I end with Sartre. But I began with his thought, and I end with his commitment to action. Until the very end, both his life and thought tell us, no obstacles are final or fatal. In the end, only praxis can decide what human beings will make of what they have been made into. In the end, neither history nor inert structures can decide; only human beings will decide. This is, after all, the ultimate Sartrean message.

Notes

1. See Ronald Aronson, *Jean-Paul Sartre—Philosophy in the World* (London, 1980).

2. I develop this argument in the final chapter of *Sartre's Second Critique* (Chicago, 1987).

3. *The Emotions* (New York, 1948), 12.

4. See Ronald Aronson, *The Dialectics of Disaster* (London, 1984), and *"Stay Out of Politics!" A Philosopher Views South Africa* (Chicago, 1990).

5. Sartre's foreword to R. D. Laing and D. G. Cooper, *Reason and Violence* (London, 1964), 7.

6. The figure was approximately fifty people per square mile by 1900; the United States did not reach this until 1940, or well after Congress enacted legislation severely restricting immigration (and in effect saying to the world that the country was full). For this and a detailed discussion of what follows, see *The Dialectics of Disaster,* 221–54.

7. In the *Cahiers pour une morale* Sartre explicitly distinguishes force, which conforms to the nature of the object, from violence, which goes against the object and "takes place where force is ineffective" (Paris, 1983, 179).

8. My analysis reflects the asymmetry of both the situation and the historical struggle. The two sides have always been fundamentally unequal in terms of organization, resources, and foreign support. The Jewish practice of denial, like the Zionist project, has been complex and many-sided from the beginning and reflects what is, after all, a successful project of almost total transformation of a land inhabited by another people. The Palestinian practice of denial has been reactive, much more rudimentary, and reflects the historic weakness of the Palestinian position.

9. This is argued persuasively in Mark Heller, *A Palestinian State: The Implications for Israel* (Cambridge, Mass., 1983).

10. *Being and Nothingness* (New York, 1956), 554.

5

THE *CRITIQUE:* A VIEW FROM THE LABOR MOVEMENT

Alan Lennon

As a public sector trade unionist and no longer a scholar of Sartre, I wish to explain why I have found Sartre's ideas useful in political and trade union work.

A rank-and-file activist in the public sector has a unique viewpoint. As front-line workers in the public sector, we are the victims of bureaucracy, but we function also as victimizers of clients in the name of that bureaucracy. People experience us as exercising power over their lives while we experience an essential powerlessness through our inability to help them. This dichotomy makes it difficult to create alliances between front-line workers and clients whenever our joint interests conflict with the interests of the senior levels of bureaucracy. It is in such potential alliances that the power of public-sector unions could reside.

In the past, I studied and wrote about Sartre's version of Marxism, particularly as set out in the *Critique of Dialectical Reason*. Sartre has often claimed to be a "committed philosopher." As such, he urges us to come down from the mountain of theory and participate in the arena of politics. Any attempt to evaluate his work must look at the effects his theory has or can have on the practice of politics. Accordingly, I would like to explain how the *Critique* can and should be used in practice.

Trade unions have an institutional history and a more or less ac-

117

cepted place within the advanced capitalist social order. This place is threatened if unions go beyond "acceptable" behavior. To some, strikes appear to be outside of acceptable behavior. As a part of the system of labor relations, strikes are permitted under certain conditions, after certain processes, and they are subjected to certain limits. Like most institutional behavior, they are highly predictable and formalized.

As a traditional unionist, I do a particular kind of political work which is different from that of a business unionist. In theory and/or in practice the latter sees the aim of trade unions to be bargaining collective agreements and arbitrating resultant rights within the workplace. Business unionism is primarily interested in servicing union members, in providing them with protection through legally constituted structures— structures in which the "experts" are said to be best suited to represent the union member and define his or her interests. Of course, the protection of legal rights (rights that have to be won—there are no "natural rights" for workers on the shop floor) is important, but it is equally, if not more, important to recognize that this approach pacifies workers in the shop and in their union.

Even where collective agreements may result from collective action, such as strikes, the interpretation of any resultant rights results in conflicts between the individual and the employer. The union sees to the protection of its members' rights *as individuals* and, in so doing, creates the impression for the rank and file that they are powerless and dependent because they are individualized. Rank-and-file unionists may believe that the solution to a problem can be provided only by an "expert" who is able to work within a legally formalized system.

What I seek to do as a political trade unionist is to empower the workers on the shop floor and, through their union, within society. I see unions as the practical means through which the workplace can be transformed into a democratically controlled expression of individual and collective freedom and power. In that manner they can express the enlightened collective self-interest of working people. Too often, unions concentrate on the solution for the individual and not enough on the overall interest of all workers. If the unions are enlightened, they deal with the collective interests of all workers and not just union members. All unions deal with problems of individual members, but they should do so with an eye to solving the cause of the problem for all working people.

My political work is to mobilize individuals within the trade union movement to take action collectively to solve their own problems— whether work-related or more broadly defined. After all, when working collectively, individuals are responsible not only for their actions but also for the collective impact of those actions. In acting in concert, these individuals must unite in terms upon which they agree. Otherwise the notion of the collective is a false one—an imposed unity that does not belong to the individuals who comprise it. By acting in their collective self-interest, they can broadly define their solidarity and affirm it through their action.

Regardless of how one perceives Sartre's own political history, he obviously paid heed to the necessity of collective action, and he tried to illuminate its meaning for those involved in it. From the time of *The Ghost of Stalin,* in which he attacked the French Communist Party for depoliticizing its members, to his support for the rebellions of May 1968, and after, Sartre supported the importance of and the necessity for working people to act on their own behalf rather than to be spoken for by a self-appointed organization. For Sartre it became important to politicize people rather than to pacify them.

I want to discuss two ideas from Sartre's *Critique.* They can help us understand the political nature of certain kinds of organizing. These are central ideas in the *Critique* I: the practico-inert and the group-in-fusion. I wish to suggest that they illuminate certain features of organizing and mobilizing groups of people which must be fully understood to avoid political mistakes and political failures. I am not suggesting that a knowledge of Sartre's work is a prerequisite to political organizing but simply that such knowledge can aid the organizer in his or her analysis and strategy and make his or her work easier and more efficacious.

The practico-inert. According to Sartre, the notion of freedom in *Being and Nothingness* was a classless and abstract notion; in the *Critique* I, he attempts to explain how freedom can exist but free actions turn out badly for the actors. The practico-inert is the key to understanding Sartre's explanation of how humans can be both free and yet in need of liberation.

Individuals who act in order to meet their needs create out of their given environment a new modified environment, the practico-inert. When human projects are incorporated into this new environment, however, it, the practico-inert, modifies these projects and mediates their results, making them different from what was expected. Matter in this form is actively passive; it reflects the projects of individuals back onto them but in forms and with meanings they do not recognize and/or had not foreseen.

Practico-inertia also means that the projects of individual people or groups can be modified by the results of the projects of other people.

119

Sartre uses the example of Chinese peasants who, individually, felled trees in order to cultivate additional land. Each peasant's project, to expand production, was rational by itself. However, when all the peasants did it, the land was deforested, causing flooding and erosion and a subsequent reduction in production. The free project of the individual peasant rebounded back on every peasant with negative and totally unforeseen results.

While human praxis creates the practico-inert, it, in turn, creates the human being. It does so because, being the condition within which we live, it is internalized by individuals and then externalized in and through our projects. In a bus queue, for example, each individual, all of whom share a common goal of getting on the bus, has internalized the external structure of queueing so that each expresses his or her goal by acting according to that practico-inert structuring. Each risks the failure of his or her project (that is, not getting on the bus) in accepting the praxis determined by the practico-inert (the manner in which one queues for a bus in such and such a town). But normally no one takes the risk of crashing the queue in order to ensure getting a place on the bus.

Obviously, then, the practico-inert is not simply the reaction of natural laws and forces but also the social structures in which we live our daily lives. These structures are not totally rigid. They can change and be changed. Many of us act in order to change the practico-inert as we would like or wish. The viscosity of the practico-inert distorts our projects into results we did not intend or into results we do not even recognize as our own.

We are all familiar with stories of people trying to deal with bureaucracies and being caught in Catch-22 situations, and probably we have all been caught in them ourselves. But let us look at the bureaucracy as an example of the practico-inert, from the point of view of the front-line worker with such a bureaucracy and not from the point of view of the outsider or victim of the bureaucracy.

Institutions such as the Department of Employment and Immigration have two goals: one is to serve the clients of the institution (this is the publicly proclaimed goal); the second is to justify itself to its masters, for example, by maintaining performance as it is measured statistically. These goals are not always compatible.

Front-line workers discover the power of the practico-inert by living the contradictory demands of the institution. It is not the supervisors who create the contradictions but rather the contradictions that are part and parcel of the practico-inert itself. The project of the front-line worker, which is to provide public service, comes back to the worker as a demand for increased statistical output; this results in the sacrifice of quality for quantity. (In turn, the institution pretends that quantity is quality.) The sense of power that lies at the front line, in terms of discretionary decision making to help people, disappears into a total sense of powerlessness before the institutional demands for output. The front-line worker learns over time that even the limited ability to help a few individuals gets overwhelmed by the demands of the practico-inert, and it makes clear that gaining control over such institutions is not a possible solution. If front-line workers expand their discretionary power, it does them little good given the way their power gets distorted within the practico-inertia of the bureaucracy. Regardless of how much discretion exists at the front line, the institutional demands for statistically measured productivity, which are necessary to justify the existence of the bureaucracy, will rebound on that power as demands for lower quality but higher quantity. What is clear is that "the long march through the institutions" cannot be a viable solution. In my opinion, the only solution must be to escape the logic of the practico-inert and to rebuild from the beginning in a manner that does not recreate the need to liberate the front-line worker once again.

Anyone who wishes to organize workers within a bureaucracy, or even to understand what happens to them, must analyze the institution as a practico-inert structure and grasp how it legislates behavior for workers. The practico-inert does not force anyone to do anything. It merely makes a certain kind of behavior appear reasonable and efficacious. It is conceivable to behave differently and not follow the path as laid out by the practico-inert. But why would one? The practico-inert provides specific paths of behavior in certain situations. To not follow them requires a justification. It also requires a willingness to pay the cost of doing what is not normally done. The path of least resistance is that provided by the practico-inert. That is how it legislates behavior, while providing individuals with the illusion of freedom and choice.

The notion of the practico-inert provides us with a concept and an analysis of the structures in which we have to live. It suggests that it is misleading and not useful to think that large bureaucratic institutions simply serve the interests of a few powerful individuals or groups. It suggests that it is no more useful to blame the vagaries of bureaucracies on low- and middle-level bureaucrats. Sartre's notion provides a tool to understand the bureaucracy as legislative of internal and external behavior and as actively passive in distorting attempts to reform or overcome it.

Another important lesson Sartre provides is that the power of the practico-inert is not based on false consciousness. As Sartre remarks: "When the woman in the Dop shampoo factory has an abortion in order to avoid having a child she would be unable to feed, she makes a free decision in order to escape a destiny that is made for her; but she carries out the sentence [of the machine] . . . which deprives her of free mother-hood."[1] But even if she knew exactly what had happened and why, what difference would it make? Life does not change because one clearly identifies the forces that deny one's liberation. Obviously knowledge here meets the need for praxis, effective praxis. The effectiveness of praxis when dealing with political and social issues is directly related to the level of understanding of the situation. But Sartre also shows that this insight needs more than just individual praxis and understanding to be effective. Individual insight produces only frustration and ineffective-ness. It produces the possibility but not the necessity for change.

2. *The group-in-fusion.* Sartre's paradigm is the Quartier St. An-toine in July 1789 at the time of the storming of the Bastille. Its residents were serialized by the insularity of their homes and the shortage of food. This seriality left them facing their situation as individuals and, conse-quently, impotent. However, Paris was united from the outside by the monarchy, as its enemy. The people of Paris, therefore, faced a common direct threat from the king's guns mounted on the Bastille's battlements as well as an indirect threat emanating from the planned policies of the monarchy. In this situation, even the most selfishly individualistic act of a resident trying to save his own life would be taken by the king's forces as a threat. The individualistic act of arming oneself in order to save one's own life became in the eyes of the regime the arming of the people of Paris against the king. The situation of the Parisians was, according to Sartre, "the impossibility of the impossibility of living."[2] The initial situation was impossible for the residents of Paris who, as poor, had been designated as expendable by the regime. Now their ability to act was denied to them by the king and his forces who perceived as a threat any of their acts and counterattacked murderously. As their situation became impossible, they united in the spontaneous common project of storming the Bastille. "The Bastille became the common interest insofar as it both could be and had to be not only disarmed but also made a source of supply of arms. . . . The task defined itself for everyone as the pressing revelation of a . . . common freedom."[3] In the group each recognized the free project of the others as his or her own and therefore found freedom in this reciprocity. Although freedom could be expressed in individual praxis, it became efficacious only in a group. The apocalyp-tic fusion of the individuals into a group is, according to Sartre, the

beginning of humanity through the reclamation of freedom. That reclamation can only occur through the collective praxis of groups (made up of free individuals), because only through such praxis can the active passivity of the practico-inert be overcome.

Sartre next discusses how the group decays back into the seriality from whence it came. It has been suggested that Sartre's essential individualism or asociality is at the basis of this decay. However, it must be said that forces exist for such a decay regardless of Sartre's assumptions and/or starting points.

The forces exist because the group-in-fusion is a group and not a fusing of individuals into sameness. The group-in-fusion is not a collective consciousness, nor does it deny individual freedom of action. The group continues to exist within the legislated patterns of the practico-inert, but its unity changes because individuals need to meet their own individual needs (food, clothing, shelter, etc.). These are satisfied individually even if the means are produced socially. The resultant dispersion into individuality then simply becomes the ultimate expression of the legislated behavior imposed by the practico-inert.

However, in my view, Sartre is far too pessimistic here. He has failed to examine the experience of the individuals who have been part of a group-in-fusion. For a trade unionist, strikes are probably the best example of such groups. As I said earlier, some strikes are simply part of a formalized collective bargaining process. The necessary moves are made; the union walks out, and round-the-clock bargaining leads to a settlement. But there are also strikes that represent the impossibility of an impossible situation for workers. An example is the Canadian federal clerks' strike in 1980 in which fifty thousand clerical regulatory workers (mostly women) struck—to the surprise of their employer, their managers, and also their union. The leadership of the union was angry with the members, because after a year of negotiations they struck spontaneously instead of following "proper procedures." For these individuals and for this union, things will never be the same. This is evident from the remarks made by the participants about the strike and its significance.

The collective taking of action against a common enemy for a common end brings people together in a way very few will ever experience. What can be said about strike action is that, after the fact, people are not the same. They have had a taste of their own power and their own strength against their common adversary. "One of the good things of the strike, it's sort of hard to explain, the sort of warm, nostalgic memories we all have. . . . I think that for a brief moment in time there was a kind of collective spirit that we could do almost anything."[4] That sense of collective power does not disappear when the strike is over. When people return to work, they go back not as the kind of employees the company had before but as a group of people who have stood together against a common enemy and who know their own ability to deal with their own problems.

They know that they are, if not in total control of their own destiny, responsible for the actions that will create, and rebound around, their destinies. Even if the strikers are not victorious, the people are still changed. "I remember a young woman in my local and in the work relationship, her supervisor exerted a lot of control over her and had a great deal of power over her. But when she was on that picket line, she was her own person, she became very strong. After the strike we had a local meeting. . . . And at this local meeting, this young woman stood up and challenged the values and beliefs of that supervisor."[5]

Solidarity, like the practico-inert, has its own inertia, but it is a positive inertia. This is well recognized within the trade union movement. It is one reason why, in its business-unionist form, the movement wants to keep strikes only as a part of an orchestrated, legally defined process of collective bargaining. Unions, like employers, are afraid of workers fusing into groups and acting against the legislated patterns of the practico-inert labor relations system. Empowering people, even for a moment, has effects on those people that may never end. These effects may return to haunt those who seek to keep power over others, regardless of the institution to which they belong. Because of the strike, people "are questioning the structure of the whole union and I think it's because of some of these things that happened that we're going to see a lot of change in the next 5 or 10 years."[6]

The notion of the group-in-fusion gives us a means with which to analyze what happens to people in collective action. What is the sense of power that they develop? Since the fusion does not continue to exist in the same form after the return to work, what form does it take? After all, strikers claim that the feeling continues to exist. What do people gain from their defeats?

As individuals, people unite. We need to understand the fact that they do not stay united, but more importantly we need to understand why people fuse, as opposed to just getting together at a meeting, and how this can be made into the most empowering experience possible. Can it be maintained as a possibility over a long period of time—that is, can they fuse, disperse, and re-fuse with some degree of regularity and with consciousness about the political need for it? Such questions must be answered because they are a key to political organizing. However, like all questions concerning organizing, they must be answered in practical terms and for specific cases. Broad generalizations are not adequate—analytical tools are required, but to be useful they must be applied to specific cases. All these questions can become clearer through the use of the concept of the group-in-fusion.

In thinking about how to organize and do political work, the question of Sartre's own political theory and practice remains. Nowhere in his work, particularly in the *Critique* I, does he provide a clear answer to the question of the permanent overcoming of seriality and the possibility of human liberation. Was his work a theoretical dead end in its inability to provide an argument for progress in politics?

If we think of politics not as consisting of a series of small victories and defeats that lead up to the great revolutionary overthrow of capitalism but as consisting of people empowering themselves before, during, and after the revolution, then one can see that Sartre is not a pessimist. He helps us to see politics differently.

In my view, the group-in-fusion, even if it collapses into seriality, can do so not in a circular way but in a way that can fundamentally change people. Similarly, the practico-inert points to the malleability of social reality—which suggests that it may be won over, even if this victory is neither a simple one, an easy one, nor ever clearly won. After a group of people have acted against it, the practico-inert is different, as are the people themselves. This process is itself political, because it reveals to people their own power, even in its limitations. Self-empowerment is the political process that can lead to a better world. Victories will not always be won, but it is hoped that the mole will continue to undermine the bourgeois, bureaucratic, and patriarchal forms of power within today's and future societies. Sartre gives us tools to understand the politics of this praxis-process—tools that we hope can help us to succeed.

Notes

I would like to thank Robert Stone for his encouragement. He is, of course, not responsible for the content. This article is dedicated to Graeme and Jan.

1. Sartre, *Critique of Dialectical Reason*, I, trans. by. Alan Sheridan-Smith, ed. by Jonathan Rée (London, 1976), 235.
2. Ibid., 349.
3. Ibid., 361.
4. *50,000 Strong* (Toronto, 1985), 39. This analysis of the clerical workers' strike was commissioned by the Canada Employment and Immigration Union (CEIU) as part of its ongoing attempt to create the conditions for a group-in-fusion to appear within the Public Service Alliance of Canada (PSAC) and the labor movement in general. The strike,

in September and October 1980, was an unauthorized walkout by fifty thousand clerical workers, mostly women, employed by the Canadian government. It represented the clerks' attempt to win not only increases to raise their wages above the poverty line but also the respect of their employer, their fellow workers, and their union—all of whom believed the clerks would not take action on their own behalf. As the strike spread spontaneously across Canada, it began to express the shared militancy and common goals of the rank and file. Unfortunately, the strike fell under the control of the union bureaucracy, which directed it back within "procedures" and undercut the strikers' unity. While victories were won, the return to seriality was facilitated and then reinforced by the union assuming the role of an institution.

5. Ibid., 38.
6. Ibid., 37.

6

NUCLEAR CITIES:
THE BASTILLE ANALOGY

Robert V. Stone

> The H-bomb has a sort of negative universality; it can have an
> effect on anyone no matter how far away. [Therefore] . . .
> permanent and universal danger has given a concrete, precise
> meaning to that formerly vague term, the human species. The
> human species is no longer a biological but a historical, social,
> political term: it is made up of those hundreds of thousands of
> men who, although still separated by very different interests and
> beliefs, are united by a common danger and a common will to
> escape catastrophe at any cost.
>
> —Jean-Paul Sartre, 1955[1]

In New York City on June 12, 1982, starting at the United Nations,
between 750,000 and 1,000,000 people marched up Manhattan's Fifth
Avenue and choked Central Park in what was probably the largest single
anti–nuclear war demonstration ever. The event marked an awakening
by New Yorkers to being "totalized" as residents of a nuclear city, and
yet it was *also* a positive popular response to that fact. But what is it like
to live in a nuclear city?

It is being thrown together with neighboring strangers by the shared
mortal threat of a nuclear missile—whose explosion might replace all of

them with a crater. We can set in relief this persistent structure on the horizon of our consciousnesses by bringing out its similarities and dissimilarities to Sartre's description of Paris prior to the storming of the Bastille on July 14, 1789.

Let us start with "totality," the pivotal concept on which the analogy turns, and its correlative, "totalization," as developed in Sartre's theory of society and history, his *Critique of Dialectical Reason*. A totality is a finished product of human action—a tool, a painting, a city—which *seems* to unify its parts in an enduring whole but whose inert and passive divisibility perpetually erodes this apparent unity. Ongoing human activity itself alone has the power to internally link its subordinate parts, that is, to "totalize." But such activity effects these linkings or "totalizations" only because it is situated, that is, only while under way within history.[2] Paris in the days before July 14 is for Sartre the "totality" that is being "totalized" by the guns and the repressive project of Louis XVI's government at Versailles:

> The government constituted Paris as a totality from outside. . . . And on the morning of Sunday 12 July, the city was full of posters "by order of the king," announcing that the concentration of troops around Paris was intended to protect the city against bandits. Through these notices the city was designated for and within itself. Thus the place, as the practico-inert tension and locus of the Parisian gathering, was constituted by an exterior *praxis* and organized as a totality. . . . The *rumors,* the *posters,* the *news* . . . communicated their common designation to everyone: *each was a particle of sealed materiality.*[3]

Each Parisian thus becomes a potential "bandit," a bit of warm matter that might be caught in a crossfire by the king's troops—a situation fraught with fear and impotence. Sartre remarks, "At this level, the totality of encirclement can be described as being lived *in seriality.*" This means that at least for a while after awakening to their common subjection to an external threat, Parisians still proceeded according to the formula "every man for himself." "Seriality," for Sartre, is seeing oneself in the other not as oneself, as in solidarity, but as other. It refers to the lawlike if passive relationships among externally collected persons that are instituted when those persons don't *want* to be related to each other. Reciprocity isn't banished by serialization, it just turns negative: being in a series (a bus line, a radio audience, a market, etc.) means being aware of the other as *subject,* but in order *not* to interact with him as such.[4]

Unlike a group, whose unity is internal, the unity of a series of persons is external to it, residing in some aspect of the "practico-inert." This is Sartre's term for the world of totalities—of humanly worked matter—insofar as they are used and therefore burden living praxis with built-in imperatives from the past.[5] The posters awakened Parisians to the Bastille's mortal threat not because it was a prison but because it was an arsenal on whose roof were heavy guns capable of leveling, at the king's command, the surrounding area, the Quartier St. Antoine. As products of past labor these guns are the practico-inert through which residents of the Quartier are totalized by the king.[6] It is also with regard to these guns that these residents serialize themselves. Seriality is here a choice that, inasmuch as it takes the king's power as "natural," internalizes in "bad faith" the king's negation of them.[7] Being posited in a common death with a stranger can provoke free abandonment of seriality and a challenge to the system-totality itself. But if individual escape seems possible, such a totalization can also be an occasion for further flight from others, that is, for intensified serialization.

Initially, in fact, Parisians responded to the king's threat by increasing seriality. Perceiving otherness rather than likeness in each other, they fled each other, since, if "others" were targets of the king's bullets, avoiding others was tantamount to avoiding his bullets. But because it seems virtually every person thought this of every other, serial behavior, especially looting of arsenals, became rampant. Each tried to beat the others to rifles since "everyone's attempt to get a rifle became for the Others the risk of remaining unarmed."[8]

Increasing the seriality of a crowd would seem to increase its impotence. But because the king's encirclement of the city foreclosed the flight from others implicit in all seriality, the serialized random "action" of the crowds of Parisians took on a collective character unintended by their members. "In its very disorganization," Sartre writes, the huge but impotent crowd discovered in itself "an irresistible mechanical force for destroying sporadic resistance at the arsenals."[9] Individual agents learned of the strength they acquired within crowds from keepers of the king's arsenals who took them to be threatening *as members of crowds*. Accordingly, the keepers of the arsenals offered little resistance to the crowds. Being treated as participants in intentional groups, individuals in the crowds internalized this collective being-for-others. Thus, as the impossibility of individual escape brought home to the Parisian crowd the real danger of death, participants realized that their *absence* from the crowd was rather itself their authentic and sole risk of death.[10]

This free dialectic of grouping together within the revolutionary crowd proceeded swiftly, once under way. Sartre calls this process "fusion." Empowered by each other, participants realized that the very same practico-inert they had previously elected to live serially—the Bastille, as the major instrument of the king's threat *within* the city—also points to a future community, created by the same formerly serialized individuals once they renounce seriality. A threat that had been an occasion for serialization and impotence becomes, when fear is pushed to its limit and inverted, a path that leads to strength for the people, in the form of arms wielded with a common purpose.[11] Consider the true statement "The people have taken the Bastille." It implies neither a melding of distinct agencies into a purported organic group-subject, as in fascism; nor a converging of interests that have been developed in isolation, as in utilitarianism; nor even an overcoming of fear by courage. Rather, it implies a practical realization, "rotating" among a crowd's participants, that one's survival, if it is possible at all, will be attained only through collective action with the crowd.[12] During such fusion—itself a free choice of freedom—Sartre says seriality is "dropped" as one would drop a mask; falling back into it is universally rejected; each person becomes a leader and a spokesperson.[13]

There are nuclear-age equivalents to many of the structures and processes Sartre uncovers in revolutionary Paris. Our century's nuclear cities, like the Quartier St. Antoine in 1789, are local foci of a more general mortal threat. And our cities show similar internal dynamics: (1) Large masses of urban residents are totalized by the threats of powerful governments that wield, from relatively safe havens, the weaponry of indiscriminate death. (2) Faced with this nuclear threat, taken as practico-inert, the initial response again has been an *increase* in seriality in the form of various purely individual defenses: "survivalism"; Rambo-style machismo, both cultural and political; the postnuclear aesthetic of working-class youth culture; and, more generally, that combination of internal flight and passivity that has been called "psychic numbing"[14] but which is the simple banishment of global perspectives from all discourse lest the frustrating question of nuclear omnicide be raised. (3) The threat of nuclear winter—global climatic changes that would exterminate life in the Northern hemisphere in an all-out nuclear war[15] is the nuclear-age equivalent of Louis XVI's siege of Paris: both the siege and nuclear winter rule out all forms of noncollective escape.[16] (4) Yet amidst aggravated seriality, events like the 1982 march, while not itself a group-in-fusion, nevertheless attest to the possibility of a new revolutionary fusion. Sartre focuses on a *section* of Paris in treating the totality of the encircled city. Similarly, but on the scale of the nuclear age, a *particular city* will be our opening onto the totality of our nuclearized globe.

New York City was to have a nuclear-sized "Bastille" placed in its midst by 1990. By the end of that year a major force of medium-range nuclear cruise missiles on seven ships of a "surface action group" (SAG) was to be moved from Norfolk and berthed in its new homeport, a portion of Staten Island a quarter-mile from the ferry slip for Manhattan. The berthing would have been in 1989, the bicentennial of the storming of the Bastille, but for popular resistance. The devastating weapons were to be housed within city limits, near the middle of a metropolitan area of 9 million people, itself the center of a wider region containing 20 million people.

Now it may be said that unlike the Bastille's guns, New York's missiles are to be *aimed at* external enemies in defense of New York area residents. But is that their only or even their most important role? The Bastille analogy holds if we ask a slightly different question about the weapons in both cases: Whom do they *totalize?* What groups—foreign or domestic—fall within the reach of their power?

Because the SAG is *designed* to single-handedly totalize three groups—primarily, the Soviet bloc, and secondarily, other ships and the Third World[17]—its gunboat-style missiles are "the most versatile weapons in the U.S. arsenal."[18] As previous arms control treaties have done, the 1987 Gorbachev-Reagan intermediate-range missile agreement may legitimate even wider deployment of such cruise missiles at sea (where European disarmament movements cannot demonstrate against them), in proportion as their land-based counterparts are withdrawn from Europe. I give the following four evidences for the thesis that, added to these three types of potential adversaries, the people of the New York City area as a whole are themselves also "totalized" by these weapons, much as the people of the Quartier St. Antoine were in 1789.

1. Were New York itself hit by air bursts of warheads on the SAG's missiles—roughly twenty megatons' worth[19]—there would be 3.6 million immediate deaths. Virtually all remaining 5.4 million metropolitan area persons would die of wounds, fires, or direct radiation in the subsequent months.[20] After that, depending on climatic conditions, fallout could kill many millions more in the region, through leukemias and other radiation-caused diseases.[21] I am excluding for the moment nuclear winter effects.

2. The primary danger of the new base to the New York City area is, of course, strategic. According to Admiral Eugene J. Carroll Jr. (retired), were the SAG base loaded to its fullest nuclear capacity it would become "a major military target for the Soviet Union."[22] If the city itself, without the SAG base, is presently a *first or preemptive strike* target for the Soviets, then, of course, berthing nuclear missile ships

there will *add* no new danger. But such a strategy is not only inconsistent with the "counterforce" policy of aiming at military targets which the Soviets have persistently espoused,[23] but it is prima facie unlikely since it would leave Soviet cities open to a retaliatory United States second strike. So let us consider only non–first-strike targeting of New York City, that is, Soviet strikes against New York in retaliation at some point *after* nuclear war is under way. In this perspective we encounter the following dilemma. As of now, prior to the nuclear SAG emplacement, New York City either is a retaliatory target of a certain priority for offshore Soviet nuclear missile submarines, or it is not. If New York City *is* currently such a target, then if the nuclear SAG base is installed, New York will be attacked at an *earlier stage* of nuclear war than it otherwise would have been.[24] If it is not now a target, then siting the base in New York City will surely make it one, according to the Soviet's professed counterforce targeting policy. In neither case does the siting make sense in terms of *defense* of New Yorkers. The decisive point is that even though we do not know whether New York is or is not now a retaliatory target, it is *certain* that the Staten Island base either makes the city such a target or raises its target priority, and *either way* (and laying aside nuclear winter) the SAG base *adds* such risks to the lives of 20 million U.S. citizens as to be incompatible with their defense.

3. Added to strategic risks are those of wind-carried plutonium leakage from fire, terrorist acts, or Navy involvement in one of the 152 large-ship accidents that occur on average in New York Harbor every year.[25]

4. Just as Louis XVI's encirclement of Paris was not in answer to any popular request for protection by Parisians, so the Reagan government did not inquire whether New York area residents wished to undertake these added risks to their lives. New Yorkers were to be asked in a 1985 referendum whether city land and money may be given for the nuclear base, but local politicians—sure the homeport would be rejected—got it wiped off the ballot at the last moment through a successful legal action. Of course, a vote to grant the land would not have constituted the circumspect, first-person risk taking by all totalized citizens, as would be required to legitimate the base. However, siting it amidst New Yorkers without even such a mild exercise in formal democracy is certainly an *imposing* of risks, an asymmetrical and illegitimate totalization incompatible with democratic government. In theory, at least, such government is supposed to protect and not *itself* imperil the lives of its own citizens.

Thus, New York, like Paris in the late 1780s, is being totalized by its own ruler from a relatively safe haven. Under the pretense of defending them, a death-dealing force is moved toward both cities, a force that, far from protecting them, further endangers their residents.

But why would a U.S. government place its own citizens in harm's way? The question becomes the more urgent and homeporting policy the more puzzling when we consider that it is inconsistent with Washington's own "counterforce" strategy, put in place in August 1980, when President Carter announced that Soviet missiles, not Soviet cities, would be targeted in future. Why, if we propose to spare the Soviet cities, do we aim at their missiles from amidst our own most populous urban areas, thereby subjecting our own cities to counterforce attack?

The main reason the Navy gives for "strategic homeporting" of sixty-four ships to around a dozen new harbors is that "dispersal" of the growing fleet from San Diego on the West Coast and from Norfolk on the East Coast will improve "defense posture" by avoiding Pearl Harbors.[26] This is a canard according to Admiral Carroll, who points out: "There is no navy in the world with the conventional naval war-fighting capacity to bring off, undetected, a Pearl Harbor type of attack against the U.S. Navy in its present configuration, that is, to sink our ships in their ports."[27] Are Norfolk and San Diego so full that there is literally no other place to put the six hundred–ship Navy that was Reagan's goal? No. A 1986 General Accounting Office report shows that there is ample room for such expansion in these existing, already-targeted harbors.[28] Indeed, our nuclear deterrent in general was quite adequate *before* the Reagan buildup. (There is inadequate space here to discuss internal military dynamics on the Soviet side or the Reagan administration policy of going beyond *deterrence* to capacities for *fighting* and *winning* such a war.) If homeporting has *no military benefits* in meeting the Soviet threat, but only costs, then what is its real point?

To make sense of strategic homeporting we must widen our perspective. The mechanism of political economy that has typified the Reagan and Bush era can be called "socialism for the rich." It makes use of a war economy and has the following four elements: (1) Tax breaks for the wealthy and heavy taxation of working people, accompanied by diminution of the "social wage" (welfare, unemployment insurance, college loans, housing, food stamps for striking workers, etc.), weakens workers' bargaining power relative to their bosses and increases their dependence on wage labor for their lives. (2) Huge administration arms budgets stand ready to redistribute this wealth upward to non–wage earners, via the government as conduit, into the hands of those workers' bosses—directly in the case of defense contractors. (3) The congressional support needed if these budgets are actually to effect this movement of wealth has been

133

forthcoming if, in an otherwise sluggish economy, a congressperson could envision returning to his or her constituents with some meager scraps in the form of military-related jobs. (4) Having sold the Congress on spread-the-defense-wealth schemes such as homeporting and the Strategic Defensive Initiative, the Reagan government was able to directly benefit its basic constituency, namely, the owners and managers of the largest U.S. multinationals, an overwhelming percentage of which experience large infusions of tax funds through defense contracts.[29] Reagan, after all, was himself for years the paid mouthpiece of General Electric, always in the top ten for the defense dole. No doubt Reagan, Bush, and their supporters in this class are sincere in opposing communism and socialism, but stigmatizing others with these labels seems to have blinded them to the fact that the system they actually practice is itself a peculiar form of socialism—a use of the federal government's taxing power to further enrich those who are already wealthy.

The scheme has worked. In 1986, compared with 1979, the poor and most middle-income families were worse off, while the rich made large income gains; indeed, in the United States the gap between the richest and the rest of us has never been wider.[30] The immediate effects of this high spending were huge government indebtedness on the one hand and stimulation of an otherwise torpid economy on the other—much as Roosevelt's "pump priming" did before and during World War II. It is by no means certain, as Seymour Melman and others have argued,[31] that stimulation by military spending is bad for capitalism, unless, of course, one counts the greater risk of the deaths of capitalists in nuclear war as bad for profits. Reagan's spending was certainly better for capitalism than Roosevelt's in terms of preserving capitalist *relations* of production since it stimulated the economy broadly while decreasing workers' bargaining power.[32] Of course, the costly goals of a six hundred-ship Navy and homeporting fit nicely into this scheme—which may explain Congress's joining in pursuing them despite their flimsy military rationales.[33]

But socialism for the rich explains only the general overproduction of warships impelled by profitable production speed-ups. It does not explain why, against the precepts of naval strategy, nuclear SAG bases were planned for New York and San Francisco rather than for existing Navy ports. (Boston successfully rejected nuclear SAG "protection"—with no help, incidentally, from then-Governor Dukakis, who sought the base.) Noting how the threat of nuclear annihilation provides rulers East and West with a wonderful tool for stifling internal class struggle and challenge to their rule, Ronald Aronson remarks, "The American bombs are meant for the American people and the Soviet bombs are meant for the Soviet people."[34] Evidently the SAG missiles are "meant" for New Yorkers. But how? Why?

While the Staten Island siting makes no sense as a defense of New Yorkers, it does make sense as an indirect threat to them. I submit that these missiles are "meant" for New Yorkers in much the way Sartre shows Louis XIV "meant" his soldiers' weapons for the Parisians. The analogy with the weapons atop the Bastille is instructive for New Yorkers precisely in implying that Ronald Reagan's "evil empire," like Louis XVI's "bandits," actually included *ourselves,* the people. If, in the fear caused by being totalized by our ruler's weapons, we should fail either to welcome the "shelter" provided by his arms or to align ourselves with his threats, those failures would become evidence that we are ourselves members of the vast and subtle underworld. In neither of the two cases does the ruler threaten his domestic population directly. However, the coercive *indirect* messages are clear in both cases, namely, since only if I wield my weapons freely will I be able to save you from our common enemy, you must not burden me with dissent from my policies and wishes, for, as the proximity of my weapons makes clear, I hold over you the power of life and death.

Why have New York and (until recently) the Bay Area been the objects of such coercive messages? William L. McBride deepened the Bastille analogy in his comment on an earlier version of this article when he found a possible answer to this question in the behavior of Louis XVI toward the Quartier St. Antoine. I quote at length:

> It is no accident that the confused but dramatic events that Sartre recounts and that we now, from our distant temporal vantage point, refer to as the start of the French Revolution occurred where they did. There was a confluence of ideological and strictly material factors. As for the latter, the Quartier St. Antoine occupies a big bend area described by the River Seine, with the fortress of the Bastille located near the middle of the Quartier's single nonriver boundary line. Given the large guns mounted on it that Stone mentions, this material situation meant that the stationing of troops along that line to prevent escape by land also opened up the feasible strategic possibility of a subsequent slaughter of the inhabitants in a simple sweep operation. Indeed, rumors that just such a military operation was being planned helped trigger the events that are now history. On the *ideological* side, the Quartier St. Antoine was what might be called a proto-industrial area, dotted with small manufacturing establishments and the residences of people who worked in them. It therefore had, unsurprisingly, the reputation of being a hotbed of civil discontent. What better candidates for mass slaughter could the royalist forces have found?

Returning to the present-day nuclear situation with which we are now concerned, we do well to ask the question, which Stone also raises, "Why New York?" One may also ask, of course, "Why San Francisco?" But isn't the answer to the latter question fairly obvious to us—*especially* in these days of AIDS? In terms of the vague ultra-conservative ideology—coldly hostile to human compassion and yet deeply emotional, not necessarily shared by all the strategic planners as individuals and yet facelessly coercive in its pervasive influence over them—that dominates and has long dominated American policy in these life-and-death areas, San Francisco appears as a little hotbed of deviants and malcontents by comparison with the general population of the country. And so, I am sorry to report, does New York. The *perception* of New York from elsewhere in the country is of a city with a combination of lots of poverty and lots of dissidence. What better place to subject to the immediate nuclear threat?[35]

Yet pure ideological resentment is not the whole story. We must add the crucial third, political, step mentioned above in order to complete the cycle of socialism for the rich. For there are clear *political* benefits from the terroristic messages of the SAGs, apart from party affiliation. The 1984 Democratic presidential candidate, Walter Mondale, saturated New York City's airwaves with an ad showing a red scramble phone that asked the ominous question "Which man would you rather have in charge of this phone?" Evidently New Yorkers preferred Mondale overwhelmingly to Reagan in this role. But was this sound politics? The trust based on fear which such ads evoke is fully transferable to the political opposition. Serialized New Yorkers *must* trust *anyone* in charge of that phone, as a hostage must trust his captor of the moment.

The Reagan government's unilateral decision to site nuclear missiles amidst New Yorkers surpassed this ad in coercively seizing such "trust." Perhaps as a response to such waves of resistance as the 1982 march, the SAG homeporting would compel us, like hostages, to identify with our captors and to identify our safety with our captors' weapons. If the SAG is installed, its very existence might cause New Yorkers to inwardly *accept* the new and much higher levels of risk, the proximate terror of nuclear holocaust, "as a continuing presence, an everyday fact of urban life."[36] As William James said, the first move toward accepting God is to bend the knee. The same may apply, in negative terms, to the tacit but morally enormous acceptance by New Yorkers of nuclear weapons in their midst. That acceptance made, New Yorkers—then believing they must share the risks of the common defense, that the Navy means jobs, and so on—could be expected in future to vote more readily for politicians favoring increased arms budgets. Of course, this would only repeat the jobs-for-defense dollars exchange that congresspersons have for decades been selling their constituents elsewhere in the country. Bruce Russett's voting analysis shows that military emplacements carry prodigious political benefits.[37] "It was clear when Secretary Lehman announced the homeporting policy," Admiral Carroll has remarked, "that it was nothing more or less than a blatant push to increase political support for the U.S. Navy budgets in the Congress."[38] Thus, once New Yorkers can be eased past this political hurdle by silent acceptance of a quietly installed SAG, arms makers will enjoy greater, more reliable infusions of New Yorkers' tax dollars, and the socialism-for-the-rich cycle will be complete. In the SAG's case it is important to notice that these political benefits, and the economic benefits that flow directly from them, would not be to Reagan or to Bush personally but to the vast military-industrial complex supported by both parties that aims to outlast them.[39]

By subjecting New Yorkers (and San Francisco Bay Area residents) to higher-priority targeting by the USSR, the barricaded U.S. government would push these urban-area residents out front the way a common terrorist would, daring the USSR to hold to its announced targeting policy. But the SAG siting is no simple hostage taking. Let us say that in all hostage taking there are a minimum of three participants: the hostage taker, the hostage, and the adversary. In conventional hostage taking the hostage is directly threatened in order to exact benefits from the adversary. In the SAG case, however, the adversary is directly threatened, and the main point of the hostage taking is to exact benefits from the indirectly threatened *hostage*. Since U.S. *direct* threats to the Soviet Union could drive the Soviets to bomb New York, such threats to the Soviets *indirectly* threatened New York. Deriving political and/or economic power from indirect nuclear threats to friendly serialized populations, under cover of protecting them, is *nuclear hostage taking*. How, then, were the SAG bases "meant" for these dense urban regions? Coercively converting these traditionally liberal regions to reliable political acceptance of the socialism-for-the-rich system—underwriting arms profits of multinationals by taxing wage earners[40]—seems to be the main point of the totalizations that will be effected by these new Bastilles, again, as with Louis XVI, in order to "defend" these regions.

Aside from other regions of the United States, the main precedent for deriving political-economic benefits from such nuclear hostage taking is in Europe. Truman first nuclearized Europe in June 1948 by sending "atomic capable" B-29s to Britain and Germany. This was ac-

137

companied by a campaign against the growing movement in Western Europe for neutralism. The result was the geopolitical and economic subordination of Western Europe to the United States.

In the late 1940s Jean-Paul Sartre and George Orwell already recognized and denounced the effect of this earliest nuclear hostage taking. As Orwell showed in *1984,* published in 1949, so helpful is the threat of an external enemy for assembling adversarial blocs of nations under their respective elites (who themselves are fully aware of this threat's vacuity) that if this threat did not exist, each bloc's elite would have to invent and institutionalize it. And, in fact, as economist Tom Riddell shows, the U.S. militarization of European nations in the late 1940s stabilized international trade on terms favorable to the United States, resulting in the subsequent U.S. economic growth in the 1950s and 1960s. Indeed, Riddell's uncovering of the directly beneficial economic effects of U.S. nuclearism provides the needed complement to the socialism-for-the-rich hypothesis. He argues that "nuclear weapons are a fundamental part of U.S. militarism, [which] has been a key to U.S. hegemony and prosperity in the post–World War II period."[41] Sartre—believing true peace required a neutral, unified Europe free of both blocs, and that this neutrality in turn required indigenous socialisms that would loosen the hold of both U.S. capitalism and Soviet state socialism on European economies— helped organize a neutralist, explicitly non-Communist political party in 1948.[42] In 1949, though, when some of the party's leaders took sides in the Cold War, the party itself fell victim to the very polarizing effects of nuclear hostage taking it was meant to oppose.[43] In 1950 Sartre wrote to his U.S. readers: "Western Europe cannot serve as a buffer zone between America and the U.S.S.R. unless she does not belong to either one. . . . From the moment you stop seeing us as soldiers, you will find we are your friends again. As neutrals determined to resist *all* aggression, we would be more useful to the cause of peace than, as belligerents without the means, we are at present to your war."[44] But such a neutralist "third way" policy would clearly be unhelpful either to preserving the domestic stimulus of "military Keynesianism" by militarizing Europe or to benefiting U.S. multinationals through U.S. dominance of international trade.[45] When Sartre argued in 1952 that the Soviets wanted peace he was wrongly interpreted as having himself taken sides in the Cold War whose fundamental dichotomy he had earlier rejected.[46] While increasingly Sartre's hopes lay in the Third World rather than in Europe, as is consistent with his taking sides only with the oppressed and exploited, I find no evidence he ever gave up his European neutralism.[47] Thus, since installing nuclear weapons in Europe compelled economically beneficial conformity by foreign friends and marginalized neutralists among them like Sartre and Orwell, a similar effect on the liberal citizens of New York and San Francisco may be anticipated—were Washington to threaten the Soviets and totalize the world from within *these* cities rather than from within Norfolk and San Diego.

Sartre's philosophizing was itself significantly shaped by his struggle for peace. In the 1955 article from which I have quoted above in the epigraph, Sartre says humanity becomes historical, social, and political as a result of the "negative universality" of the bomb. Thus, humanity's nuclear threat to itself may be all we concretely have in common as *historical* beings. This projection against ourselves of our own annihilating power is the sad, all-too-real totalization of humanity that replaces God, our former positive if ahistorical and unreal totalizer. Since neither God nor nature will save us from nuclear self-immolation, we are condemned to find a solution within history, which means surviving by inventing one ourselves. Sartre was suggesting in 1955 that we must apprehend human history in secular, nonreductivist, but global terms in order to dismantle the terroristic structures of the nuclear age. But it is precisely this idea of history as "a totalization without a totalizer" that animates Sartre's *Critique of Dialectical Reason,* begun in 1958.[48] Evidently this philosophy of history is born of and for the nuclear age. Is the historical totalization of humanity by its global conflict initially effected *by means of the bomb*—taken as the practico-inert with regard to which, like the world market, we serialize ourselves on a world scale? A case can be made for such an interpretation of the *Critique,* Volume I. And Volume II's precise analysis of the unity constituted by the adversaries in a boxing match provides formal elements of a theory of intergroup conflict that could help in understanding East-West power games.[49] Sartre's unfulfilled plan in Volume II to follow the analysis of the Soviet Union with one of Western societies clearly indicates his project had a global—though emphatically concrete and nonuniversal—scope suitable for nuclear-age problems.[50] (To be sure, these problems require a wide perspective in which precision is difficult, but thinkers like Michel Foucault, who refuse to talk of "totalizations"[51] or of "the whole of society,"[52] make it hard to comprehend, much less to stop, the macro-oppressions of nuclearized superpowers.)

The recently uncovered threat of nuclear winter confirms Sartre's 1955 insight that nuclear weapons do indeed negatively unify humans. Yet the humanism Sartre uncovers in such facts does not unite individuals through a priori participation in an eternal human essence, as in past humanisms. Instead, for his dialectical humanism, unity is the ongoing, nonidealist, historical *project* of constructing a meaningful human history out of particular rebellions against existing oppressive situations.[53] Obviously the most widely shared of such situations is worldwide nuclear terror. Sartre's plays *Nekrassov* (1955)[54] and *The Trojan Women* (1965)[55] must be counted as part of his nonpacifist struggle for true peace and against Cold War terror, begun in 1946.

It may be said that the Bastille analogy collapses when we consider that most of the royalist forces might plausibly envision escaping with their lives, having slaughtered the residents of the Quartier St. Antoine, while our present-day nuclear warriors can certainly expect, especially given the threat of nuclear winter, to themselves ultimately perish in an all-out nuclear war—an enormous apparent dissimilarity between the two cases. However, as Joe Cuomo has painstakingly documented, the Reagan leadership evidently believed it would *not* itself perish in this holocaust. It seems that Ronald Reagan and some of his advisors, along with several "born-again" Protestant Christian leaders such as Pat Robertson and Jerry Falwell, believed that we are living in the earth's last days and that the final battle of Armageddon would soon be fought as prophesied in the Bible, but that those who are born again (as Reagan said he was himself) would be directly "taken up" into heaven in an event called "the rapture," rejoining others with similar beliefs and leaving the rest of humanity to annihilation.[56] Obviously unafraid of nuclear war, which indeed appears to be God's will on this view, such a leadership was not unlike the coterie of royal counselors at Versailles who believed divine support made Louis XVI invincible.

Of course, the *class* of owner-managers that was behind Reagan (and outlasts him) might logically be expected to be more realistic about threats to its continued existence. Indeed, isn't the Cold War at an end? Aren't such threats obsolete? But residents of nuclear cities cannot count on this. Having amassed vast wealth and power through nuclear hostage taking, this class may not yield the practice up readily, even if its ostensible target has softened and its suicidal character is evident. Sartre makes almost the same point in one of his greatest plays, *The Condemned of Altona* (1959).[57] Written against France's suppression of Algeria, the drama scathingly portrays a German capitalist family whose postwar wealth issues from loyalty to the Nazis and then the Americans. So hemmed in by its crimes that divestment or suicide are its only ways out, it becomes evident that this family, and its class generally, would clearheadedly elect to take the audience along in its suicide, were it able to do so, *rather than yield any of its power and wealth.*[58] Sartre is cautioning France against identifying its destiny or its humanity with such families. The point applies doubly and globally to the United States in the nuclear era, even in its supposedly Post–Cold War phase, for until the political economy of nuclearism is fully dismantled it, and not just East-West tensions, structures our living space.

Sartre is clear that Parisian crowds had no diabolical plan, contrary to what the king thought. They became revolutionary not through irreverence to him, and certainly not through heroic courage or moral supererogation, but simply through fear of death. The wealth of contemporary New Yorkers as a population—a dissimilarity with the *sans culottes* of the Quartier St. Antoine—conceals the exploitation of its working classes by the system of socialism for the rich. But this disanalogy is perhaps compensated for by another: the fact that, however great it may now be, *no* privilege will survive the equalizing carnage of nuclear holocaust, a history-stopping destructiveness far more final than the French king's cannons, a point that Sartre makes, though in the context of a discussion of effects of technology on history.[59] Practically speaking, application of Sartre's analysis to the present situation in New York leaves us this stark choice even in the era of Gorbachov and a "kinder, gentler America": either die serialized in the nuclear holocaust prepared by our rulers or fuse into the revolutionary group that will disempower the small class that benefits from the continuing nuclear hostage taking.

In theory, however, the contrast I have drawn between the series and the group is too sharp; Sartre envisions many intermediary social forms. The huge 1982 march, for example, is midway between the group and the series: it represents the result of action of the group *upon* the series, that is, of the collective organizers upon the vast public of the city and the nation.[60] The same is true of the "Nuclear Gridlock" campaign, one of the more successful anti-SAG efforts, described as follows in a 1987 peace movement publication: "Since July, teams of activists have been stationed during rush hour at high-traffic sites throughout the city, holding giant banners reading 'CAN YOU IMAGINE FIGHTING THIS TRAFFIC TO ESCAPE A NUCLEAR ACCIDENT?' Gridlocked motorists have been suitably impressed. The response has been wonderful."[61] These interventions show the variety of forms imaginative action can take. As in the example of 1789, if the series is *treated* as a group, it may gradually begin to act as such in its own right.

Just as the danger of slaughter by royalists was greater than that of being attacked by bandits in the Paris of 1789, so the danger of nuclear war at the hands of the world's rulers totalizes more residents of nuclear cities today than does that of being mugged or homeless on the streets of such cities. Moreover, since nuclearism widens the gap be-

141

tween classes, the latter danger is *a function of* the former. Without such a prioritizing of dangers nothing is possible in terms of political action; *with* such a conscious awakening by citizens of such cities, anything is. Workers, especially defense-related workers, who think peace can be got by voting for politicans who make nuclear threats to distant Communists, also thereby move wealth through taxation from workers (including themselves) directly to owner-managers—especially those in the arms industry—thus not only increasing the latter's social power qua capital but also giving them an objective interest in further nuclear threats, with the unhappy result that such workers not only lose relative social power qua real wages but also make war *more* rather than less likely! Thus, like the French of 1789, Americans two hundred years later already possess in themselves the means needed to solve their own problems. It would not be enough either to allow the Navy to quietly move the base elsewhere or to force it to do so by declaring New York and San Francisco nuclear-free zones. Aside from leaving homeporting, the six hundred-ship Navy, and socialism for the rich unchallenged, such half measures would not greatly reduce the danger of nuclear holocaust any more than taking a stolen musket to one's home would have done in Paris—so long as that home remained in range of the Bastille's cannons. Peace requires nothing less than disempowerment of the class built on nuclearism, the class that uses SAGs to terrorize the dissident residents of nuclear cities into abetting the system of socialism for the rich, since it is in the *interest* of this class, still dominant, to perpetually risk nuclear holocaust—precisely in the name of those residents. Armed with this knowledge, a vast newly invented group-in-fusion made up of these residents would be irresistible and could nonviolently dismantle the system that continues to bring them homeports in particular and nuclear holocaust in general.

There is a precedent in New York City's own history for such a conversion of the series into the group. On the evening of July 9, 1776, after public readings of the Declaration of Independence, crowds of New Yorkers converged on Bowling Green. A fleet of British warships supporting the king's army on Staten Island—ships that could level the city[62]—lay at anchor in New York Harbor. A huge statue of George III dominated the green, flaunting the crown's ability to extract surplus value from colonists' labor and return it to them in the form of larger-than-life symbols of their exploitation. Knowing that Washington's army needed lead, and that the statue was lead under its gilt, the crowd pulled it down with horses. It did so not just to affirm freedom but in order to turn the statue into shot for use against the British.[63] As in the storming of the Bastille, this spontaneous turning of a symbol of oppression to revolutionary ends was done directly under the hostile guns of the legitimate government. In our militaristic era, the system of socialism for the rich makes SAG missiles today's symbols of the system's power to extract surplus value.[64] Unlike the statue's lead or the Bastille's rifles, the new plutonium totalizers are toxic and useless and can't be turned to human purposes. However, the future national wealth that goes into creating such nuclear installations certainly could be.

This small New York preview of the Bastille assault (there were similar incidents in Boston and Philadelphia in July 1776) opens a possible revolutionary future for nuclear cities. If the Bastille analogy holds, we can say that a revolutionary path is implicitly already laid down by the practico-inert itself, a path that future groups-in-fusion might decipher and follow in responding to such bases. For the group is a fusion of a previously serialized gathering of people who serialized themselves in response to a totalization effected through a practico-inert entity that was taken as more essential than they.[65] Fusion reverses this priority. Since such fusion, if it occurs, will be a free upsurge based on circumstances then existing, its character is impossible to predict. Indeed the very meaning of such bases will be decoded by those who then emerge from seriality in order to assume responsibility for the situation. Given the continuing risks of the nuclear age, it should be sooner rather than later.

Notes

I thank William L. McBride, Elizabeth A. Bowman and the editors of this volume for editorial help and the C. W. Post Research Committee for research support.

1. "The Peace We Want Must Not Be Like the So-called 'Time between the Wars,' " *L'Humanité*, June 27, 1955; quoted in Michel Contat and Michel Rybalka, *The Writings of Jean-Paul Sartre*, Vol. I: *A Bibliographical Life*, trans. by Richard C. McCleary (Evanston, Ill., 1974), 312. For guidance to other statements by Sartre on nuclear weapons and World War III, see 157, 165, 177, 181, 205–7, 243–44, 271–72, 275–79, 310, 312, 460.

2. Jean-Paul Sartre, *Critique of Dialectical Reason*, Vol. 1: *Theory of Practical Ensembles*, trans. by Alan Sheridan-Smith, ed. by Jonathan Rée (London, 1976), 45–46, (hereafter *CDR*).

3. *CDR*, 353; Sartre's emphasis. In this cases, the translation is mine.

4. *CDR*, 255–58.

5. *CDR*, 67, 187–92, 247n.

6. *CDR*, 358, 360–61.

7. *CDR*, 308–9, 351. See my "Sartre on Bad Faith and Authenticity," in *The Philosophy of Jean-Paul Sartre*, ed. by Paul Arthur Schilpp (LaSalle, Ill., 1980), 246–47.

8. *CDR*, 354.

9. *CDR*, 355.

10. *CDR*, 369.

11. *CDR*, 360–61, 364, 366–67, 376.

12. *CDR*, 370–73, 384, 396–400. For clear accounts of this shift, see Thomas R. Flynn's *Sartre and Marxist Existentialism: The Test Case of Collective Responsibility* (Chicago, 1984), 113–19; and Joseph S. Catalano's *A Commentary on Jean-Paul Sartre's Critique of Dialectical Reason* (Chicago, 1986), 169–73.

13. *CDR*, 357–58, 366–67, 389, 401.

14. Robert Jay Lifton, "Imagining the Real," *Indefensible Weapons: The Political and Psychological Case against Nuclearism* (New York, 1982), 13–22.

15. "The Climatic Effects of Nuclear War," by R. P. Turco, O. B. Toon, T. P. Ackerman, J. B. Pollack, and Carl Sagan, in *Scientific American,* August 1984. In a new 1990 article, in light of their analysis of recent research, these authors now say, "The magnitude of the effects has been modulated somewhat," although "the basic physics we proposed turned out to be correct." See the *New York Times,* January 23, 1990.

16. The threat of nuclear winter accomplishes this with novel finality, a significant dissimilarity between Paris of 1789 and New York of 1989.

17. Simeon A. Sahadachny, *Nuclear Trojan Horse: The Navy's Plan to Base Nuclear Weapons in New York Harbor* (New York, 1985), 15, 18, 20.

18. William M. Arkin and Richard W. Fieldhouse, *Nuclear Battlefields: Global Links in the Arms Race* (Cambridge, Mass., 1985), 125. See also 54–56.

19. Sahadachny, *Nuclear Trojan Horse,* 23.

20. William Martel and Paul Savage, *Strategic Nuclear War: What the Superpowers Target and Why* (Westport, Conn., 1986), 120–21.

21. Helen Caldicott, *Missile Envy: The Arms Race and Nuclear War* (New York, 1984), 289.

22. "Nuclear Trojan Horse," in *New York Times,* August 8, 1983. Carroll is deputy director of the Washington-based Center for Defense Information, which advocates a strong military without excessive spending. In an interview of May 5, 1988, Carroll told the author: "Whenever you go out of your way to create a facility lacking military justification, but which represents a threat against the Soviets that justifies their targeting the most densely populated urban center in the U.S., you really are creating risks that are totally unnecessary. Were I a Soviet targeteer assigned to find targets for ten thousand warheads but told that I couldn't attack urban centers, only military or military-related facilities, it would delight me to have the U.S. suddenly plot the USS *Iowa* with nuclear cruise missiles on it in the middle of New York Harbor. I would then have no compunction whatsoever in knocking out that military capability of the U.S. The fact that it would take out a few million people in the process is what we call 'collateral damage.' That's a nasty break, but that's the way the cookie crumbles." The USS *Iowa's* forward gun turret exploded April 19, 1989, killing forty-seven sailors. It was withdrawn from the seven-ship SAG complement in the Pentagon's December 1989 budget for the White House. This will probably not affect the SAG's priority as a target. It is noteworthy that even *after* the Iowa was withdrawn for mothballing it was scheduled for a $26 million maintenance layover in Norfolk. Secretary of Defense Richard Cheney says the nukeport, which is well under construction, is not scheduled for being cut. *New York Times,* January 18, 1990.

23. U.S. strategists Martel and Savage also find that "counterforce remains the guiding light of Soviet [strategic] thinking," in *Strategic Nuclear War,* 19. The Naval Weapons Station at Earle, New Jersey, across from Staten Island, is not a priority counterforce

target, being primarily a nuclear weapons storage facility. The Bay Area in California, by contrast, contains obvious counterforce targets, including the Air Force Satellite Control Facility at Sunnyvale and the Naval Air Station at Alameda. See Arkin and Fieldhouse, *Nuclear Battlefields,* 198, 175, 180.

24. To see that this alternative indeed adds net risks, it is enough to consider that to directly aim at New York City because of its SAG port would result in more destruction to it than to aim directly at nearby strategic bases, such as McGuire Air Force Base in New Jersey.

25. W. Jackson Davis, *Nuclear Accident Aboard a Naval Vessel Homeport at Staten Island, New York: Quantitative Analysis of a Hypothetical Accident Scenario* (New York, 1988); Coalition for a Nuclear-Free Harbor, *No Safe Harbor: The Consequences of a Nuclear Weapon Accident in New York Harbor* (New York, 1988); see also Sahadachny, *Nuclear Trojan Horse,* 41.

26. Vice Admiral William J. Cowhill, as quoted in Sahadachny, *Nuclear Trojan Horse,* 14. The irony that cancels this rationale is that one of the nuclear-armed battleships is to be homeported in Pearl Harbor itself, on Battleship Row, where the Japanese sank two such ships on December 7, 1941. See the *Wall Street Journal,* June 16, 1989.

27. Interview, May 5, 1988.

28. "Naval Ships Information on Benefits and Costs of Establishing New Homeports," GAO report, June 1986.

29. Michael Reich and David Finkelhor, "Capitalism and the Military-Industrial Complex," in *The Capitalist System: A Radical Analysis of American Society,* ed. by Richard C. Edwards, Michael Reich, and Thomas E. Weisskopf (Englewood Cliffs, N.J., 1972), 394.

30. "The average family in the bottom 40% of the population (below $24,000 a year income) had $918 less yearly income in 1986 than in 1979, after adjusting for inflation. Even the average family in the middle 20% (income of $24,000 to $35,000 a year) ended up behind, with $228 less than in 1979. But the typical family in the top 40% ($35,000 and up) received $2,775 more, and the wealthiest 5% of families raked in an average of $12,648 more in yearly income." "The Economy in Numbers," based on U.S. Census Bureau reports, in *Dollars and Sense,* no. 131 (November 1987).

31. Seymour Melman, *The Permanent Arms Economy* (New York, 1974).

32. Reich and Finkelhor, in *The Capitalist System,* 399. See also James M. Cypher, "A Prop, Not a Burden: U.S. Economy Relies on Militarism," *Dollars and Sense,* no. 93 (January 1984), 7.

33. Carroll interview, May 5, 1988. Several congressional leaders, including conservative senator Barry Goldwater, have made the same point. Senator James Exon (Democrat of Nebraska) has remarked: "The large number of ports . . . is clearly intended to scatter the wealth. . . . How can bases for three or four ships make any sense other than from a political perspective? Let's face it, the Navy's plan should be called the home-porking plan." *Congressional Record,* May 1986.

34. Ronald Aronson, *The Dialectics of Disaster: A Preface to Hope* (London, 1983), 287.

35. Comment delivered April 9, 1988, at the 6th Annual Socialist Scholars' Conference, Borough of Manhattan Community College, New York.

36. Sahadachny, *Nuclear Trojan Horse,* 32.

37. *What Price Vigilance?* (New Haven, Conn., 1970), chap. 3. The case of Congressman Joseph Addabbo of the Queens borough of New York City is a case in point even closer to home. Addabbo supported the freeze on nuclear weapons and opposed the MX

missile on grounds that they were unnecessary to maintain U.S. deterrent capacity. However, when the prospect of homeporting in New York City came up, with its (very likely exaggerated) prospect of jobs and federal dollars for his constituents, his critical eye for truly necessary and strategically wise defense endeavors seems to have clouded over, since he gave it his full support. See Terence Kivlan, "A Republican's Democrat," *Staten Island Advance*, September 16, 1984.

38. Interview, May 5, 1988. Simply as a deal, New Yorkers would be unwise to accept the exchange of defense jobs for votes offered by their political leaders. The mere four hundred or so permanent civilian jobs the SAG homeport would create would do virtually nothing to rebalance the $5 billion excess New Yorkers paid for defense (in 1982) in taxes over the amount the Defense Department spent in New York State—which, projected into the future, would come down to a net loss of 288,200 jobs annually in New York, the largest such loss of all fifty states, as calculated by Employment Research Associates, an economic research group in Lansing, Michigan (source: "Nuclear Trojan Horse," cited above in note 22). If the aim is to create jobs, a straight taxation-for-jobs exchange, without going through the military-industrial complex, would instantly create full employment in New York—but, of course, this would undermine socialism for the rich and capitalist relations of production generally.

39. Saul Bloom, director of the Arms Control Research Center of San Francisco, reports: "It is our evaluation that the aim of Reagan military programs, strategic homeporting and Star Wars in particular, is to complete the infrastructure needed to institutionalize the Reagan military machine beyond the term of the Reagan administration. It takes ten to fifteen years to get any given military program in place. Consequently, you must create an infrastructure of local interest and local political influence to ensure that these programs, and the general military buildup, are sustained to completion. By the mid-1990s they would like to be able to fund by congressional district rather than by project." Interview with the author, May 10, 1988.

40. Reich and Finkelhor, in *The Capitalist System*, 400–401.

41. Tom Riddell, "Militarism: The *Other* Side of Supply," *Economic Forum* 12, no. 1 (Summer 1982), 55–56, 60–63; Teresa Amott and Tom Riddell, "The Freeze, Militarism, and the American Economy," *Socialist Review*, no. 74 (March–April 1984), 109.

42. Contat and Rybalka, *Writings*, 204–10.

43. This failure was not the result of a mere personality conflict. Sartre's movement had not escaped the U.S. government's attention, which secretly funneled money to France through the international arm of the AFL-CIO in order to encourage the pro-U.S. drift that effectively destroyed the party, which was called the Rassemblement Démocratique Révolutionnaire. See Annie Cohen-Solal, *Sartre: A Life* (New York, 1987), 307. The U.S. government was determined to head off European neutrality during this era. See Riddell's account of the secret 1950 National Security Council document on European neutrality, in "Militarism," 51–52, 56.

44. Contat and Rybalka, *Writings*, 244.

45. Riddell, "Militarism," 54–57.

46. In *The Communists and Peace*, trans. by Martha H. Fletcher and John R. Kleinschmidt (New York, 1968). A disinterested reading will reveal that Sartre is at each turn concerned to defend the *sincerity* of Soviet and French Communist Party calls for international peace and the *legitimacy* of the French CP as a representative of the French working class, and that he is not defending as a partisan Soviet or CP policies or internal structures.

47. See, in *The Communists and Peace* itself, his defense of European neutralism

against Raymond Aron's attack on it, 16–17. It is noteworthy that the idea of a united, neutral Europe has again seized the imagination of western European youth, even though the movement's impetus seemed to come from the desire of European multinationals to consolidate power by giving up certain forms of infra-European competition.

48. *CDR*, 817.

49. *Critique de la raison dialectique*, Vol. II: *L'intelligibilité de l'histoire*, text established by Arlette Elkaïm-Sartre (Paris, 1985), 26–60.

50. *Critique* II, 436–43.

51. Michel Foucault, "Politics and Ethics: An Interview," in *The Foucault Reader*, ed. by Paul Rabinow (New York, 1984), 375–76.

52. Michel Foucault, "Revolutionary Action: 'Until Now,' " in *Language, Counter-Memory, Practice: Selected Essays and Interviews*, ed. by Donald F. Bouchard, trans. by Donald F. Bouchard and Sherry Simon (Ithaca, N.Y., 1977), 232–33.

53. Sartre, *Search for a Method*, trans. and intro. by Hazel E. Barnes (New York, 1963), 90: "Our historical task, at the heart of this polyvalent world, is to bring closer the moment when History will have *only one meaning*, when it will tend to be dissolved in the concrete men who will make it in common." Humanity as its own project, or "making the human," is the central, positive theme of Sartre's unpublished works on ethics and history of the mid-1960s. See in this regard the following articles by Robert V. Stone and Elizabeth A. Bowman: "Dialectical Ethics: A First Look at Sartre's Unpublished 1964 Rome Lecture Notes," *Social Text* 13–14 (Winter-Spring 1986); " 'Making the Human' in Sartre's Unpublished Dialectical Ethics," in *The Future of Continental Philosophy and the Politics of Difference*, ed. by Hugh J. Silverman (Albany, N.Y., 1989); and, chapter 2 in this volume, "Sartre's *Morality and History:* A First Look at the Notes for the Unpublished 1965 Cornell Lectures."

54. Trans. by Sylvia Leeson and George Leeson, in *The Devil and the Good Lord and Two Other Plays* (New York, 1960).

55. English version by Ronald Duncan (New York, 1967).

56. Joe Cuomo, "The Armageddon Network," *Penthouse*, July 1987; and, also by Cuomo, the radio documentary "Ronald Reagan and the Prophecy of Armageddon," WBAI-Pacifica.

57. Trans. by Sylvia Leeson and George Leeson (New York, 1967).

58. This point comes from Elizabeth A. Bowman, *The Moral Impasse and the Possibility of the Human: A Study of Jean-Paul Sartre's Ethics and His Political Theatre*, Ph.D. dissertation (Ann Arbor, Mich., 1987), 246–52.

59. "[Cannons] belong to him who is already the strongest and they reinforce that strength. Exactly similar situation to that of the atomic bomb. . . . If the future is conceived starting from the lived situation with its limits, and if the clean future is denied by the true future, itself defined by technical revolutions, then the future outlined by Marx with revolution at its end is precisely denied by the 'atomic' revolution. At the start, revolution has become impossible and is replaced by war. This is followed by bureaucratic and technical dictatorship which bit by bit replaces capitalist oppression. . . . In the very name of Marxism, the most important event in the last fifty years is not the Russian Revolution, it is the atomic bomb. . . . It cannot be shown, for example, that using atomic energy will not produce a State socialism with a dictatorship of technicians and bureaucrats, simply because atomic energy cannot be allowed to be in private hands." *Cahiers pour une morale* (Paris, 1983), 87–89; my translation. Sartre is thought to have written these notes in 1947–48.

60. A march like the 1982 effort, but with somewhat broader focus, occurred on June

11, 1988, in New York and in the Bay Area, again along with a UN Special Session on Disarmament.

61. *N.Y. Mobilizer* 4, no. 8 (September 1987).

62. Bruce Bliven Jr., *Under the Guns: New York: 1775–1776* (New York, 1972), 345–46.

63. A newspaper reported a week later: "The lead wherewith this monument was made, is to be run into bullets, to assimilate with the brains of our infatuated adversaries, who, to gain a pepper-corn, have lost an empire." *New York Historical Society Quarterly Bulletin* 4, no. 2 (July 1920), 50.

64. E. P. Thompson, "Notes on Exterminism, the Last Stage of Civilization," in *Beyond the Cold War: A New Approach to the Arms Race and Nuclear Annihilation* (New York, 1982), 55.

65. *CDR*, 364.

III

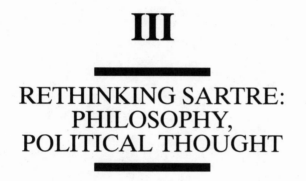

RETHINKING SARTRE: PHILOSOPHY, POLITICAL THOUGHT

7

THE ROLE OF THE EGO
IN RECIPROCITY

Hazel E. Barnes

Most of what Sartre wrote about the ego is negative. He expelled it from consciousness, describing it as a structure imposed *by* a consciousness rather than the structure *of* a consciousness. My ego, as a psychic object, stands as open to the judgments by other consciousnesses as to my own. The feeling it gives me of special intimacy is the result, not of an ontological status different from that of other objects, but of familiarity of presence, as is the case with the house I have lived in or the book I have written. It is only out of fear or in bad faith that I try to believe that my consciousness *is* my ego. My freedom and my responsibility for my life both derive from the fact that consciousness and ego are *not* the same. The Sartrean imperative to make oneself is addressed to consciousness, and it is a directive to act in the world. The ego neither makes nor acts. It does exist, of course (though not as a substance); it is not a fiction. But Sartre spoke of it chiefly as an obstacle to authentic choice of action. To reject this view of the relation between consciousness and the ego would be to repudiate Sartre's philosophy. I have no wish to challenge or to tamper with the fundamental thesis of *The Transcendence of the Ego*.

Nevertheless, I am going to argue that there are reasons for attributing a more positive role to the ego if Sartre's psychology is to make any sense. Moreover, there are relevant passages in the posthumous *Cahiers*

151

pour une morale[1] which seem to me to necessitate some rethinking. Implicitly, if not in so many words, these show that the ego is not only a possible trap and an evasion; it is also the instrument that allows Sartrean *comprehension* to function.

Without disputing Sartre's claim that the other's ego and my ego are equally objects for both of us, it seems to me evident that the practical problems that a consciousness confronts with respect to them are quite different. Consequently, I will speak first briefly of my consciousness's relation with my own ego—my ego for me—and then more fully of its relation with the other's ego.

The ego is my practical objectification in the world.[2] In itself this is a neutral statement. A consciousness cannot exist without making itself be in the world. By my actions I carve out my being-in-the-world. "You are your life," Inez tells Garcin. What worried Sartre is the fact that just as my actions in the material world may, in the form of a counterfinality, turn back against me to distort my project, and may do so either directly or through the intervention of others, so the self-image that emerges from an undertaking of mine stands at the horizon of any future enterprise. It returns to me as other and would do so even if (as it almost always does) it did not carry with it the imprint of the attitudes of other persons to what I have done. Sartre's fear is that the ego as self-image may contaminate any praxis; for example, instead of acting in order that an end that requires courage should be achieved, I will act because I want to be a courageous person or, worse yet, to be what others would consider a courageous person. Though Sartre devotes a fair amount of space in the *Cahiers* to this kind of argument, none of what he says is new. It relates to one of the conducts in bad faith that Sartre discussed already in *Being and Nothingness* apropos of sincerity. In the *Cahiers* it leads him to a more radical conclusion. At one point he states flatly that our goal should be to get rid of the "I" and the "me" (433) and to live without ego (430). I submit that this is nonsense. Indeed, Sartre himself apparently felt that he had gone too far, for he quickly suggested that he could accept living with the ego if it were redefined. He says that subjectivity (by which he means the lateral reference of prereflective consciousness to itself, *conscience* [*de*] *soi*) and the ego together have "moral and temporal ontological priority" over any alienation (433). In other words, the ego is not necessarily linked with inauthenticity. By ego, Sartre here refers not to a fully developed psychic "I" and "me" but to "that always open *Moi*, always open and always in suspense, which is referred to by the enterprise at hand." It is an ego that exists in order to lose itself—or

152

be lost (*se perdre*). What does he mean? What is the nature of the purified ego that Sartre finds acceptable? He seems to claim here that it is only the temporal unity of the immediate project, the surpassing in action of the given toward an end. Since it is devoid of an "I" and a "me" in the usual sense, we might want to conclude that it is nonreflective; but we have been taught by Sartre that the ego appears only with reflection. Furthermore, there is an ambiguity regarding whether pure praxis itself is or is not necessarily nonreflective. At times Sartre appears to think that pure praxis limits itself to the simple performance of tasks to be done—like the streetcar to be caught, the kindling to be stacked, and so on. But can we really extend our examples to include the Bastille to be taken, the war to be fought, the revolution to be made? Granted, there is neither profit nor need to cloud action here with the resolve to *be* a taker of the Bastille, a combatant, or a revolutionary. But just as obviously, not to reflect at all would immerse us in the "Serious World." Surely, the praxis that results from any choice of a task as one that is to be done must frequently involve, or at least be the result of, reflection. If praxis is a movement to establish a not yet existing reality in place of what is there now, it may well be founded on a reappraisal of one's own relation to both the present and the projected situation. In the *Cahiers* Sartre says that "the existent [that is, the human individual] is a project, and reflection is a project of assuming this project." Reflection "is itself a project; it is a project sprung from the nonreflective project and a decision to suspend or to pursue the project" (495). Surely, the ego is included in the material and mental data that consciousness considers in making the decision.

The essential and helpful part of Sartre's new definition of ego lies in the words "always open and always in suspense"—*en sursis*, perhaps better translated as "always in the making." But I do not see why this ego needs to be devoid of the "I" and the "me." The famous conversions of which Sartre wrote are neither necessarily nor usually nonreflective detachments from the past, lived in pure immediacy. They entail new kinds of action toward new ends because they offer a revised hodological map of one's life and of the world. Sartre's remark that a person's greatest creative act is perhaps the creation of values by which to live does not refer to the formation of a closed system to be created as soon as possible.[3] It is illustrated rather by Sartre's own existential project— to think against himself, which was certainly not a mere introspective self-reevaluation but what I would call a restructuring of his "I" and "me" in their relation to action in the world. Sartre said in *The Transcendence of the Ego*, "The ego is to psychical objects what the World is to

153

things."[4] I suggest that the ego is always at the horizon of my choices as a kind of imposed ordering (imposed by consciousness, of course) which must be taken into account but can be modified, just as my notion of "the world" is. (In phenomenological terms, "the world," too, is the structure of consciousness.) Though the relation my consciousness sustains with my ego is not identical with that of my consciousness to my body, that "psychic object par excellence,"[5] I think that it is comparable in important respects. In my contact with the external world, my ego, like the body, is to some degree the past and the passed by and the projected ground of my projected future. It may be suggested that what I offer is revisionist Sartre. Possibly it is. In any case much more needs to be said on the subject, but I will leave it now and turn to the question of my encounter with the other's ego and of the other's with mine.

Ignoring completely the vast and much discussed area of the subject-object conflict in human relations, I will consider now the new dimension of reciprocity. My focus here will not be on the social philosophy of the *Critique of Dialectical Reason,* which is based on common praxis, but rather on reciprocity in individual relationships, which Sartre discussed in *Cahiers pour une morale.*

Part of what Sartre says refers to a benign exploitation of the basic conflict for the mutual advantage of the two persons (300). This anticipates the discussion we find early in the *Critique.* In a mutually beneficial use of one another as objects, we may each one use the other as a means to an end sought by both of us or even to different but nonconflicting ends desired by each of us. Sartre goes beyond this amiable utilitarian contract to an internal bond of reciprocity—in his discussion of, first, my response to the other's appeal and, second, the meaning of authentic love.

"To explain is to throw light on causes; to comprehend is to throw light on ends" (287). To comprehend is to grasp intuitively the other's network of means and ends together with the meaning the other assigns to them. Such empathetic understanding does not necessarily mean the approving acceptance of the ends (287), as Sartre demonstrated in his study of Flaubert. But one logical and natural consequence of comprehension is the will to assist the other. When I respond positively and authentically to the appeal, neither of us is made an object to the other. Sartre writes, "I *recognize* the other's freedom without being paralyzed by it as by a look. Indeed I posit that his end is my end but not because it is an unconditioned end or an end which I posited first, but because he posited it as an end" (291). It is his freedom that has given the end its

154

value. That is, I make the other's end my end, neither by objectifying it nor by stealing it but by willing that the end should be achieved by the other. I do not forfeit my own ends, but, so to speak, I make room for the other's end in the midst of my own. I fit it in. Sartre neatly illustrates this point with an everyday example. I say to the one who asks my aid, "I'd like to help you, but I just don't have time. Oh, what the Hell! The work can wait till tomorrow. I'll go along with you" (295).[6]

The difficulty in which that other freedom finds itself is now part of my concern. I am involved. I care. The other's project will remain wholly his but will contain within it a structure that is mine. "The other's freedom is . . . the extension of my freedom in the dimension of otherness" (291). But it is not an alienating otherness. Through the other I have a future in a new direction, and with my full consent. Implied in my positive response to an appeal Sartre sees a more general affirmation: "that the world may have an infinity of free, finite futures, each of which is directly projected by one free will and indirectly supported by the will of all others" (292). Sartre does not want to make of this an abstract ethical imperative. He does insist that "to replace a closed, subjective totality as the ideal of unity by an open diversity of outlets depending on each other is to posit that in any case freedom is better [vaut mieux] than nonfreedom" (292).

Sartre claims as well that appealing (in contrast to demanding or begging) is itself a reciprocity. The man who appeals puts himself at risk when he offers the gift of his freedom to another. Recognizing the gratuity of the other's response, he says, in effect, not "You ought" but "You can" (295). Sartre believes, whether correctly or not, that the appeal is also to promise reciprocally that one can be appealed to. But beyond that, the appeal is an invitation to the other to realize the possibility of a human unity based not on work in common toward a single goal but a "supple unity of diversity," a recognition of the conditioned character of each person's ends and the unconditioned character of each one's freedom" (297).

Ignoring the engaging ethical implications here, I return to the question of the nature of the comprehension on which such reciprocal empathy must depend. In the Cahiers Sartre says that he has already discussed comprehension as "an original structure of the perception of the other" (288). He refers to the section, in Being and Nothingness, on the second dimension of the body, my body for the other—or the other's body. "I perceive the other's body in light of its end" (288). Already there is a rudimentary reciprocity, Sartre says now, for I can understand the gesture as a thrust toward its end only if I mirror it in myself, so to

155

speak, viewing it as if I were to adopt the other's end. What Sartre means, I think, is that in perceiving the other I comprehend him in terms of his hodological space, constructed analogously to the way I live my own but with the other as centering center. Sometimes, as in Sartre's example of extending a hand to someone climbing onto a bus, contact is restricted to the immediate and the impersonal. Most often, in the complex interaction of the appeal, much more is involved than a perception of bodily movement and its goal. Sartre notes that I lend my aid to another's project only when, to a greater or lesser degree, I approve of its end—at least as being right for the other. This requires a comprehension of the other's psychic space; that is, of his ego, not as something fixed but as an ongoing project which, as in any praxis, relates the three temporal dimensions and colors and gives meaning to what he is doing. I maintain that in what Sartre calls "the imbrication of the two freedoms" (297), when I interact with the other so as to aid him, the other's ego and mine are both essential parts of the gestalt, even though the focus is on my free act to further the other's free project. They are present just as our bodies are. One could perhaps say that it is by means of my comprehension of what both egos have been that I act to modify what they will become in their ongoing creation by each of our consciousnesses.

That I value the other's freedom as it is expressed by his ego is demonstrated more clearly in Sartre's discussion of authentic love. Contrasting this with the Hell described in *Being and Nothingness*,[7] he declares that to love authentically is not to try to appropriate the other (523–24). It is not reducible to the desire to be loved. Yet while authentic love must be founded on the recognition of the other as an absolute freedom (515), such recognition is not precisely its origin. Sartre is quite emphatic on this point. He writes, "Freedom as such is not lovable, for it is nothing but negation and productivity. Pure being, in its total exteriority of indifference, is not *lovable* either. But the other's body is lovable inasmuch as it is freedom in the dimension of being. And to love means here something other than a desire to appropriate. It is first of all a creative revelation" (523). In loving comprehension I care about and care for the other's precarious being-in-the-midst-of-the-world. Sartre writes, "This vulnerability, this finitude *is the body*. The body for the other. To reveal the other in his being-in-the-midst-of-the-world is to love him in his body" (517). (What Sartre says is not limited to erotic love. The other's embodied consciousness, the other's person, is the object of my concern in friendship, in response to the other's appeal, even in my support of the political leader I favor.)

Sarte's evocation of the second dimension of the body is extremely significant. Even without the *Cahiers* I had always felt that it is in this dimension that reciprocity must emerge. To understand the other's body as the meaningful object that it is demands that I recognize the subject expressing itself in gestures and words even if I cannot grasp it as it is for itself. In *Being and Nothingness* Sartre pointed out that the other's body reveals to me his "character."[8] Sartre almost, though never quite, equates this with the other's ego. In the *Cahiers* he says that through his gestures (which must surely include words as well as bodily movements) the other delivers to me his being, by means of "that twofold malady of Being: motion and the project" (518). The other's body and the other's ego are to me what he is. It is through them that I involve myself. But I do not thereby limit him to being only what he is. Through his body and ego, as expressions of his consciousness, I comprehend the other "in terms of his enterprise, that is, in terms of what he is not" (517–18). My awareness of the other as body and as ego does not ensure my respect for him as subject, but here is the only pathway to such recognition. That the authentic encounter of freedoms is via their objectification Sartre makes clear by comparing my active comprehension of the other's project with my perusal of a work of art (516). In both contexts I do not deny the other's freedom; I willingly lend my own to the discovery and pursuit of the creative revealing of the other's ends.

Sartre's own ideal for what human relations can be is expressed in the notion of transparency, which he described not only in the late interviews but many years earlier in the *War Diaries*.[9] Obviously, the mutual waiving of inhibitions, repression, and need for secrecy on which transparency depends requires an openness that is impossible without the respectful recognition of each one's freedom. But there is nothing either abstract or impersonal here. The relation is highly personal. While it would be destroyed by the mistaken demand that each other identify with a completed ego, that he be what he is, still what gives interest and value to the relationship is the evolving product of the other's consciousness and the comprehending acceptance of one's own. It is the body that individualizes, Sartre told us.[10] It is the ego that personalizes, albeit as the expressive product of an ongoing consciousness.

To look at the ego in the way I have suggested does not reinstate Sartre's *bête-noire,* a world of closed monads seething with inner subjectivity. It responds to the charge that the abstract Sartrean consciousness is like an empty bubble rising up from the mass of Being. The ego, seen in this new way, personalizes the human world without reducing us to fixed personalities. It allows us to harvest the promise of Sartre's early

157

claim that the other's and my ego are both out there in the world for our comprehension.[11] I like Stuart Charmé's comparison of the Sartrean fundamental project to the story one tells oneself about oneself.[12] But if consciousness is the author, the ego is the first-person narrator that a consciousness invents as it writes. Without the ego there would be no story. Without the ego, other persons would be largely undifferentiated by us, if indeed they could be said to exist for us in any way at all. At most, they would be simply creatures strange to us. Moreover, Sartre's later stress on the *being* of the other person as expressed in body and ego seems to me to give a new and richer meaning to his old claim that every freedom is situated.

Finally, I see a possible bridge between Sartre's philosophy, as I have interpreted it here, and the new emphasis on contextual ethics, contextual knowing, and contextual thought which dominates much of recent feminist writing.[13] I am not arguing that there may be after all a strong femininity in Sartre, which would be far more foolhardy than my attempt to rescue the ego from obloquy. But neither do I believe, as some feminists have suggested, that the prepersonal consciousness, which Sartre claims to be the origin and essential core of our freedom, dehumanizes. By giving meaning to being, consciousness makes us persons.

Notes

1. *Cahiers pour une morale* (Paris, 1983). Translations are my own. Numbers in parentheses are page numbers.

2. Sartre stated this in so many words in a manuscript concerned with what has been called "Dialectics of Ethics in History," which Robert V. Stone kindly allowed me to read. The concept itself was present already in *The Transcendence of the Ego* and further developed in *Being and Nothingness*.

3. *Baudelaire*, trans. by Martin Turnell (New York, 1950), 44. Sartre's precise words are: "Absolute creation—the creation of which all other forms are simply a consequence—is the creation of a scale of values."

4. *The Transcendence of the Ego: An Existentialist Theory of Consciousness*, trans. by Forrest Williams and Robert Kirkpatrick (New York, 1957), 75.

5. *Being and Nothingness*, trans. by Hazel E. Barnes (New York, 1972), 455.

6. I have translated a bit freely in order to retain the colloquial flavor.

7. Sartre refers to *Being and Nothingness;* most of us would think of *No Exit*.

8. *Being and Nothingness*, 457.

9. *Life/Situations: Essays Written and Spoken*, trans. by Paul Auster and Lydia Davis (New York, 1977), 11–12; *War Diaries*, trans. by Quintin Hoare (New York, 1984), 273–74.

10. *Being and Nothingness*, 409.

11. *Transcendence of the Ego*, 95.

158

12. Stuart L. Charmé, *Meaning and Myth in the Study of Lives: A Sartrean Perspective* (Philadelphia, 1984).

13. I am thinking particularly of three works: Carol Gilligan, *In a Different Voice: Psychological Theory and Women's Development* (Cambridge, Mass., 1982); Nel Noddings, *Caring: A Feminine Approach to Ethics and Moral Education* (Berkeley, Calif., 1984); Mary Field Belenky, Blythe McVicker Clinchy, Nancy Rule Goldberger, and Jill Mattuck Tarule, *Women's Ways of Knowing: The Development of Self, Voice, and Mind* (New York, 1986).

8

SARTRE AND MARXIST EXISTENTIALISM

Monika Langer

A recurrent theme in the philosophical literature of the last quarter-century has been the relationship between Sartrean existentialism and Marxism. Much of the discussion has centered on the unorthodox nature of Sartre's Marxism as presented in his *Critique of Dialectical Reason,* and on the connection between that work and his earlier *Being and Nothingness.* Thomas Flynn's book *Sartre and Marxist Existentialism* constitutes one of the most interesting recent contributions to the debate. Flynn contends that "Sartre's is an authentic, though 'revisionist,' Marxism" which, in combining "salient features" of existentialism and Marxism, incorporates "the morally responsible individual into the sociohistorical context."[1] My essay takes issue with Flynn's position on the grounds that Sartre's Marxism as articulated in the *Critique of Dialectical Reason* is basically at odds with authentic Marxism—whether classical or revisionist. I contend that the lately published second volume of the *Critique* retains the fundamental features of the first, and hence does not significantly alter the nature of Sartre's Marxism. Despite my disagreement with his interepretation of Sartrean Marxism, Flynn's focus on responsibility[2] reopens for me the intriguing question of whether Sartrean existentialism can provide the requisite foundation of freedom for Marxism.

My essay argues that Marxism indeed requires a philosophical foundation,[3] not because it *lacks* freedom—as Sartre claimed—but because it *presupposses* that "free, conscious activity is man's species character" and that "estranged labour estranges the *species* from man."[4] In other words, Marxism, which bases itself on an unclarified conception of freedom, must spell out and clarify its own conception. Accordingly, I will reconsider Sartre's own intricate argument for the freedom of human reality (in *Being and Nothingness*). That argument seems to supply precisely the kind of philosophical basis that Marxism so sorely lacks—all the more so as Sartre himself anticipates and counters numerous objections. A closer scrutiny, however, reveals flaws that render Sartre's argument ultimately untenable. Yet those flaws are fruitful in disclosing a possible corresponding weakness in Marxism and underlining the need for an adequate phenomenological analysis of freedom. While Sartre's alleged Marxism and his existentialism are unable to provide the necessary philosophical grounding for Marxism, the reconsideration of his position sheds light on what remains to be done if Marxism is ever to have a genuinely firm footing.

At the time he was writing the *Critique of Dialectical Reason,* Sartre thought this work provided the necessary foundation for Marxism:

It is *inside* the movement of Marxist thought that we discover a flaw of such a sort that despite itself Marxism tends to eliminate the questioner from his investigation and to make of the questioned the object of an absolute Knowledge. . . . And to come to the most important point, *labor,* as man's reproduction of his life, can hold no meaning if its fundamental structure is not to pro-ject. . . . Existentialism, too, wants to situate man in his class and in the conflicts which oppose him to other classes, starting with the mode and the relations of production. But it can approach this "situation" in terms of *existence*—that is, of comprehension. It makes itself the questioned and the question as questioner. . . . Thus the comprehension of existence is presented as the human foundation of Marxist anthropology . . . the foundation of Marxism, as a historical, structural anthropology, is man himself inasmuch as human existence and the comprehension of the human are inseparable. . . . Marx's own Marxism, while indicating the dialectical opposition between knowing and being, contained implicitly the demand for an existential foundation for the theory. Furthermore, in order for notions like reification and alienation to assume their full meaning, it would have been necessary for the questioner and the questioned to be made one. . . . It is necessary that the questioner understand how the questioned—that is, himself—*exists his alienation,* how he surpasses it and is alienated in this very surpassing.[5]

Fifteen years after the publication of its first volume, however, Sartre himself acknowledged that "the *Critique* . . . is *not* a Marxist work" and that he had been mistaken in regarding existentialism as "*only an enclave of Marxism*": "It cannot be an enclave, because of my idea of freedom, and therefore it is ultimately a separate philosophy. I do not at all think that ultimately this philosophy is Marxist. It cannot ignore Marxism. . . . But now I do not consider it at all a Marxist philosophy."[6] At the same time, Sartre noted the lack of freedom that "would be on the same level, a mixture of theory and practice, as Marxism—a philosophy in which theory serves practice, but which takes as its starting point the freedom that seems to me to be missing in Marxist thought."[7] Sartre was correct in contending that Marx's own Marxism required a foundation, and in realizing that the *Critique of Dialectical Reason* "is really *non*-Marxist." He erred, however, in maintaining that the *Critique* "is not opposed to Marxism."[8] Before reconsidering whether an appreciation of "the questioner" can supply the requisite foundation of freedom for Marxism, we must note the major factors that disqualify the *Critique* for that task.

Ronald Aronson points out that it is imperative that the first volume of Sartre's *Critique* be reconsidered "in light of the project as a whole."[9] By the same token, Merleau-Ponty's scathing criticisms of Sartre's pre-1955 philosophy must be recalled in any such reassessment, for Sartre almost certainly had Merleau-Ponty's strictures in mind while writing the *Critique*. As Flynn noted in "Merleau-Ponty and the *Critique of Dialectical Reason*," it is impossible to prove that Sartre was in fact responding to Merleau-Ponty's attack contained in the latter's *Adventures of the Dialectic;* nevertheless, the nature of the two philosophers' personal relationship and the substance of their respective texts make such a supposition reasonable.[10] Aronson, going beyond Flynn, argues that once one moves "into Sartre's and Merleau-Ponty's intellectual-political universe of the 1950's, it is impossible *not* to read the *Critique* as a reply to the challenge of Merleau-Ponty." As Aronson explains, that challenge is highly complex, for Merleau-Ponty sought to disclose the inadequacies of Sartre's ontology and politics, while himself criticizing Marxism from a "post-Marxist" stance. According to Merleau-Ponty, Marxism was itself fatally flawed philosophically and had in any case been invalidated by history. Aronson points out that in response, Sartre distinguished "dogmatic dialectic" from "critical dialectic" and employed the latter to make comprehensible why praxis had become divorced from theory in Stalinism. Further, Sartre embarked on an inquiry into history as a "totalization without a totalizer." Not only did Sartre's monumental project remain unfinished, but its very formulations of the dialectic displayed a fundamental dualism. Aronson argues that the actual historical separation of theory from praxis left Sartre without "the basis for thinking his way beyond the dualism at the heart of his thought." Certainly, as Aronson points out, the problem of the gap between philosophical reflection and active politics is not Sartre's problem alone; and the limitations of his project do not prevent its being a remarkable achievement.[11] Yet it does seem to me that the dualism in Sartre's ontology, as it manifests itself in his *Critique,* precludes the work's fulfilling its intended purpose of providing a philosophical foundation for Marxism. In order to reassess the *Critique,* it will be useful to recall in some detail a number of Merleau-Ponty's earlier objections.

In *Adventures of the Dialectic* (French original published 1955), Merleau-Ponty contended that despite appearances to the contrary, Sartre's philosophy lacked any genuine intersubjectivity and interworld and, hence, any genuine appreciation of the real nature of action and history. According to Merleau-Ponty: "In Sartre there is a plurality of subjects but no intersubjectivity"; "there is no hinge, no joint or mediation, between myself and the other"; "there is an encounter rather than a common action because, for Sartre, the social remains the relationship of 'two individual consciousnesses' which look at each other"; "commitment in Sartre's sense is the negation of the link between us and the world that it seems to assert; or rather Sartre tries to make a link out of a negation"; for Sartre it is a question of "either him or me."[12] Merleau-Ponty acknowledged that

> Sartre, however, is not unaware of the historical field in which the revolution, and consequently all Marxist politics, is established. The apparent paradox of his work is that he became famous by describing a middle ground . . . between consiousness and things—the root in *Nausea,* viscosity or situation in *Being and Nothingness,* here [*The Communists and Peace* with *A Reply to Claude Lefort*] the social world—and that nonetheless his thought is in revolt against this middle ground and finds there only an incentive to transcend it and to begin again *ex nihilo* this entire disgusting world.[13]

That Sartrean world, alleged Merleau-Ponty, is one in which "whether as a permanent spectacle or as a continued creation, the social is in any case before consciousness and is constituted by them." Thus, "Sartre's effort to annex history to his philosophy of freedom and of the other" means that, for him, history "is a history of projects"; "history and revolution are nothing but a pact of thought or of wills . . . it is con-

163

sciousness which gives meaning." In Merleau-Ponty's assessment, "what continues to distinguish Sartre from Marxism, even in recent times, is therefore his philosophy of the *cogito*. Men are mentally attached to history."[14] In short,

> the social can enter [Sartre's] philosophy of the *cogito* only by way of the *alter ego* . . . the other can have the status of a self only by taking it away from me, and I can recover it only by reacting to the magic of the gaze with the countermagic of pure action. . . . Although the enlarged *cogito*, the philosophy of For-Others, does not confine itself to the perspective of self on self, it is inside this perspective that it must introduce what puts this position into question. The social never appears openly; it is sometimes a trap, sometimes a task, sometimes a menace, sometimes a promise, sometimes behind us as a self-reproach, sometimes in front of us as a project. In any case, it is never perceived or lived by man except as incompleteness and oppression, or in the obscurity of action. It is the absolute of the subject who remakes himself when he incorporates the point of view of others, which he was dragging along behind him like a hardship. . . . With Sartre, as with the anarchists, the idea of oppression always dominates that of exploitation.[15]

Sartre's insistence on depicting things through "the eyes of the least-favored" tends to obscure the dominance of the idea of oppression over that of exploitation in his philosophy, noted Merleau-Ponty. The latter cautioned that centering on "the gaze of the least-favored . . . can ground any kind of politics," and that Sartre effectively subordinates "doing to seeing."[16] Sartrean philosophy lacks "the landscape of praxis" in which "my tasks are presented to me, not as objects or ends, but as reliefs and configuration," a world in which action fully "inhabits its field." Instead, Sartre reduces "history and the social . . . to a series of instantaneous views"; common action collapses into invention on the part of a few, with complicity on the part of the rest. Sartrean praxis is tantamount to continual intervention in history, rather than being "an activity immanent in the object of history" as stipulated by Marx's *Theses on Feuerbach*. For Sartre "we are what we contrive to be and, as for everything else, we are as responsible for it as if we had done it"; moreover, our de facto complicity "is always for the worse."[17]

Thus, Sartrean freedom remains fleshless "and tends toward violence"; it initially "presents itself trapped and powerless. . . . It is as if at each moment everything that has made us, everything from which we benefit, and everything which will result from our life were entered into our account. . . . To live is to wake up bound like Gulliver at Lilliput."Since "we are responsible for everything before everyone as if we had done it with our own hands," "our relationship to a world already there" is violence; and our attempt to break out of "the original trap" will likewise "be violence"—this time, that violence is a matter of "conquest."[18] History thus understood is devoid of objective meaning—or, rather, "what one calls 'objective meaning' is the aspect taken by one of these fundamental choices in the light of another, when the latter succeeds in imposing itself." History becomes "a melodrama" in which "there is only a single monotonous fight, ended and begun at each moment, with no acquisition, no truces, no areas of abatement." Society, according to such a view, is rife with "rivalry" and "false fraternity"; it is the leader who confers meaning on the situation and "the path chosen is the only one possible and is *a fortiori* the best." The relationship "between the proletarian and the militants, between the militant and his leaders . . . is literally an identification"; nonetheless, "the workers' unity is always to be remade . . . they have not many more ties among themselves than with the bourgeoisie, and the problem is to erase by means of the class Other and through struggle the ineffaceable otherness of the individual Other." By force of will, the militant "molds or manipulates" the proletariat.[19]

Merleau-Ponty conceded that Sartre's "analyses have the benefit of helping one understand how backward forms of sociability and the cult of the leader have re-emerged even in communism," but pointed out that they leave us "far from Marxism." In fact, "the 'objective' critique of capital hardly enters into Sartre's study. Inside an immediate or moral relationship of persons, he deliberately focuses on those that capitalism ruins." Further, "he never evokes the basic Marxist hope of resolution in *true* action, that is to say, action fitted to internal relations of the historical situation, which await nothing but action to 'take,' to constitute a form in movement.' In "this substantial action . . . which, in its culmination, is called revolution," there is no imposition of "impalpable" meaning on blind being—"there is neither pure authority nor pure obedience." Such true action is not Sartrean "pure action, which is to say, force." Merleau-Ponty concluded emphatically that "certainly [Sartre's] philosophy is the opposite of Marx's."[20]

Although it was not only the Sartrean denial of an interworld that led Merleau-Ponty to this conclusion—as is evident from the foregoing presentation of his criticisms—the latter's clearest pronouncements regarding that particular issue should be noted:

> Marx . . . thought there were relationships between persons "mediated by things." . . . For Marx there was, and for Sartre there is not, a

coming-to-be of meaning in institutions. History is no longer for Sartre, as it was for Marx, a mixed milieu, neither things nor persons, where intentions are absorbed and transformed and where they decay but are sometimes also reborn and exacerbated, tied to one another and multiplied through one another; history [for Sartre] is made of criminal intentions or virtuous intentions and, for the rest, of acceptances which have the value of acts.[21]

Merleau-Ponty cautioned that the recent Sartre "has not gotten any closer to Marx" despite his apparent distance "from his [original] dichotomy between things and men." Unlike for Marx, "for Sartre, the social whole never starts moving by itself, never yields more movement than it has received from 'inassimilable' and 'irreducible' consciousnesses." In the Sartrean world, any "escape from equivocalness" can be brought about only "through an absolute initiative" whereby subjects transcend the weight of the social whole.[22]

Any endeavor to distill "the 'essence' of Marxism" is "perilous" indeed, as Flynn notes;[23] yet Merleau-Ponty's criticisms highlight fundamental features whoses absence spells a distortion—rather than a development—of Marx's own Marxism. Already in 1946 Merleau-Ponty had argued that for "authentic Marxism . . . everything has a meaning. . . . In the movement of history, man, who has alienated himself for the benefit of his fetishes and has been drained of his very substance, regains possession of himself and of the world."[24] Emphasizing that "*for Marx, the vehicle of history and the motivating force of the dialectic . . . is concrete human intersubjectivity,*" Merleau-Ponty had ruled out any definition of the human being as consciousness. He had argued that Marxism recognizes the interior tie between a society's specific "ideological formations" and "the way this society has set up its basic relationship with nature." For Marxism, "it is a matter of understanding that the bond which attaches man to the world is at the same time his way to freedom."[25]

In *Adventures of the Dialectic,* we must not forget, Merleau-Ponty was saying farewell to Marxism. Nevertheless, he reiterated that a philosophy that despite appearances to the contrary, lacks any genuine interworld and intersubjectivity, is basically at odds with Marxism. As we saw above, the latter's incompatibility with Sartre's philosophy centered on the following features of Sartrean thought: emphasis on oppression rather than exploitation and, hence, relatively little critique of capital; focus on the encounter of rival individual consciousness (moreover, usually the least-favored) whose self-assertion requires a negating transcendence of—or, at best, false fraternity with—the other; reduction of social life and history to projects constituting a melodramatic fight with no real hope of resolution in common action; portrayal of praxis as violent response to initial entrapment and as incessant intervention in history; predominance of invention by a few, with pure compliance and burdensome complicity for the rest; prevalence of spectacle, instantaneous views, and the pact of thought or wills; lack of any agency on the part of the social whole, other than the movement imparted by inassimilable consciousness—in short, lack of that *genuinely* "mixed milieu" which *is* history for Marxism.

Does the *Critique* meet Merleau-Ponty's objections, or does it in fact manifest the same fundamental features that occasioned this sharp attack on Sartre's pre-1955 philosophy? Sartre himself indirectly shed some light on that question in the 1975 interview to which I alluded earlier. When asked whether he had ever abandoned phenomenology, Sartre replied in the negative and added: "I have never thought as a Marxist, not even in the *Critique de la raison dialectique.*"[26] Later in the interview, in response to the question "Can one consider that there is an interworld in your philosophy?" Sartre said: "I admit neither that I have the same philosophy as Merleau-Ponty nor that there is this element of interworld." He went on to say that the difference between Merleau-Ponty's philosophy and his own had to do with "a fundamental incompatibility" rather than a simple misunderstanding:

> I am not much of a continuist; the in-itself, the for-itself, and the intermediary forms . . . that is enough for me. For Merleau-Ponty, there is a relation to being that is very different, a relation in the very depths of oneself. . . . I do not see any reason to speak of intersubjectivity once subjectivities are separated. Intersubjectivity assumes a communion that almost reaches a kind of identification, in any case a unity. . . . I see the separation but I do not see the union.[27]

In the first volume of his *Critique of Dialectical Reason,* Sartre argues that from the beginning of history up to the present, humans have found themselves in a situation of scarcity experienced as need. All social structures are rooted in this situation. In a field of scarcity, each individual regards all others as rivals whose presence prevents there being enough for oneself. Compromise is the only feasible solution, given this mutual hostility. Prompted by fear of the others' violence, each agrees to a mutual limitation of freedom and to collaboration—with its accompanying division of labor—aimed at the joint elimination of scarcity. This collaboration requires the dissolution of the "series," which is an inert, loose aggregate of individuals who all have the same aim but lack any collective purpose. When confronted with an external enemy posing a common danger that the individual as such cannot counter, all members of the series recognize that their only hope for survival lies in common action. This recognition, which transforms each one from serial "Other" into "third party," signals the formation of the "group-in-fusion," as all simultaneously direct themselves toward a common project. Each member interiorizes the emerging integration, and the latter spontaneously finds expression in a common praxis. The joint opposition to the perceived enemy takes the form of revolution. As soon as the revolutionary tension abates, however, the newly constituted group is in danger of relapsing into seriality. Further, once the immediate danger from the external foe recedes, the group's members become aware of the potential menace from within their own ranks. To counter this perceived internal threat to the group, the members pledge to limit their own freedom voluntarily, so as to work together instead of destroying one another. To forestall the others' betrayal, each freely consents to the institutionalization of terror, thus authorizing the exercise of violence against anyone (including oneself) who threatens to break the group's paradoxical solidarity. For Sartre, in short, the original situation is one of conflict caused by scarcity: individuals encounter each other as rivals in a field of scarcity, and their apprehension of a common menace leads to the formation of a group whose continuing cohesion after the revolutionary moment rests on the threat of violence against defectors. Individuals can continue to work together only in what increasingly becomes a hierarchical structure reinforced by terror. Since it is unclear whether, and how, scarcity can ever be eliminated, it remains correspondingly unclear whether oppression can ever be overcome.[28]

We can see already that the basic argument of *Critique* I retains the traits that rendered Sartre's pre-1955 philosophy incompatible with Marxism. The primacy of scarcity—to be considered in more detail below—mystifies the Marxist contention that a *society establishes* its fundamental relationship with nature and that *exploitation* characterizes contemporary social formations. Featuring the encounter of mutually threatening individuals whose fear of each other gives rise to an uneasy pact institutionalizing terror, Sartre's account remains irreconcilable with Marxism. The section on "the third," which presents one of the most arresting descriptions in *Critique* I, shows just how firmly Sartre remained committed to his earlier philosophizing despite appearances to the contrary. The situation depicted centers—typically—on *looking* and provides an instantaneous view of two least-favored individuals. The "concrete historical bond of interiority," which Sartre intended to reveal through this particular situation, explicitly involves *negation*—more specifically, mutual robbery and repulsion. Looking down from a window, Sartre sees a road mender and a gardener who are both busily working on either side of a wall and are unaware of each other's presence. It is the *passive viewer's* need to *project* himself through the two workers whom his look *confronts*, in order to *distinguish* their ends from his own, which prompts him to realize his membership in a particular society. Moreover, the two workers' reality affects him insofar as "it *is not* [his] reality." He "[sees] the *two people* both as objects situated among other objects in the *visual field* and as prospects of escape" who *rob* him "of an aspect of the real" and reduce him to "a living object" in turn. Their unity is predicated on reciprocal *limitation* and *deprivation,* on "seeing what the Other does not see"; it is the third's perception that mediates "between [the] two molecules." The "mutual theft," the "reciprocal negation" of the two manual workers, spells a profound "complicity against" the intellectual spectator. In short, here "the only true bond is negation."[29] As in *Being and Nothingness,* so in *Critique* I Sartre insists on the ineradicability of this negation: "it is impossible *to exist amongst men* without their becoming objects both for me and for them through me, without my being an object for them . . . the foundation of the human relation as the immediate and perpetual determination of everyone by the Other and by all . . . is simply *praxis.*"[30]

Sartre does, it is true, employ crucial Marxist notions in his description of the mediating third. Thus he notes that the gardener is working on "bourgeois property," that the observing intellectual rediscovers "class struggles," that "the worker produces himself through his work," that *praxis* always arises "at a definite moment of History and on the basis of determinate relations of production."[31] Nevertheless, Sartre's philosophy remains as remote from Marxism as it was at the time Merleau-Ponty penned his incisive criticisms. By then, the latter had himself abandoned Marxism in favor of "a noncommunist left," convinced as he now was that revolution is inherently doomed to failure, that the Marxist notion of a self-suppressing class precludes self-criticism, and that the idea of a dialectic rooted in "pre-existing relationships such as they are in things" renders Marxism dogmatic and germinates oppressions.[32] Sartre, likewise, was to reject the idea of the dictatorship of the proletariat; yet, in his case, that dismissal was not to involve a farewell to Marxism—at least, not in his own eyes. On the contrary, as we know, while Merleau-Ponty was definitively taking his leave of it, Sartre was considering himself to be more firmly aligned than ever with Marxism. However, this in no way renders Merleau-

Ponty's criticisms invalid. The core of the fundamental incompatibility of Sartre's philosophy with that of Marx lies in the fact that Sartre never managed to let go of his Cartesian premises. In *Jean-Paul Sartre—Philosophy in the World,* Aronson explains why Sartre's account in the *Critique* remained so "patently unhistorical [and] unsocial."[33] The crux of the problem is Sartre's fundamental assumption of "isolated individual *praxis,*" which precludes his arriving at historical and social reality. Aronson correctly points out that the simple multiplication of separated individuals—as in Sartre's leap from one to three (intellectual, road mender, gardener)—cannot yield social relations. Such an approach distorts individuality and human activity by failing to recognize that any individual can *be* such only as part of a particular society in which each one's activity implies that of all others. Not surprisingly, the second volume of the *Critique* similarly fails to show "how a *multiplicity* of hostile or unrelated *praxes* cohere . . . even at their most penetrating, the analyses of the *Critique* remain wholly within the pre-existing limits of Sartre's thought."[34] Once again, fundamental sociality is conspicuously absent, while rivalry and conflict— everywhere conditioned by scarcity—continue to occupy center stage. Sartre's intriguing description of a boxing match will serve to highlight the extent to which *Critique* II, like *Critique* I, is fundamentally at odds with Marxism.

In *Critique* II as in *Critique* I, Sartre begins with mutually opposed individual *praxes* and—unsuccessfully—seeks to show how a plurality of such irreducibly conflicting *praxes* composes a synthetic unity. The first concrete study in the second volume is particularly significant insofar as it not only sets the tone for the remainder of the work but also provides its clearest expression of those features that Merleau-Ponty, though himself no longer a Marxist, correctly condemned as incompatible with Marx's philosophy. Like the road mender and gardener in the previous volume, the boxers Sartre now depicts belong, typically, to the least-favored segment of society. The physical violence each boxer inflicts on the other is, according to Sartre, their response to the perceived powerlessness of their initial status in society. Sartre points out that the boxers' managers exploit this situation for the sake of profit, and that "boxing is an economic enterprise."[35] He notes that most boxers come from the working class and have experienced "the violence of oppression, of exploitation" all their lives. Having interiorized this violence, they attempt to escape from their oppressive condition by venting their anger in aggression against one of their own class. While a few champions succeed in fleeing their class, most boxers do not significantly improve their situation by agreeing to sell their violence in exchange for wages. This *pact* means, moreover, that the "liberating power" of these workers becomes alienated in the very marketing of their bodies, for the rules governing boxing ensure that the combatants' explosive violence simultaneously "unleashes and derealizes itself" in becoming a spectacle.[36]

This appeal to Marxist notions (such as the working class, exploitation, alienation, capital) unfortunately does not signal a Marxist study of boxing, any more than Sartre's use of such notions in his discussion of "the third" indicated genuine compatibility with Marx's philosophy in *Critique* I. It is true that Sartre places the boxing match within a larger socioeconomic system and emphasizes the boxer's desire to succeed economically (by winning the match, the championship, and thus leaving their socioeconomic class). Nonetheless, oppression still takes precedence over exploitation in Sartre's presentation. As in *Critique* I, the focus is ultimately on the hostile encounter of individuals whose self-assertion necessitates negating the other—indeed, Sartre stresses that the boxers "find their own life only in the destruction of the other's life," and that they reproduce the regime's social structure in their conduct.[37] Given Sartre's insistence that the boxing match not only retotalizes all matches but also publicly incarnates "*all*" conflict," we have here the graphic reduction of history and social life to a melodramatic fight. Nor should it be thought that Sartre's reference to workers' "liberating power" and "will to unite against exploitation" indicates any genuine hope of resolving the conflict through joint action. Sartre contends in *Critique* II, as he did in *Critique* I, that conflicts—be they "single fights" or "social struggles"—"are *all* conditioned by scarcity, negation of man by the Earth interiorizing itself as negation of man by man."[38] Describing the universe "as field of scarcity," Sartre maintains that within this framework relations are "fundamentally antagonistic" and that struggles "represent the very way in which men live scarcity in their perpetual movement to go beyond it."[39] Although he acknowledges that ours is only one history among all possible histories, and that it is impossible to demonstrate a priori "that all possible histories must be conditioned by scarcity," Sartre claims that any history free of scarcity (whether it be scarcity of products, tools, titles, or humans) "is as unknown to us as that of another species living on another planet."[40] These alleged limitations to our knowledge and affirmations effectively dash Marxism's basic hope for a positive human coexistence.

Sartre implicitly equates action with continual *intervention* in history, by focusing on the two boxers' ferocious effort to break free of the oppressive condition into which both have been born. Their competition

171

for titles constitutes a *spectacle* which supplies an instantaneous view and involves a *pact*, of wills. Further, the boxers *invent* their responses to each other, while the onlookers—who form the vast majority—become accomplices. So total is the spectators' complicity that (according to Sartre) this collective "participates" in the incarnation of violence—and even "*produces the boxers.*" In observing the boxers' fight, the public simultaneously becomes unified into a group and torn "full of holes" by the bets which "transform each neighbor into an adversary of his neighbor or (if they wager on the same fighter) into brothers-in-arms."[41] Any such unity is, of course, extremely unstable, and, as in Sartre's earlier work, it is predicated on the rivalry of mutually opposed individuals who remake themselves by a negating transcendence of the Other. Moreover, Sartre continues to insist on the oath taking and fraternity-terror he had described in *Critique* I. Here, as there, he tries to unify mutually adversarial individual projects; yet he fails to see that his Cartesian starting point still precludes any such unification.[42] Thus he distorts the *positive* awareness of social existence that was so essential to Marx's philosophy. The "indissoluble unity of the human and the anti-human," which Sartre claims exists "even outside all alienation," is destructive (rather than constitutive) of that "mixed milieu" in which—according to Marx—"nature [exists] . . . as a *bond* with *man* . . . as the *foundation* of his own *human* existence."[43] Unlike for Marx, for Sartre there is no "*genuine* resolution of the conflict between man and nature and between man and man—[no] true resolution of the strife . . . between objectification and self-confirmation . . . between the individual and the species."[44] For Marxism, Sartre's *Critique* is a profound distortion of both our actual and our potential situation.

Earlier, I noted that in both volumes of his *Critique* Sartre insists that scarcity conditions all conflicts. This insistence on scarcity plays a central part in his distortion of Marxism. Sartre himself readily admitted, when questioned about his overemphasis on scarcity, that this notion "is not Marxist thought. Marx did not think that primitive man or feudal man lived under the rule of scarcity.[45] In the *Critique,* Sartre castigates Marx (and Engels) for failing to stress scarcity; yet Marx himself emphatically rejected such emphasis, alleging that "abstract and contradictory notions like scarcity and abundance" are useless for understanding the class struggle.[46] In fact, for Marxism such notions mystify that struggle by obscuring the exploitation that underlies it. Why, then, does Sartre make scarcity central? I suggest that the answer is to be found in his continuing adherence—appearances to the contrary notwithstanding—to the philosophy of freedom elaborated in *Being and Nothingness.* There Sartre had argued that the apprehension of *lack*—the nihilating rupture with plenitude—is constitutive of the very being of human reality. In the *Critique,* Sartre attempts to annex history to this ontological freedom by recasting lack as scarcity. As William McBride has pointed out, "it would be difficult for readers of the *Critique* to exaggerate the prominence of its role in Sartre's account."[47] Although he was referring to Volume I, McBride's point applies equally to Volume II. The term *scarcity* is inherently vague, in the *Critique* Sartre identified the overcoming of alienation with the unqualified elimination of scarcity, and the inherent impossibility of achieving the latter effectively ruled out the attainment of a genuinely socialist society.[48]

Klaus Hartmann, too, has argued persuasively that "Sartre's principle of scarcity merits only dubious theoretical status," and that "the theory of the *Critique* deprives itself of acceptable social solutions by dint of its very theoretical foundations; its lack of ultimate affirmativity is a function of these foundations."[49] The latter consist of highly abstract principles centering around the notions of scarcity, rivalry, otherness, the third, and the practico-inert. These principles preclude any durable affirmative communion or union and prevent the nonantagonistic nascent group (the *"groupe en fusion"*) from ever becoming more than a fleeting phenomenon. As Hartmann argued, Sartre moreover submerges "the economic specificity of alienation" in his nexus of negative principles.[50] Like McBride, Hartmann was commenting on the first volume of the *Critique.* It is clear, however, that his argument holds for the second volume as well.

Marxism, unlike Sartre's *Critique,* posits the original situation as one of cooperation rather than confrontation and emphasizes the socioeconomic origins of the subsequent historical antagonisms. The division of labor initially occurs quite spontaneously, and it is tribes or families, rather than individuals, who encounter each other on an independent footing. Far from being rooted in an inevitable scarcity and in the very nature of human activity, alienation arises from the fact that some human beings appropriate the means of production, thereby putting themselves in a position to control the others' labor power. The relationship between employer and worker is based on the former's desire to make a profit, rather than any deliberate will to negate the other's freedom. Marxism very carefully distinguishes between alienation and objectification, whereas the *Critique* implicitly collapses that distinction.[51] In acting to satisfy their needs, so Sartre argues, humans work upon inert matter and initiate a process that strikes back at them as an alien force. Marxism, by contrast, emphasizes that only under conditions of exploita-

173

tion does humans' objectified activity become an alien force that turns against them. Those conditions can, and must, be eliminated through the abolition of the entire system of production and exchange that brought them into existence. Sartre is unable to offer any such solution to the problem of alienation, given the ineradicability of human need, the de facto existence of others, the apparent inevitability of scarcity, and the inescapable ossification of all revolutionary activity.[52] No matter how intriguing, Sartre's *Critique* thus clashes with Marxism and cannot possibly provide its foundation.

The notion of freedom lies at the core of Marxism; yet unfortunately the meaning and status of freedom are not at all clear. Marx himself appealed to "human status and dignity" for labor and the worker, in calling for "universal human emancipation."[53] By "human status and dignity," Marx seems to mean our "spiritual essence, [our] *human* being"; and this in turn seems to hinge on the contention that, unlike animals, we do not *coincide* with our "life-activity" but rather are *conscious* of it. The *human* being is thus a being *for itself;* and only because of this is it "a free being." What distinguishes it from other species—its "species character"—is therefore "free, conscious activity":

> The whole character of a species—its species character—is contained in the character of its life-activity; and free, conscious activity is man's species character. . . . The animal is immediately identical with its life-activity. It does not distinguish itself from it. It is *its life-activity.* Man makes his life-activity itself the object of his will and of his consciousness. He has conscious life-activity. It is not a determination with which he directly merges. Conscious life-activity distinguishes man immediately from animal life-activity. It is just because of this that he is a species being. Or rather, it is only because he is a species being that he is a conscious being, i.e., that his own life is an object for him. Only because of that is his activity free activity. Estranged labor reverses this relationship, so that it is just because man is a conscious being that he makes his life-activity, his *essential* being, a mere means to his *existence* . . . in degrading spontaneous, free, activity, to a means, estranged labor makes man's species life a means to his physical existence. . . .
>
> But man is not merely a natural being: he is a *human* natural being. That is to say, he is a being for himself. Therefore he is a *species being,* and has to confirm and manifest himself as such both in his being and in his knowing.[54]

These words were written in 1843–44. Over the next forty years, Marx does not give any argument in support of these claims. In fact, in reiterating the fundamental distinction between humans and animals in

Capital, Marx explicitly makes that distinction *a presupposition* of his critical analysis of capitalist production: "We pre-suppose labor in a form that stamps it as exclusively human."[55] Marx notes that whereas "mere" animals operate purely instinctively, humans labor purposively. Thus the latter imagine the product to be made, subordinate their will to the modus operandi for its construction, and by doing so realize a purpose of their own. The more distasteful the task, the closer must be their attention in carrying it out.[56] Purpose, imagination, will, and attention have to do with *consciousness,* surely; hence, the crux of Marx's contrast between animals and humans is unchanged. Our very being as humans seems to hinge on the freedom that is constitutive of noncoincidence, that is, consciousness, being for itself—in short, "spontaneous, free, activity." Ontological freedom thus appears to be Marx's pivotal presupposition in unmasking capitalism and calling for an end to exploitation and alienation.

A presupposition can always be challenged; consequently, Marx's basic assumption concerning the being of humans renders his sustained critique of capitalist society at least somewhat dubious. Ironically, the non-Marxist and earlier Sartre of *Being and Nothingness* may hold more promise for solving this problem. Sartre's early philosophy could conceivably come to the rescue. The foregoing has, I hope, revealed a rather striking similarity between Marx's claims regarding the *"human being"* and Sartre's claims in *Being and Nothingness.* Unlike Marx, however, Sartre provides an intricate argument to support those claims— rather than leaving them simply as presuppositions.

It seems to me that the whole of *Being and Nothingness* constitutes a detailed argument for humans' "original, ontological freedom."[57] Our very ability to question—in the everyday sense of the word—reveals that freedom defines our existence as humans, contends Sartre. The crux of his argument is that all questioning presupposes the noncoincidence of the questioner and the questioned—the detaching, "nihilating withdrawal" that supposes rupture with the causality of self-identical being-in-itself. Questioning is not restricted to the posing of actual questions in our usual sense of the term; rather, it is synonymous with "the being of consciousness qua consciousness." Moreover, "the ontological foundation of consciousness" is the "ontological act" whereby being-in-itself "deteriorates" into that "presence to itself" which is constitutive of being-for-itself, or "human reality." The for-itself is the original, perpetual project of noncoincidence; it "is the being which determines itself to exist inasmuch as it cannot coincide with itself."[58] This project, this primordial nihilation which is the foundation of "empirical freedom," is the very being of humans—namely, pure spontaneity. Ontological freedom is simply this "nihilating spontaneity." To preclude an infinite regress we must recognize the nonsubstantial absoluteness, the "immediate self-consciousness" of human reality. Thus Sartre argues that "man is free because he is not himself but present to himself."[59]

Paradoxically, the absoluteness of ontological freedom does not entail the elimination of motives, causes, obstacles, and limits. According to Sartre, the for-itself by its very upsurge as freedom structures undifferentiated being-in-itself into a world; and any specific action expresses that fundamental project. To act is to choose, and the for-itself's choice of ends "carves out" objective configurations and brings about the emergence of causes in the world. Motives are merely the apprehension of such causes, inasmuch as this apprehension is nonthetic self-consciousness. Far from being internal or external *givens,* end, cause, and motive are therefore indissoluble terms of a project—that is, of a particular way of being-in-the-world. Any deliberation is itself part of the primordial project; while any reflective decision is predicated on the fundamental choosing which is nothing but the for-itself's very existence as freedom. The latter's structure rules out caprice because freedom as project, as nihilating spontaneity, precludes instantaneity and lack of restrictions. Nihilation requires that there be something to be nihilated, or surpassed; moreover, if that something were simply created ex nihilo by freedom, the fundamental project—the for-itself as noncoincidence—would collapse. Thus human reality everywhere encounters obstacles it has not created; but those obstacles can reveal their resistance only in the context of a (human)) project. Freedom exists solely in a *situation;* and the latter is such only through freedom. By its very upsurge, freedom confers meaning and value on brute being according to its fundamental choice of itself. This ontological freedom, or "autonomy of choice," supports empirical freedom—that is, physical, religious, social, political, and economic freedoms. *Being and Nothingness,* however, concerns itself exclusively with analyzing ontological, rather than empirical, freedom.[60]

Despite its ingenuity, Sartre's analysis is flawed. As Merleau-Ponty points out in the final chapter of his *Phenomenology of Perception,* the very notion of *ontological* freedom actually destroys freedom—such freedom is a contradiction in terms. If humans' very being is freedom, then it is impossible to detect its appearance anywhere—for no matter what we feel or do, that primordial freedom remains the same. If "freedom is total and infinite," as Sartre claims, then it lacks any background of nonfreedom from which to stand out. Consequently, it cannot *be* anywhere. If "choice and consciousness are one and the same thing," the

176

notion of *choice* becomes utterly meaningless. To declare all acts free is effectively to declare none of them free and to do away with the very idea of action. Sartre's contention that humans are "wholly and forever free or . . . not free at all" presents us with a specious either/or; for to be infinitely and eternally free is to have nothing to choose, nothing to acquire, nothing to do.

The heart of the problem is discernible in Sartre's own stipulation "that the choice, being identical with acting, supposes a commencement of realization in order that the choice may be distinguished from the dream and the wish." If choice is infinite and omnipresent, it is difficult to see how there can be any such distinction. Further, as Merleau-Ponty notes, there is an unresolved difficulty in the very notion of a global choice of ourselves and our way of being-in-the-world: since that primordial choice is synonymous with our very upsurge in the world, it is perplexing how it can even be considered *our* choice. Ultimately, such an originating choice spells a fundamental contradiction insofar as choice implies an antecedent commitment, or acquisition. Despite Sartre's insistence on the contrary, freedom cannot be absolute; it must indeed have a "support" and a "springboard." Human reality must be *receptive* if there is to be "concrete and actual freedom" at all. There must be—as Merleau-Ponty maintains—a transformatory, prereflective interaction, between "a power of initiative," that is, a bodily intentionality, and an intersubjective world that *solicits* favored forms of response without *dictating* any of them. Sartre's conception of freedom as a nihilating spontaneity masks our primordial *bond* with the natural and cultural world, our fundamental *inherence* in prereflective coexistence with other incarnate subjectives who share a particular situation. All of them live through, and modify, that situation. There is thus a dialectical relationship in the emergence of historical events: history offers meanings for humans to take up and carry forward. The historical situation elicits responses—but it is humans who actually respond. Merleau-Ponty reminds us that, as Saint-Exupéry said, we are "but a network of relationships." It is by assuming those relationships and carrying them forward that we realize our freedom.[61]

Earlier I contended that, its centrality notwithstanding, the meaning and status of freedom are by no means clear in Marxism. In light of the foregoing critique, that ambiguity could turn out to be a boon for Marxism. If the latter is in fact claiming *ontological* status for freedom, then Merleau-Ponty's criticism of Sartrean freedom applies—rendering Marxism likewise fatally flawed. As I indicated, there are passages in Marx's writings that seem to authorize such an interpretation of freedom. A number of other passages, however, suggest an interpretation more in keeping with the notion of freedom that emerges in Merleau-Ponty's own philosophy. Thus, for example, Marx criticizes Feuerbach for presupposing "an abstract—*isolated*—human individual," and argues instead that "the human essence is no abstraction inherent in each single individual. In its reality it is the ensemble of the social relations."[62] Similarly, in his famous critique of Bruno Bauer's position "on the Jewish question," Marx challenges the notion of "individual freedom" which "lets every man find in other men not the *realization* but rather the *limitation* of his own freedom":

> Far from viewing man here in his species-being, his species-life itself—society—rather appears to be an external framework for the individual, limiting his original independence . . . the sphere in which man acts as a member of the community is degraded below that in which he acts as a fractional being, and finally man as bourgeois rather than man as citizen is considered to be the *proper* and *authentic* man. . . .
>
> The *political revolution* dissolves civil life into its constituent elements without *revolutionizing* these elements themselves and subjecting them to criticism. . . .
>
> Only when the actual, individual man has taken back into himself the abstract citizen and in his everyday life, his individual work, and his individual relationships has become a *species-being*, only when he has recognized and organized his own powers as *social* powers so that social force is no longer separated from him as *political* power, only then is human emancipation complete.[63]

Similar passages stressing that freedom has to do with the *realization* of human *potentialities,* and that such realization can occur only in and through *community* with others, are to be found in other early works as well as in Marx's later writings.[64]

If freedom is *not* synonymous with the *being* of humans, for Marx—and that is the more plausible interpretation—where does that leave Marxism? I have argued that neither Sartre's *Critique of Dialectical Reason* nor *Being and Nothingness* can provide a philosophical foundation for Marxism. The criticism of the Sartrean conception of freedom would suggest that one might draw on Merleau-Ponty's phenomenological philosophy. Yet is it viable to bring the "post-Marxist" Merleau-Ponty to the rescue of Marxism? Even if one were to answer in the affirmative, one would look in vain for a full-fledged phenomenological account of freedom in Merleau-Ponty's writings. The final chapter of the *Phenomenology of Perception* is explicitly devoted to the topic; yet Merleau-Ponty's treatment is primarily critical and fails to offer more than the barest outline of a positive conception of freedom. Further, not only does the meaning of freedom within history remain quite undeveloped, but it is by no means clear that Merleau-Ponty's phenomenology can serve as a fruitful point of departure. Geraldine Finn, for example, has claimed that "phenomenology is especially vulnerable to [feminist] critique because it has assumed that the phenomenology of male-consciousness is tantamount to the phenomenology of consciousness as such."[65] It remains to be seen whether Merleau-Ponty's phenomenology can survive such a feminist critique or whether a specifically feminist phenomenology will ultimately need to be developed. Similarly, it remains an open question whether Marxism itself can withstand contemporary feminist critiques. As is well known, a number of feminists have argued that Marxism fails to deal with women's oppression, and that is is not philosophically feasible to amend the theory with respect to women—"the exclusion or denigration of women is integral to the system, and to give equal recognition to women destroys the system."[66] The question whether Marxism can accommodate contemporary ecological concerns, or whether the domination of nature is integral to it, similarly remains open. In short, it is not certain that marxism *can* be given a genuinely firm philosophical footing. What *does* seem certain, however, is that any such footing would need to include an adequate phenomenological analysis of freedom.

Notes

1. Thomas R. Flynn, *Sartre and Marxist Existentialism: The Test Case of Collective Responsibility* (Chicago, 1984), xi, xiii–xiv.

2. The focus on responsibility is not, of course, entirely new. Already in 1957, Leszek Kolakowski sought to combine Sartrean existentialist insights with Marxism in emphasizing that "the essential social engagement is moral" and that "every individual's access to . . . any . . . form of political life is a moral act for which he is fully responsible." From "Responsibility and History," in *Existentialism versus Marxism: Conflicting Views on Humanism*, ed. by George Novack (New York, 1966), 292–93. Far from reiterating Kolakowski's moral individualism, however, Flynn explores the notion of responsibility in Sartre's philosophy and argues that Sartre combined existentialist and Marxist features in articulating a satisfactory theory of collective responsibility.

3. An examination of arguments for and against the claim that Marxism requires a philosophical foundation lies beyond the scope of this essay. For a consideration of some recent work on this issue, I refer the reader to Supplementary Volume VII of the Canadian Journal of Philosophy, *Marx and Morality*, ed. by Kai Nielsen and Steven C. Patten (Guelph, Ont., 1981).

4. Karl Marx, *Economic and Philosophic Manuscripts of 1844*, trans. by Martin Milligan, ed. by Dirk J. Struik (New York, 1964), 112–13.

5. *Search for a Method*, trans. by Hazel E. Barnes (New York, 1968), 175–80.

179

6. "An Interview with Jean-Paul Sartre," in *The Philosophy of Jean-Paul Sartre*, ed. by Paul Arthur Schilpp (LaSalle, Ill., 1981), 20.

7. Ibid., 21.

8. Ibid.

9. Ronald Aronson, "Sartre and the Dialectic: The Purposes of Critique II," *Yale French Studies*, no. 68 (1985), 95. Aronson makes the same point in chap. 1 of *Sartre's Second Critique* (Chicago, 1987).

10. Thomas R. Flynn, "Merleau-Ponty and the Critique of Dialectical Reason," *Hypatia* (Boulder, Colo., 1985), 248.

11. Aronson, *Sartre's Second Critique*, 11–32.

12. Maurice Merleau-Ponty, *Adventures of the Dialectic*, trans. by Joseph Bien (Evanston, Ill., 1973), 205, 142, 152, 193, 200.

13. Ibid., 137–38.

14. Ibid., 158–59, 161.

15. Ibid., 155.

16. Ibid., 147, 194, 168, 153–54, 198.

17. Ibid., 199, 198, 163, 132, 192, 193.

18. Ibid., 196, 161, 193, 163.

19. Ibid., 146–51, 123.

20. Ibid., 151–53, 181, 122, 124.

21. Ibid., 124.

22. Ibid., 139–40.

23. Flynn, *Sartre and Marxist Existentialism*, 173.

24. Maurice Merleau-Ponty, "Marxism and Philosophy," in *Sense and Non-Sense*, trans. by H. L. Dreyfus and P. A. Dreyfus (Evanston, Ill., 1964), 128.

25. Ibid., 126, 129–30. By 1960, Merleau-Ponty had become convinced that "the Marxist link between philosophy and politics" had ruptured, and that it therefore no longer made "much sense" to ask whether someone was or was not still a Marxist. "Introduction," *Signs*, trans. by Richard C. McCleary (Evanston, Ill., 1964), 8–11.

26. "An Interview with Jean-Paul Sartre," 24.

27. Ibid., 43–44.

28. In "An Interview with Jean-Paul Sartre," he declared: "In any case, there is a difference between supply and demand that arises from the way man is made, from the fact that man demands more, whereas the supply is limited . . . need is not an oppression; it is a normal biological characteristic of the living creature, and he creates scarcity. . . . Scarcity is social to the extent that the desired object is scarce for a given society. But strictly speaking, scarcity is not social. Society comes after scarcity. The latter is an original phenomenon of the relation between man and Nature. Nature does not sufficiently contain the objects that man demands in order that man's life should not include either work, which is struggle against scarcity, or combat," (ibid., 31–32). When asked whether he saw "a possible end to scarcity," Sartre replied: "Not at the moment." He added that socialism "would not lead to the disappearance of scarcity" (32). See also *Critique of Dialectical Reason I: Theory of Practical Ensembles*, trans. by Alan Sheridan-Smith, ed. by Jonathan Rée (London, 1982), 105, 112–13, 127 ff., 140 ff., 318 ff., 735 ff. In the original French text, the corresponding pages are *Critique de la raison dialectique I: Théorie des ensembles pratiques* (Paris, 1960), 186, 192, 204 ff., 214 ff., 358 ff., 688 ff.

29. *Critique* I, 100–106.

30. Ibid., 105–6.

31. Ibid., 100, 101, 103, 106.

32. "Epilogue," *Adventures of the Dialectic,* 203–33. See especially 207 ff., 219, 226–27, 231–32.

33. Ronald Aronson, *Jean-Paul Sartre—Philosophy in the World* (London, 1980), 243–92. See especially 263–68. See also Aronson's article "Sartre's Return to Ontology: *Critique* II Rethinks the Basis of *L'Etre et le Néant,*" *Journal of the History of Ideas* 48, no. 1 (January–March 1987), 99–116.

34. Ibid., 264, 285, 286.

35. *Critique de la raison dialectique II; L'Intelligibilite de l'histoire,* ed. by Arlette Elkaïm-Sartre (Paris, 1985), 45–54. Here and in subsequent quotations from *Critique* II the English translation is my own. Ronald Aronson's article "On Boxing: 'Incarnation' in *Critique* II" provides a useful summary of this part of *Critique* II; *Revue Internationale de Philosophie* 39, nos. 152–53 (1985), 149–79; republished as chap. 3 of *Sartre's Second Critique.* However, Aronson's interpretation of Sartre's study of the boxing match is more sympathetic to Sartre than is my own view. While the placing of the specific conflict within a larger socioeconomic system can be seen as a step forward for Sartre, the study itself constitutes a singularly clear expression of the very features that render Sartre's philosophy incompatible with Marxism.

36. Ibid., 45, 46, 51–53, 56.

37. Ibid., 46, 57. Sartre says that his aim "cannot be to outline here a historical and dialectical interpretation of boxing" (45); nevertheless, his study of a boxing match is not only limited in scope but antithetical to any genuinely Marxist account of such a match.

38. Ibid., 29, 32, 37, 57, 22.

39. Ibid., 22–23.

40. Ibid., 22, 23, 26, 32, 58, 349, 394–95n.

41. Ibid., 35, 36, 22.

42. Ibid., 76, 106, 61, 71, 194, 239–40, 301.

43. Ibid., 301; Marx, *Economic and Philosophic Manuscripts of 1844,* 137–38.

44. Ibid., 134–35.

45. "An Interview with Jean-Paul Sartre," 30.

46. *Critique* I, 144 ff.; and Karl Marx, *The Poverty of Philosophy* (Moscow, 1955), 37.

47. William Leon McBride, "Sartre and Marxism," in *The Philosophy of Jean-Paul Sartre,* 621.

48. Ibid., 621–24.

49. Klaus Hartmann, "Sartre's Theory of Ensembles," in *The Philosophy of Jean-Paul Sartre,* 636–37, 648–49.

50. Ibid., 636–41, 649.

51. Marx, *Economic and Philosophic Manuscripts of 1844,* 175 ff.; and Karl Marx, *Grundrisse: Foundations of the Critique of Political Economy,* trans. by Martin Nicolaus (Harmondsworth, 1973), 211 ff., 831–32.

52. See, for example, *Critique* I, 81–83, 122 ff., 222 ff., 333 ff., 661 ff., 735–48, 804–5, 811–12. *Critique* II, 21 ff., 58 ff., 76 ff., 106, 131 ff., 198, 248 ff., 298 ff., 349, 364, 394 ff.; Marx, *Economic and Philosophic Manuscripts of 1844,* 106 ff., 137 ff., 170 ff.; Karl Marx, *Capital: A Critical Analysis of Capitalist Production,* trans. by Samuel Moore and Edward Aveling, ed. by Frederick Engels (Moscow, n.d.), I, 76 ff., 340 ff., 667 ff., 686 ff., 702 ff.; *Writings of the Young Marx on Philosophy and Society,* trans. and ed. by Loyd D. Easton and Kurt H. Guddet (New York, 1967), 144, 272, 281–82.

53. Marx, *Economic and Philosophic Manuscripts of 1844*, 118.

54. Ibid., 112–14, 182. I am hyphenating "life-activity" in keeping with 113, line 3, and with the 1959 edition also translated by Martin Milligan (Moscow, 1967).

55. *Capital* I, 174. Incidentally, I would question Marx's radical dichotomy between humans and animals. Sartre prudently refrained from considering the being of animals; but when asked directly, he stated that "animals have consciousness." See "An Interview with Jean-Paul Sartre," 28.

56. *Capital* I, 173–74.

57. *Being and Nothingness*, 569, 583.

58. Ibid., 16, 58 ff., 124–26.

59. Ibid., 12 ff., 60, 84, 567 ff.

60. Ibid., 16, 84, 564 ff., 575 ff., 594 ff., 612 ff., 619 ff., 635 ff., 645 ff., 675 ff., 705 ff.

61. Ibid., 60, 473 ff., 534–59, 562–63, 568 ff., 595, 616 ff., 654–80; and Merleau-Ponty, *Phenomenology of Perception*, trans. by Colin Smith (London, 1962), 434–56. Note that Sartre's emphasis in *Being and Nothingness* is on separation rather than interconnectedness. The recurrent notions of "rupture," "wrenching away," and "conflict" are indicative. Thus he says, for example: "Human-reality is free because . . . it is perpetually wrenched away from itself and because it has been separated by a nothingness from what it is and from what it will be. . . . But this power of nihilation cannot be limited to realizing a simple withdrawal in relation to the world. . . . This means evidently that it is by a pure wrenching away from himself and the world that the worker can posit his suffering as unbearable suffering and consequently can make of it the motive for his revolutionary action. This implies for consciousness the permanent possibility of effecting a rupture with its own past, of wrenching itself away from its past . . . so as to be able to confer on it the meaning which it has in terms of the project of a meaning which it does not have. . . . To come into the world as a freedom confronting Others is to come into the world as alienable. If to will oneself free is to choose to be in this world confronting Others, then the one who wills himself such must will also the passion of his freedom. . . . Thus the Other's freedom confers limits on my situation. . . ." It is "useless for human-reality to seek to get out of this dilemma: one must either transcend the Other or allow oneself to be transcended by him. The essence of the relations between consciousness is not the Mitsein; it is conflict."

62. Karl Marx, "Theses on Feuerbach," in Karl Marx and Friedrich Engels, *The German Ideology and Supplementary Texts*, ed. by C. J. Arthur (New York, 1970), VI, 122.

63. Marx, "On the Jewish Question," in *Writings of the Young Marx*, 236–41.

64. See, for example, *The German Ideology*, 83; *Economic and Philosophic Manuscripts of 1844*, 137 ff., 181 ff.; Karl Marx, *Capital: A Critique of Political Economy*, ed. by F. Engels (Moscow, 1971), III, 820; *Grundrisse*, 487 ff.

65. Geraldine Finn, "On the Oppression of Women in Philosophy—Or, Whatever Happened to Objectivity?" in *Feminism in Canada: From Pressure to Politics*, ed. by Angela Miles and Geraldine Finn (Montreal, 1982), 155.

66. Ibid., 151. See also such works as Mary O'Brien, "Reproducing Marxist Man," in *The Sexism of Social and Political Theory: Women and Reproduction from Plato to Nietzsche* (Toronto, 1979); Lydia Sargent, ed., *Women and Revolution: A Discussion of the Unhappy Marriage of Marxism and Feminism* (Boston, 1981); Mary O'Brien, "Hegemony and Superstructure: A Feminist Critique of Neo-Marxism," in *Taking Sex into Account: The Policy Consequences of Sexist Research* (Ottawa, 1984).

9

SARTRE'S EARLY ETHICS AND THE ONTOLOGY OF *BEING AND NOTHINGNESS*

Thomas C. Anderson

For decades there has been controversy over whether the ontology Sartre sets forth in *Being and Nothingness* is compatible with an ethical theory. Some have claimed that its pessimistic portrayal of human existence—as a useless passion doomed to failure, an unhappy consciousness which cannot escape its unhappy state[1] and its negative account of human relations—as inevitably conflictive[2] rendered ethics meaningless or impossible. Others have maintained that Sartre's denial of all objective moral values inevitably resulted in complete moral relativism.[3] Still others, myself included, have contended that such conclusions involve serious misinterpretations of Sartre's early phenomenological ontology, and that the latter in fact provides the foundation for a coherent (though not flawless) ethics whose general outline is suggested by Sartre himself in some early published works.[4]

All interpreters agree that Sartre frequently took public moral stands and that he employed notions having a moral character, notions such as bad faith, authenticity, radical conversion, the city of ends, and so on. But disagreement remains about both the meaning of these concepts and their compatibility with his early ontology. Of course, these controversies would presumably have been resolved long ago if Sartre had finished the work on ethics that he promised at the end of *Being and Nothingness*.

183

Fortunately, three years after his death Sartre's adoptive daughter published two of his notebooks, entitled *Cahiers pour une morale* and written in 1947–48, which are part of the ethics he was then working on as the sequel to his ontology. While these six hundred pages of notes do not constitute a completed text and comprise only about one-fifth of a larger collection which was lost, they still furnish a great deal of insight into the ethics Sartre was developing complementary to, and grounded in, his early ontology. My purpose is to show how the *Cahiers* (in spite of its inevitable ambiguities and inconsistencies) can help resolve many of the contentious issues surrounding that Sartrean ethics.

Of course, this article concentrates on two early works in Sartre's career, and he later modified some, though certainly not all, of the positions he adopted in this period. However, in order to assess the extent of any such modification it is necessary to determine exactly Sartre's early position. It will be my contention in what follows that the *Cahiers* shows that many standard interpretations of the ontology of *Being and Nothingness* are erroneous and, as a result, that they see the later Sartre shifting more radically than he did in fact. On the other hand, insofar as Sartre does significantly modify his early positions in some areas, especially his understanding of interpersonal relations, it is important to recognize that the changes actually begin very early, in the *Cahiers* (as well as in other published works of this period).

Speaking of the latter, I should note that the notebooks we have were written at the same time as *What Is Literature?* and shortly after the publication of *Existentialism Is a Humanism* and "Materialism and Revolution." In my analysis I will briefly refer to these works where appropriate and point out some of the interesting parallels between positions taken in them and in the *Cahiers*.[5] Let me add that even though these early published works contain some of the same positions that are found in the *Cahiers,* the latter offers far more explanation of, and justification for, these positions.

Actually, the *Cahiers* was the first of three ethics Sartre worked on in his lifetime. While I believe that a number of the basic positions Sartre adopts in it (for example, the primary moral ideal and goal he proposes) are maintained throughout his career, I will not pursue this point here except to note that in interviews toward the end of his life Sartre stated he was "returning" to this first morality "enriching" it and not rejecting it.[6] In this article, I intend rather to focus on three important issues of interpretation of *Being and Nothingness,* issues about which commentators have been in sharp disagreement. These issues are central to understanding *Being and Nothingness* and, therefore, must be resolved if one is to determine the extent to which Sartre's later positions constitute a shift from his earlier ones. Specifically I will seek to answer the following questions: (1) Does the ontology of *Being and Nothingness* doom human existence to inevitable failure and meaninglessness, thus rendering ethics pointless? (2) Since Sartre rejects all objective values in *Being and Nothingness,* can he offer any coherent reason for preferring one value or set of values over another in his ethics? (3) If conflict is the very "essence" of human relations, as *Being and Nothingness* claims, what is the significance of ethical norms?

My procedure in treating each question will be first to present the often conflicting positions of Sartre's commentators, then to use the *Cahiers* in an attempt to resolve their disputes, and finally to offer some evaluation of Sartre's position and that of his commentators.

Does the ontology of *Being and Nothingness* doom human existence to inevitable failure and meaninglessness, thus rendering ethics pointless? Those who answer affirmatively point to the extremely pessimistic statements Sartre utters in his conclusion to *Being and Nothingness:* "all human activities are equivalent . . . all are on principle doomed to failure. Thus it amounts to the same thing whether one gets drunk alone or is a leader of nations."[7] A basic ontological reason for this nihilism is, of course, that Sartre believes that every human being's fundamental urge is for the impossible, namely, to be God. We desire to be a being that would be necessary, that is, exist by right rather than by contingency, but one that would preserve its freedom and consciousness by being itself the cause or foundation of its own necessity. Putting it in terms of freedom and choice, Sartre writes, "my freedom is a choice of being God and all my acts and all my projects translate this choice and reflect it in a thousand and one ways."[8] Again, referring to man's fundamental project, he says, "he can choose only to be God."[9] Since we can never achieve the status of an *ens causa sui,* no matter how much money, power, or virtue we attain, this fundamental desire or choice renders our existence a "useless passion," and the for-itself is "by nature an unhappy consciousness with no possibility of surpassing its unhappy state."[10] What sense, then, does ethics make in the face of this inevitable failure?

In reply, defenders of Sartre point to other early published works that indicate that he did not think that human existence was inevitably a useless failure. *What Is Literature?* proposes that in the creation of the aesthetic object man's existence is not in vain but meaningful, even joyful. And neither it nor "Materialism and Revolution" is pessimisitic in tone, for in both Sartre suggests that it is eminently worthwhile to strive to achieve the city of ends, the classless society of democratic

185

socialism.[11] Equally important is the general position he asserts in *Existentialism and Humanism,* namely, that our existence will possess as much meaning and significance as we ourselves give it[12]—a position certainly compatible with the ontology of *Being and Nothingness* which insists that human beings are the sole creators of meaning and value in a universe that itself possesses no objective or transcendent values.

Furthermore, on the last few pages of *Being and Nothingness* Sartre seems to hold out the possibility that human beings do not have to choose the project of being God as the primary value and goal of their lives. (And the statements he makes there about the failure of all human pursuits, as well as his remark about the unhappy state of the for-itself, refer precisely to the vain desire and futile search for that impossible goal.) Of equal importance, and overlooked by most critics, is a crucial distinction Sartre makes early in that same work between goals that one seeks as values on the prereflective level and goals-values that one reflectively chooses.[13] Being God is a goal-value in the first sense for Sartre, for contingent human beings inevitably, structurally, desire to be *ens causa sui.* But goals-values in the second sense are those one freely chooses, and at the end of *Being and Nothingness* Sartre seems to allow for the possibility that being God need not be reflectively chosen as the primary goal-value one actively pursues. However, since he suggests this possibility only briefly in a couple of pages, and only through a series of questions, and since, as we saw, he also claims that man "can choose only to be God," his position is not altogether clear.

By comparison the *Cahiers* is quite clear. Though in it Sartre reasserts his view that human beings on the unreflective level inevitably aspire to be God, he leaves no doubt that they need not *reflectively* choose this as their supreme goal, nor should they if they wish to avoid failure (or "Hell," as he now calls it). The following selection, written in 1945 and published as an appendix to the *Cahiers,* makes this plain. Sartre writes: "the first project or original choice that man makes of himself . . . is to join an *en-soi-pour-soi* [in-itself-for-itself] and to identify himself with it, briefly to be God and his own foundation."[14] This project, or choice, he goes on, is made unreflectively, and to live according to it is Hell (inevitable failure), and so the question becomes "will one exit from Hell" and attain "salvation"? This question can be posed "only at the reflexive level." The question is, he continues, "whether reflection will accept responsibility for the first project of freedom or not accept it, and will be purifying reflection refusing to have anything to do with it."[15] And, he concludes, "accomplice reflection is only the prolongation of the bad faith which is found at the heart of the primitive

186

nonthetic project [to be God], whereas pure reflection is a rupture with this projection and the constitution of a freedom which takes itself for an end."[16] This distinction between a pure reflection, which breaks with the God project, and an accomplice (or impure), which simply goes along with it, is not new but was present in *Being and Nothingness* and earlier in *The Transcendence of the Ego,* although both places treated in detail only impure reflection.[17] In fact, in *Being and Nothingness* Sartre stated explicity that he was not going to discuss pure reflection and the conversion that attains it. The study of "the nature and role of purifying reflection," he said there, "cannot be made here [in a work of ontology]; it belongs rather to an *Ethics.*"[18] Of course, the *Cahiers* is, or was to be, that ethics, and it does indeed contain an extensive treatment of pure reflection, its rejection of the God project, and its grasp of human freedom.

The *Cahiers* also unequivocally identifies pure reflection with the radical conversion from bad faith that Sartre occasionally refers to in *Being and Nothingness,* and like *Existentialism and Humanism,* it states that it is up to human beings, the only sources of meaning and value in the universe, to provide meaning (salvation) for their lives. Even though there are no transcendent or objective values that confer meaning on our existence, it is not a failure (Hell) if *we* choose to value it. In itself our existence is neither meaningful nor meaningless, neither justified nor unjustified, Sartre says. It is up to us, and to us alone, to justify it: "Man, the unjustifiable foundation of every justification"; and, again, "It is me, who nothing justifies, who justifies myself."[19] Thus, according to the *Cahiers,* a meaningless existence can be avoided by human beings if they choose something other than being God as their primary goal and value. (We have yet to see what this something should be.)

Unfortunately, what complicates the issue is that the *Cahiers* also repeats the assertion made in *Being and Nothingness* that men can *choose* only being God as their ultimate value. In the same appendix quoted from above, Sartre also says the following about the project to be God: "This project is first in the sense that it is the very structure of my existence. I exist as choice, but this choice [of God] . . . is made on an unreflective plane."[20] Though he insists that this unreflective choice is "freely made," he also maintains that "it can do nothing but posit the in-itself-for-itself."[21] It is true that Sartre immediately goes on to indicate, in passages cited earlier, that on the *reflective* level human beings need not choose the God project; nevertheless, such a reflective choice cannot erase my unreflective choice since it is "the very structure of my existence."[22] In other words, Sartre's position in the *Cahiers* (as in *Being*

187

and Nothingness) is that the project to be God both must be (nonreflectively) freely chosen and need not be (reflectively) freely chosen as man's primary goal-value. But I would argue that to speak of a free choice (whether unreflective or not makes no difference) when no other fundamental options are possible than the project to be God is simply to misuse the term. A free choice with no options is self-contradictory. It makes better sense to speak of man's basic unreflective structural desire, passion, or project (all Sartre's words) to be God as just that, a desire, passion, or project, but not as a free choice. If one limits this latter term to its ordinary sense (which, Sartre admits, means an ability to select among at least two possibilities),[23] we find, as we saw above, that in the *Cahiers* he clearly holds that it is possible, and even necessary if one is to avoid failure, to choose some other fundamental goal than the unattainable one of being God.

I suspect that it was Sartre's overwhelming desire in his early ontology to protect human freedom against all comers that explains his overextended use of terms such as *choice* and *freedom*. Recall, for instance, that at this stage he insisted that *every* conscious act was a free choice, as were such "states" as emotions and desires. In fact, consciousness was *identified* with freedom and choice, and its free projects were often said to be *totally* responsible for the world and its structures.[24] Though the Sartre of *Being and Nothingness* admitted that human freedom was immersed in facticity, he tended to minimize the power of facticity to restrict and curtail freedom. The later Sartre made no such mistake, for he emphasized the power of social and political structures created by others to constrain one's freedom.

I have argued that in the *Cahiers* Sartre advises human beings to cease choosing God as their primary goal and value. However, some commentators claim that Sartre's position is that human beings should pursue this unattainable goal even though they realize that it is unattainable. We should become an *ens causa sui* in an analogous or "symbolic" way, István Mészàros says, and Linda Bell asserts that Sartre wants men to keep this impossible goal as a "regulating ideal" to guide their behavior.[25]

The problem with this interpretation of Sartre's position is that it seems to ignore his own wish at the close of *Being and Nothingness* that we "put an end to the reign of this value [the project to be God]," not to mention his advice in the *Cahiers* that we "renounce" the God project and "refuse to have anything to do with it." Furthermore, Sartre himself indicates in *Being and Nothingness* that his lengthy descriptions of symbolic ways of becoming an *in-itself-for-itself,* through doing and appropriation (having), are descriptions of activities of those who have not undergone the "purifying reflection" necessary for ethics.[26] And the *Cahiers* goes even farther and explicitly labels as "inauthentic" the attempt to symbolically become *causa sui*.[27]

The response of the *Cahiers* to our first issue, then, is that human existence is not inevitably a failure or a useless passion, since human beings can reflectively choose freely to renounce (though not eradicate) their fundamental passion to be God. They can choose as their primary end and value something other than the *ens causa sui*, even though they can never cease structurally to desire that impossible goal. But what should be chosen in its place according to Sartre? This brings us to our second issue: Since Sartre rejects all objective values in *Being and Nothingness*, can he offer any coherent reason for preferring one value or set of values over another?

Critics of Sartre claim that since for him all values are created by human freedom, all are equally arbitrary or subjective. For example, Sartre himself may prefer human freedom and the classless society, but since the value of these objects comes only from his free choice, anyone can freely choose to value the exact opposite. Because he denies objective values, Sartre has no basis for claiming that one person's moral values, including his, should be preferred to any others.[28]

On the other hand, many have noted that on the last two pages of *Being and Nothingness* Sartre appears to suggest that human freedom is the goal one should choose in place of being God. Certainly it is generally recognized by defenders and critics alike that in *Existentialism and Humanism*, "Materialism and Revolution," *What Is Literature?* and elsewhere (including some very late interviews) Sartre does propose human well-being and, more specifically, human freedom as his primary goal.[29] Many have also observed that *Existentialism and Humanism* appears to offer a very concise argument in support of such a choice, an argument that, his critics notwithstanding, is rooted in Sartre's ontological denial of objective values. This cryptic argument has been analyzed elsewhere in some detail, and so I will only repeat it briefly here. *Existentialism and Humanism* suggests that since human freedom is in fact the source of all value, "strict consistency" requires that that freedom be chosen by the individual as his or her primary value.[30] Sartre's point appears to be that if any other object is chosen as one's value, such a choice and value would have little worth if the freedom from which it issued is not itself valued more basically. Needless to say, there is controversy about the validity of this argument, which I will address below.

As for the *Cahiers*, freedom is clearly proposed as an alternative goal to God. Thus, in a text cited above (note 16), Sartre states that pure

189

reflection refuses to have anything to do with the project to be God and, instead, is "the constitution of a freedom which takes itself for an end." Actually, Sartre refers to the goal or end of his morality in various ways in his notebooks, but all are intimately connected to freedom and most are practically equivalent to it. Thus, while he speaks of the final goal of humanity as the freedom of all, the whole or totality of freedom, and of men's ultimate end as "establishing a reign of concrete freedom," "the human reign,"[31] he also calls this reign and goal the city or realm of ends, where each treats the other as an end and all live in intersubjective unity.[32] This city is in turn identified with a socialist society in which there is no ruling class. And the classless society in its turn is designated as the place where "freedom is valued and willed as such."[33] In one passage he goes so far as to say that the ultimate goal of man is not mutual love or respect, nor even a classless society or city of ends. Rather, "the person is his goal under the form of *ek-stase* [i.e., freedom] and gift."[34]

However, this reference to the human person as gift confuses matters by suggesting another ultimate goal than freedom. And indeed the *Cahiers* does say that the human being's "absolute end" after pure reflection or conversion is the creation of the world, and even the "salvation" of the world by making freedom its origin. It states that the "task" and "destiny" of man in generosity, that is, to give oneself to Being so as to make it appear as a world.[35] It is true that to choose as one's absolute end the creation of the world means to choose man as free (for it is precisely because man is free that he is the creator of the world); nevertheless, to make one's goal the free revelation of Being as world is not identical to making human freedom one's goal. For the latter makes *man's* being its goal; the former makes *being's* appearance and foundation primary. Unfortunately, in different places the *Cahiers* affirms each one as the converted person's primary goal.

In fact, this second goal, the free creation of the world, remains extremely formal in the notebooks and sounds much like the goal of all artistic creation for Sartre, namely, the presentation of an object as totally founded by freedom. Just as freedom is always the foundation of every human work of art, so the converted person wills freedom to be the foundation of the real world.[36] The problem with this is that freedom always is just such a foundation no matter what world it makes appear— one of peace, justice, and beauty or one of war, brutality, and ugliness. Unlike the goal of freedom for all in a classless society, which has content to it, the goal of creativity offers no guidance about what kind of world human beings should create. I suspect this is one reason Sartre later labeled the ethics of the *Cahiers* pejoratively a "writer's ethic" and criticized it for being too abstract.[37]

Fortunately, there are rather clear indications that freedom for all is really the primary goal of the notebooks. In some passages Sartre suggests that the reason human beings freely create a world, and thereby give meaning and justification to being, is to attain meaning and justification for their own free existence.[38] Since human reality is fundamentally a being-in-the-world ontologically grounded in being, it can have meaning ultimately only if the world and being have meaning. Thus, though the *Cahiers* proposes two somewhat different primary goals for the ethics it sets forth, creativity seems to be basically a means, while human reality, or human reality as free, is its ultimate end. It is worth mentioning that *What Is Literature?* also discusses the relation between creativity and the classless society or city of ends. However, it mainly considers the creation of works of art; the *Cahiers* is mainly concerned with the creation of the world. *What Is Literature?* argues that since literature is an appeal of freedom to freedom it can "only realize its full essence in a classless society" which will be "the reign of human freedom."[39]

But why should a free human reality be the ultimate end of Sartre's ethics? Certainly not because it possesses some objective or intrinsic value, for Sartre's ontology denies this. The argument of the *Cahiers,* the most elaborate ever offered by Sartre, is put in terms of meaning and justification. As we have already noted, in his universe only human beings, or, more precisely, human beings as free, create all meaning and value. But if any human creations, of self or world, are to possess an *ultimate* (or absolute) value or significance, their source or ground itself must especially be of value. After all, how significant would be a meaning that came from and rested on a valueless source and foundation? As the *Cahiers* often puts it, creation must be justified, given an *absolute* foundation. But man is precisely such a foundation, for he is the absolute—that is to say, irreducible and only—source of all justification in the universe. Man alone can supply a meaningful foundation or justification for his own existence, by accepting in pure reflection his ontological freedom and conferring value on it. If he does so it will thereby possess value and justification, and whatever it creates will in turn be grounded in meaning and so also justified. Thus Sartre argues that freedom should be valued above all else, for only then will it and its creations receive an ultimate (absolute) meaning and justification.[40] (Note that this extended argument of the *Cahiers* is quite similar to the one briefly indicated in *Existentialism and Humanism.*)

A number of critics, while admitting that Sartre does propose freedom as his primary moral value, complain that he remains extremely vague in these early years about the concrete content to be included in such a goal. And Sartre himself later voiced this criticism of his early work. As we noted, the *Cahiers* does identify the reign of freedom with the classless society and socialism, but neither is discussed in any detail. Similarly, when he speaks of creativity as man's goal, Sartre asserts that our task is to reveal the maximum amount of being, for doing so will give maximum meaning to the world and to human existence. Yet, since he admits that all human attitudes create meaning, and that whatever happens to a human being allows him to create more, it is unclear just what creating the maximum amount of being actually entails.[41]

The most powerful suggestion the notebooks offer is their insistence that freedom must be willed concretely, and this means willing human reality not as pure freedom but as freedom immersed in facticity. It is precisely my facticity that makes my freedom and its projects concrete, that gives shape and direction to the goals I seek and the values I create. It is also my facticity that expands or contracts my freedom. It follows that if the social conditions in which I live are oppressive and restrict my freedom, a choice of freedom entails the change or removal of these oppressive structures.[42] To will freedom concretely means to structure the personal and social facticity or situation of human beings so that they have more freedom. The most freedom for all will be available in a classless society where each treats the other as an end. Thus, Sartre's goal here, while lacking in specific details, is not totally contentless.[43] Some years later Sartre's insistence that human freedom is always enveloped in facticity will lead to emphasizing human needs and their role in specifying our goals. This will give even more content to freedom as a goal, for choosing freedom will then mean making attainable those many and various goals that can fulfill human needs. But that is later; needs have only minor significance in the *Cahiers* and in other works of this early period.[44]

It remains to evaluate Sartre's argument that human beings should choose freedom as their primary value. A number of authors have observed that this is persuasive only if one first values logical consistency, rationality, or consistency with reality.[45] Recall that Sartre's argument, developed at some length in the *Cahiers*, maintains that freedom should be valued because it is in fact the source of all values and meaning in the world, including that of my own life. He suggests that it would not be rationally consistent or consistent with the facts of the matter ("consistent" is Sartre's very word in *Existentialism and Humanism*) to value some goal and not value that freedom through which that goal is valued in the first place. But, of course, in Sartre's universe one may freely choose to value irrationality or inconsistency instead of their opposites, for neither possesses any intrinsic or objective value. Is Sartre, in spite of his ontology, presupposing in his argument that rational consistency and consistency with reality have objective value? Some critics have made this charge. I believe rather that Sartre fully recognizes that in the final analysis consistency has value because one freely gives it value. As he says in *Being and Nothingness,* the choice to be rational is "beyond all reasons" and "prior to all logic" because it is precisely by that choice that one confers value on logic and rational argumentation.[46] Indeed it is impossible to give reasons in support of valuing logical consistency or rationality without begging the question!

On the other hand, Linda Bell has claimed that Sartre's argument for freedom rests on the fact that in order to freely value anything whatsoever one must first value freedom: "the choice of anything as a value entails the more fundamental choice of freedom as a value." This is true, she asserts, because "he who wills the end wills the means" and because in Sartre's world freedom "bears a unique position of means to every other value."[47]

But what does it mean to say that "he who wills the end wills the means"? If Bell is claiming that one cannot *in fact* will an end without also willing the means to it—in other words, that willing the end must actually "entail" willing the means—I believe she is incorrect. Surely I can will a goal, such as a healthy body, and yet not will the means to it, such as daily exercise or a low-cholesterol diet. People do this all the time. It may be illogical or stupid to will ends without willing the means to them, but we can in fact do so. To say that "he who wills the end wills the means" can only mean that it is irrational, logically inconsistent, to will an end and not also will the means, because one logically (though not factually) "entails" the other. I agree that he who wills the end (a meaningful life) should, to be reasonable, will the means to it (free-dom). However, I repeat, for Sartre human beings have no absolute obligation to be reasonable or logically consistent, for being or doing so has no objective value. To claim, as Bell does, that "one who allegedly wills the end without at the same time willing the means is not in earnest about willing the end" may also be true. But this does not mean that one cannot really will one without willing the other; moreover, "earnest-ness" has no more objective value for Sartre than does consistency.

A somewhat similar argument is offered by Thomas Flynn.[48] Admit-ting that Sartre's own defense of the need to be rationally consistent is "weak," Flynn suggests that Sartre should have referred to "existential" rather than "logical" consistency. Thus, Flynn says, for a person to freely choose "unfreedom" is not logically inconsistent but "a futile and empty gesture; in fact a nonact." To freely choose unfreedom is "impossible in practice"; it is like choosing not to choose. I think Flynn is correct; it is existentially, or practically, inconsistent to freely choose unfreedom (though it is too strong to claim it is "impossible in practice," for it is evident that people often do freely choose unfreedom, for example freely choosing to enslave themselves to drugs). However, the notion of existential inconsistency does not address the main conclusion Sartre wishes to defend, namely, that freedom should be the *primary* value one chooses in place of being God. Granted, it is existentially inconsistent to freely chose *un*freedom; but it is not existentially inconsistent to freely choose power or pleasure or God (rather than freedom) as one's *fundamental* value, so long as one still awards some lesser value to freedom. Thus I do not think that Sartre can appeal to existential consistency in order to demonstrate that freedom should be one's primary value. Instead, he seems to be correct in suggesting that it would be logically inconsistent, and inconsistent with reality, including human reality, to desire a meaningful existence and not first and foremost value human freedom.[49]

In the *Cahiers* Sartre argues for human freedom as the primary value one should choose in place of being God. The person who undergoes a pure reflection, a conversion, and chooses freedom as his end is called the "authentic" individual.[50] And the authentic individual, Sartre says, does not choose just his own personal freedom as his goal; he chooses to recognize and support as well other freedoms in the city of ends. This brings us to the third and last issue to be discussed: Sartre's view of human relations. If conflict is the essence of human relations (as *Being and Nothingness* apparently maintains), what is the point of ethical norms, especially any that would oblige me to respect and promote the freedom of others?

Countless critics have maintained that Sartre in *Being and Nothingness* holds that all human relations are essentially conflictual.[51] They point out that he describes in great detail a panorama of relations, including love, and shows that ultimately all involve conflict inasmuch as they are attempts at domination and subjugation of oneself by others and/or of others by oneself. Does not Sartre himself state, "Conflict is the original meaning of being-for-others," at the very beginning of his discussion of concrete human relations? Likewise, at the end of this same discussion, even after admitting that human beings do occasionally cooperate and work together, he insists that this does not "modify the results of our prior investigation," namely, that "the essence of the relations between consciousnesses is not the *Mitsein,* it is conflict."[52]

Of course, other early works such as "Materialism and Revolution" and *What Is Literature?* speak of mutual recognition and even collaboration of freedoms,[53] but does this more positive view indicate a radical shift from *Being and Nothingness,* or is Sartre's position there not as negative as it appears? Some commentators have singled out the extremely intriguing footnote he places at the end of *Being and Nothingness.* "These considerations," he writes, "do not exclude the possibility of an ethics of deliverance and salvation. But this can be achieved only after a radical conversion which we cannot discuss here."[54] These commentators claim that this footnote indicates that the human relations Sartre describes there in detail are intended to be relationships only among individuals who have not undergone a conversion, in other words, individuals who attempt to be *ens causa sui* and so react negatively to others who confer on them an object status that they cannot control. Of course, it is tenuous to base such a claim on a footnote. Let us turn to the *Cahiers* to see if it throws any light on how we should interpret Sartre's early view of human relations.

The *Cahiers* reveals the second group of commentators to be correct, for Sartre tells us that *Being and Nothingness* was attempting to set forth not the essential nature or necessary structure of all human relations but only the relationships among unconverted individuals, among inauthentic persons, those who have not undertaken a pure reflection. Early in his notebooks Sartre writes that "the struggle of consciousnesses [only] has meaning before conversion." "After conversion there is no longer an ontological reason for remaining in struggle." Elsewhere he asserts that conversion means "morality without oppression," and in an explicit reference to *Being and Nothingness* he states that conversion can transform the "Hell" of human passions described there.[55] Likewise he stresses repeatedly that oppression or domination is not an inevitable ontological condition, nor a necessary result of history, but a free human decision.

Conversion removes domination and conflict because a converted individual renounces the God project. He no longer attempts to be in total control of his own being like an *ens causa sui.* Thus Sartre states that he is not "troubled" by the fact that others objectify him and give him a dimension of being, his being-object, which he cannot control. By conversion or pure reflection I not only accept my freedom, "I accept my being-object" as an inevitable part of my human condition. As a

195

result my objectivity need not be a cause of alienation and conflict: "It only becomes so if the Other refuses to see in me also a freedom. If, on the contrary, he makes me exist as existing freedom as well as being-object . . . he enriches the world and myself."[56] If both the others and I undergo conversion, reject the God project, and choose our mutual freedoms as our goal, our objectification of each other is not oppressive, nor a source of conflict, but a positive enhancement of our existence. We can cooperatively work together, adopting each other's free projects in intersubjective relationships, which Sartre here calls "authentic love." Relationships of this kind constitute the city of ends or reign of freedom which is the ultimate goal of his morality. Indeed, not only is conflict not a necessary component of human relations according to the *Cahiers;* it can in principle be totally overcome, Sartre says, by a "conversion of all," "an absolute conversion to intersubjectivity," which would involve the transformation of present society into a classless one where each individual would recognize and will the freedom of all.[57]

The problem with the more benign view of human relationships in the *Cahiers,* in which each one wills the freedom of all, is that it appears to be radically incompatible with fundamental epistemological positions of *Being and Nothingness.* For Sartre speaks there as if knowledge of others inevitably involves objectifying them, necessarily entailing an alienation of their free subjectivity. To objectify a subject is to reify it, that is, to "degrade" it to the status of a thinglike object; "objectification is a radical metamorphosis."[58] This is the reason Sartre states that even if I should want to take the other's freedom as my end, the fact that I do so turns it into an object and thus "violates" it. *Being and Nothingness* goes even farther and denies the possibility "of the simultaneous apprehension of [the other's] freedom and of his objectivity." It limits human relations to those of subject to object or object to subject. Sartre writes that we can never achieve "the plane where the recognition of the Other's freedom would involve the Other's recognition of our freedom."[59]

Though the *Cahiers,* as I noted earlier, does stress the possibility of overcoming conflict and oppression, it also repeats many of these themes. It, too, speaks of objectification by others as the "negation of my subjectivity" and thus as a "sin against freedom" because objectification involves freedom's alienation, an alienation "from which man cannot exit." In the same vein the *Cahiers* states that "reification [is] the first ontological phenomenon" between human beings and asserts that to take freedom as an end is to "substantialize" it.[60] However, unlike *Being and Nothingness,* Sartre does not say in his notebooks that a human being can be grasped only as an object or as a free subject.

Rather, he asserts that these narrow alternatives of his earlier work "can be transformed by conversion," which enables us to apprehend each other as both freedom and object, and even primarily as freedom. Because it described human relations before conversion, *Being and Nothingness* lacked, Sartre says, an understanding of the "reciprocal recognition" or "reciprocal comprehension" of freedoms.[61]

The *Cahiers* does indeed contain a rather lengthy discussion of comprehension (or recognition). This explains that unlike knowledge or the look, which simply objectify the other subject, comprehension grasps the other as freedom by sympathetically involving itself in his pursuit of his goals. Comprehension is not merely a passive contemplation or viewing of the other's freedom and its projects, but rather "anticipating" in myself the operation of the other toward his ends. I "outline," Sartre says, "the adoption of the other's goal by myself." I freely "engage myself" in the other's free projection toward his ends and in so doing "preontologically" (i.e., prior to knowledge) grasp his freedom without objectifying it.[62]

For Sartre this sympathetic engagement in the freedom of the other suggests a unity between persons that was totally missing in *Being and Nothingness*. Though he insists that such unity is not an ontological fusion of individuals into some superindividual reality, he does describe it as a "certain interpenetration of freedoms" where "each freedom is totally in the other." Relations of this kind are also present in authentic love and friendship, he says. They involve a "unity of diversity" or a "sameness" that respects the other free individual and overcomes radical separation and otherness; in them, "otherness is recaptured by unity, even though it always remains ontically."[63] This unity enables me to apprehend and will the other's freedom as such, without degrading or reifying it. The inevitable objectifcation of the other that still occurs is, then, not primarily a debasement or a source of conflict, since it is objectification by one who is "the same," one who comprehends the other person primarily as a free subject.

The *Cahiers* constitutes a significant advance beyond the narrow subject-object human relations described in *Being and Nothingess*. It allows for and explains the possibility of comprehending and willing others, as both freedoms and objects. It also significantly supplements other early published works which, although they assert the possibility of subject-to-subject relations, contain no discussion of conversion or comprehension which make such relations possible. Still, Sartre leaves unanswered a question crucial for ethics. Even if one can eliminate human conflict and oppression, and the degrading forms of objectivity, even if one can unite with other subjects and will their freedom, why, according to Sartre, should he do so? What, if any, moral obligation requires me to respect and will the freedom of others rather than seek to dominate and destroy it? Why not choose just my own freedom and ignore that of others? Sartre's answer in his notebooks is anything but clear, but to pursue these issues will require another article.[64]

I have shown here that the *Cahiers* provides invaluable assistance in interpreting Sartre's early ontology and its relationship to morality. It unquestionably supports the view that he did not intend in *Being and Nothingness* to portray the definitive human condition as one of failure, meaninglessness, or conflict. Rather, as he says on the third page of the notebooks, *"Being and Nothingness* is an ontology before conversion." I might add that with its treatment of pure reflection, conversion, comprehension, and justification, and its argument for valuing freedom, the *Cahiers* also contains far more explanation of the bases for positions taken in other early works than do these works themselves. Thus the *Cahiers* shows that even in these early years Sartre believed that if persons renounced the God project and instead willed concretely their mutual freedoms, they could create a life that overcomes despair and conflict. This would be a life in which human beings unite in comprehension and authentic love, act to give meaning and justification to their existence, and strive to realize the human reign, the city of ends.

Notes

1. The following have advanced such criticisms: R. Bernstein, *Praxis and Action* (Philadelphia, 1971); R. Jolivet, *Sartre: The Theology of the Absurd,* trans. by W. Piersol (New York, 1967); I. Mészàros, *The Work of Sartre* (Atlantic Highlands, N.J., 1979); A. Philonenko, "Liberté et mauvaise foi chez Sartre," *Revue de Métaphysique et de Morale* 86 (1981); R. Williams, "The Problem of God in Sartre's *Being and Nothingness,"* in *Phenomenology in a Pluralistic Context,* ed. by C. Schrag and W. McBride (Albany, N.Y., 1983).

2. Recent authors who have maintained that the early Sartre held that human beings are inevitably in conflict are: P. Caws, *Sartre* (Boston, 1979); R. Aronson, *Jean-Paul Sartre—Philosophy in the World* (London, 1980); C. Brosman, *Jean-Paul Sartre* (Boston, 1983); T. Flynn, *Sartre and Marxist Existentialism* (Chicago, 1984); W. Schroeder, *Sartre and His Predecessors* (Boston, 1984); J.-L. Chrétien, "Une Morale en suspens," *Critique* 39 (November 1983); F. Elliston, "Sartre and Husserl on Interpersonal Relations," in *Jean-Paul Sartre, Contemporary Approaches to His Philosophy,* ed. by H. Silverman and F. Elliston (Pittsburgh, 1980); R. Good, "A Third Attitude toward Others: Jean-Paul Sartre," *Man and World* 15 (1982).

3. Caws, *Sartre;* M. Warnock, *Existentialist Ethics* (London, 1967); H. Veatch, *For an Ontology of Morals* (Evanston, Ill., 1971); R. Frondizi, "Sartre's Early Ethics: A

Critique," in *The Philosophy of Jean-Paul Sartre,* ed. by P. Schilpp (LaSalle, Ill., 1981); Chrétien, "Une Morale en suspens"; H. Spiegelberg, "Sartre's Last Word on Ethics in Phenomenological Perspective," *Research in Phenomenology* 11 (1981).

4. T. Anderson, *The Foundation and Structure of Sartrean Ethics* (Lawrence, Kan. 1979); H. Barnes, *An Existentialist Ethics* (Chicago, 1978); F. Jeanson, *Sartre and the Problem of Morality,* trans by R. Stone (Bloomington, Ind. 1980). Others who have defended Sartre from one or more of these criticisms are: L. Bell, "Sartre, Dialectic, and the Problem of Overcoming Bad Faith," *Man and World* 10 (1977); T. Busch, "Sartre's Use of the Reduction; *Being and Nothingness* Reconsidered," in Silverman and Elliston, eds., *Jean-Paul Sartre, Contemporary Approaches;* Flynn, *Sartre and Marxist Existentialism;* P. Knee, "Le Problème moral comme totalisation chez Sartre," *Dialogue* 23 (1984); A Manser, *Sartre, A Philosophic Study* (New York, 1967); Spiegelberg, "Sartre's Last Word."

5. *What Is Literature?* trans. by B. Frechtman (New York, 1966) (hereafter *WIL*); "Materialism and Revolution," in *Literary and Philosophical Essays,* trans. by A. Michelson (New York, 1962) (hereafter *MR*); *Existentialism and Humanism,* trans. by P. Mairet (London, 1973) (hereafter *EH*). An extensive comparison of these works with the *Cahiers* would, of course, be most valuable, but that is not the purpose of this essay.

6. *Sartre by Himself,* filmscript trans. by R. Seaver (New York, 1978), 42–43; "The Last Words of Jean-Paul Sartre," trans. by A. Foulke, *Dissent* (Fall 1980), 398–400.

7. *Being and Nothingness,* trans. by H. Barnes (New York, 1956), 627 (hereafter *BN*). See note 1 above.

8. Ibid., 599

9. Ibid., 566. See also 93–94. We might point out that Sartre apparently held the view throughout his life that human beings naturally desire to be God, for he asserts it in some very late interviews, such as "Self-Portrait at Seventy," in *Life/Situations,* trans. by P. Auster and L. Davis (New York, 1977), 61.

10. *BN,* 90

11. *WIL,* 24, 25, 37, 187, 191, 192; *MR,* 250, 253–55.

12. *EH,* 54.

13. *BN,* 93–95.

14. *Cahiers pour une morale* (Paris, 1983), 577 (hereafter *CM*). I take responsibility for all translations, but I must acknowledge the valuable assistance of Patricia Radzin and Ann Owens. Also see 491, 492, 495, 498–502.

15. Ibid., 578.

16. Ibid.

17. *BN,* 159 ff. *The Transcendence of the Ego,* trans. by F. Williams and R. Kirkpatrick (New York, 1957), 99.

18. *BN,* 581. The same statement is made on 628.

19. *CM,* 22–23, 498. See also 455, 463–64.

20. Ibid., 577.

21. Ibid., 578.

22. Ibid., 577.

23. Ibid., 339.

24. *BN,* 462, 553–56, 599. A good recent article on this topic is by D. Follesdal, "Sartre on Freedom," in Schilpp, ed., *The Philosophy of Jean-Paul Sartre.* In my opinion, a similar overemphasis on freedom is present in *WIL;* see, for example, 23, 28, 33. *MR,* on the other hand, gives significant weight to materiality as limiting freedom, 245 ff.

25. Mészàros, *The Work of Sartre*, 242; L. Bell in her review of my *The Foundation and Structure of Sartrean Ethics* in *Man and World* 14 (1981), 223–24.

26. *BN*, 581. His whole discussion in Part IV, chap. 2, sec. 2, is said to be "aimed only at accessory reflection."

27. *CM*, 536. Page 495 advocates "renouncing" the God project; 578 refers to a "rupture" with it and "refusing" it. Actually, when Bell speaks of guiding our behavior by the regulative idea of God, she is not, in my opinion, using the term *God* in the strict Sartrean sense, namely, as an *ens causa sui*, a conscious being that is the foundation of its own necessity. Her main point seems to be that Sartre believes that a harmony, a unity, both within the various aspects of the self and in the self's relation to its being for others, is achievable and desirable. I have no quarrel with this; Sartre does advocate such harmonies (see *CM*, 467, 484; *WIL*, 37–38); but I do not see how they involve his notion of God in any strong sense.

28. Some of these critics are listed above in note 3.

29. *EH*, 51; *WIL*, 108, 192; *MR*, 245, 253; *Critique of Dialectical Reason*, trans. by A. Sheridan-Smith (London, 1976), 673: "Self-Portrait at Seventy," 84; *On a raison de se révolter* (Paris, 1974), 347; *BN*, 581, 627. Given such texts, I am amazed that Joseph McMahon would write that "Sartre never believed that men should seek to be free," *French Review* 54, no. 6 (May 1981), 879.

30. *EH*, 51. Thomas Flynn has analyzed this argument in detail in chap. 3 of *Sartre and Marxist Existentialism*, as have I in chap. 3 of *The Foundation and Structure of Sartrean Ethics*.

31. *CM*, 483, 406, 302, respectively.

32. Ibid., 17, 95, 174, 177, 302, 416–17.

33. Ibid., 434. See also 109, 169–70, 302, 421. *WIL*, 105, 108, 187, 191, 192; and *MR*, 253, also identify the reign of freedom with democratic socialism. Even in very late interviews Sartre continued to make this identification. See *On a raison*, 347; "Self-Portrait at Seventy," 84.

34. *CM*, 177. *WIL* also states that socialism is not the end but the (last) means before the end that is to place the human person in possession of his freedom, 192.

35. *CM*, 137, 463–64, 490, 499–502.

36. Ibid., 461. Compare with *WIL*, 23, 24, 36, 37, 107.

37. M. Contat and M. Rybalka, *The Writings of Jean-Paul Sartre, A Bibliographical Life*, trans. by R. McCleary, (Evanston, Ill., 1974), I, 228, 295; interview with C. A. Van Peursen, "In gesprek met Jean-Paul Sartre," in *Wending* (The Hague) 9 (March 1954), 18–20, 22–24; *On a raison*, 77–78.

38. *CM*, 135–37, 455, 463–64, 499–504, 512–13, 549–52.

39. *WIL*, 105, 108. Aronson discusses this in chaps. 2 and 3 of his *Jean-Paul Sartre— Philosophy in the World*.

40. *CM*, 465, 498, 502, 514, 543.

41. Ibid., 500–507, 513, 522.

42. Ibid., 148–49, 346–52, 487, 522. *WIL*, 43–45, and *MR*, 252, make the same point.

43. Flynn, *Sartre and Marxist Existentialism*, 38, while admitting that Sartre argues for "choosing freedom," claims that this freedom "is neither the object nor the specific content of our choice. Rather it is what Sartre terms the form of our choice, the ultimate meaning of our actions." This statement is perplexing, for how can one choose freedom as the ultimate meaning of action and not make it the object or content of his choice?

Granted, in *EH* Sartre does refer to freedom as the form of his morality and state that it is a form that admits of a variety of concrete contents. Nevertheless, this form cannot be totally contentless, else one could never determine what matter (specific content) is or is not compatible with it. I do agree, however, that in *EH* (and *CM*) Sartre gives little detail about what concrete contents are compatible with freedom.

44. In a lengthy collection of unpublished notes used for a lecture he gave in 1964 at the Gramsci Institute in Rome, Sartre claims that human need is the *root* of morality and of moral norms. This manuscript is now at the Bibliothèque Nationale, Paris. I thank Robert Stone, Elizabeth Bowman, Michel Rybalka, and Madame Mauricette Berne of the BN, for their assistance in making it available to me.

45. Anderson, *The Foundation and Structure of Sartrean Ethics*, 50–65; Bell, "Sartre, Dialectic, and the Problem of Overcoming Bad Faith," 298; Bernstein, *Praxis and Action*, 154–55; Jolivet, *Sartre: The Theology of the Absurd*, 66; Veatch, *For an Ontology of Morals*, 76–77; S. Lee, "The Central Role of Universalization in Sartrean Ethics," *Philosophy and Phenomenological Research* 46 (1985–86), 63–64.

46. *BN*, 479, 570.

47. Bell, review, 225–26.

48. *Sartre and Marxist Existentialism*, 37–39.

49. Let me add that I do think Sartre's argument here is sound but, to repeat myself, only if human beings first value rationality and consistency. And Sartre himself concedes that we have no absolute obligation to do so.

50. *CM*, 488–92, 497, 577–78.

51. See above, note 2.

52. *BN*, 364, 429.

53. *MR*, 250, 254; *WIL*, 29, 30, 32, 35.

54. *BN*, 412. In the pages that precede his treatment of human relations (361–64), Sartre also states that the relations to be discussed are those that occur in the context of the God project.

55. *CM*, 16, 26, 515. Places where he states that oppression is a human choice are 13, 353, 395–96.

56. Ibid., 515. See also 17–18, 26, 91, 113–14, 293–94, 433–34.

57. Ibid., 17–18, 54–55, 95, 421, 430, 487, 522–24.

58. *BN*, 273.

59. Ibid., 408–10.

60. *CM*, 18, 136, 177, 398, 429, 484.

61. Ibid., 515, 430. In my opinion Chrétien's review of *Cahiers*, "Une Morale en suspens," gives far too little weight to the role of conversion and comprehension in overcoming human conflict. Of course, conversion does not eradicate our desire to be God; it simply refuses to value that impossible goal. Thus there will always be a *tendency* for the converted individual to "fall" by going along with his fundamental desire and so again enter into conflict with others.

62. The *Cahiers* discusses comprehension at 285–303. *BN* mentions comprehension (lxiii, 251, 289, 291, 439) but does not use the term primarily to refer to the apprehension of others but of oneself.

63. *CM*, 16–17, 300, 303, 417, 430.

64. I discuss Sartre's arguments for choosing the freedom of others in "The Obligation to Will the Freedom of Others According to Jean-Paul Sartre," *The Question of the Other*, ed. by A. Dallery and C. Scott, (Albany, N.Y., 1989).

10

SARTRE ON EVIL

Peter Royle

Throughout all the changes in Sartre's career, what remains constant is the nexus of basic philosophical doctrines on which his theory of good and evil depends. I would like to show here how these doctrines are relevant to an understanding of evil in the world, and also (because they are not fully explicit in his writings) to a completer understanding of Sartre himself. The portraits I shall paint do not purport to be exhaustive but are designed to show how certain philosophical conundrums can be clarified by a Sartrean approach. The examples I have chosen are all taken from Sartre's work up to and including 1952 (including the posthumously published *Cahiers pour une morale*). It is in these earlier writings that Sartre's basic moral themes emerge most clearly.

In *Saint Genet,*[1] which used to be considered to be in many ways Sartre's substitute for the promised ethical treatise, he states that for the good citizen "Evil is the Other and it is himself insofar as he is for himself Other than himself, it is the will to be Other and that everything be Other, it is what is always Other than what is."[2] Furthermore, "if it wishes to become absolute, Evil must become an object of detestation for the person who commits it."[3] "Nobody, of himself, before being recognized as guilty, will say: I want Evil . . . *for us,* Evil is impossi-

202

ble."[4] On the same subject in *Being and Nothingness,* where more philosophical language is used, Sartre elaborates:

> To apprehend myself as *evil* can't be to refer to what I am for myself, for
> I am not nor can be evil for myself. First of all because I *am* no more
> evil, for myself, than I "am" a civil servant or a doctor. . . . Next,
> because if I were to *be* evil for myself. I should have to be it in the mode
> of *having to be it,* that is, I should have to apprehend and will myself as
> evil. But that would mean that I must discover myself as willing what
> appears to myself as the opposite of my Good and precisely because it is
> Evil or the opposite of my Good. I must therefore expressly will the
> opposite of what I will in one and the same moment and in one and the
> same respect, that is, I must hate myself insofar precisely as I am
> myself. And, to realize fully, on the ground of the for-itself, this essence
> of wickedness, I should have to assume myself as wicked, that is, ap-
> prove myself by the very act that makes me blame myself.[5]

I cannot, then, be evil for myself, unless, like the "good citizen," I
simply identify good with an established order, and evil with what is
outside it, while casting myself beyond its pale. This is because, however
much I may try to hide the fact, I am generally aware that I myself am
the origin of my values. For Sartre, as for Socrates, what I want is, for
me, good; and what I don't want is bad. How, then, could I want the
bad? It seems certain that some people are weak-willed and do want for
themselves what they themselves recognize as bad; and if they do the
bad things they feel like doing, they are liable to feel remorse, and they
may be driven to repentance. This is what happens to the citizens of
Argos in *The Flies.* And there are surely strong-willed people who want
for themselves what they recognize as bad for themselves, such as masochists. There are many characters in Sartre's work who fall into this
category: Inès in *No Exit* is a prime example, and Baudelaire and Genet
were, according to him, people who willed evil for themselves. How can
such people be accommodated by his theory?

Let us start with people who, without necessarily feeling remorse or
repenting, sincerely admit that they are evil. "Isn't it obvious," writes
Sartre,

> that the sincere man constitutes himself as a thing, precisely to escape this
> thinglike condition, through the act of sincerity itself? The man who
> admits to himself that he is evil has exchanged his disquieting "freedom-
> for-evil" for the inanimate character of an evil being: he *is* evil, he ad-
> heres to himself, he is what he is. But by the same token, he escapes from
> this *thing,* since he is the one who contemplates it, since it depends on him
> to maintain it under his gaze or to let it collapse into an infinity of

particular acts. He derives *merit* from his sincerity, and the deserving man is not the evil one, insofar as he is evil, but insofar as he is beyond his evil. At the same time, the evil is disarmed since it is nothing, except on the level of determinism, and since, by admitting it, I posit my freedom in relation to it: my future is clear, all is permitted me. Thus the essential structure of sincerity doesn't differ from that of bad faith, since the sincere man constitutes himself as what he is *in order not to be it.*[6]

What makes possible sincerity (a bad thing, as opposed to authenticity) is, then, the same thing that makes possible bad faith, or self-deception, of which it is an example: the structure of our consciousness. In its unreflecting or prereflexive state, it is consciousness (thetic or positional consciousness) of its object and at the same time consciousness (nonthetic) of itself. But it can become, in impure or conniving reflection, a quasi-object for itself. The very notion of self-deception implies, in fact, that there are a deceiving self and a deceived self, and that these two selves are ultimately the same (this is one dimension of what Sartre means when he says that we are what we aren't and aren't what we are).

What is humility, particularly the sort of humility associated with a deep sense of moral unworthiness? If one chooses to be humble, perhaps on account of a sense of one's insignificance when compared to God, or a belief in original sin, one will perhaps persuade oneself to believe that one is corrupt, intrinsically evil, not merely a being capable of doing evil but one who sins of necessity. And conversely, if one thinks oneself to be evil by nature, it will be because one has chosen humility as a solution to the problem of being. But to believe that I am evil can only be an act of faith, since, as we have seen, for me, what I want is good. In other words, in regarding myself as evil I shall be in bad faith, for while believing it I shall also not believe it. Everything assures me that what I am doing is good, but my faith warns me that I am nonetheless a sinner. All that I do is thus both good and evil: good, otherwise I shouldn't have done it—and in the last analysis I can do only what appears to me to be good—and bad because it is I, a bad person, who has willed it. The humble man lives constantly on the reflexive level. He is not really interested in others; he is himself the end of all his acts. If I am hungry, I want to eat; but I lie in wait for my desires, which must in principle be bad. So I fast. This leads to a conflict between my reflexive consciousness and my reflected consciousness. However, in fasting I am still doing what I want. Could it then still be evil? The only reply, if we wish to avoid a vicious see-saw, is no. So I identify myself with my unreflecting consciousness, which is the source of evil, and my reflexive consciousness becomes my conscience, that is, the look of the Other. "I," there-fore, am evil, but because I outsmart myself, with the grace of God, the good that I do can be appreciated in a spirit of humility. But what happens if I am proud of my humility, which is inevitable if indeed I consider humility to be a virtue? This will only confirm me in my view of myself as a person who sins of necessity, a person who in this instance appears to be steeped in pride; for I'll consider myself guilty of having attributed to myself something I owe to myself indeed, but which accord-ing to my principles I ought to recognize as an effect of God's grace, and the vicious process will start all over again.

But humility is not remorse. It is to be situated halfway between true self-affirmation and repentance. There is remorse only when a person feels really guilty, in other words, when he recognizes himself as the author of an act that his chosen judges condemn. Unlike willed humility, remorse, if genuine, is not action but passion. That is to say, it is not an emotion of the kind described in *The Emotions,* where emotions are seen as actions, but actions upon oneself. It is a feeling, such as shame, which arises unbidden from one's interaction with others, a passion in the classi-cal sense. But it is a passion that can be transformed forthwith—and, in the case of the humble person, generally is—into action for psychological reasons that vary from individual to individual.

Is remorse then always to be shunned? Not at all. When Electra asks Orestes if the Corinthians, whom Sartre contrasts favorably with the people of Argos, ever feel remorse, he replies: "Sometimes. Not often." The fact is that there is a distinction between remorse action and re-morse passion. We are all open to remorse, whether we assume our freedom or not. But whereas the self-deceived person may turn this passion into a pattern of behavior, the authentically free person will never do so. Moreover, his remorse will never stem from lacking the courage of his acts, as in the case of the person who steeps himself in it, but will depend either on a "bona fide" mistake or on a free change of project, in the light of which a certain act from his past will be seen as reprehensible.

What about the repentance to which I may be driven by remorse? In general its secret goal is to hide from myself my responsibility as a creator of values. To say "I have done evil," given that for me evil is what I don't want, must mean that I have done something that I didn't want to do. But it could be said, provided we distinguish the conse-quences of an act from the act itself, that I always want to do what I do. Thus, if I say that I have done evil, I thereby show, unless I have had a change of project, that I deny all responsibility for the creation of my

205

values. For I leave it to others to define good and evil according to their will, and thus place myself in their power. And, according to Sartre, the absolute Other, who guarantees the values of an alienated society, is God.

We must, however, distinguish clearly between the notion of guilt and that of responsibility. The former is imposed upon me by the other (including the other I may have become for myself), the latter derives from my essential freedom, and must be assumed. The main theme of *The Flies* is the need to replace guilt and remorse by a sense of genuine responsibility; and the person who courageously accepts his responsibility, which means in the case of Orestes a readiness to remain true to his acts, will, according to Sartre, be beyond such excuses.

Now, what about the person who genuinely wills evil and is proud of it? It is possible, of course, that in willing evil he is merely aiming to shock, to challenge through rebellion values he really accepts, and which are dictated by others. Such is no doubt the case with much youthful rebellion. But in this case there is no challenge to Sartre's theory, since such a person merely wants what others don't want while still defining himself morally in relation to a system he has not intellectually overthrown. What is interesting and significant in Sartre's theory is the fact that it can accommodate, on account of his theory of consciousness, the phenomenon of people who are genuinely evil for themselves, a phenomenon that has traditionally been overlooked or thought to constitute an almost insoluble paradox.

Let us look at what he has to say about Baudelaire:

And it is not by accident that Baudelaire sees in Satan the perfect type of suffering beauty. Defeated, fallen, guilty, denounced by . . . Nature, exiled from the Universe, overwhelmed by the memory of the unexpiable fault, devoured by unassuaged ambition, transfixed by the look of God freezing him in his diabolical essence, constrained to accept in the depth of his heart the supremacy of Good, Satan yet wins over God himself, his master and his conqueror, through his suffering, through this flame of sad dissatisfaction which, in the very moment when he consents to this crushing, shines like an unexpiable reproach. In this game of "loser takes all" it is the vanquished who, *qua* vanquished, carries off the victory. Proud and defeated, filled with the feeling of his uniqueness in the face of the world, Baudelaire compares himself with Satan in the secret recesses of his heart. And perhaps human pride has never gone farther than in this always stifled, always contained cry which resounds throughout Baudelaire's work: "*I am Satan!*" But what is Satan, at bottom, if not the symbol of disobedient, sulky children demanding to be frozen in their singular essence by the paternal look and who do evil in that framework of good in order to affirm their singularity and have it consecrated?[7]

What we see here is that for Sartre evil is parasitic on good, just as nothingness depends on being. This can be the good according to others, or the good according to oneself, but in either case it is the good that comes first; and in either case the person who wills evil also wills his own defeat—which for Sartre is the essence of vice. In the case of the person who rebels against the values of others without having anything to put in their place, he devotes himself to defeat in bad faith. If he doesn't choose, like the "salaud," a justified place in a society that he consecrates, it is because, like certain intellectuals, he prefers, as his fundamental justification, the place of the critic. This means that he doesn't really want to change society; for it is society, precisely, in its present form, that provides him with the opportunity to oppose it and thus to justify himself. He will therefore have to beware of effective action and devote himself surreptitiously to failure. Such people, like Garcin in *No Exit*, are often pacifists.

But as I have said, it is also possible to reject one's own good, to want for oneself what one doesn't want for oneself, and to do so in complete good faith. Such a person was Genet, on whom Sartre casts a much more favorable judgment than he does on Baudelaire; and such is Inès in *No Exit*. Because she is a lesbian (and this is a pattern of behavior that she has chosen), Inès is damned by society and decides, in total lucidity, to damn herself. This is why she is at home in Hell, which reflects her former domestic situation, and in which, given her sadomasochistic tendencies, she is the torturer (and self-torturer) in chief. Profoundly wounded by society's demand that because she is a woman she should transform herself into an object, she devotes herself solemnly to the humiliation of the male. This takes the form of trying to transform herself into a male to give herself as an object of pleasure to a woman. Hence she becomes a masochist; and hence also she confers on sex a ritual and symbolic role. This project is obviously doomed to failure. For it is impossible in principle to *use* the free transcendence of a genuine subject. Like all masochists, according to Sartre, Inès will end by treating her partner as an object. And to the extent to which she has identified herself with the other woman, she will suffer her degradation as her own and will be conscious of having yet further humilated the sex that she wished to avenge.

This explains her sadism. Feeling that she has humiliated her part-

207

ner without having attained any of her goals, and having forgotten, no doubt, the very object of her activity, she feels rancor not toward herself but toward her partner—for having allowed herself to be manipulated and thus having contributed to the degradation of their sex. She now tries to make her partner horribly aware of this degradation.

Sadism, however, for Sartre, is also doomed to failure. For the sadist is seeking to appropriate the transcendent freedom of the victim; and this remains, by the very nature of things, out of reach. Furthermore, the more the sadist persists in treating his victim as an instrument, the more this freedom escapes him. Inès, however, is fully aware that her enterprises are doomed to failure; and as a masochist she seeks failure itself as her principal goal. She does this because her hatred of men is stronger than her love of freedom. Provided she can involve men in her downfall, she doesn't worry about failing. And that is precisely what she is trying to do, symbolically, in her sexual relations. They represent a desperate effort to mutilate men, which means that for her a male must always be at least symbolically present during her sexual acts. For her, as for Baudelaire (and also, in a different sense, for Sartre himself), sex is not a duet but a trio.[8]

Inès's attitude conceals, in effect, a profound contradiction. Nobody will ever be able to realize, according to Sartre, the impossible synthesis of the in-itself-for-itself. But Inès, instead of recognizing this as an ontological truth, attributes it to the position occupied historically by women in a society dominated by men. At the same time she has recourse to a historical, indeed magic, means in her attempt to resolve the problems posed by this situation. Since Being—that is, Paradise—is out of reach, instead of opting for authentically human existence (which, for Sartre, is on the other side of despair and involves a radical conversion), she chooses Hell. It is obvious that for a woman of her intelligence it would have been better, on the contrary, to fight in company with other women, and no doubt also with enlightened men, to transform historically the situation of women. Instead, she chooses not revolution but, like Baudelaire, revolt. As we have seen, one of the characteristics of this type of rebel is to rejoice finally in the status quo. It's in vain, therefore, that one begins by being evil in the mode, as Sartre says, of having to be so. After all, one chooses one's own values: in wishing to preserve the status quo, one inevitably becomes it in the mode of the in-itself. This is equivalent to delivering oneself up body and soul to the oppressive Other. Thus, from being a tortured victim one becomes a more or less open accomplice of the oppressor.

It is realizing the futility of evil that motivates Goetz, in *The Devil and the Good Lord,* to try to become the only person in history to accomplish genuine good. Unfortunately, however, he is more concerned with putting on an act for God, to whom he leaves the task of defining the good, than with achieving practical goals in the real world. Ultimately his good is simply another form of evil, treachery in a new guise.

> Listen, *curé;* I had betrayed everybody and my brother, but my appetite for treason wasn't assuaged: so one night, under the ramparts of Worms, I came up with a plan to betray Evil, that's the long and short of it. Only Evil is not to be so easily betrayed: it wasn't Good that came out of the dice shaker: it was a worse Evil. Anyway, what does it matter: monster or saint, I didn't give a damn, I wanted to be inhuman.[9]

What Goetz realizes at the end of the play is that the only legitimate morality for human beings is one that is based on the understanding that they themselves are the source of their own values. "I wanted pure love: foolishness; to love one another is to hate the same enemy: and so I shall espouse your hatred. I wanted the Good: stupidity; on this earth and in this time, Good and Bad are inseparable: I agree to be bad in order to become good."[10]

To be bad in order to become good is obviously not really to be bad at all. It is, however, possible to argue that we must choose real evils in order to overcome the obstacles that keep our good from becoming a real and not merely imaginary good, the good of which we desire to be the foundation. To act for or refrain from acting against evil in accordance with this insight is to be really bad. Such a person, says Sartre,

> *likes* Evil as the adversary which allows him to affirm himself. . . . But we see immediately (and he refuses to see) that he likes *for himself* a moderate evil . . . and especially the Evil *of others.* . . . [S]ince Evil becomes the essential means of realizing the Good, Evil becomes the essential and the Good the inessential.[11]

Since evil is, according to Sartre, what by our own definition must be eradicated, and since man will always be movement and transcendence, our only coherent attitude to evil is to try to abolish it. It is for future generations to decide their own good, thereby encountering their own obstacles. If Goetz describes himself as being bad in order to become good, it is because objectively, as Sartre says, revolt is crime; and because subjectively, an account of the necessary suffering it entails, it is experienced as evil.[12]

These portraits owe their interest to the fact that they embody at-

209

tempts to grapple with some of the difficulties in the logical definition that what I want is, for me, good. More than perhaps any philosopher, Sartre is able to accommodate and to illuminate the puzzling phenomena I have discussed. Even if his theory brings with it a whole new range of problems, it represents an obvious challenge to all those who would try to explain why we choose evil.

Notes

1. *Saint Genet: comédien et martyr* (Paris, 1952), 31. All references in this essay are to the French editions of the works cited, and all translations are my own.
3. Ibid., 32.
4. Ibid., 39.
5. *L'Etre et le néant* (Paris, 1943), 332–33.
6. Ibid., 105.
7. *Baudelaire* (Paris, 1947), 113–14.
8. For Sartre (witness his descriptions of *le Tiers*—the Third—in *Being and Nothingness* and *le tiers régulateur*—the regulatory third—in *Critique de la raison dialectique*) the basic structure of human reality is triadic. Whereas normal lovers try to escape the gaze of the Third (they inevitably fail, and this is one of the reasons why, according to Sartre, love is doomed to failure), perverts like Inès take pleasure in his presence.
9. *Le Diable et le bon Dieu* (Paris, 1951), Act III, dixième tableau, scène IV.
10. Ibid., Act III, onzième tableau, scene II.
11. *Cahiers pour une morale* (Paris, 1983), 108.
12. Ibid., 416.

11

THE REVOLUTIONARY HERO REVISITED

Pierre Verstraeten

At the end of *Violence et ethique* I stumbled upon an aporia, which I attributed to the development of Sartre's dialectial works: theater, philosophy, and political essays. Those who make the revolution are necessarily personally motivated by reasons that are suspect from the point of view of its universal meaning, and those who give the right reasons to carry out the revolution don't make it. In other words, the project of concrete universality, the revolution, is sustained by people who remain attached to their particular individuality while those who are detached from everything and from themselves by the idiosyncrasy of their psychological development are not willing to undertake it. Those who think that they are concerned with the public good are incorrigible individualists, while those who have eyes only for their own souls are naturally ascetic and therefore singular enough to be already in touch with the universal. In short, those whose detachment from desire is obvious remain attached to their own profile, while those who are driven by desire are detached from the larger scheme of things by the very content of their personal problem. The individualism of the first nourishes itself on the public welfare; the singularity of the second nourishes itself on the culture of their inner nothingness. The first consider their individuality synonymous with a universal cause; the second expand their inner life by

211

negating the world. The first construct in the positive; the second dissolve in the negative. But it seems as impossible to build by radical negativity as by negating the world while reconstructing it.

Nevertheless, the same freedom is involved, and the one path is apparently as radical as the other. But the opposing destinies have little in common, whether they point to the active freedom of the man of action—including Sartre himself in his public activism—or the passive freedom of the artist—including Flaubert insofar as Sartre speaks about him—or whether the militant or the adventurer. On the one hand we have the doctrinaire, the ideologue, or the militant; on the other hand, the aesthete or the self-experimentation of the beautiful soul. To further generalize these oppositions, the first reflects the dialectic of the for-itself and the in-itself or of praxis and inertia; the second reflects the Being of this dialectic in "universal contingency." We move from one freedom to the other, or from one inauthenticity to the other.

Sartre long dreamed of a synthesis of the two characters as being the dialectical synthesis par excellence. But through the revolutionary hero, this synthesis reveals itself as vague, if not illusory. I had thought that Goetz would do, that he constituted the synthesis of interior negation become conscious of the necessity of transforming the world from this preliminary experience, while conserving its negating radical nature. Indeed, until *The Devil and the Good Lord* Sartre's theater gave us the alternative of the "moralist" and the "dialectician," with the dialectician being favored: Hoederer as against Hugo in *Dirty Hands*. Orestes as against Electra in *The Flies*. But this priority was psychological only. Sartre's dramatic effectiveness made it attractive, but we were left with a purely critical dialectic. With Goetz the duality interiorizes itself in his own experience, and we follow his becoming a dialectician through the trials of good, of evil, and of ascetic, purely internal, mortification. At the end of a decisive and crucial trial this leads to a fight to the death and to seeing him preserve and transcend his prior experience and so end up with a properly dialectical vision. I named this, in keeping with the first plays, a critique of dialectic.

From this perspective the paradox of *The Condemned of Altona* lies in the fact that the same structural itinerary, now pursued by Frantz, did not lead to the same synthesis—but rather to a meaningless impasse, that of death. This play yields no other message than an individual and historical failure. At the most the message was to exonerate the century, a non-dialectical message destined for future centuries.

Certainly one could make a positive diagnosis of *The Condemned of Altona* by an outside witness or spectator, as Michel Contat has done by

212

noting Sartre's lucidity about the murderous destiny of inhuman causes in which a nation engaged its sons (specifically, in France the Algerian war). But this ignores that the play itself delivered another message, the message of failure, and that it delivered it from a structure of dialectical becoming identical to Goetz's. In short, the very principle of a dialectical synthesis developed in *The Devil and the Good Lord* could be retrospectively canceled or contested by this new destiny. It was still possible to prop up *The Condemned of Altona*'s nondialectical destiny in a dialectical way, by referring to the historical situation temporarily imposing an impasse on the dialectical ambition. But this would grant no autonomy to the force of conviction that led Sartre to recasting the problematic through an identical structure of development in Goetz and Frantz.

In this sense, we can just as well see *The Condemned of Altona* as Sartre's abandonment of the goal of dialectical synthesis and the return to an unbridgeable duality between the man of action, engaged in the world according to a moral, ascetic, realistic, and even dialectical perspective; and the artist, the adventurer—again, Flaubert's passive freedom compared to Sartre's active freedom.

Frantz's delirium, and especially the punishment that he derives from it, reactivates as the very enemy of freedom the separation and the heterogeneity Sartre had attempted to introduce as the starting point of political theater. The realistic figures of Slick and Nasty, which serve as foils to the man of action in his successive stages, attempt to reabsorb the opaque and contingent aspect of being that is pre- and anti-human. This is the being revealed by *Nausea* in its irreducible necessity of fact and which the artists Sartre studied had attempted to penetrate in their clairvoyance, if not to capture it with their art (see, for example, the beauty, in spite of their phenomenological falsity, of the works of Faulkner, Wols, etc.).

In other words, we are once again left to face a split between the being in immanence of man, of meaning, of history, and the being in transcendence of that immanence. The ontological argument of *Being and Nothingness* bore witness to this impasse as the in-itself's necessity of being: *Critique* II indicated it as the being of the "totalization of envelopment." This was the being itself of the relationship of the for-itself and the in-itself—not the phenomenon of being, still indebted to the intentional correlation, but the being of phenomena, the basis of the ambition of the phenomenological ontology of *Being and Nothingness*.

This duality is revealed by the end of *Critique* II and simultaneously resolves a series of tensions about the work and even the man Sartre, or rather it displays them clearly enough to measure the full extent of the split. I think this is because it neither expresses an unhappy conscious-ness nor a consciousness dialectically driven by contradictions, but more properly a conscience torn between the terms of an alternative lived by one and the same man and yet lacking a common link, between two dimensions of human existence that are at once inevitable and irreconcil-able. The unhappy conscience postulates misfortune as redemption, be-cause misfortune bears witness to a religious absolute; the contradiction bears witness to an antagonism, hence to a final triumph of one thesis over another, and even eventually to their synthesis, now becoming a "thesis" for an eventual new contradiction. As for the divided conscious-ness displayed in *Critique* II, it presupposes the common fabric being torn apart.

Traditionally this means the man of action and the respectable man, the philosopher and the marginal man, Faust and Mephisto. But with the "separated" or "cleaved" conscience in unity, in one and the same person, the terms of the separation present neither the same goal nor the same ambition, and hence they do not become an effective alternative to each other. At stake, rather, are two irreducible dimensions. They con-demn the philosopher to endless swingings, from one to the other. For as much as he wanted to act on the world without stopping to think about it, in other words, giving in to his wish to transform it without abandon-ing his desire to change life, to transform the world, like Marx, means to act with others according to a universal project. To change life, like Rimbaud, means to live one's life in contingency and to feel oneself awry in the awareness of the absence of all legitimacy.

In this sense what could appear as dualism developing itself in time, according to the successive stages of the man of action facing the realist's obstinate opacity, opens out at the end of *The Condemned of Altona* into an unbridgeable separation, with no other synthesis than a balancing. There is no sense of man in his relationship to others, but a sense of the absence of sense. Or rather it is still possible for man to create one that will always remain precarious, temporary, transitory, and ultimately use-less: "History is revealed to fighting individuals and groups as *riddled;* its deaths are billions of holes which pierce it; and each time, through this fundamental porousness, the fragility of praxis-process is given in experi-ence, as the universal presence of its being-in-exteriority."[1] This is *Cri-tique* II. And again: "A man dies always too early or too late."

But it is important to recall the successive stages that have led to this aporia whose status I have just reinterpreted. The problem was to inter-pret the impasse of the dialectical model, at the very level of the specific originality of a dialectical ethics: in a fight to the death. This allowed the hero to reveal himself while sweeping away the idealistic scruples of his moral vision of the world, and while mediating the meaning of a universality achieved through this risk of death, assumed through the very violence of the defeat inflicted on his adversary. This offered a model of the intelligibility of the revolutionary conversion, through the daring sacrifice of his most personal interests and the discovery that man is ready to die for a human "cause."

This rests on the most modern forms of "conversion": Hegel's struggle of master and slave, Marx's class struggle (assumed by the class that has suffered an absolute wrong), Lacan's symbolic assumption of the risk of death with the test of castration, and the mortifying conquest of man's status. These writers perfected the tradition of the Platonic philosopher's bodily death, the redeeming death of Christianity, the Kantian sacrifice of one's own specific interests in order to rise to the height of moral law. In short, they perfected a timeless tradition in philosophy, marking the intellectual or existential mutation to truth or the absolute.

Certainly Sartre criticized the Hegelian model of the struggle of consciousnesses as proof of the other's existence. But he was far from having despised the risk of death, put forward as proof and affirmation of the unconditionality of freedom in situations of exploitation or oppression. Very much to the contrary, in impossible situations, death is the always possible recourse to freedom at the cost of life.

When he brilliantly affirms in *Critique* I that the possibility of death is not given with life (whose only reality resides in the perpetuation of its being),[2] he immediately makes clear that from then on, if the hypothesis of death is envisioned or even adopted, death is in some way the continuation of life, exemplary and unsubjugated. Even Foucault made this lyrical formulation about revolutionaries, in speaking of Iranians: "Because the man who rises up is ultimately without explanation, there must be a tearing away which interrupts the thread of history, and its long chains of reasons, so that man can 'really' prefer the risk of death to the certainty of having to obey."[3]

As I have said, *The Condemned of Altona* ended with conflict between the hero, who had run the greatest risks, and the identity of self and being, without hope of synthesis. Frantz's self-identity with being assumes the guilt of the age and renders all human agitations ridiculous. Throughout the play, the unfolding of such inhuman identities submerges the protagonists' vain attempts to inscribe their intentions on the world. This is expressed in many places: "The innocent were twenty years old, they were the soldiers; the guilty were fifty, they were the fathers." ". . . I am no longer sure which of us made the other. . . . He

215

created me in his image—unless he has become the image of what he created." "Mine? But I never choose, my dear girls! I am chosen. Nine months before my birth they had chosen my name, my career, my character, and my fate." "What are you telling me? Your life story or mine?" "I am mankind, Johanna. I am every man and all mankind. I am the century. . . . Like anyone." "You wanted to build ships and you built them—I built them for you.—What! I thought you made me for them. . . ." And so on.[4]

Nevertheless, in *Violence et ethique* I tried to save the model of attaining dialectical ethics in order to safeguard Sartre's original contribution to the dialectical intelligibility of the revolutionary hero. In respect to Robert Jordan in *For Whom the Bell Tolls* or Kyo in *Man's Fate*, Merleau-Ponty thought that, deprived of God and of an assured end of History, the contemporary hero—"One always lives with others, but one dies alone" (Hemingway)—saw no other meaning than "faithfulness to oneself" in commitment to others. Robert Jordan makes Maria the depository of his image after his death as a guerrilla. A moving psychology, but without philosophical justification. Certainly, in *Humanism and Terror*, Merleau-Ponty tried to justify the vile dialectic of the Moscow trials and of spontaneous admissions of guilt, in the name of a progressive universalization of history to be realized in socialism, if not communism. Because universal freedom was to be created, or because it could only come about in a permanent revolution, the essential thing was to preserve its "principle" against any and all denials. Otherwise history is abandoned to "the sound and the fury," empty of all meaning. But again, demanding a horizon of reconciliation has no other philosophical legitimation than the negative one of rejecting the present situation, or the positive but irrational one of a vow presumably guaranteed by one's own commitment to a universal society.

Hence, in *Violence et ethique* I argued that Sartre's great contribution lay in rationally elucidating the conditions for existentially arriving at that will to commitment. I called this the logic of the "tempering" of the hero by becoming dialectician.

Thus it was necessary to try and save the model in spite of Frantz's failure, and to begin by denouncing the religious atavism of the conversion model, as well as the traditional aporias involved in the transmission of grace. If grace is freedom and spreads only as a result of the Holy Spirit's return after Christ's sacrifice, we must ask not only how the hero achieves liberation but, equally, how he will make others achieve it, under his own personal guarantee. Certainly I thought that the religious mortgage on the question did not disqualify its solution. After all, the spirit's immanent becoming in Hegelianism was not undermined by the fact that spiritual ambition, in the course of the history of Western civilization, had been unduly projected into the heaven of a religious transcendence.

Nevertheless, the religious genealogy of the conversion should not have left its intellectual structure untouched; there must, after all, be a meaning, a good, a true, a horizon of reconciliation, in order that the conversion can be considered as deserving a critical examination.

Besides, Sartre was not fooled by it. In our interview, "I Am No Longer a Realist," he showed a very clear resistance to this dialectical model which he had in some sense instigated. He expressed a profound suspicion of the meaning and content of its revolutionary goal:

> One can always suspect it, in fact I still dispute it! For example, I have chosen something at this very moment [an alliance with Maoists]; I have chosen in a certain way, but I am not sure it is the right way. Freedom is all the time! It is there, and when it fails, this means it has alienated itself all over again! . . . I know what I must tear myself away from, but I do not quite know what for. Or to put it another way, the thing that is the least well founded in me is optimism, the reality of the future. I have this optimism but I cannot find a basis for it. And that's the heart of the matter. . . .[5]

Throughout the interview, I resisted for the sake of the possibility of revolution, without realizing that it was not an obvious "fact" whose possibility (individual and heroic) I was attempting to establish. At least it was not obvious for Sartre, because for him this fact and its opposite were totally in suspense.

Deep down, I based myself on the almost ad hominem argument of the persistent theme of *conversion* in his work. It was present abstractly in the idea of a still-incomplete ontological freedom, and concretely in his intellectual biographies of Genet and Flaubert. We know how Sartre resolved the problem in both cases: by recourse to a detailed synthesis showing a conditioning of freedom, by freedom, to freedom. Flaubert's conversion is what Sartre called (1) the *reversal* of the role of actor for others. Flaubert moves to the exclusive interior scene of his own subjectivity after the second castration inflicted by his father. It is also (2) the transformation of his project of actor by assumption-defiance of the paternal sanction in the modality of its self-cancellation at the heart of its interiority. In other words Gustave intensified his imaginary life, or his life as imaginary, through his negation of the world in and by his ego-for-nothingness. He simultaneously underwent the test of the "essential poverty" of an imaginary realm reduced to his volatile fantasies, and discovered the super-significance of graphemes as support for his demi-urgical will-for-evil. (3) Finally, we come to the *conversion,* which according to Sartre leads to a "modification of structure" of his "private games."[6] This time it is a quasi-mechanical result, namely, the exploitation of the natural power of the graphemes as hallucinogenic satisfaction of his desire, and thus as budding writer. This acutely raises the question of why Sartre so firmly rejected the idea of "conversion."

One can guess that he did not want to throw the baby of socialism out with the bathwater of the conditions for bringing it about, that is, the revolutionary hope with the absence of historical perspectives, a fortiori with the absence or failure of the "revolutionary hero." Sartre's ethical radicalism is applied to universal reconciliation: it should simultaneously be affirmed and recognized as impossible under prevailing historical conditions. At bottom this is the opposition of Lucien and Jean in the screenplay *In the Mesh*—Lucien, the just one who is intransigent about principles and refuses all consideration of conditions, opposes Jean's ethical radicalism, which gauges the impossibility of any absolute principle, even a revolutionary one, and thus accepts his actions' relativism or ambiguity. At the same time Jean preserves his people's revolutionary anger, at his own expense, rather than letting it sink into the sad morass of poverty or of heroic struggle, doomed in advance, against a great power. In short, Jean is a hero subject to public disgrace because he affirms and defends a horizon of reconciliation as well as its historical impossibility. He dialecticizes the impossibility with the necessity and vice versa, into the "politics of the lesser evil." As a result, for Sartre there is no question of a model of attaining dialectical tempering. This is because its eventual failure—obvious in Frantz's case—would lead to abandoning any possible socialist perspective. Jean is only an "immediate" dialectical hero, meaning that he is legitimate only from a psychological point of view. This changes nothing about the central question I raised in attempting to structure the conditions of revolutionary possibility. This is precisely the ambiguity of *Critique of Dialectical Reason,* which tries to establish the conditions of possibility of a single history, while accumulating the "theoretical" obstacles to its realization. As long as what is constraining is "the fact," one can hope that the obstacles will be overcome. But when the "fact" itself becomes blurred or is effaced, the obstacles reveal themselves as foreshadowing an impossibility—of creating the desired conditions for achieving the "fact" of a reconciled society, a world revolution.

The theoretical explanations follow clearly from the text of "I Am

No Longer a Realist": one knows what one must reject, but it is not possible to make blueprints or a designer's model for what one must do. One can always propose viewpoints, but one must be conscious of the impossibility of imposing them on future generations.

The model entailed a struggle beginning with the projection of an ideal, the mediation of this idealism by violence, and universalization. Taking into consideration its difficulties did not involve questioning its Christian genealogy, but diluting its revolutionary character in the more general, and hence trivializing, problematic: the problematic of attaining culture, or interiorizing the "symbolic order." This order is a discursive and rational one, and Oedipal identification is signified through it by an interposed ideal, be it of an imperative or a value. In other words, in a decisive struggle situation it appears in that initial stage which motivates Sartre's definition of man as son-of-man in the moral treatises after the *Critique*. The crucial conflicts, during which the hero defined himself decisively as "dialectician," reactualize the first struggle, carried out in childhood against the father. They do so in the nature of ideals supposedly at stake in the challenge: imperatives and values to be interiorized under the threat of castration. But a more radical double criticism soon attacked this development, rejecting the model's principle, even in its generalized and banalized form. The Oedipus complex not only stopped having any rights as a royal road to attaining man's humanity, but it also found itself radically denounced as a typically classical model by the generation of May 1968.

The first step consisted in a sort of neutralization of the Oedipal model in the name of a more radical universalization of the status of man. This went beyond man as paradigm of the tradition. Foucault did this by showing its character as historically determined and dominated by the philosophy of finitude, which draws the whole of man's biological, economical, and cultural experience into an anthropological dogmatism. This was also done by multiplying the paths to achieving the "symbolic order" (different types of neuroses: hysterical, obsessional, and phobic). This cast doubt on the paradigmatic function of the classical hero, insofar as he might belong to one of the categories that psychologically defined the typology of the differing possible discourses: the hysteric's discourse, that of the academic, of the expert, or of the analyst. More radically, we must not forget the placing in orbit of a generalized rationality through the psychological modalities of "avoiding" the Oedipus complex (psychoses and perversions). In short, these two levels of criticism abandon any kind of hierarchy concerning the order of the multiple norms governing the different types of human existence. The generationally inspired denunciation by May 1968 attacked the very principle of privilege granted to the "symbolic order," linked its rationality with the dominant interests of society, and attacked its function of socially reproducing privileges favoring the "heirs" of the holders of power. More generally, the denunciation focused on the blatant "triumphalism" of the image of the hero as the strongest. The hero as ideal type rejects any way of life not centered exclusively on the criteria of efficiency, of optimum production, and of the endlessly increasing reproduction of "this" man's hold on the world. This was the Nietzschean and Marcusean influence on the May 1968 movement.

Hence my model went astray, because it concerned itself only with attaining the classical image. I therefore concluded my postscript to *Violence et ethique* (for myself and for Sartre, who was moreover rapidly moving to align himself with the Maoists) with the resurgence of a "realistic idealism." I was referring to thousands of Hugos taking to the streets in the name of pure principles, who rejected the dialectical model of the lesser evil by demanding a purer universality. They tried to be more radical, as well as more effective in their simple mass uprising: They were the pure force of a purified universality. I wrote an article that became the editorial of *Les Temps Modernes* for those months, which said specifically: "It seems therefore that we are being dealt a new set of cards. There is a relatively general revision of the rules of the game. In short, the philosophical and political cards have been completely reshuffled." In fact, it was a rather confused situation, which would not be without consequences. . . .

First of all, Sartre revises his classical conception of the intellectual: he no longer simply opposes him to "the theoretician of practical knowledge" as in the lectures in Japan[7] and in the interview he had given to the Belgian journal *Le Point*.[8] In order to claim the title of intellectual, it is no longer enough to radically proclaim the universality of one's properly theoretical activity, in opposition to the "practitioner of knowledge" who applies his knowledge in the "specific" framework of his own society's systems of norms and values. Therefore, it is no longer enough to commit oneself alongside society's victims, the dispossessed, the exploited, and the oppressed, in the name of the same universality. Nor is it enough to be faithful, with the greatest possible lucidity, both to the party of the exploited and to evaluating the truth of its discourses. No, one must completely abandon that outmoded conception of the intellectual—so very inactive and unmilitant, so elitist and privileged—and, as Sartre says in "I Am No Longer a Realist," in borrowing Mao Zedong's formula, "get off one's horse." This means not "visiting" the people from atop one's intellectual knowledge, but placing oneself at the people's level, and beginning by renouncing the caste or class privileges of the intellectual's dominating role.

This position, as can be seen immediately, reinforces the generational criticism of reason. And, in fact, of all the militant movements, Maoism, with all its ex-intellectuals and academics, seems to carry the day in France. Its organization. La Gauche Prolétarienne (The Proletarian Left), meets with Sartre's approval, and he maintains special links with Pierre Victor, one of its leaders. Finally, the creation of the newspaper *Libération,* of which Sartre is the titular director, completes the militant transformation of the classical intellectual.

But if we evaluate the intrinsic philosophical tenor of this "mutation" rather than looking at it with the eyes of the revolutionary enthusiast eager to renew his ideological arsenal, we observe an astonishing reversal of the situation. And the first observation, itself obvious, is that it is *as an intellectual* that Sartre proposes the model of the "new" intellectual. In short, it is in "classical" terms that he specifies the conditions for scuttling the classical intellectual. How to avoid suspecting in this an ambiguity that undermines the proclaimed originality of the ambition? But even more, and to some extent essentially, the "new just ones," whose reappearance on the historical scene could be celebrated, are the Hugos ruled out in *Dirty Hands,* now countless and relegitimized by the force of their new "intervention." These "new just ones" invent a revival of "realistic idealism" by creating an institution that is in itself original, namely, "the establishment"—that is, the most "responsible" among them abandon their university status and become factory workers.

But this original and radical invention of a new activism simultaneously reveals a more timeless philosophical mood: the resurgence of a sacrificial project in the struggle, namely, the Christian "paradigm" of the sacrifice of Jesus the just into Jesus the crucified, or Jesus Christ. In an essentially revolutionary tone, Hegel showed this as the dialectic of the philosopher and the man of action, of the sacrifice of the son by the father, or of evil and of its pardon—in the mutual sacrificing of the just man to the necessity of action, and the efficiency of action to the universal vocation of his commitment in the world. This resulted in restoring some legitimacy and some relevance to the model I had originally proposed, while simultaneously ruling out its pretense of revolutionary exclusivity: it always deals with the technique of taking over the minds of the world's victims by the "righters of wrongs." Its genealogy is perfectly revealed by Nietzsche with regard to the ascendancy over the world by the great

221

ascetic priest. This represents the appropriation of twenty centuries of our history by Christianity, in short, a religious secularization of the worst kind. Yet at the same time Sartre gave us the countermodel of this specious and underhanded militant, the properly negative face of this postclassical and triumphalist intellectual, of this "just one" who mortifies himself in his most obvious interests in order to rediscover them a hundredfold in the form of sociohistorical compensation for his sacrifice, this crucified one, monopolizer of the destiny of minds. We recognize here the portrait of Flaubert as the portrait of what Sartre affirmed or recognized himself as *not* being, because he was, as a child, "the opposite" of Gustave: "the child whose portrait I implicitly draw in contrast to the young Gustave, the little boy who is sure of himself, who has profound convictions because in his first years he had all the love that a child needs in order to become an individual and self that dares to affirm itself—that little boy is me."[9] This perfectly sets the tone for the "postclassical" intellectual, the one whose strength of mind can go as far as to sacrifice his most internalized advantages. He will always draw an increased benefit from it, because whatever projects he undertakes, the broadening of his psychosocial as well as social-economical and economic-symbolic reproductions is irreversibly inscribed in him. He retains the possibility of the project, the possibility of doing, while the portrait of the little Flaubert is precisely that of passivity, or of the impossibility of declaring oneself in a project. In short, Gustave reveals the absence of the very possibility of projecting and therefore of accumulating or broadening his existential "profits."

What sounds the mourning bells (or the bells of resurrection, whichever you prefer) for those who are "established," such as Sartre himself, in terms of their ambition to do better, and other, than all the great "converts" of the history of Western culture is that they always stand before the tribunal of eternity, beginning with the one of their own age. In this sense there are only happy ones who "have it made"—or suicides, which is another way of taking possession of history. There are the repentant ones who have it made in prison, like Frantz, who must be considered happy in his schizophrenia because he chose it over death; or those who have it made who are dead, such as Hugo, since he returned from his suicide under the present form of countless "just ones" (who prematurely have it made). There are, finally, those who have it made who, having given up the game, are thoroughly happy, such as Sartre— who preserves isolation in his work while paying the public price of his commitments, tranquil in his dual vocation, giving up no advantages, neither of the present nor of the future, but accumulating profits on both fronts.[10]

And indeed he simultaneously contributes the theory of this destiny to this somewhat double "practice":

First it is necessary to be deceived, to believe in one's mandate, to confound purpose and reason in the unity of maternal love, to live out a happy surrender; and then to have this false happiness gnaw away at itself in order to allow alien infiltrations to be dissolved in the movement of negativity, of project and praxis, to substitute anguish for surrender. . . . Truth is intelligible only at the end of a long, vagabond delusion; if it is handled before, it is only a real delusion.[11]

Truth examined closely through the negative, through the sacrificial test, thus purified of its dross of errors . . . another victory! And, in fact, what to do now? Unless to play on both fields and accumulate profits— his Flaubert and his alliance with the Maoists are "a good example of this mixture; one goes as far as possible in one direction, but in the other one finishes what one has to do."[12]

But one of the terms of the aporia appears in this "mixture." If for the dialectician a humanism will be built on need, revolutionaries and their militant consciousness will rise up against the possibility of the impossibility of its satisfaction.[13] Sartre will say also, but this time speaking for his alter ego, Flaubert: "On the nothingness that engulfs or will engulf all that exists, on the permanent and objective challenge, to the heirs by the very existence of the disinherited, on the void which is irrepressible need . . . is based an authority that gives the unworthy, the disenfranchised, invisible and nocturnal rights by affirming the supremacy of the negative."[14] But need met by revolution will necessarily see a resurgence of the chains of serial inertia in the victorious group. Conversely, the "invisible and nocturnal" rights of the disinherited will never make themselves real and will remain, on account of this, the irretrievable heterogeneity of the way of the world, at its best for artists, at its worst for anonymous ones, a problematic grave for those who are unknown. Sartre does not despair of sustaining the two terms of the aporia, but certainly not of unifying them, this heterogenous and separate consciousness. To gain new advantages?

Notes

1. *Critique de la raison dialectique* II (Paris, 1985), 324.
2. *Critique de la raison dialectique* I (Paris, 1985), 300; trans. by Alan Sheridan Smith, *Critique of Dialectical Reason* I (London, 1976), 190.
3. *Le Monde,* May 11, 1979.

4. *Les Séquestrés d'Altona* (Paris, 1960); trans. by Sylvia Leeson and George Leeson, *The Condemned of Altona* (New York, 1963), 31, 80, 84, 92, 133, 171.

5. "I Am No Longer a Realist," Chapter 3 in this volume.

6. *L'Idiot de la famille* I (Paris, 1971), 911; trans. by Carol Cosman, *The Family Idiot* II (Chicago, 1987), 251.

7. "Plaidoyer pur les intellectuels," *Situations* VIII (Paris, 1972); trans. by John Matthews, "A Plea for Intellectuals," *Between Existentialism and Marxism* (London, 1974).

8. "L'Intellectual face à la révolution," *Le Point*, no. 13, (January 1968).

9. *Le Monde*, May 14, 1970; trans. by Paul Auster and Lydia Davis, "On *The Idiot of the Family*," *Life Situations* (New York, 1977), 114–15.

10. Which corresponds to the historical reality of the distribution of the different fates of the established ones. There are the "repentant" established ones, in prison or in private confinement, and, consequently, content to have avoided the worst; there are the "terrorist" established ones, not showing repentance, dead to history or to themselves, but proud to be eternal witnesses of the value of their cause; finally, the fate of the prosperous and happy established ones, who have made their sacrifice the very humus of their historical adaptation, or even of their social success according to the simultaneous idea history has made of them.

11. *L'Idiot de la famille* I, 143; trans., 136.

12. "L'Ami du people," *Situations* VIII (Paris, 1972).

13. *L'Idiot de la famille* I, 433; *trans.*, *420*.

14. Ibid., 429; trans., 417, translation changed.

IV

RETHINKING SARTRE:
FICTION, BIOGRAPHY

12

NAUSEA:
PLUNGING BELOW THE SURFACE

Adrian van den Hoven

What is one to make of a protagonist to whom it seems that he is filled with lymph or lukewarm milk,[1] who compares a friend's hand to a "fat white worm" (9), and who feels that an old man is "forming thoughts of crabs or crawfish in his head" (14)? Then again, how is one to judge a protagonist who calls Bouville's bourgeoisie "swine" (113) because it imposes a distorted portrait of itself on society, but who does not seem to be morally perturbed by the behavior of a pederast who fondles schoolboys and by an exhibitionist-rapist-murderer? And how can one interpret the phantasmagoric imagery of an author who rejects all forms of conventional art, including narration, but who nevertheless projects the writing of an impossible adventure that "would have to be beautiful and hard like steel and that would have to make people ashamed of their existence" (210)?

These seemingly disparate levels of the text of *Nausea* can indeed be integrated, and they have their common source in an overarching vision of man, society, the arts, and the entire universe. First, when Roquentin's mind's eye plunges below the surface of people and objects, he perceives instantaneously beneath this gloss the multiple evolutionary stages, from the most primitive to the most evolved, undergone by man and creation.[2] These various stages remain copresent and coexistent to Roquentin's imagination.

Secondly, Roquentin's angry rejection of bourgeois values, both moral and artistic, is intertwined with his materialist view of the universe: a world he sees as being hidden from view by the bourgeoisie, who cover it up, distort it, and reverse its temporal flow. Thirdly, Roquentin's fascination with lower life forms and his unwillingness to condemn any animal-like or instinctive form of behavior (specifically that of the pederast and the exhibitionist) are also related to the fact that he sees these again as being no more than manifestations of the physical and material universe.

Ultimately, Roquentin proposes a positive solution to the psychosexual obsessions that permeate *Nausea*. It is embodied in the cooperative relationship of the Jewish composer and the black singer. Together they produce a new art form that enables Roquentin to transcend contingency. It inspires him to envision an impossible adventure, a purely fictional creation, which can perhaps justify his existence retrospectively and compel his readers to view their own existence critically and thereby go beyond it.

This metamorphosis is the result of the fact that the various levels of *Nausea* interact with one another: even if they can be analyzed in their own terms, the novel clearly possesses a distinct and coherent vision within Sartre's oeuvre. This does not mean that *Nausea* must be viewed as standing utterly apart from Sartre's other writings. But rather, such an approach, a careful analysis of its specific salient features, can lead us to view this novel—including its controversial ending—as a positive and significant milestone in the author's artistic *and* psychological development.

I will begin by dissecting *Nausea*'s nightmarish vision of the world. In order to do that, I will focus on the etymological, literary, artistic, and scientific origins of some of the novel's key elements, such as its original and its ultimate title and the protagonist's and the city's names. I will relate these findings to the imagery of the text in order to uncover the precise nature of the phantasmagorical universe Roquentin inhabits. Since he views human relationships in a similar abhorrent fashion, I will then turn my attention to Roquentin's psychosexual quest to show that his homo- and heterosexual obsessions (as they are carried out through his alter egos) lead him ultimately to entertain the possibility of a creative, cooperative relationship. This relationship is illustrated by the collaborative activities of the Jewish composer and the black female singer. He discovers this new possibility after having first passed in review, and rejected, the various distorted bourgeois art forms and after having pondered the jazz melody—a cooperative creation by these two 1930s outcasts.

The intertextual relationship that *Nausea* entertains with Sartre's childhood readings is laid bare in *The Words* and, within *Nausea* itself, by the reading habits of the Autodidact and of Anny in her younger days. These indicate that at the source of Roquentin's nightmarish descriptions of man and the world are the many illustrated volumes contained in the library of Karl Schweitzer (Sartre's grandfather). These made up young Sartre's "scientific" and pictorial education. In the copiously illustrated works of Michelet and Jules Verne, and in the dictionaries and encyclopedias by Larousse and others (some with such revelatory titles as the *Encyclopédie Autodidacte Quillet,* by a self-confessed autodidact), Poulou (the young Sartre's nickname) learned about art, about history, about man's origins, and about the physical nature of the universe.

The many drawings, engravings, and colored plates of these tomes provided young Sartre with instant pictorial glimpses of man's primitive beginnings, and they permitted him to absorb in a flash the abhorrent life forms that populate the bottom of the ocean and from which all presently "evolved" forms have sprung. These nineteenth-century popularizations made the entire universe's history coexistent and copresent for him. By simply flipping from one illustration to another, young Sartre could envision the overlapping of past and present and of the most primitive and the most evolved forms of life. The famous illustrated Hetzel editions of Jules Verne's novels such as *Twenty Thousand Leagues under the Sea* also provided young Sartre with a graphic illustration of men seated "on the back of a submarine," which initially they mistake for a gigantic whale. It shows these men marveling at the submarine life forms through the windows of the *Nautilus* (its name is etymologically linked to *nausea*) as it floats through the ocean. These experiences parallel those of Roquentin. He describes himself as being seated on the back of a "donkey's carcass" as he floats through Bouville in a streetcar, and through the windows he views Bouville passing by as if he is seated in a submarine. Similarly, Roquentin plunges below the water's surface in a fashion parallel to the *Nautilus*'s visits to the bottom of the ocean.

Roquentin's uncompromising materialism can be traced to these nineteenth-century texts. I would suggest that they are the source of the constant degradation of man's higher functions and the hybrid nature of the imagery he uses to describe his fellow man. The Autodidact is regularly compared to a dog and to a chicken. Sartre sees such social activities as eating and lovemaking in purely instinctive, physical terms. Poulou's graphic "scientific education" has permeated all of Roquentin's language, and it provides the parameters of his hallucinatory vision. Just as Poulou was able to grasp man's horrifying origins from an instant glance at the colored plates and illustrations of his childhood reading, so Roquentin permits the reader to envision instantly the universe's total evolution by using imagery that treats all levels and stages of creation as being coeval and coextensive.

What, after all, is at the origin of Roquentin's superiority over the other characters in the novel? It lies in the fact that, unlike them, he constantly sees through the idealized surfaces of man and the world. He can expose, below these surfaces, the horrifying crawling creatures that inhabit the primitive physical universe. Similarly, Roquentin reduces man's psychosexual impulses to the crude physiological level underlying our artificial, idealized images. Just as he instantaneously sees the physical origin of all of man's idealistic posturings, so does he persistently reduce all hetero- and homosexual pulsations, such as those of the Autodidact and the exhibitionist, to their primitive physiological origins. Roquentin refuses all idealistic distinctions between love, humanism, desire, and instinct. Instead, the degrading imagery Roquentin uses to describe man's ostensibly higher impulses is intended to provide us with instantaneous glimpses of man's various evolutionary stages. In the same way, Roquentin's hetero- and homosexual obsessions, as they are played out by his alter egos, the exhibitionist and the Autodidact, are integrated in his phantasmagorical vision. Roquentin does not morally condemn their conduct, because their behavior fits within his vision. After all, he is trying to return to what is most basically biological: the natural and the physical. Roquentin saves his anger for the bourgeoisie, because it is indulging in a wholesale idealistic cover-up of the real, physical nature of man and the universe. Roquentin's review of the conventional arts (architecture, sculpture, painting, music, theater, and narration) exposes how the bourgeoisie hides, distorts, and rearranges reality by way of idealization in order to suit its own needs.

Other key elements of *Nausea*—its original and final title, the protagonist's and the city's names—also demonstrate how the text's phantasmagorical vision permeates all of the novel's elements. As is well known, Sartre intended to entitle his novel *Melancholia*, after Albrecht Dürer's engraving. It is likely that he saw this engraving first in the Larousse dictionary, but it is equally possible that he read about it in

230

Michelet's *Histoire de France* (the work that also inspired Anny) or in the works of Gérard de Nerval, Théophile Gauthier, or Charles Baudelaire. This engraving had become a nineteenth-century commonplace, inasmuch as melancholy and spleen were in vogue. Sartre's initial decision to entitle the text *Melancholia* also indicates how firmly his education was rooted in the nineteenth century. In the engraving we see an angel, compass in hand, seated among scientific paraphernalia as well as geometrical shapes and other objects, while the waters stretch out before and beside the angel. Geometrical shapes such as triangles and circles are essential components of Roquentin's abstract but "unreal" other world which is provoked by the jazz melody. In addition, the angel's compass makes us aware of the importance of perspective in the explorer's universe, and, of course, it also plays a significant but negative role in this text. Roquentin immediately rejects perspectivism as a method for coming to grips with objects: "Here is a carton box which contains my ink bottle. I should be able to say how I saw it *before* and how at present I . . . Well! It is a rectangular paralleliped which detaches itself from—it is ridiculous, there is nothing to say about it" (5). Roquentin also denounces the abuse of perspectivism practiced by the painter Blévigne, who had deliberately enhanced Parrotin's physical size.

The ocean plays an equally important role in *Nausea*. But once again, unlike the angel, Roquentin is not satisfied with melancholy musing while he glances at the sea's smooth surface. For example, when Roquentin describes the sea at low tide, he calls it first "a puddle of light" (63), using imagery that is reminiscent of Rimbaud's "Bateau ivre." Second, his realistic description invokes Dürer's "Melancholia," as when he refers to the cubes of stone that protect the pier from the waves. Immediately thereafter, he points out that the waves are "full with swarming holes" (63), filled no doubt with primitive life forms.

Up to this point Dürer's engraving has been a largely negative counterpoint to Sartre's text, but the etymology of the word *melancholia* is relevant in positive terms. It signifies "black bile" and refers to one of the four humors or of fluids that, according to ancient physiology, are contained in man's body and determine his temperament. Consequently, the original title already stresses the physical and material origin of man's state of mind: man is a hybrid made up of solid matter such as flesh and bone but also of fluids. Whenever he is in a state of disequilibrium, one of the fluids dominates both his body and his mind. Of course, Roquentin's universe is dominated by fluids, and whenever he describes the physical world around him it tends to dissolve into a fluidic state:

All these men in overcoats seemed to float slowly a few inches from the ground. From time to time the wind pushed shadows on us which trembled like water, the faces extinguished themselves for a moment and became chalklike.

It was Sunday; framed between the balustrade and the fences of the holiday cottages, the crowd flowed away little by little, to go and lose itself in a thousand brooks behind the big hotel of the Compagnie Transatlantique. (63)

The semisolid nature of Roquentin's universe is also underlined by the title Gallimard imposed on the text. *Nausea* derives from the Greek word *nautia*, the seasickness suffered on a *naus* (a ship) by the *nautilos* (the sailor). Already it is not difficult to envision Roquentin, in the manner of Jules Verne's hero, as a hypochondriac Captain Nemo gliding in his submarine *Nautilus* (which in the novel takes the shape of a streetcar) through the streets of Bouville, and describing with fluidic imagery the objects, the buildings, and the streets that float by him:

Behind the windows bluish objects pass by in a jerky fashion, all stiff and abrupt. People, walls. Through its open windows a house offers me its black heart: and the windows go pale and turn blue all that is black. Turns blue that big building made of yellow brick which advanced hesitantly while shivering and which stops all of a sudden while pointing its nose. . . . The yellow building leaves again, it slides in one leap against the windows. . . . (147)

Roquentin's aquatic meanderings remind one again of Rimbaud's "Bateau ivre." This is not surprising, given that the imagery for both works derives from childhood readings, and since Rimbaud's work functions as a pertinent intertext for *Nausea,* whose protagonist, as we will show below, is also very much a "man-boy."

The etymology of the protagonist's name, Roquentin, also provides clues to the phantasmagorical imagery of the text. First of all, Larousse's *Grand dictionnaire de XIXe siècle* indicates that the correct spelling is *rocantin* and not *roquentin,* the variant used by Brueys and Balzac, among others. Before we turn to the extended meaning to which Balzac puts the word, and which most likely inspired Sartre, let us focus first on the three definitions provided by Larousse.

First, it is a name that was given in the past to songs composed of other songs. This definition permits us to understand Roquentin's fascination with the jazz melody "Some of These Days," of which he records fragments in the text. It also explains the inclusion in *Nausea* of fragments of other texts, such as *Eugénie Grandet.* Finally, it gives a clue to the fragmentary nature of the "private diary," the entries of which can be composed of a word or two, such as "Nothing. Existed" (122), or of lengthy and detailed descriptions of an entire Sunday. In fact, as is the case in *rocantin*-type songs, this text is largely composed of and inspired by other texts while simultaneously commenting on them.

The second definition Larousse provides is "a name given in the past to the veterans charged with the defense of a *roc* or a citadel."[3] This suggests a link between Roquentin and Bouville, a city being invaded or threatened by the surrounding vegetation. It is Roquentin's function to be on guard against the city's instability.

Finally, the Larousse indicates that by extension one also spoke in the past of *un vieux rocantin*, "a dirty old man." It then cites Brueys and Balzac, who both misspell the word as *roquentin*. Balzac uses the word on three different occasions to refer to old men who are obsessed with young women. It is most likely that Sartre stumbled upon it in his readings of *Le Père Goriot*. Not only is it Vautrin who states of old Goriot "he is a gallant fellow, this roquentin"; it is also he who insists to Eugene Rastignac that "you have to get your hands dirty." If this hard-bitten philosophy suggests Hoederer's outlook in *Dirty Hands,* Balzac's Mme. de Beauséant is closer to Hugo's: "The world is a quagmire, let's attempt to remain on high ground." The filiation with old Goriot helps to explain Roquentin's fascination with young girls, as expressed through his alter ego, the exhibitionist. During Roquentin's imaginative recreation of the young girl's rape and murder, he clearly identifies with the exhibitionist. Only when he meets Anny again and realizes that she is no longer a little girl does his obsession with her begin to wane: "But now she no longer looks like a little girl. She is fat, she has a big chest" (161). In *Nausea* the hetero- and homoerotic obsessions come into violent conflict with reality, tragically in the case of Lucienne's murder and pathetically in the case of the Autodidact who is publicly exposed. In both cases, the obsessions also die a symbolic death for Roquetin. In regard to Roquentin's heterosexual obsessions, it is not until he finds a different model in the cooperative venture of the composer and the singer that he can actually begin to conceive of different social relationships.

The city's name, Bouville, also partakes of the hybrid nature of Roquentin's universe. The word *bouville* can be decomposed into three primary elements—clay, water, and stone—therefore, it is not surprising that Bouville regularly threatens to revert to a semifluidic state. Of course, the essentially unstable nature of this citadel makes it all the harder for Roquentin to defend it.

Roquentin's lack of sexual maturity is also stressed in *Nausea*'s epigraph, borrowed from Céline's *L'Eglise*. It immediately highlights the psychosexual impact of his quest by stating that "He is a boy without collective importance, he is just barely an individual" (1). Simultaneously, it also brings out his social marginality, a characteristic he shares with his cohorts the Autodidact, the Jewish composer, and the black singer. Roquentin, the solitary bachelor, has remained a boy. By analogy, physical immaturity can be translated into sexual immaturity and ambivalence, and in this manner the epigraph subtly foregrounds Roquentin's hetero- and homosexual obsessions "through which he must see clear" (5). In the text these inclinations are treated as immature because they invade and overwhelm him and make him ill. They also prevent him, until nearly the end of the novel, from entertaining relationships that are productive and cooperative rather than obsessive, violent, and exploitative.

Now that we have outlined the phantasmagoric nature of Roquentin's universe and have seen him as an immature and sexually ambivalent submarine voyager who wants to "see clear" through his obsessions, let us follow him through the text and analyze some of the encounters that provoke his nauseous state. The first description of this state occurs precisely when this "man-boy" wishes to emulate some boys on the beach who are skipping stones off the water:

> Saturday the boys were skipping stones and like them I wished to throw a pebble in the water. At that moment, I stopped, I let the pebble drop and I left. I must have looked peculiar, probably, because the boys laughed behind my back.
> That is all for the outside. What happened within me has not left any clear traces. There was something that I saw and which disgusted me, but I do not know anymore if I was looking at the sea or the pebble. The pebble was flat and dry on one side, damp and muddy on the other. I held it by its edges, with my fingers very much spread out to avoid dirtying myself.(6)

The novel's first dramatic incident immediately portrays the protagonist as a ridiculous old man who wishes to play "with the boys." He seeks to be a boy again and begins to feel nauseous when he links the primitive world of the sea, from which all life springs, with that of the pebble. It is a microcosm of Bouville since it is at once damp and muddy and hard like a stone. The fact that he has his attack of nausea while wishing "to play with the boys" links his subconscious sexual ambivalence and immaturity back to the phantasmagorical submarine origins of man. Titillating the pebble prevents him from returning it to its origins. It provokes in him a vision similar in its primitivity to the one he has later when he touches the pederast's hand.

The sensation of touch that provokes the attack can be associated with two other sensations, those of sight and of smell, which were responsible for the original attack six years ago in Indochina when Mercier invited him on an archeological mission: "I was staring at a little Khmer statuette on a green carpet, beside a telephone. It seemed to me that I was filled with lymph and tepid milk" (9). And some moments later Roquentin adds: "Before me, presented with a sort of indolence, there stood a voluminous and dull idea. I do not know very well what it was but I could not look at it so much it disgusted me. All that mixed itself up for me with the perfume of Mercier's beard" (10). For Roquentin synesthesia, another state idealized in the nineteenth century, does not lead to the discovery of an other-worldly paradise as it did for Baudelaire in "Correspondances." Rather, it sickens him and takes him back to a basic infantile stage, invoked by his use of the words *lymph* and *tepid*—that is, mother's milk.

Roquentin's first encounter with the Autodidact again describes him in terms of those primitive life forms that can be either terrestrial or aquatic and which precede man in the life chain: "I saw an unknown face, barely a face. And then there was his hand, like a fat white worm in my hand. I immediately let go of it and the arm fell back softly" (9).

Later on, when Roquentin describes the seduction scene in the library between the Autodidact and the two schoolboys, the link between this primitive shape and sexuality is again brought out. As was the case with Roquentin when he wished to emulate the boys, he perceives laughter: "Half hidden behind his shoulder, the white-haired boy raised his ear and laughed quietly" (193). Moments later, the actual seduction scene is described; it features "a little white hand," "a brown hairy object," and "and a fat finger yellowed by tobacco and which possesses, next to that hand, all the gracelessness of a male sex organ" (195).

It is at this moment that "the young boys stopped laughing" (194–95). The two parallels between this scene and Roquentin's encounter with the boys on the beach and between the initial description of the Autodidact's hand and this final encounter of digitals firmly establish Roquentin as an ineffectual and ridiculous version of the pathetic Autodidact. As Roquentin's alter ego, he suffers the ignominious consequences of his sad attempt at "humanism": he is publicly exposed, humiliated, and expelled from the library. As if to underscore the sexual nature of his crime, Roquentin remarks that "the Autodidact's nose

235

began to piss blood" when the librarian hit him (197). Roquentin's outrage at the treatment the Autodidact receives makes the librarian wonder "if he too is perhaps a fag" (198). This remark suggests an indirect explanation of Roquentin's sympathy for the Autodidact. But the latter's miserable fate also rules out this kind of behavior as a viable future alternative for Roquentin.

The protagonist's heterosexual obsessions are also linked directly to his hallucinatory vision of the universe. He sleeps with the hotel owner, but "she disgusts him a little, she is too white and she smells like a newborn baby" (71). Afterward he experiences a surrealistic nightmare. It may be inspired by Henri Rousseau's "primitive" landscapes and also by Jules Verne's descriptions of the submarine flora and fauna, such as he provides, for example, in *Voyage to the Center of the Earth*. This is Roquentin's description:

> I suddenly saw a little garden with low and broad trees from which hung immense leaves covered with hairs. Ants, centipedes, and ringworms ran everywhere. There were even more horrible beasts: Their bodies were made of a slice of toast like the ones you place under roast pigeons; they walked sideways with crab feet. The large leaves were altogether black with beasts. (72)

Again the sensation of sight and smell do not lead him into an extraterrestrial paradise, but they make him descend into a hallucinatory universe. Even when he encounters a female with whom he is in sympathy and who makes him happy, he quickly descends into a submarine universe composed of mud and nauseous odors, of decomposing bodies—and thence finally to the bottom of the ocean. This is how he describes the universe he perceives inside the Café Mably through its steamed-up window:

> The room is full. The air is blue because of the cigarette smoke and the steam which emanates from the damp clothes. The cashier is behind the counter. I know her well: she is a redhead like me: she has a disease in her belly. Slowly she is rotting away under her skirts while showing a melancholy smile, similar to the odor of violets which bodies in decomposition sometimes give off. A shiver runs through me from top to toe: it is . . . it is she who is waiting for me. She was there, pointing her immobile bust above the counter, and she smiled. From the depth of the café something spreads over the isolated moments of the Sunday and welds one to the other, gives them a meaning; I have traversed this entire day to end up there, with my forehead against that window pane, in order to contemplate that delicate face that radiates against the red curtain. Everything has stopped, my life also; that big window, that

236

heavy air, blue like water, that fat, white plant at the bottom of the water and I, we form one complete and static unit: I am happy. (67–68)

This redhead, Roquentin's female soul mate, drags him back to the origins of creation when all was chaos. It is precisely for this reason that Anny detests his red hair. It advertises too blatantly his sexuality, it takes her back to a primitive universe without order and planning, and it places him in conflict with her nicely ordered surroundings.

But before we discuss Anny's final rejection of Roquentin, we must look at the description of little Lucienne's rape and murder. Her violent death prefigures the end of Roquentin's boy-girl relationship with Anny. Also, Lucienne's death is described in terms that contain some of the same elements as those used for the homosexually inspired encounters: fingers, mud, earth. They indicate that the primeval origin of both types of sexual inclinations is the same:

> Little Lucienne has been raped. Strangled. . . . A soft bloody desire for rape takes me from behind . . . a finger scratches my shorts, scratches and pulls on the little girl's finger which is covered with mud . . . slowly, softly, the fingers of the girl scratch less strongly, shameful individual, scratch the mud and the earth less strongly, the finger slides softly, the head falls first and caresses rolled warmly against my thigh. . . . (120)

After the little girl has been physically eliminated, Roquentin notices that all Anny's girlish attributes have also disappeared. "At present, I clearly distinguish her face. All of a sudden it becomes pale and drawn. A face of an old woman, absolutely fearful . . ." (182)

She remarks to Roquentin: "The first good-looking boy who comes along will do just as well as you" (182). And Roquentin has indeed been replaced by another young man, as he notices the next day at the train station: "The guy wore a camel-haired coat. He was tanned, still young, very tall and very handsome" (183). However, obsessions are tenacious, and when Roquentin decides to leave Bouville and to say good-bye to "la Patronne" (with whom he used to sleep), he discovers that she too has taken on enormous proportions: "How have I been able to press my lips on that broad face" (203)?

Now that Roquentin is bereft of his sexual illusions, what is he left with? He has already systematically dismissed all conventional aesthetic solutions that would have allowed him to find consolation in the arts. First, narration reverses the chronological unfolding of events by structuring all events in terms of the eventual ending. Consequently, this social activity does not contribute to uncovering true temporality and contingency. Instead, it results in their being obscured. Architecture, in the shape of Bouville's cathedral, becomes a monument to financial success which suppresses the squalid and odorous origins of the bourgeoisie's wealth. Sculpture—Impétraz's statue—is exploited to reinforce platitudes and the moral order. Blévigne has distorted Parrotin's real stature. He has carefully exploited the laws of perspectivism in order to make Parrotin seem taller. Theater, as embodied in Anny's "privileged situations" and "perfect moments," leaves no room either for the contingent aspects of reality. Classical music is incapable of consoling anyone, and the artificial paradise created by Baudelaire's poetry turns into a nightmare, as do the childhood dreams of Rimbaud's "Bateau ivre."

The scathing denunciation of nineteenth-century aestheticism is paralleled by the abrupt and violent demise of exploitative relationships. The positive conclusion of *Nausea*—which points toward a new art form as well as a preferable form of human interaction—stands in contradiction to the phantasmagoric universe Roquentin is leaving behind. But since it is generated by it, it is consistent with the text and artistically justified. Consequently, it can be said that the various layers of *Nausea* complement each as they conflict with one another. Roquentin's hallucinatory vision of the coeval coexistence of all life forms makes him reject violently all conventional artistic and moral attempts to cover up or distort the absurdity of reality. At the same time, his imaginative materialism makes him view all physical and instinctive manifestations of man with a scientific eye which precludes moral indignation even in the case of the child murderer. On the other hand, both the homoerotic and the heterosexual adventures end in violence, and, as a consequence, he is compelled to abandon these inclinations and reassess his social relationships. He has already had to abandon biography because he knew he could not resuscitate the past, and on philosophical grounds he has just dismissed conventional narration. Yet at the same time he has also exploited the technical possibilities of the highly autobiographical genre of the private diary. The heteronymous nature of *Nausea*'s journal entries so perfectly exhaust the contingent nature of reality that he can not go beyond futile attempts to reconstruct the past, or to create a distorted copy of the present, and explore a new genre and attempt a new life. Neither is unrelated to the present ones, but they are nevertheless radically different from them and exclude the possibility of his falling into the same traps again.

The jazz melody provides Roquentin with a future artistic model. It is a pure product of the imagination; it has its own structure and, like mathematical abstractions, *can* be said to owe nothing to reality. The impossible adventure Roquentin would like to create would possess its own coherence and structure, and yet it would retain a social function. It would provide a negative mirror to the reader to whom it would expose at once his contingent nature and his inauthentic attempts to cover up this reality. In purely human terms this fiction could provide a retroactive justification for Roquentin's existence. It would compel the reader to actively denounce his bad faith and to metamorphosize himself into a person willing to create a purely human existence and universe. This is precisely what Roquentin would like to do in his projected novel.

In terms of his social relationships, the Jewish composer and the black singer propose to Roquentin a potential model that is also radically different. Theirs is a cooperative and productive relationship not mired in exploitation and obsession but creative and mutually interdependent. As such, it foreshadows the relationship of writer and reader as Sartre outlines it in *What Is Literature?* Just as the singer is essential to the composer so that his music may be performed and appreciated, so the reader is a necessary complement to the writer. It is in the reader's mind that the writer's unveiling of the world will lead to a conversion and to a subsequent metamorphosis of the world itself.

The conclusion of *Nausea* represents two steps forward. It represents a sloughing off of old psychosexual dependencies and of distorted and redundant art forms, and it proposes to replace them with a more positive human relationship and an innovative art form. The new couple of composer and performer, of writer and reader, will produce a work that will function as a two-edged sword. It will cut us loose from this contingent, false, and absurd universe and introduce us to a universe that is coherent, translucent, and totally rigorous.

Notes

1. *Oeuvres romanesques,* ed. by Michel Contat and Michel Rybalka with Geneviève Idt and George H. Bauer (Paris, 1981). All references to this text, the Pléiade edition, will be identified by page number in parentheses at the end of the citation. All translations are mine; however, these have been checked, where pertinent, against the American translation: *Nausea,* trans. by Lloyd Alexander (New York, 1949).
2. See also Geneviève Idt, *La Nausée: analyse critique* (Paris, 1971), 44–45.
3. Michel Contat and Michel Rybalka remark in the "notice" to the *Oeuvres romanesques* that, according to von Wartburg's standard French etymological dictionary (*FEW*), this definition is not correct. However, since it is quoted in the *Larousse de XIXᵉ Siécle,* it has acquired a fictional legitimacy and can be incorporated as part of the interpretation.

13

THE RESURRECTIONIST,
OR NOVEMBER IN LE HAVRE

Robert Wilcocks

"On entre dans un mort comme on entre dans un moulin," writes Sartre in the preface to *The Family Idiot*[1] (translated by Carol Cosman as "A corpse is open to all comers"). This almost untranslatable idiom has the sense that it matters little where one begins the exploration of a dead man, for all will eventually be grist to one's mill. It was in this brilliantly devious sense that Sartre investigated the early experience and writings of Gustave Flaubert. From this apparently haphazard approach will emerge a synchronic kind of construction, or reconstruction, giving sense and value to the diachronic lived details encountered in the research.

There are those who wonder at such labor—over twenty years on and off—devoted to a man who had not yet written *Madame Bovary*. I think they may have been misled and that Sartre's public statements about *The Family Idiot* may have contributed to this. I do not think that Sartre began this monumental study of Flaubert's evolution (and *continued* it in the face of almost insurmountable difficulties, not the least of which were intermittent bad health ending in virtual blindness and the busy schedule of public commitment that his political persona demanded) in order to show *how Madame Bovary* came to be written. I think he took for granted that *Madame Bovary* was a prose fiction masterpiece of the nineteenth century; I further think that, having taken this for granted, Sartre felt himself to be dealing with an equal. And this equal had left sufficient public and private literary remains for a rigorous examination of the early years of apprenticeship. Sartre would do in this work what Roquentin had failed to do with the Marquis de Rollebon in *Nausea:* he would give life and substance and significance to a being whose existence was now only of a historical and documentary nature. What was flesh and the living chaos of sensation and had not been reduced to words—the books, the notebooks, the letters, the scribbled confidences—would by *words* become again, for him in his act of writing them and for us as we read them, a tangible, palpable presence with all the imagined glories and all the tremendous fears of its untried youth upon its head. This is the *magic* to which Sartre aspired.

In early-nineteenth-century Edinburgh those who disinterred bodies from their graves for the dissection tables at the medical school were ironically called "resurrectionists." Sartre, with perhaps less irony, may be called a resurrectionist. He does not deliver a body. He, the arch-materialist, strangely, delivers a consciousness. And this consciousness, seen through the testimony of itself and its peers, traced carefully through its developmental stages, will be dissected with all the imaginative and yet analytical attention of an expert anatomist. In his review of *The Condemned of Altona* Pierre Marcabru had already invented the analogy for Sartre's forensic skills: the great French anatomist Xavier Bichat.[2] The work on Flaubert and Sartre's emerging awareness of his empathy for the man will allow him to go beyond a mere literary Bichat. In *The Family Idiot* the dissection (though it is, of course, almost the opposite of this in that Sartre puts flesh *on* bones long since dead) is double. The apparent subject—Flaubert—with whom Sartre had publicly claimed to have little in common, whether on the intimate family level or on the broader political level, reveals another subject: the formative experience of Sartre himself.[3] In my view Sartre was fully aware of what attracted him to this project. One may recall his comments in the program notes for his adaptation of *Kean* (1953), where he explains the success over the years of Dumas's play—its ability to allow great actors to tell the truth about themselves, their lives, and their art, "but according to the rules of their trade: discreetly and modestly, that is to say, by slipping into the skin of another person."[4]

The remembered and deceptively dissected Poulou of *The Words* is not *quite* Gustave struggling with the ambitions of the powerful father in charge of surgery at the Hôtel-Dieu in Rouen, although the young (and indeed the later) Sartre might well have accepted for himself this description of the hero of *November:*

> He was not cunning enough to be a philanthropist, and his natural decency drove him away from medicine; as for business, he was incapable of calculating and the mere sight of a bank frayed his nerves. In spite of his madnesses he had too much sense to take the noble profession of advocacy seriously; moreover *his* justice would never have accommodated itself to the laws.[5]

The Flaubert discussed in *The Family Idiot* is not merely the emerging infant with his recorded traumas; he is also the young writer in his late teens and early twenties cutting his teeth as a creative artist. The Sartre who contemplated the writing of a factum on contingency in Le Havre is as much present in these pages as the magical child exhumed in *The Words.* We find, in fact, in these marvelous pages a presence of Roquentin-Sartre as much as a memory of Poulou's childish games with literature.

One may ask indeed (and the question is not as frivolous as it appears), *why* is Antoine Roquentin more than six feet tall? The traditional answer has been posited as either melodramatic overcompensation for Sartre's diminutive stature or else as a novelistic contrariety to throw "autobiographical" readers off the scent. There is a more cogent and a more worthwhile explanation. It involves us, inevitably, in that complex construct devised by Sartre before the war in *The Psychology of the Imagination,* the *analogon.* When perception is confused and the consciousness is inhabited by an imaginative (or imagined) *alterity* the safe principles of empiricism dissolve and the world, like the self, becomes haunted. In Volume III of *The Family Idiot* Sartre even uses the religious term *transubstantiation* to describe the phenomenon. Having declared that "it is by projecting himself into another that he informs us best about his own state" (*IF* III, 658–59), Sartre elaborates an interpretation of Flaubert's recorded reactions to the last illness, death, and burial of Théophile Gautier.

The documentary evidence, the correspondence with George Sand, furnishes Sartre with the material for an impromptu *explication de texte* in which he demonstrates with verve Gustave's complicated network of attitudes toward himself, his correspondent, Théophile Gautier (an ambiguous double for Gustave in Sartre's view or, rather, an *analogon* for what Gustave imagined himself to have been), and finally but by no means least, since this aspect gives significance to the rest, his century and its society. Gustave, for Sartre, sees himself in the grave in the guise of Théo (*IF* III, 659). What killed Théo? Or, better, what killed Théo the lover of Art for Art's Sake? There is no doubt in Gustave's mind— "la bêtise," that quasi-universal malediction, human stupidity, and, more particularly, French bourgeois stupidity. This is not entirely a brilliantly rhetorical perversion practiced by Sartre upon Gustave. For he quotes extensively from the letter to George Sand of October 23, 1872, in which Gustave observes of Théo, inter alia: "Car il [Théo] est mort, j'en suis sûr, d'une suffocation trop longue causée par la bêtise moderne" ("For he died, I'm certain of it, of an overlong suffocation caused by modern stupidity") (*IF* III, 659). The first sentences of Sartre's commentary on this letter are worth quoting *in extenso* because they throw light on the rich ambiguities of the triad Flaubert-Sartre-Roquentin, and because they bring us back to one of the problems of *November* which so fascinated Sartre: its double narrative device (first person followed by third person):

> A striking text. Théo's death allows Gustave *as Other* to grasp his own love of Art; it is no longer a subjective feeling, it is an objective virulence, no longer merely a *pathos* but an *ethos* which, in its corrosive absence, spontaneously disqualifies the bourgeois of Rouen. But, in order for him to thus devalue the thick stupidity of these good folk, it must first have been responsible for his assassination. Here then is Gustave crucified, dead and risen just like narrator No. 2 of *November*. (*IF* III, 659)[6]

Why, then, is Antoine Roquentin more than six feet tall? The question should now appear less frivolous. One might say that as Gustave is to the dead Théo, so is Jean-Paul (not Poulou) to the dead Gustave. But this would embroider simplicity into a text that cries out for the sinuous complicity of the artful arabesque. And Sartre was too conscious a writer (too conscious of his craft, too conscious of his cultural heritage) to have *accidentally* or *unconsciously* chosen the stature of a Gallic chieftain for the first-person narrator who broods in provincial Normandy on madness, art, lost love, and contingency. It seems to me that a closer intertextual reading of *Nausea, The Words,* and *The Family Idiot* cannot but bring into focus the image of that tormented giant, the author of *November*.

One may bring this home more immediately than any list of common themes, though these have a contiguity on more than one level that may surprise, given that *Nausea* is written by a philosopher in his thirties and *November* by a much younger man who was *not* (Sartre insists on this) a philosopher. One may do so by reading consecutively and then

243

contrapuntally the last pages of *Nausea* (from the meeting with Anny to the end) and the hundred or so pages of *The Family Idiot* II that examine the evolution in Gustave's life and writing from *Smarh* to *November.* To hop from page to page and from book to book produces an extraordinary sensation of discovery and familiarity. What one discovers, apart from objective documentation about Flaubert and its evaluative assessment, is how much this study of a literary and existential apprenticeship reads like a mature reflection on the possible multiple motivations of Roquentin by one who knew him well (from *within,* as it were). The tone and obsessions are familiar. This, perhaps, should not surprise us. After all, in the last pages of *The Words* Sartre writes, with emphasis on the verb, "I *was* a Roquentin, I showed in him, without complacency, the thread of my life."[7] We have thus declared authorial identification; but, as Michel Contat and Philippe Lejeune have pointed out, *The Words* is a text full of traps, and not just for the unwary. In admitting his authorial complicity with his character, Sartre is indulging in the literary equivalent of the Dance of the Seven Veils, and this admission is by no means the last veil.

It may well have taken Sartre the years of study and reflection that produced *The Family Idiot* to grasp fully what he himself had understood by the phrase "I *was* Roquentin." The deception, that is, the partial and ludic revelation taken for a complete and authentic revelation practiced in *The Words* may not have been a deliberate trap. Sartre may have known at that time (the late 1950s to the early 1960s) what he *meant* by the phrase and yet may have realized that such a meaning, with the fullness it now had for him, could not be elaborated in that autobiographical text—better the lapidary admission. After all, the chief subject of *The Words* is the precocious actor, Poulou, and the "possession" of the fifty-year-old writer by this Ariel. It is *not* the anguished young man, Jean-Paul, aware of the meaninglessness of existence and doubting his ability to transcend that contingency. So the question remains: who, or what, was Roquentin? And the ancillary question: Who, or what, was the Sartre who took himself to be Roquentin?[8]

Sartre's observation about Flaubert ('it is by projecting himself into another that he informs us best about his own states") is true for him, too, so much so that, for those who know Sartre's writings well, any reading of *The Family Idiot* necessarily becomes polyphonic. To the extent that this study is a "biography," one can equally read the following commentary on the final third-person narrative section in *November* as a remarkably accurate statement about Sartre's writing of *The Family*

Idiot itself: "However, the biographer portrays himself in his enterprise: his unadorned phrases betray the constant concern to refuse any *pathos*. But beneath the affectation of impartiality, beneath the condescending irony, one discovers violence and a strange, jolting, precipitous rhythm" (*IF* II, 1721).

Sartre does not immediately offer any quotation to justify this reading of a latent violence (presumably toward the first-person narrator) in the rhythm of the third-person narrative; but he does provide an observation about the mixed *telos* of this second narrator which accords well with Sartre's own role in *The Family Idiot:* "this man is not detached . . . he has been called in, one might say, to give a diagnosis. . . . If he plays at being impartial, if he blocks his feelings, it is because he is conducting an enquiry: seeking to understand the motives of the accused or the patient, he prohibits himself, at first, from sharing them" (*IF* II, 1721). But the Sartre of *The Family Idiot* stands, in these very volumes, in relation to the Sartre who "was" Roquentin in much the same way that Flaubert's second narrator stands toward the first, or, as Sartre argues, as Flaubert of October 1842 did to the Flaubert of the spring of that year. The differences that appear the moment one posits an analogous relationship—for example, that with Sartre we are dealing with a period of many years of reflection and with his youthful ambitions amply fulfilled in the interim, while with Flaubert we are dealing with a crisis of mere months and with still no certainty of glory—do not matter when one takes into consideration the essential polyphony of *The Family Idiot*. A living presence within the writerly mind of Sartre is coming to terms with itself; the long haunting by Flaubert-Roquentin is beginning to make sense and may be, by this act of exorcism through comprehension, beginning to come to an end. But "this man is not detached." The latent violences are his, more than the second narrator's, as are the odd, jolting rythms.

In his analysis of *Memoirs of a Madman,* Sartre mentions Flaubert's platonism of the imagination (*IF* II, 1589) and discusses the well-known trap of "bovarism": "There's the trap: we believe we *recognize ourselves* in a character in a novel, whereas we only install in ourselves the impossible demand to be the synthetic product of a divine totalization" (*IF* II, 1590). That this was one effect of Karl Schweitzer's library and Anne-Marie's liberality with Nick Carter we know (or may believe) from our reading of *The Words*. In that autobiography Sartre speaks of his own platonism and his desire to make things and people become *words* where they would endure on a plane removed from quotidian fallen

245

reality. Flaubert was also subject to this temptation. But Sartre, together with Flaubert, questions whether this taking of the literary for the essence of the real is *merely* a trap: "But *is it only a trap?* No: for this imperative leads us to work upon ourselves and to deepen ourselves" (*IF* II, 1590). Thus, by derealizing ourselves through identification with an *analogon* for an individual whom we take as ourselves, we may achieve through this double act of fictionalization (recognizing ourselves, the real, in the fictional, and seeing in the fictional a transcended mode of the real) an amelioration of our present state and self-awareness. Sartre was foxed by this one for a long time and has had the grace to admit it. So was Flaubert: but he also changed. The above quotation (*IF* II, 1590) shows Sartre paraphrasing Flaubert, albeit in an ambiguous way. He wishes to lead us to the part in *Memoirs of a Madman* where Flaubert appears to deny this ethical utility to art. He wishes to introduce what he calls "the curious and revealing passage" (*IF* II, 1590) in *Memoirs of a Madman* where art no longer expresses, or mimes, or is the image of, but where it simply *is*. The passage to be quoted is, in fact, revealing about Flaubert. It marks a transitory refusal of facticity and utility (even in their transcendent aesthetic modes) which was to remain an aspect of his aesthetic yearnings even in mature years. But, in a way, it is even more revealing about Sartre, given the significance he accords this fragment of juvenilia, given the way he isolates the passage and then expounds at length upon it. One can imagine the resonances it produced in the young Sartre of Le Havre (who is present and quoted here *only* through Flaubert), and one can imagine further—indeed the very choice of quotation obliges us to—the resonances produced in the old Sartre by the memory of those resonances. What is the aesthetic demand of Flaubert in *Memoirs of a Madman* that so excites Sartre?[9]

"I would want," writes Flaubert, quoted by Sartre, "something that had need neither of expression nor form, something pure, like a perfume, something hard like stone, something intangible like a song, and that it be at the same time all of this and none of these things" (*IF* II, 1590). One can hear already in this quote the nasal lifting of the saxophone high above the needle scratches of "Some of These Days." In the station the train to Paris is waiting as Roquentin notes *his* aesthetic ambition:

> Another kind of book . . . one would have to guess, behind the printed words, behind the pages, something which would not exist, which would be above existence. A story, for instance, such as cannot happen, an adventure. It would have to be beautiful and hard as steel and it would have to make people ashamed of their existence.[10]

246

And, one recalls, "behind the pages" is precisely where Roquentin has just imagined—in a little impromptu fable (*un apologue*) inspired by the song—that he would feel most at ease. He is wishing for more than to live in the world of art, or to *live* the world *for* art—as any artist might as a refuge from philistinism, or from his own facticity, or in order to live with joyous, meaningful awareness of his possibilities of producing the *significant irrealization* that a painting is for Sartre. He wishes to live *inside* the world of art in order to become an irrealized presence inhabiting a significant irrealization. What is more essentially Flaubertian than to persuade oneself that one "lived elsewhere, *behind* the canvas of the paintings with Tintoretto's doges, with the grave Florentines of Gozzoli, *behind* the pages of the books with Fabrice del Dongo and Julien Sorel" (*OR*, 207; my emphasis)? Not a desire, be it noted, to be part of a work of art, but a desire *per impossible* to correspond, within an achieved aesthetic vision (that of Tintoretto, Gozzoli, or Stendhal), with those *creatures* in the literal sense (the doges of *Tintoretto*, not those of history) within a world shaped by aesthetic necessity.

In Roquentin's fable, as in the young Flaubert's frustrated efforts at flight from reality, there is a rude awakening. There is a fear, lived as it is recounted within the confines of the fable (perhaps the *only* example of aesthetic and ontic contiguity in *Nausea*[11]—a fear that is the consequence of the invasion of the authentic and unrelenting contingency which it is Roquentin's lot to deal with. There is, in short, the realization that one had "played the fool" (*avoir bien fait l'imbécile*), that there had been a "misdeal," and that one was, indeed, sitting physically and contingently in a bistro in front of a glass of warm beer.[12]

The "warm beer" is perhaps a case of literature overreaching itself, an example of the Hemingwayesque "nostalgie de la boue," where the "little true detail" must be sufficiently sordid to evoke by itself the disease of the narrator. *Nausea* has many of these tricks, and they weaken the text far more than the inconsistencies of, for example, temporal realism (the longest sunset in literature) that Denis Hollier complained of in *Politique de la prose*.[13] Or, rather, they alert the reader to something unresolved in the state of mind of the author (Sartre-Roquentin), which requires that any lived or living experience be subjected to depreciation in order for it to become an example of the triumph of literature over the lived. Would a return to the reality that one was sitting in front of "an ice-cold lager" have affected the point of the fable? The answer would probably be yes, because the mineral, crystalline resonances of "ice-cold" would have diminished the shock of the "nauseous disgust" which is, according to the Sartre of *Psychology of Imagination*, sine qua

247

non of the "realizing consciousness"—especially after a return from the *irréel* world of the imagination. "Ice-cold" would have allowed an intrusion of a semblance of the purity of the *irréel* into the contingent reality of which people should be ashamed (*OR,* 210). It would not have provoked nausea, nor would it have provoked disgust or shame; therefore, the beer must be "warm." What may be said to weaken the text "as a work of literature" in fact strengthens it if we assume that behind Roquentin lurks the deprived and miraculous Poulou, no longer certain whether he is a "mémoire d'outre-tombe" of Gustave or a man called Jean-Paul Sartre engaged in becoming himself.

There is, within this fable of Roquentin, a concise presentation of the conflict between the two states of "being" that tore at Gustave's stability. On the one hand, what one may call a kind of "angelism" (the projection of the self into the status of created nonbeing "behind the canvas") and, on the other, its opposite, the "imbecile" identity of the daily round. In his fable, Roquentin sees, as did Flaubert, imbecility as a mark of untranscended self. Elsewhere in *Nausea* it is his hypersensitivity not to his lack of intelligence but to what he takes to be his own physical ugliness that is the focus of attention in the description of disintegration during the depressive crises. Indeed, it is less his ugliness than the simple fact of the gratuity of his own *unloved* flesh—and unloved, that is, unvalued, flesh is, as Lacan later observed with all the trenchant cruelty of a trained divine, merely *meat.* Even the savage games of subversion of the Cartesian *cogito* do not test his intelligence. They do, however—this is the significance of those set pieces where the intellect goes on the rampage against itself—test his sanity. And here his temptations join with those of Gustave. "I see *clearly,*" writes Roquentin, "into the apparent disorder of my life" (*OR,* 206). Elsewhere he notes that he will keep a diary in order to see *clearly* into his life, and this in spite of the scarcely credible comment at the end of the undated page that opens the novel: "What is curious is that I am not at all disposed to believe myself mad" (*OR,* 6).

It is difficult not to recall these phrases when one reads the footnote that Sartre appends to his discussion of Flaubert's *Memoirs of a Madman,* in which he quotes from the correspondence to Louise Colet of August 9, 1846: "I had seen *clearly* into things and into myself. . . . I had understood all within myself, separated and classified (before seeing you)." To this he adds an acerbic commentary (equally applicable to some of the contradictory self-judgments of Roquentin): "In other words Flaubert never decides completely whether to know himself or ignore himself" (*IF* II, 1552).

II

Complete self-knowledge such as some think obtainable through "self-analysis" is not possible, said Sartre in the interview with Contat and Rybalka on *The Family Idiot*.[14] On the philosophical level there cannot be totalization of a living evolving entity; the attempt at totalization with Flaubert was possible "because the life of Flaubert is a completed totality."[15] On the psychological level there will always be gaps and the intrusion of unrecognized value-laden material: "if I seek to study myself presuppositions will slip in; this is inevitable because of the adhesion or adherence to oneself."[16] In the same paragraph Sartre mentions Merleau-Ponty's stated intention to write an autobiography and his later change of mind. He would draft a novel, not an autobiography. Sartre quotes his former colleague as giving this explanation for the change: "No, basically, it would be better if I were to write a novel. Why? Because in a novel I would be able to give to periods of my life which I don't understand an imaginary sense." A similar kind of assessment was no doubt partly responsible for the decision to write *The Words* on the level of the imaginary (in the double sense of granting unusual significance to the unraveling of Poulou's imaginative constructs and using the mature imagination to flesh out the external circumstances of the childhood world). Sartre did this within a form that owes more to the novel than to the traditional autobiographical enterprise. As Philippe Lejeune concludes:

> The invention of the dialectical *récit* in *The Words* is . . . a doubly important event. In the perspective of the evolution of the autobiographical genre, it is one of the rare renewals of technique and vision that we have seen for a long time. As far as Sartre's work is concerned, *the Words* is the most "totalizing" he has ever produced . . . because within it are fused into *one single form,* in a perfect synthesis, the two modes of philosophical discourse and narrative, a fusion many times sketched out in different manners, either in the fictions of *Nausea* and *The Age of Reason* . . . or in the biographical enterprises, but in all these attempts, admirable of their kind, the equilibrium was not attained, or else the joins remained visible.[17]

Lejeune's criteria are not entirely aesthetic or formal because he is also concerned for the kinds of truths that are being told (or hidden). In this respect, he is far more rigorous with Rousseau's *Confessions* than with Sartre. With Sartre one gets the impression that he is so overwhelmed by the aesthetic success of *The Words* that he misreads the profound meaning that he, generally, attaches to the adjective *dialecti-*

249

cal. These comments, for instance, on *The Family Idiot* seem to me to betray the kind of "common-sense" approach to the work that misses completely the dialectical dialogue with the self, on the transposed level of the imaginary, that is at the heart of the enterprise:

> and the real lived experience (especially for early childhood) escapes in large part from the biographer. The more the information is lacking, the more the analysis develops, proliferating into monstrous expansions: the less one knows about it, the more one is obliged to calculate, to deduce, and to replace the singular by the universal, and the more one takes pleasure in doing it.[18]

In fact, Sartre is very careful *not* to replace the "singular" by the "universal." Many is the time in *The Family Idiot* when he warns against this tendency at work in Flaubert, particularly in the latter's moments of despair. Of his many criticisms of doctrinaire Freudianism, and beyond those methodological and philosophical inadequacies he first learned from Jasper's *General Psychopathology,*[19] the notion that one can, and should, universalize from a specific individual history is perhaps the most firmly and consistently rejected. What Sartre *does* do, and one is surprised that a reader as sensitive as Lejeune has not noticed it, is to insinuate into the other "singular" about whom he is ostensibly writing his own "singular."

Early on, in the first few pages of Volume I, Sartre writes of the eight- or nine-year-old Gustave: "he was learning the use of the symbol" (*IF* I, 16). The next sentence, which could easily have found its place in *The Words,* reads: "A child, if he incarnates himself as Don Quixote from early on, installs in himself, unbeknownst to him, the general principle of all incarnations: he knows how to find himself in the life of another, how to live like another his own life" (*IF* I, 16–17). To read this as a universalizing statement about children is to forget which book one is reading, who its author is, and what he has achieved in dialectical autobiography. It is true that such a statement from another pen *could* indeed have an air of the sage generalization of the pediatric expert writing a guidance manual for young mothers. But such a manual is not likely to be signed "Jean-Paul Sartre" or to be 2,800 pages long. The statement refers to two imaginary children: Gustave and Poulou. Like so many statements about Gustave's interior life, the network of referentiality extends in two directions: explicitly it is a commentary, itself the result of an imaginative construction, on Gustave; implicitly it points toward a continuation of that strange public dialogue with the self called *The Words.* This time, however, the displacement is such that the interior life of another writer mediates the dialogue with the self. In some respects, at least, Gustave is an *analogon* for Poulou as, later, Flaubert will be for Sartre.

In *The Words* Sartre unveils, with capricious sincerity and with the necessary defense strategy of a double-edged humor, those various childhood reveries of heroism, salvation, and glory—all of which are glimpsed, or achieved, within the domain of literature. The double-edged humor is used to distance the child and his circumstances from the consciousness investigating them *and* to attack in the bud any temptation in reader response to a fraudulent, disguised self-pity via a maudlin compassion for Poulou. Reflecting on his dreams of posthumous glory at the age of nine, Sartre uses a curiously feminine image to convey the tortured aspirations of the nine-year-old: "I was a frigid woman whose convulsions solicit then attempt to replace orgasm. Will one say that she is simulating or just that she's trying a bit too hard?"[20] He continues, emphasizing the gap between the lived experience and the desired experience: "In any case I would get nothing from it, I was always a little ahead of, or a little behind, the impossible vision which would have discovered me to myself and I used to find myself, at the end of my exercises, doubting and having gained nothing except a few fine nervous frenzies."[21] When he was twenty-one, Sartre recalled these boyish imaginings in a letter to Simone Jollivet: "On the one hand I'm extremely ambitious. But of what? I imagine glory as a dance-hall filled with gentlemen in evening dress and ladies with plunging necklines who raise their glasses in my honor. It's quite corny, but I have had that image since my childhood."[22] Alongside these passages one might read the following fragment from "Pensées intimes" written by the nineteen-year-old Gustave Flaubert sometime during 1840:

> When I was ten I already dreamed of glory—and I composed as soon as I knew how to write. I painted, expressly for myself, ravishing scenes—I would imagine a theater full of light and gold, hands clapping, shouts, laurels. The author is called for,—the author is, of course, me, it's my name, me-me-me,—I am sought in the corridors, in the boxes, people lean over to see me,—the curtain rises, I step forward,—what intoxication! They look at you, they admire you, they envy you, they're close to loving you![23]

This passage could also, by virtue of its provoked vision, have come from the Poulou *redivivus* sections of *The Words*. That, at any rate, would be an understandable response at first reading. Then one realizes on a second reading that Gustave is more frank, more gauche perhaps,

251

more honest in his self-mendacity than the Poulou of *The Words*. And he is not playing at dialectics. He is a puzzled young man writing for himself in order to situate some of the origins of his present puzzlement. It is the end of the paragraph, the climax of the piled-up verbs culminating in "they're close to loving you!" that reveals, with conscious awareness perhaps, the anguish of the unloved. It admits, with a clumsy un-awareness, that the search for a deep affective security has for a long time been, unsuccessfully, displaced into a search for fantasmic public recognition of artistic merit. On the level of its affective significance there is a touching, almost humble modesty to the final acceptance that, even with worldly acclaim achieved, "they" (*on*) are still only *close to loving you*.

It may not surprise us that Sartre seems blind to the possibilities of this particular text from the "Pensées intimes." Even the use of Gustave as *analogon* does not remove the coyness from Sartre's text. What Sartre does comment on, and with a mordant jocularity that should arouse our suspicions, are the lines following this passage: "Ah! what pity, what pity to think on it, what greater pity to write it down for oneself, to say it to oneself.—Yes, I am a failed great man [*un grand homme manqué*], the species is common today."[24] Seizing on the rhetorical opportunities for displaying the virtuosity of his analytical abilities while thrusting the soiled linen of revealed emotion deep into the bottom of the laundry bag, Sartre spends a brilliant page (*IF* II, 1627–28) deconstructing the supposed logical flaws of the phrase "a failed great man." For this to have any meaning there must be a hierarchy among men: "one must in good logic say that there are very great men, fairly great men, and little ones. And a little one couldn't be a failed great one: he is what he is, neither more nor less" (*IF* II, 1627). Sartre adds a prim, housewifely footnote to this invention: "It goes without saying that these conceptions are completely foreign to me" (*IF* II, 1627). I say "housewifely" because of the comic displacements of the admission of emotional need that are hard at work here. Sartre may be bold about sexuality and its various manifestations (even within himself); but once the idea of the need for emotional security rears its ugly head, Sartre folds his arms, scowls on the doorstep, and goes into analytical and literary overdrive. We are offered a startling version of the La Fontaine fable of the frog who wished to puff himself up to the size of an ox: "the frog who wants to make himself as big as the ox is not a failed ox, he's a mad frog" (*IF* II, 1627). Yes, indeed! In the meantime we may have forgotten that in its common acceptance the phrase used by Flaubert has no need whatever, logical or linguistic, of a concept if hierarchy among men. It is employed in precisely the same sense as the familiar examples given by *Harraps:* "C'est un médecin manqué" (he ought to have been a doctor) or "C'est un garçon manqué" (she ought to have been a boy; she's a regular tomboy). Sartre *knows* this, of course, and he probably knows that we know that he knows.

Why then the parade of logical legerdemain? To answer this question we also need to ask why the first part of this passage from "Pensées intimes" is not subjected to the same rigor, is not, as far as I can recall, subjected to *any* discussion. The answer, or *an* answer, lies in the proximity of experience and the verbal icons used to transpose this experience onto paper. Poulou is not recorded as having written that he was a "failed great man," but we do know how much the first part of the Flaubert passage corresponds to Poulou's imaginings. When the *analogon* gets too close for comfort its ontological status changes and it becomes a substitute self in which the self still recognizes itself. The magical release, the playground area of the imaginary, is absent, and the old resistances and repressions reassert themselves.

It is to Sartre's credit, I believe, that he was aware of these risks and was, by the fact of publishing *The Family Idiot,* prepared to live publicly by them. *The Words,* whatever Sartre may have said in interviews, was not the farewell to literature that he claimed it to be. That farewell, destined like so much of his work to be unfinished, was *The Family Idiot.* There, monumentally, but in a style as sparklingly deceptive as that of *The Words,* he crafted a carefully researched and documented biography which would also be a displaced autobiographical investigation. This "true novel," as Sartre called it, needs to be read with all the philosophical and aesthetic caution one accords to that other novel, *The Words.* When the text is amusing, or jocose, or philosophically *outré,* we may be sure that we have hit upon a *noli me tangere* of the Sartrean psyche. It says much for Sartre's courage that he should have persevered with *The Family Idiot,* given what he knew the alert reader would discover about him, those things Flaubert called *"l'indisable"* (the unsayable), those things that, in order to be discovered, would require the dismantling of a sequence, or the antiphonal rendering of a tone, or unmethodically (but with empathetic intuition—and hence following in Sartre's footsteps?) the dismembering of the methodological apparatus of the enterprise.

What is the methodological apparatus of *The Family Idiot?* We have to go back to a comment in the *Cahiers pour une morale* where, in order to grasp the method of psychological investigation at work within the larger "totalizing" context, Sartre contrasts the explicative procedures of Freud with the *verstehende* (or comprehensive) approach of Karl Jas-

253

pers. Sartre notes that the whole difference between the *verstehen* (which he translates as *comprendre*) of Jaspers and the *erklären* (which he translates as *expliquer*) of Freud is that the former includes the project and the situation of the subject in all their virtuality, whereas the latter eliminates these aspects and concentrates on the explanation of causes without regard to the existential ends. He writes:

> Here the problem of comprehension is posed. It has been badly posed and it is very simple: to explain is to illumine through the causes, to understand is to illumine through the ends. All of Jaspers's examples are reducible to this model. *To understand* how family oppression engenders the hypocrisy of the subject is to follow the behavior of the subject posing his own ends in the transcendence [*dépassement*] of this oppression and, in particular, via the means at his disposal.[25]

The existential (as opposed to Freudian) psychoanalysis sketched out at the end of *Being and Nothingness* follows to the letter Jaspers's model and is, by and large (with some excursions into the field of Freud's Oedipal theories), the method adopted for the descriptions of Flaubert's personal journey into literature.

The "larger *totalizing* context" in which he sets this psychological method is Sartre's well-known "regressive-progressive" approach, less a "method" than a complex combination of methods. Sartre allows himself, in fact, a fairly broad eclectic approach which is difficult to categorize succinctly. Perhaps the best description is that given by Pierre Daix in his three-part review in *Lettres françaises* in 1971:

> In fact, Sartre proceeds by a spiral analysis, taking up in turn each of the stages at another level, so as to always illumine a delimited present by its immediate future, and both of them, sometimes, by the more distant future, then, starting off once more from this present, he goes again to encounter the immediate future with more precision.[26]

This description is accurate only as far as the *intellectual* structure of *The Family Idiot* is concerned. What is missing in this description, and what is essentially the thesis of this article, is the significance that one should attach to the *affective* structure of the work. This is, of course, not a self-standing structure as such plastered onto a preexisting intellectual one. On the contrary, the tensions behind it provided the profound motivating forces for the whole work and are woven almost inextricably into the texture of the whole. As the patterns in an Oriental rug are not printed upon a preexisting substance but are integrally formed with the very fibers of the rug as it is being made, so Sartre's affective presence informs *The Family Idiot*.

Among the many examples this text offers, we can examine the presence of ghosts in the sections entitled "Gustave and His Double" and "Appearance of the Preneurosis" (*IF* II, 1711–66). This is a detailed account of the "double" genesis of *November* and an ingenious and convincing demonstration of the significance *for Flaubert* of the radical shift from the first-person narrative of the greater part of the manuscript to the third-person narrative of the last part, begun after a silence of six months in August 1842. Sartre's investigation is conducted with brio. These pages on the genesis of *November* and on Flaubert's discovery of alterity within himself are, like most of the other major sections of *The Family Idiot,* saturated with literature and with intertextual literary references. Sartre has made himself intimately familiar with those texts read by Flaubert in his formative years, and to this cultural background he has added his own dimension of literary reference. Furthermore, a teasing referentiality to discussions of literature within his own fiction completes the elaborate palimpsest.

Roquentin's reflections in *Nausea* on the act of writing and on the significance of that act are present, implicitly, beneath Sartre's analysis of the opening paragraphs of *November.* There are four aspects, or moments of focus, to this analysis, all of them interconnected. In the first instance, Sartre examines Flaubert's early text and suggests its significance for Flaubert *as he was writing it;* second, Sartre probes the shift in significance for Flaubert conveyed by what he calls the "brutal break" (*cassure brutale*) of the third-person voice of the concluding narrative. Third, as a corollary to this, he leaps forward to the famous "objectivity" of the works of Flaubert's maturity and to the meaning that the evidence of the "brutal break" adds to our understanding (as readers in the twentieth century) of Flaubert's works. Finally, Sartre is reflecting upon (and, implicitly, inviting us to reflect upon) Sartre-Roquentin's ruminations on the necessary duplicity of writing. By giving form to that which was formless, and an end to that which was open, writing changes existence into adventure. Or, as we shall see in the case of Roquentin-Sartre, changes present existence back into the nearest equivalent of lost adventures. Sartre writes: "No doubt that Gustave, a mortal subject wishing for death, wished to exhibit himself in his singular universality. The first words that he writes are decisive: 'I love autumn.' Just like those which begin the second paragraph: 'I have just returned from my walk in the empty meadows' " (*IF* II, 1714). The sense of the imminent extinction of desire, of ambition, and of any kind of authentic sense of future— conveyed almost entirely by the evocation of landscape, climate, and season (an instance of Ruskin's pathetic fallacy)—is paramount in these two opening paragraphs. But two phrases, the last of each paragraph, do not effect this displacement of mood into surroundings: "it is sweet to watch the extinction of all that which, only recently, burned within you," and "I was cold and almost frightened."[27] Each of these personal references serves to reinforce the affective atmosphere created by the displacements. Sartre continues his commentary:

> A personal taste—a dated, irreversible event, an individual moment of his story [*histoire*]. From then on, the chips are down: the young writer will render through words the taste of his daily life. Not the least "distancing" in the relationship between the lived and the reflected: each phrase is a brushing of the self against the self. Total adhesion: the author insists he is right, i.e., that he accepts himself and wished to be as he feels. (*IF* II, 1714–15).

In *Nausea* the entries for Friday three P.M. and Saturday midday (*OR*, 39–50) concern the richness of the memory of past events, largely in Morocco (which Roquentin eventually dismisses as *verroterie*—glass trinkets—using the same term that Sartre will use in *The Family Idiot* to dismiss the imaginings of the hero of *November*); the realization that his present has "no secret dimension," that it is limited to the body ("I am rejected, abandoned in the present. I try in vain to rejoin the past; I cannot escape myself"—*OR*, 42); the brief visit of the Self-Taught Man whose naive comments on "adventures" provoke further reflections ("Something begins in order to end: adventure allows no extension; it has meaning only by its death. Toward this death, which will also, perhaps, be mine, I am dragged with no return" (*OR*, 47); and, finally, the whole entry for "Saturday midday" is devoted to a sardonic discussion of the dichotomy to live/to recount. The last paragraphs of Friday offer an anticipatory epiphany of the "Some of These Days" vision on which the novel ends ("I am so happy when a Negress sings; what summits would I not attain if my *own life* were the matter of the melody"). This theme is taken up with a somber admission of impossibility in the very last paragraph of "Saturday midday," where, between the line, may be heard a two-part invention on the "retrospective illusion" (see *IF* II, 1598, and, of course, *The Words*). This is its aesthetic component, and on lost childhood this is, even more darkly hidden, its psychological counterpart: "I wanted the moments of my life to follow each other and to be ordered like those of a life which one recalls. One might as well try to catch time by the tail" (*OR*, 50).

Although in many senses Roquentin is *not* Sartre, we have enough documentation on—and *by*—Sartre, especially the important *Psychol-*

ogy of Imagination, to know that those passages in *Nausea* on the relationship between life and literature allow for a complete concordance between what Roquentin is made to write and what Sartre was actually thinking. Of these passages we may say, as Sartre does of the opening of *November:* "not the least 'distancing' in the relationship between the lived and the reflected: each phrase is a brushing of self against self."

The deception provoked by the *real* and the risk of self-deception that the *imaginary* may hold are as present in Sartre's reflections on Flaubert as is naïveté in Roquentin's reactions to the Self-Taught Man. If the real provokes deception, it is only because there has been a prior encounter with the imaginary. Sartre's words "the chips are down: the young writer will render through words the taste of his daily life" imply a meaning in Flauibert's narration exactly the same as Roquentin's "but the end is there, which transforms everything. For us the guy is already the hero of the story" (*OR,* 50)—except that for the first-person narrator of *November* the "heroization" has already occurred. He has constituted himself as a *personnage,* or, rather, he is a *personnage* in whom Flaubert, using the first person, has constituted a part of himself. By contrast, Roquentin is a "personnage" in whom Sartre has constitued a part of himself, but with an ambiguity (far richer than the young Flaubert's) that will permit him an extraordinarily unstable use of "I" with a shifting valency, itself dependent upon the many heteroclitic narrative modes employed in the text.

Given the totality of the text of *November,* including the sudden later shift to third-person narrative, the first part conceals an ambivalence of meaning in relation to its creator. There is the significance of the text at the beginning with the hero-narrator implying his own end and the end (or ends) of his text in the act of writing it; but there is also the significance the text assumes once the third-person narrator intervenes. On the aesthetic level, Sartre sees in this shift a successful salvage operation:

> But Flaubert *does not disown* the beginning of *November* . . . however displeased he may have been with his former work, it is precisely in order *to complete* it that he has introduced the second narrator. Better: having succeeded with the conclusion, it seems that this ending, in his eyes, by a strange retroaction, transforms the beginning without touching it, changes defects into beauties, and saves, in some way, the pages written before February. (*IF* II, 1718)

On the psychological level, Sartre recognizes the value of the "brutal break" as something giving a dynamism of living human crisis to the text far more moving than the *amphigouri* of the first two parts. Flaubert

257

has realized that he no longer coincides with his *personnage,* that he is *other* than what he pretended to take himself to be, and that he could no longer even keep, except perhaps ironically, to this earlier pretension. He may not have discovered what he *is,* but he has discovered what he is *not.*

As we know Sartre always refused to consider literature as texts divorced from the human enterprise responsible for their production. However devious the author, his writing would, ultimately, always bear silent witness to his circumstances and to his relationships with them. A crisis transcended through literary production will not necessarily remove the neurotic conflict that engendered it; but the literary production will inevitably bear the traces of the conflict from which it emerged. Of the malaise that the "brutal break" effects on the reader, Sartre notes:

> But this is precisely what gives it its value; this failure of narration strikes even more deeply, the less it seems, on the surface, to be willed. Something begins to live under our very eyes: a real event that has happened to the author and that we read between the lines. If we are asked what this event is, we shall say that Flaubert took up his manuscript with the intention of completing it at the moment when he perceived that he *could no longer* speak of himself in the first person. It is this rupture of adhesion to lived experience, this brusque distancing swelling in the intimate relation of self to self, that allows us best to understand how Flaubert felt, at a deep level, the experience of the eight previous months. (*IF* II, 1716–17)

What Sartre does *not* mention is that the text to which he grants chronological and aesthetic authority—the concluding third-person narrative—is written in a style very close to that used in many parts of *The Family Idiot* (which itself sometimes gives the impression of being a third-person transposition of *The Words*). He uses nominative absolute constructions ("Passionate for what is beautiful, ugliness was repugnant to him like crime"),[28] one of the most frequently employed opening gambits in the period of *The Words*. He uses delicately balanced double-phrased sentences, where an irony, lurking unrecognized in the first half, explodes in our faces at the end of the second half (a technique Voltaire had employed to great effect in *Candide*): "He had the vanity to believe that men did not love him; men did not know him."[29] These and other classical literary devices, and indeed the very cadences and rhythms of the language, make a reading of this third-person narrative into an exercise in *déjà vu!*

Sartre sees in this stylistically recorded crisis the origin (or at least a literary evidence of *one* aspect of the origin) of the famous impersonality of the writings of the mature Flaubert:

At the end of the summer of '42, when he comes back to *November,* he doesn't get angry, never raises his voice: simply, he no longer enters into his work and the first narrator seems a stranger to him; he speaks of him—i.e. of himself—as of *another,* an acquaintance rather than a friend. . . . The style is taut, hardened, often striking but cold; for the first time Gustave produces a work which could lay claim to what he will call "impersonalism" and—which says a lot about the meaning of this literary doctrine—he himself is the object of this impersonal tale. (*IF* II, 1717)

For Sartre this "impersonality," so aesthetically and psychologically successful, was a solution that had its own dialectical ambiguity. It was not merely the result of Flaubert no longer coinciding with his *personnage,* it was also a recognition of, an interiorization of, and an aesthetic mastery of the effects of his passivity toward the world and its hold on him: "Manipulated from early childhood by others, Gustave, at the heart of the infinite accord of self with self, has always felt himself to be a finite object for others. The successive employment of 'I' and 'he' appears to him to be the best way to indicate himself as a concrete object—that is to say as a singular universal" (*IF* II, 1719). Sartre has left us several published "versions" of the echoes of his own childhood and of the subsequent difficulties of the adult in coming to terms with it. The first, in which the golden-haired angel makes his first travestied appearance, is *The Childhood of a Leader* (1938). This story, clearly crafted as a fiction rather than as a displaced autobiography, is written in the third person with the narrator sardonically distanced from Lucien Fleurier. Nearly a quarter of a century later Sartre returned in *The Words,* using a specious adaptation of first-person "confessional" narrator. In the interim he had begun to amass the documentary material for what was to become *The Family Idiot,* the third and most complex version of this obsession with the "unfinished business" of the early years of personalization for a creative consciousness. Sartre's choices of narrative technique, where important aspects of his psyche are invested in the text, do not seem to correspond to Gustave Flaubert's as hypothesized in *The Family Idiot.* Nor should we expect absolute congruence, even with the partial displacement of Poulou onto Gustave. However, we have not yet considered the earliest of the published "autobiographical" fictions, *Nausea.* The time has come to consider the deep significance of that little mischievous phrase from *The Words:* "I *was* Roquentin."

What is remarkable in this work, a young writer's first novel written in the confessional first person, is the total absence of reference to an actuality, a remembrance, or even a "legible" transfiguration of childhood. Roquentin seems to have sprung like a dragon's tooth fully armed into his author's consciousness. Neither childhood, adolescence, nor the recollection of the complex ambivalences toward parental figures have any place in this book. The "ablation" is total.[30]

In *November,* by contrast, after the evocation of the melancholy of autumn in the opening pages, Flaubert proceeds to elaborate upon the unbiquity of infantile, childhood, and adolescent fantasies of sexuality provoked by the touch, smell, or memory of women.[31] Sartre-as-Roquentin is silent on this subject. Whether this circumspection was the consequence of an involuntary "blocking" during the drafting of *Nausea,* it was not the result of a conscious concern for literary propriety—witness the minutely detailed, and unpunctuated, mimesis of the breathless masturbatory rape fantasy (*OR,* 120–22) or the vision of Jouxtebouville which concludes with an implicit phallic subversion of Pascal's "thinking reed" (*OR,* 188–89).

If it were not for the brief, unexpected mention of Aunt Bigeois's consolation from Chopin's *Préludes* after the death of his uncle (*OR,* 205), one might imagine Roquentin as the ultimate orphan raised among strangers to live, as an adult, among strangers. "Someone is missing here: it's Sartre!" The Sartre of *The Words* is certainly missing, unless one takes *Nausea* to be a sinister discovery of adulthood, a nightmare version of the provoked dreamworld of the child Poulou in the darkened bedroom—"I grew old in the shadows, I became a solitary adult, with neither father nor mother, neither hearth nor home, almost without a name."[32] For this reading to fit, it must also allow for the subsequent negation of Poulou's kingdom represented by La Rochelle. The innocent incest with Anne-Marie (now become the alien mother, Mme. Mancy) is here denied him; the ham acting of Karl's loving authority is replaced by a "real" adult, Joseph Mancy (is this the origin of Sartre's loathing of the *esprit de sérieux*? and, among his peers, he discovers his unattractiveness. May we accept that at some stage in early manhood (and hence well prior to the unearthing of the past in the troubled self-analysis that led—publicly at least—to *The Words*) there was such a repression of this nocturnal adventure and of its significance that they became, in effect, fused into an unconscious fantasy?

In a paper on this kind of dilemma, "On Ablation of the Parental

260

Images, or The Illusion of Having Created Oneself," the unorthodox British analyst Charles Rycroft mentions in passing his own reading of *The Words* (which he sees as the paradigmatic text of the parental ablator). He presents the clinical picture of the problem thus:

> It can generally be assumed that as children patients—and, indeed, all human beings—have had intense feelings about both their parents, and that as adults they never become entirely indifferent to them, but retain them as living images in their minds, both as living persons who are to some extent still loved or hated and as internal figures whose behavior and ideals are still used as models to be copied or deified.
>
> It would seem, however, that in some people the parental images suffer a different fate. Instead of remaining a living part of the patient's personality, they are, or appear to be, ablated or destroyed, so that the patient appears to lack parental introjects. . . . This apparent psychological discontinuity is, of course, in the last resort an illusion and a piece of unconscious self-deception, explainable by postulating the massive use of such defence-mechanisms as repression and splitting, which exclude the parental images from consciousness and from the patient's self-image and which divest all memories of father and mother, and of the self's childhood with them, of all meaning. . . . The phenomenon I am describing can also be explained as the result of an unconscious fantasy that the parents have died.[33]

As we shall see, there is evidence from Sartre's correspondence (of which Rycroft had no knowledge at the time of writing his paper) to support this interpretation. Undoubtedly the term *unconscious fantasy* can cover a wide spectrum of psychic disorders and is frequently abused in lay and even in professional analytical writings. But it does seem that in the attempt to *will* himself into adulthood by buckling on an artificial carapace that was to become an essential part of his public persona, Sartre underwent a series of intensely private crises whose force he recognized but whose sources he wished to ignore. Certainly, the presentation of self in *Nausea* demonstrates the vertigo experienced by one who cannot, yet, investigate the past and who cannot, because of this, live the present with any sense of ease or equilibrium.

For all of its cleverness, which seems on reflection to be composed of so many brilliant barricades of denial, *Nausea* reveals the profound need of humans for love. It also reveals the catastrophic, disabling effects of the denial or absence of love. Roquentin's aesthetic quest is but one more displacement of this need. The illustration and recognition that the love affair with Anny is over are powerfully conveyed; what is not said, however, *even between the lines,* is what this love may represent on a deeper

261

psychic level for Roquentin. In fact, *no* text is so watertight that it cannot be intelligently and imaginatively read *against* itself (this is, indeed, the position adopted by the Sartre who wrote *The Family Idiot*).

Much ink has been spilled on discovering the "identity" of Anny. Is she a version of Simone de Beauvoir (some of whose characteristics she appears to share)? Is she, as many Sartrean scholars now seem to believe, that earlier Simone, Simone Jollivet, to whom Sartre dedicated a typed copy of *Nausea* which was found among her papers after her death and later used by Contat and Rybalka to establish the variant edition of the present Pléiade volume? In their editorial comments, Contat and Rybalka note: "Sartre has several times confirmed to us that Anny is the one fictional character who was the most directly inspired by a real person, Simone Jollivet, the young women with whom he had his first affair from 1925 to 1927" (*OR*, 1790). Or is she a kind of amalgam of women with whom Sartre was intimate in his twenties, as the Ellénore of *Adolphe* is a composite creation by Benjamin Constant? These kinds of questions imply, alas, an analysis of the superficial.

The establishment of an apparent similarity between a person and a character on the level of their physical attributes, gestural mannerisms, verbal tics, and aesthetic preferences is only the first criterion for biographical investigation. It is only then that the real interpretive work begins. What must be examined is *what the living model represented to the living author* and what the fictional transposition represents to him in his camouflage as "self-made man" and hero (antihero?) of a confessional novel. If Simone Jollivet is the source of that romantic couple "the adventurer and the adventuress" in the days before the Fall when they both believed in their complicitous intimacy, in their "necessity," and in the reality of "adventures," what, then, is one to make of the following admission of ablation of the parental imago in the letter to her of 1926 which opens *Lettres au Castor et à quelques autres?* "Here are my two fundamental tendencies. The first is ambition. I very quickly grew displeased with myself and the *first true construction that I have made has been my own character.* I have worked at two things: to give myself will power and to repress within me the second tendency (sentimentality) of which I was profoundly ashamed."[34] Furthermore, what is one to make of the fact that this admission (which continues with a description of the circumstances in which he last received at age fourteen a box on the ears from his mother) is addressed both as a confidence and as an act of seduction to the one woman who appears to have replaced the distant, infantile, and probably "alienated" memory of Anne-Marie as the little adventurer's accomplice and aide-de-camp?

Whether Sartre was justified in his choice of substitution (Simone for Anne-Marie) we shall never know. This would require a documentation on Simone Jollivet as extensive as the one we currently possess on Sartre, and this seems, at present, an unlikely occurrence. Whether Sartre was, deviously or obscurely, aware of the act of substitution (and the psychic level at which it was being perpetrated) is another matter. Here we are able to establish a synchronic intertextuality of all of his available writings. I suspect that a synchronicity of childhood crises and pleasures can be discovered throughout the text of *Nausea,* and that the unconscious network of transpositions that profoundly motivates this text and informs its shape and structure will lead us inevitably to Paris, to Alsace, but above all to La Rochelle. La Rochelle was the introduction to solitude and contingency. At La Rochelle Sartre realized that "there are no adventures," that the adventuress had gone, that perhaps she never really was, that she was a figment of one's imagination coinciding in the days before the Fall with what one had mistakenly taken to be one's "necessity." The English title of the Proust volume *Albertine disparue* suggests the jealous despair of the Poulou who was metamorphosing into Jean-Paul: *The Sweet Cheat Gone.* Anny's absence hovers, perversely present, over the text of *Nausea.* Roquentin is mistakenly moved by it, as was Flaubert's dying Félicité by the "presence" of the Holy Ghost the Comforter—conjured on the faulty vision of the fading consciousness by the feathers of a stuffed parrot that, alive, had gone under the name of "Loulou."

III

If Simone Jollivet, "the adventuress," is the recognized source for Anny and the unrecognized displacement of the alienated infantile, or early childhood, memory of Anne-Marie, one may ponder the strange condensation operated in the choice of name for the heroine. This is especially so given the extraordinary significance that Sartre attaches to *November,* and given the long discussion (*IF* II, 1750–66) on what achieving this work meant for Flaubert (so close to what Sartre had claimed for *Nausea* in his own career). Without an awareness of *November* and its place in the mental library of the young Sartre, and without an awareness of his childhood (and nowadays one has to force oneself to realize, *artificially* as it were, that in 1938 *The Words* had been neither published, written, nor yet conceived), the name chosen for the heroine has no resonances beyond, perhaps, the hinted exoticism of the foreign—"Anny" rather than the expected "Annie."

November is a novel about (and largely "by") a highly intelligent and gifted man who appears to have failed in life because he has failed in love, or, rather, he has known a great and passionate love which has devastated him, and now that he can no longer possess her he feels completely abandoned. As Roquentin is haunted by "Some of These Days" and tries to imagine the origins and the miseries of the singer and composer, so the hero of *November* is haunted, after his mistress's disappearance, by the street barrel-organ grinder and his melancholic airs and sets to wondering what had driven this Italian peasant from his home and his corn fields to this employment.[35] As Sartre indicates, at the time of writing *November* Flaubert had known two intense love experiences: the platonic, or at any rate unconsummated, adoration of what might be called the maternal substitute, Madame Elisa Schlésinger; and the brief but profoundly sensual rutting with Eulalie Foucault in Marseilles. In the next novel, the first version of *L'Education sentimentale* (Sartre never says this, but one suspects he reads it as the Flaubertian equivalent of *The Age of Reason*), these two women are condensed into one feminine experience, Madame Emilie. Sartre notes: "E as in Elisa, LIE as in Eulalie" (*IF* II, 1759). A similar kind of deep condensation has taken place in the naming of the heroine of *Nausea*. When Sartre discusses the presence of the woman of *November* he is at pains to point out the extent to which she is seen as the feminine counterpart of the hero himself. Already in the first volume of *The Family Idiot* Sartre had introduced the notion of the feminization of self in the mode of the imaginary that was an aspect of Flaubert's character (and openly admitted by Flaubert himself in letters to women friends). What is surprising is that each time he mentions the name of the heroine of *November* Sartre gets it wrong! He writes "Maria." Her name is "Marie." It is as if, writing in his old age about his great predecessor in order to discover the tangled paths to the heart of his own labyrinth, Sartre had stumbled, quite unaware, on the literary half of that compression of "Anne-Marie" which was to give "Anny" in *Nausea*.

The resurrectionist at work in *The Family Idiot* appears at times to have come across a family vault, *his* family vault, rather than the isolated remains of a famous writer from another country. In a recently published paper (1986), "Jean-Paul Sartre, biographe de Flaubert," the eminent *Flaubertiste* Jean Bruneau is highly critical, qua *Flaubertiste,* of what he sees as the distortions, disinformation, and tendentious reading of Flaubert's early years. Having given chapter-and-verse examples of Sartre's historical and scholarly errors, he concludes on Sartre's work: "It adds nothing, I think I have shown this, to Flaubert studies in the proper sense; it even goes against the current, for research on Flaubert, before and since Sartre's work, has shown up the weakness of its hypotheses. The interest of *The Family Idiot* lies elsewhere: in the numerous and profound discussions on a key topic: the frontiers between the real and the imaginary. From this perspective, Sartre's work is a masterpiece."[36]

This encomium is wholly justified; but even more important is the *specific* "real" and "imaginary" Sartre himself, probed obliquely but intensely in his old-age revelation to us, his readers, of a youthful yet continuing—at times, one suspects, against his will—fascination with Gustave Flaubert, at once an alter ego and a ghost he could not lay to rest. The middle-aged writer of *The Words* who could cheerfully boast of the early stroke of genius that brought him to public attention— *Nausea*—is very much present in this passage on Flaubert's later admiration for *November:*

> I have said that he still enjoyed, in his forties, reading it to his intimates. If a middle-aged man has retained so much esteem for this disguised autobiography, one can imagine the enthusiasm of the adolescent who, in October '42, had just completed it. He had won his bet. The failed great man had made of his failings the source and the subject of a masterpiece. (*IF* II, 1755)

In a sense, failure transcended is the leitmotiv of the Sartrean enterprise and the most powerful source of identification with Gustave, more "real" and less "imaginary" than the constructed parallels of sexual and affective wounds. Perhaps the most moving passage of *The Family Idiot*, because of the presence of mind and strength of purpose that must have been required to write it, is the lucid and scathingly "truthful" description of the great writer (but which one?) in his old age. It was drafted when Sartre, in his late sixties and with failing eyesight, was, after some two thousand pages, approaching the end of the second volume:

> In these last years he knows that he must draw the line. He plunges into the past trying to pick up and retain in his hands this life of austerities (profitable in spite of everything), this life which has been neither successful nor ruined. He works. He pores over huge, boring books that he cannot always understand; the aridity of his endeavor repulses him; yet he had dreamed of this, in various forms, since his youth. But after '75 he is no longer equal to his hatred; even for misanthropy one needs alacrity. Prematurely aged, abandoned by his niece, he needs tenderness and accepts it with gratitude if ever it is offered him. . . . He is

cured of the neurosis which for more than thirty years has kept him alert, but, at the same time, he has lost his *personnage*—let's say his "character" for he was always "his own play-actor"—and now finds again, after a whole life of faking it, the painful and defenseless "estrangements" of his childhood. (*IF* II, 2134–35)

Notes

1. *L'Idiot de la famille* (Paris, 1971–72), three volumes (hereafter *IF*). The first volume has now been translated (in two volumes) by Carol Cosman as *The Family Idiot: Gustave Flaubert 1821–1857* (Chicago, 1986–88). All general references will give the English title; however, all specific references will give the French edition. All quotations are from the French text and are my own translations.

2. Pierre Marcabru, *"Les Séquestrés d'Altona,* drame bourgeois, analyse lucide d'une décomposition,"* Arts* 30 (September 1959), 8.

3. I do not use the dichotomy *manifest/latent* because that implies an unconscious element to which consciousness has no access except through the dubious revelations of the psychoanalytical session.

4. *Un théâtre de situations* (Paris, 1973), 283.

5. Gustave Flaubert, *Oeuvres complètes de Gustave Flaubert* (Paris), 1973), II, 667. My translation. Hereafter *Flaubert* followed by page reference.

6. One should note in passing the concision of the recognition by Sartre in that last phrase that although there are two distinct narrative voices in *November,* the second is merely a continuation of the first "by other means," as von Clausewitz might say.

7. *Les Mots* [*The Words*] (Paris, 1964), 210.

8. These questions, incidentally, have their own ambiguities since they both involve two quite distinct temporal references: On the one hand, the "identification" admitted by a mature and deeply self-conscious writer who had achieved in the real world of his contemporaries the literary glory whose quest had inhabited the daydreams of the young Poulou and, with possible ironic transposition, the last paragraphs of *Nausea* and on the other hand, the doubting provincial school-teacher assailed by his own contingency and prey to the suspicion that he may remain "some mute inglorious Milton". It takes an intertextual reading of *The Family Idiot* to resolve these ambiguities into the structure of what one may call the "spiral of displaced (and, here, transcended) repetitions" that was Sartre's life.

9. I say "excites" Sartre; perhaps I exaggerate. Nonetheless it leads to two full pages of closely-printed exegesis that could serve as an aesthetic appendix to *Being and Nothingness.* Roquentin, one might say, is alive and well and living in Paris.

10. *Oeuvres romanesques* (Paris, 1981), 210 (hereafter *OR*).

11. One can discount the artful employment of the present tense in the hotel scene with Anny which paradoxically creates the effect of a deliberate stylization, and hence aesthetic "distancing" of a deeply disturbing encounter.

12. By contrast, Anny's "privileged situations" leading to "perfect moments" are an attempt to give to existence an aesthetic quality whose formal beauty allows the participant/witness to live aesthetically. Roquentin's fable, however, requires more than a transcendence of imminence through aestheticism, for its very point of departure is already beyond the contingent world of experience or even the theatricalization of that

world. And necessarily so, for that world is one constantly subject to the menace of the possibility of disintegration via *estrangement*, or hebetude, or depersonalization, or "epilepsy"—all those somatizations of anguish for which Roquentin has but one word: *nausea.*

13. Denis Hollier, *Politique de la prose: Sartre et l'an quarante* (Paris, 1982).

14. *Situations* X (Paris, 1976), 91–115.

15. Ibid., 105.

16. Ibid., 104.

17. Philippe Lejeune, *Le Pacte autobiographique* (Paris, 1975), 242–43. My translation.

18. Ibid., 242.

19. Karl Jaspers, *General Psychopathology*, trans. by Marion Hamilton and J. Hoenig, (Manchester and Chicago, 1963). One example of Sartre's criticism of Flaubert's abuse of induction is in *IF* II, 1536: "What he calls dissection is necessarily reduced to passive observation . . . and to induction . . . whatever Flaubert discovers in himself he immediately wishes to generalize. For the terror of his 'difference' tortures him and, scarcely has he discovered a particularity, than he makes it a trait of human nature."

20. *Les Mots,* 174.

21. Ibid., 174–75.

22. *Lettres au Castor et à quelques autres* (Paris, 1983), 9. The same letter includes the following surprising admission of an overwrought emotional nature such as one might expect to find in Gustave: "I was—something which perhaps you never suspected—born with the character that fits my face: madly, stupidly sentimental, a coward and a cry-baby. My sentimentality has gone to the extent of making me sob at anything. Plays, films, novels have made me cry out. I have had fits of unjustifiable and unbelievable pity, fits of cowardice as well, of weakness of character which at one time caused my parents and friends to rank me among the greatest of failures." *Lettres au Castor,* 10. My translation.

23. *Flaubert,* 601.

24. Ibid.

25. *Cahiers pour une morale* (Paris, 1983), 287. My translation.

26. Pierre Daix, "Le Flaubert de Sartre," *Les Lettres françaises,* May 26, 1971, 4.

27. *Flaubert,* 614.

28. *Flaubert,* 666.

29. Ibid.

30. Contat and Rybalka appear to concur. See their remarks, *OR,* 1731. For a different point of view, see Adrian van den Hoven, "*Nausea:* Plunging below the Surface," Chapter 12 herein.

31. A ubiquity which, one should note, extends fantastically beyond the grave. Had Freud read *November?* I have been unable to find in his complete works any commentary on the following passage, which is one honest hysteric's admission of pansexualism, at least in his own case: "Woman, whom I was already trying to understand (there is no age when one doesn't think about it: as children we palpate with a naive sensuality the bosoms of the big girls who kiss us and hold us in their arms; at ten years, one dreams of love; at fifteen it happens to you; at sixty, one still holds on to it, and if the dead dream of something in their tomb, it is to reach out underground into the nearest grave in order to lift up the shroud of the deceased woman and to mingle oneself with her sleep); woman was thus for me a magnetic mystery which troubled my poor child's head" (*Flaubert,* 616).

32. *Les Mots,* 98.

33. Charles Rycroft, in *Psychoanalysis and Beyond* (London, 1985), 214–32. One

example of Rycroft's lack of orthodoxy is his criticism, aired in this paper, of the number of professional analysts who entered the profession precisely as parental ablators. He is also highly critical of the doctrinal devotion, especially evident in North America, paid to Freud's utterances *ex cathedra* (some of which he sees as more revealing of Freud's psychopathology than of "fact").

34. *Lettres au Castor,* 10; my emphasis.

35. *Flaubert,* 669.

36. Jean Bruneau, "Jean-Paul Sartre, biographe de Flaubert," in *Lectures de Sartre,* ed. by Claude Burgelin (Lyons, 1986), 177. Apart from specific and easily identifiable matters of error (for instance, on the electoral, financial, and cultural status of Achille-Cléophas), Bruneau is concerned to show that Sartre has misunderstood the "atmospherics" of the Flaubert household and suggests that he has confused them with some leftover sentiments about his own childhood. It seems to me that there is some justification in Bruneau's criticism; but I would suggest that rather than see Karl Schweitzer behind the father figure Gustave had to cope with in late adolescence, it would make more sense to *imagine* the duty-oriented polytechnician, Joseph Mancy. Bruneau gives evidence of the spontaneous warmth and affection among the three correspondents—"ton père et ami," Gustave himself, and the pet of them both, "le Rat," Caroline.

14

ROMANCE AND RESSENTIMENT: SAINT GENET

Walter S. Skakoon

Recently, critics have turned their attention to nonfictional texts and decided to scrutinize them for their poetics. Ignoring the traditional distinction between fiction and nonfiction in their consideration of these texts, they are analyzing nonfictional works for their tropes (their rhetorical and stylistic features) and emplotment (the configuration of the story.) From this perspective Richard Rorty can remark quite justifiably that for Derrida philosophy becomes a kind of writing.[1] In turn, Hayden White can create a poetics of nineteenth-century historiography. *Metahistory*[2] is an orchestration of Northrop Frye's theory of genres, tropic analysis, Stephen Pepper's typology of philosophical worldviews, and Karl Mannheim's classification of ideologies into a system of categories in terms of which the poetics, metaphysics, and ideologies of historians and philosophers of history from Michelet to Nietzsche can be described. In reference to biography, Leon Edel, the noted biographer of Henry James, calls for a poetics of biography when he states: "A biographer is a storyteller who may not invent his facts but who is allowed to imagine his form." Henry James had referred to this form as "the figure in the carpet."[3] It is the life myth of the biographical subject and is identical to the coherent narrative that underlies the external chronicle of events.

In Sartrean terms, the life myth or the coherent narrative in *Saint Genet* represents the *projet originel* of the biographical subject. In biography, as well as in philosophy, history, or fiction, what matters is that each genre, whether fictional or nonfictional, has a narrative (or *mythos*) and can therefore be studied for its poetics.

My goal is to study the poetics of Sartre's *Saint Genet*. First, the terms *emplotment* and *tropes,* which together constitute the poetics of the text, deserve further elucidation. *Emplotment* designates the manner in which a chronicle, a sequence of events unfolding in time, is configured into a story. This configuration takes place by virtue of the fact that the events are reencoded in order that a specific point can be made or a theme (*dianoia*) expressed. The events are reorganized so that sense can be made out of the facts by means of the technique of selectivity: the determination of the relative importance of the events in relation to each other. Selectivity and the particular positioning of the beginning, middle, and end of the events constitute the various elements that go into the operation of emplotment. Organizing the facts around a theme is necessary in order to provide them with a familiar cultural tradition within which emplotment can be carried out according to recognized patterns. According to Northrop Frye, there are four such patterns or modes in the Western tradition. These patterns, also referred to as archetypal myths, have resulted in the following narratives: romance, tragedy, comedy, and satire. Any of these patterns may be discovered in a particular work. However, a specific work may well represent a displacement in respect to the particular narrative theme expressed in the work. For example, the pattern inherent in a specific novel may be that of romance, but the work may tend toward the realistic, and as a result the tension between these two may be expressed through ironic means.

Tropes, the rhetorical or stylistic features of a text, designate the modes of discourse. The most common devices are metaphor, metonymy, synecdoche, and irony. Metaphor is employed to bring out the similarity between two objects; by means of analogy it permits one to see one term as the representation of the other. Metonymy permits one to relate two entities and view one as the substitute for the other; such an exercise can lead to a kind of reductionism. Synecdoche means that a part of an entity is made to stand for the whole or vice versa; the use of this device can result in a tendency toward contextualization and integration. Irony denies a pointed representation or metaphor by stating it and implying its opposite.

This approach will enable us to illuminate the poetics of *Saint Genet*. It is well known that in this work Sartre's philosophical discourse very much overshadows the biographical narrative.[4] However, submerged below the explicit discursive level of Sartre's analytic biography, a specific form of narrative is implied, that of romance. Both the discourse and the narrative assume certain tropic features. In his attempt to understand Genet's life—that is to say, to render it explicit in *Saint Genet* through an analysis of Genet's words—Sartre employs the formal poetic methods of emplotment and tropes. He attributes these features to an imaginary mode of consciousness which, in the case of Genet, is motivated by *ressentiment*.

In *Saint Genet* Sartre uses employment and tropes in the following manner. By means of empathy, he renders explicit Genet's own worldviews, with the result that the employment arises from Genet's own activities as these are grasped in his works. The tropic features of *Saint Genet* represent Sartre's perception of the repetitive nature of Genet's behavior. It must be stressed here that Genet's repetitive behavior assumes a spiral form. Of course, Sartre is perfectly capable of appreciating the poetic features inherent in Genet's work, but he refuses to see these texts in purely formalistic terms and thus to privilege Genet's literary and autobiographical texts. Like Marxist critics, Sartre privileges genre criticism because of the mediatory function it performs. This kind of criticism is essential if one wishes to view literature both historically and within the context of the transformation of its forms and of social relations. As Fredric Jameson asserts: "The strategic values of generic concepts for Marxism clearly lie in the mediatory function of the notion of a genre, which allows the coordination of immanent formal analysis of the individual text within the twin diachronic perspective of the history of forms and the evolution of social life."[5]

Sartre emplots Genet's life as a romance because this is a genre in which the primary binary opposition is that of good and evil. Ethics, as an instrument of power relations in society, also sorts out classes of individuals into categories of good and evil. The genre of romance makes use of these ethical and social distinctions. In addition, and in keeping with Nietzsche's and Sartre's definition, Genet's *ressentiment* allows him to maintain an ethical stance that runs counter to the dominant one: in the face of good, Genet will maintain evil.

According to Nietzsche, Christianity, the slave morality, was maintained against the dominant pagan morality; these ethical priorities reflected conflicts of social class and power. Genet, as social pariah, belongs to the margins of society. We must go beyond formalism in order to render intelligible the binary opposition between good and evil in romance, rather than permitting it to remain an immanent formal

271

feature. This allows us not only to treat the question of the poetics of Sartre's biographies but also to measure the extent to which Sartre detects *ressentiment* in Genet, specifically in respect to the closure of his biographical texts.

First I would like to explore the archetypal myth or narrative in terms of which Genet's life is emplotted. I will do this in conjunction with the dominant tropic figure that informs both the emplotment and the discourse. Then, as indicated above, I will show that Genet's recourse to the imaginary has its source in *ressentiment*.

Sartre's *Saint Genet* is emplotted along the lines of romance—in contradistinction to three other archetypal myths or narratives, namely, tragedy, comedy, and satire. Frye uses the term *mythoi* or *generic plots* to refer to these four narrative pregeneric elements of literature. These are "narrative categories of literature broader than, or logically prior to, the ordinary literary genres."[6] Frye lists four such categories: the tragic, the comic, the romantic, and the ironic or satiric.

Romance, according to Frye, "is the structural core of all fiction: being directly descended from folktale, it brings us closer than any other aspect of literature to the sense of fiction, considered as a whole, as the epic of the creative man's vision of his own life as a quest."[7] In *Anatomy of Criticism* Frye defines this quest as "the search of the libido or desiring self for a fulfillment that will deliver it from the anxieties of reality but will still contain that reality."[8] The basic tropic feature found in Genet is the metaphor, the trope of identity and representation.[9] The particular mode in which romance is reflexively reconsidered is Frye's low mimetic one of irony. The latter mode also serves as a critique of the representational power of metaphor and of the idea of identity.

Fry divides literature into two modes: high mimetic and low mimetic. High mimetic is a "mode of literature in which, as in most epics and tragedies, the central characters are above our own level of power and authority, though within the order of nature and subject to social criticism." Low mimetic is "a mode of literature in which the characters exhibit a power of action which is roughly on our own level, as in most comedy and realistic fiction."[10] Irony is bringing down the high idealized form to actuality, which reveals the greater exercise of power as illusory. According to Sartre, Genet's idealized representations are deflated by his reflexive consciousness.

Frye considers romance as the nearest form to the wish-fulfillment dream. This dream is realized by the quest and gives romance its form as a series of adventures. These adventures unfold in six stages.[11] The first phase is the birth of the hero, described as being the descendant of unknown parents who is sent to another place. The second phase is the hero's upbringing in an arcadian world, a period of innocence. The third inaugurates the quest theme, where the hero is separated from his past. This is followed by the fourth phase, that of descent, which is the agonistic period of romance. In that stage the integrity of the innocent world is pitted against the assault of experience. The next phase is one of ascent, a period of reflection in which experience, now comprehended, ceases to be mysterious. In the final phase, the hero is reunited with a community, or else he withdraws into the solitary life.

Sartre presents Genet as the abandoned child, parents unknown, who is sent to another place, from city to country. There (second phase) he lives, innocent, at one with nature. Then comes the break with nature and the introduction of the quest theme. Genet is accused of being a thief and makes this nomination his quest. The phase of descent is initiated by Genet's being charmed and possessed by representations or metaphors of identity: saints and heroes, criminals and lovers. In the ascent phase, experience is comprehended by writing, as a process of self-emancipation. In the last stage, the epilogue, we discover that Genet has not been reunited with a community, but has gone beyond being the writer-magician and become the melancholic pensive figure, *Il penseroso*.

Sartre focuses on the romance narrative rather than rendering Genet with novelistic realism. The critics who have noted this have charged him with writing a highly abstract, somewhat repetitious work. As a consequence, *Saint Genet* has been treated as a transitional work, between the early abstract study of Baudelaire and the more novelistic *The Family Idiot*. Sartre himself was critical of the abstract nature of *Saint Genet* and said that it lacked an appreciation of social forces. Yet if *Saint Genet* had been shaped as a more realistic work, it would be out of keeping with Sartre's own conception of his biographical subject.

Sartre makes the claim that Genet has no history. According to Sartre himself, for a man to have a history, he must evolve. The course of the world must change him as he in turn changes it. This reciprocal transformation of individual and environment is denied to Genet, and thus he has no place in this world. Sartre grants that between the ages of fifteen and twenty-five Genet wanders about the world and has more adventures in the space of one year than most men have in a lifetime, but they do not affect him. The events vary, but Genet's behavior does not change one iota. He does not have meaningful encounters with either circumstances or individuals. He remains the same throughout the ten-year period between the ages of fifteen, when he is first sentenced, and twenty-five, when he begins to write. His life does not make sense from the historical or novelistic perspective because he does not grow. All that one can perceive is a surface agitation. Genet himself refers to the persons, places, and circumstances only as matters of anecdotes in his life. And so Sartre himself sums up that period of Genet's life in a brief anecdotal paragraph:

> And now here is a story for an anthology of Grim Humor: an aban-
> doned child manifests evil instincts in his early childhood. He robs the
> poor peasants who adopted him. Though reprimanded, he persists. . . .
> He decides that he will do the worst in every circumstance and, as he
> came to realize that the greatest crime was not the doing of evil but the
> manifesting of evil, he writes, in prison, abominable books which stand
> up for crime, and which are punishable by law. . . . The President of the
> Republic nullifies the sentence he was supposed to serve.[12]

Genet's life can be read as a chronological sequence of seemingly unmotivated adventures where the conjunction *and then* would both join and disjoin events, as opposed to being linked by the conjunction *hence* and thus being rendered as a motivated series of events. This is in keeping with the nature of pure or "undisplaced" romance narrative.

A sequence of sentences linked by the conjunction *hence* would introduce linear intelligibility and would signal what Frye calls displacement into a more naturalistic mode. For instance, in the scientific cultural worldview of late-nineteenth-century Europe, hereditary determinism was a plausible, hence intelligible, accounting for the unfolding of a person's life. Zola's novels provide ample demonstration of this view. On the other hand, critical realism provides a more dialectical view of the unfolding of personality, seeing it as the result of an interaction between individual and society. Either of these last two explanatory principles—genetic determinism and dialectic interaction—constitutes a way of making stories plausible at particular moments in cultural time.

Today the reader will not take Zola's scientism seriously. He will, however, recognize that the scientism made the story plausible for the author's contemporaries. The story (without the deterministic explanation) is structurally the myth that has been rendered plausible for a particular audience. We may refer to this mythic structure as the deep structure of the realistic work. Frye defines myth as "an abstract or purely literary world of fictional and thematic design, unaffected by the canons of the plausible adaptation to familiar experience."[13] In narrative terms, myth is the imitation of the actions we would perform if no limitations were placed on our desire. Displacement is the action of rendering myths plausible: "The presence of a mythical structure in realistic fiction . . . poses certain technical problems for making it plausible, and the devices used in solving these problems may be given the general name of displacement."[14]

Romance is situated between myth and naturalism, taking a human direction away from the gods, but is more conventionalized in form than naturalism with its surfeit of details simulating reality.

However, the romance narrative of *Saint Genet* cannot become more novelistic because Sartre does not grant Genet a personality. He only grants him an *identity*. A verdict conferred an identity upon him, effectively circumventing the growth of a personality. The natural impulses in Genet could not be acculturated through insertion in the world, and they could not take on the nuances that would make for an interesting subject. An interesting subject would mean one who is nuanced and flexible and adjusts to circumstances.[15]

Rather than possessing a personality that he can develop in the face of circumstances, Genet must deal with the identity of thief conferred upon him by those in authority. This prevents Genet from being defined as an individual enduring and changing in time, and he is forced to accept an explanation by what he has done at a particular moment. The deed casts him in a role to be played, in a now predetermined future, until the identity is lifted from him, by his own deeds and/or the volition of others. Changes in Genet can only occur brusquely by metamorphosis, rather than gradually as when there is personality development. Sartre will thus present Genet in relationship to a role. While it can be said that one's personality is more uniquely one's own, since it is one's history, a role has a general quality. It requires some sort of assent or rejection from a particular individual—defined as the doer of a deed upon which the judgment is passed. Sartre cannot play off Genet's personality against his identity, and thus appeal to our emotions, because he has not attributed any unique personality to him. For the same reason, he cannot condemn the unfairness of any accusation against Genet by appealing to the individual's uniqueness. Therefore, personality cannot be grounds for a sentimental critique of Genet's condemnation as a thief, as in bourgeois literature.

Sartre argues that Genet could not protest at the moment of his condemnation because he does not have the self-confidence that arises from a developing personality. Because his natural instincts were barred from acculturation, Genet had to either accept the identity conferred upon him or face a void. Sartre claims that Genet's lack of socialization left him internally a wasteland. Ideally, when he was expelled from the

Garden of Eden, he should have been able to take the next step, in which libidinal energy encounters social reality and leads to a mutually satisfying resolution. However, Sartre has removed instinct and desire as the motor force for Genet's quest phase. In this phase, according to Frye, wish-fulfillment compromises with reality. But Genet, cast in the evil role of a thief, must recognize himself as having no legitimate claim on the world. He exercises the only alternative left open to him: having no option but to be a thief, he must will that metamorphosis. The object of his quest is thus not wish-fulfillment but will-fulfillment. Whereas Frye says that the mimesis of narrative serves "to link human life to the biological dependence on the natural cycle" and also "to remold nature in the image of desire,"[16] Genet's quest is rigorously antinatural. Its goal is a negative identity,[17] the pursuit of which, the reliving of the moment of being called a thief, is traced in a series of adventures which Sartre connects by referring to repetition compulsions.

In the stage of descent, however, no metamorphosis can be called permanent. Frye notes that "in descent narratives the central image is that of metamorphoses, the freezing of something human and conscious into an animal or plant or inanimate object."[18] These metamorphoses are the particular forms of enchantment.[19] The ascent phase represents a contrary action, namely, the casting off of the inhuman forms and their replacement with the original human form. If the theme of descent represents an enchantment into inhuman form, the theme of ascent represents an emancipation and separation from the enchantment. In willing the metamorphosis, Genet produces this two-stage reverse effect. By willing his metamorphosis into a thief, Genet ultimately separates himself from it, because in the very process he separates the freedom of consciousness from the object of consciousness: Sartre argues that Genet cannot at once *be* the thief object and actively *will* to be the thief. In the last analysis, Genet becomes aware of willing to will as an activity that frees him from the passive constitution of the metamorphosis. In order to realize that his active consciousness breaks the spell of his possession by others, in the role in which he was cast, Genet has to will the metamorphosis.

In maintaining the role, Genet entered the sacred world of ritual. Sartre argues that in willing to act out his negative identity, Genet wills a social reality sustained within a framework of fixed institutions, and also wills an internal modification of himself. In modifying his consciousness rather than the world, this act can be considered idealistic. The result is that in denying himself real activity upon the world, Genet enters a world where he moves as in a trance, performing predetermined gestures to predetermined ends as in a ritual. This is the result of wanting what is imposed on him. As a consequence, in continuing to steal, Genet simultaneously recreates his nature and consecrates it.

Genet's acts are really gestures in a preordained script designed to reveal the essence given to him. Through repetition he tries to present that essence to himself as it appears to those for whom he possesses the persona of the thief. Rather than dispersing himself in time and daily reality, Genet wishes to discover himself as a demoniacal and sacred being, which he can do only by provoking the reactions of others—in other words, by submitting to others. These gestures situate Genet in Frye's phase of descent. Sartre describes Genet in this stage in terms of two metamorphoses: the first into the homosexual criminal (with its counterpart, the saint), the second into the aesthete.

In the ascent stage, which reverses the previous one, Sartre describes Genet in terms of his metamorphosis into a writer. The anecdotal episodes of Genet's existence are organized by Sartre into groupings under the heading of metamorphoses. The episodes within each grouping are to be considered as similar, representing in psychological terms a repetition compulsion. In the themes of descent, where Genet is represented as thief and figure of evil and then as aesthete, the episodes grouped under each heading are also similar. Sartre proceeds by establishing analogous structures between the metamorphoses. Metaphor by analogy is Sartre's way of linking the various anecdotes of Genet's life which appear so meaningless from the novelistic or historical perspective. In a historical or diachronic perspective there would be an incremental change in the subject, an adding and nuancing of personal characteristics resulting from constant interaction with the social environment. On the other hand, as in romance, *Saint Genet* reveals sudden changes of identity, brought about by sheer exhaustion because of the repetition. The feeling that "enough is enough" results in metamorphoses that lead to more of the same, only in another form.

Genet the aesthete is still like Genet the thief. But while trying to recapure the essence of thief by returning to crime, Genet inhabits a sacred universe with moral overtones; as aesthete, on the other hand, he derealizes reality. In both instances, no actual change and no history or time are introduced into these spaces. The sacred world is the derealized world of the aesthete, and this second metamorphosis represents a secularization of the first. In both instances Genet is under the spell of static dematerialized worlds.

These dematerialized worlds testify to the absence of the vital presence of psychobiological reality, in other words, of personality, the only bearer of change. Thus, the absence of this materiality accounts for the sameness of the episodes.

The movement from the phase of descent to the phase of ascent is the result of a simple reversal. Genet the enchanted becomes Genet the enchanter. Once again the aesthete, under the spell of his derealized or dematerialized world, simply does an about face, as if by a reflex action. Suddenly he becomes aware of himself through the whirl of impressions that increasingly disorient him, as in a nightmare. As both Sartre and Frye point out,[20] the intensification of the spell brings about its exhaustion. At its frightening culmination Genet returns to himself and goes into his last metamorphosis, ascending to the form of the writer.

The reversal from enchanted to enchanter returns the metamorphosis in the stage of descent to the original enchanters, the figures of authority, who in turn can, in the enchantment of reading, experience the spell they had cast on Genet. Their dismay ends his quest of will-fulfillment in words, realizing fully in them the metamorphoses of descent that he pursued. But this realization occurs in Genet's absence: the enchanter, having enchanted, vanishes, free from identity.[21]

The irony of Sartre's emplotting Genet's life as romance lies in the ultimate treatment reserved for representation and identity. In the last analysis there is no representation or identity for Genet, for they have all been returned to the original enchanters. Now that Genet is a consciousness emptied of all obsessions, no metaphor can contain him. Purified subjectivity is not like anything.

Sartre joins Genet in *ressentiment* against *les Justes* when he imagines their scandalized reactions to Genet's own text. *Saint Genet* does not end predictably, with the last stage of the romance narrative, where a new order and a new ethic dawn. It ends instead with a plea for understanding, a plea found at the very heart of *ressentiment* itself, as Sartre states in *The Family Idiot*:

> Resentment, without ever raising itself to the level of hatred, becomes the deep *meaning* and *purpose* of submission. Which can be expressed in these terms: when aggressiveness is lacking, when the Other is already established in the subject and deprives him of his sovereignty, namely, the autonomous activity that would allow him to assume or reject a constituted character, in short when consent and revolt are equally impossible, resentment appears in the unloved child. It is a complex tactic by which he attempts to recover an impossible subjectivity by exaggerating the alienation that first makes him conscious of himself as object. In the present case the tactic consists of borrowing the force of the other through passive obedience and turning it against him;

by turning himself into the pure means of realizing the alien ends imposed on him, the resentful man lets them reveal their own inconsistency and, by their unavoidable consequences, their malignity.[22]

Sartre uses the narrative to illustrate a successful auto-psycho-
analysis by *un homme du ressentiment*. Though the romance narrative is
ultimately salvational, entry into this narrative is by way of the frustration of need and desire. As we have seen, the denial of one's nature and
of a concomitant development of personality is marked in Genet by a
series of negative life-denying identity stances (the criminal, the saint),
which Sartre designates by the term *metamorphosis* and which signal
Frye's narrative stages of descent. *Ressentiment* is the recourse to these
negative nature-denying stances that constitute Genet's imaginary world
and serve as an entry point into the romance narrative.[23]

For Sartre, *ressentiment* as a recourse to the imaginary defines not
only Genet but also the artist from about the mid-nineteenth century on,
notably Baudelaire, Flaubert, and Mallarmé. In historical terms, *ressentiment* represents, according to Sartre, the attitude of post-Romantics
who perceived the failure of the myth of Prometheus and its abandonment by their elders. This myth expressed the revolutionary ideals of the
tranformation of society in keeping with the needs of human nature. The
failure of this somewhat Rousseauean ideal, whose realization would
ultimately have been political, led the younger generation to adopt a
stance that denied nature as a reflection of their elders, a reflection that
also served as a rebuke. Forsaking the myth of the Revolution entailed
substituting the imaginary, and led to the art-for-art's-sake movement.
Ressentiment is the attitude that serves historically to demarcate the line
between the Promethean revolutionary man and the artist as imaginary
man.[24] The imaginary man sees himself as already old and sterile because his life is already prefigured before him in a twilight world. It is
this inheritance from the elders which is accepted with *ressentiment*, that
is to say with dignified obedience and silent reservation.

In philosophical terms, the forsaking of the Promethean ideal meant
the separation of being and negation. Instead of the dialectical relation
between the two, which brings about change through negation and transformation, being becomes seen as good and negation as evil. Their
separation expresses a denial of change and a projection of evil into
others, perceived as disturbers of society's order and stability. It is in this
context that Sartre situates the lives of his writers and poets.[25] In their
ressentiment, their creativity cannot be that of the deed but only of the
imaginary. The figures of Genet's metamorphoses in the stage of descent

are analogous to the stoic response of the slave in the master-slave relationship in Hegel's *Phenomenology of Mind,* a text Sartre takes as a model.[26] Genet as a thief and the slave as a stoic both seek to assume what they have been condemned to. In either case these solutions are illusory. Eventually, as the slave becomes the skeptic, so likewise Genet will become the aesthete, both attitudes being universal negatives and equally illusory because of their denial of external determination. This is partly in keeping with Nietzsche's own famous definition of *ressentiment* in the *Genealogy of Morals:* "The slave revolt in morality begins when *ressentiment* itself becomes creative and gives birth to values: the *ressentiment* of natures that are denied the true reaction, that of deeds, and compensate themselves with an imaginary revenge."[27] It is also in the context of *Saint Genet* that Sartre answers Nietzsche's call, "I need a critique of the *Saint.*"[28]

The emplotment of the life-denying identities of good and evil in the romance narrative, then, reveals an aestheticization of values where self-interest is suppressed in favor of values given as objective and universal. This signals the dominance of the past through morality, which is a sedimentation (the term is Nietzsche's) of the past practices of a group. In the case of Genet this morality is the quasi-internalized morality of the just. The salvational aspect emerges when suppressed self-interest acknowledges itself (Sartre's "doing") over and against "being" and risks de-aestheticizing or de-platonizing values frozen in morality.

Genet's auto-analysis is the recognition of the logical impossibility of reconciling "being" and "doing." The break with morality signals what Frye terms the "themes of ascent": Genet is disenchanted and freed by recognizing the inadequacy of the identities, the definitions within which he tried to hold himself. However, recognizing logical aporia in maintaining "being" by "doing" does not lead to a future of ethical conduct. Though Genet is disenchanted by morality, Sartre deems that ethical conduct as conduct according to values oriented toward the future, necessary as it may be, is impossible at the present time. The impossibility (but necessity) of ethics, like the initial impossibility (but necessity) of activity gratifying need and desire, signals the return of *ressentiment.* However, given the impossibility of ethics today, *ressentiment* must remain the most authentic response.

Notes

1. See Richard Rorty, "Philosophy as a Kind of Writing," *Consequences of Pragmatism: Essays 1972–1980* (Minneapolis, 1982), 90–109.

2. See Hayden White, *Metahistory: The Historical Imagination in Nineteenth-Century Europe* (Baltimore, 1973).

3. "The Figure in the Carpet," in *Telling Lives: The Biographer's Art*, ed. by Mark Pachter (Washington, D.C., 1979), 20.

4. "In the criticism of literature, we often have to 'stand back' from the poem to see its archetypal organization." Northrop Frye, *Anatomy of Criticism* (New York, 1968), 140.

5. Fredric Jameson, *The Political Unconscious* (Ithaca, N.Y., 1981), 105.

6. Frye, *Anatomy of Criticism*, 162.

7. Northrop Frye, *The Secular Scripture* (Oxford, 1976), 15.

8. Frye, *The Anatomy of Criticism*, 193.

9. Kenneth Burke, "Four Master Tropes," in *A Grammar of Motives* (Berkeley, Calif., 1969).

10. Frye, *Anatomy of Criticism*, 366.

11. Frye, *The Secular Scripture*, 97–157.

12. Jean-Paul Sartre, *Saint Genet* (Toronto, 1964), 612.

13. Frye, *The Secular Scripture*, 47.

14. Frye, *Anatomy of Criticism*, 136.

15. "Thus Genet lives outside history, in parenthesis. He no more cares about his individual adventure—which he contemptuously calls 'the anecdote'—than did an ancient Egyptian about his national history. He deigns to take notice of the circumstances of his life only insofar as they seem to repeat the original drama of the lost paradise. He is a man of repetition: the drab, slack time of his daily life—a *profane* life in which everything is permissible—is shot through with blazing hierophanies which restore to him his original passion, as Holy Week restores to us that of Christ." *Saint Genet*, 13. The quote reveals Sartre's debt to Mircea Eliade's distinction between sacred and profane time; see *The Myth of the Eternal Return*, trans. by W. R. Tresk (London, 1955).

16. Frye, *Anatomy of Criticism*, 106.

17. "He is forbidden from the beginning to desire. All societies castrate the maladjusted. This castration can be actually physical or can be achieved by persuasion. The result is the same. The desire of Genet, who is condemned, outside of nature, impossible, becomes a desire for the impossible and for what is against nature." *Saint Genet*, 95.

18. Frye, *The Secular Scripture*, 140.

19. Sartre quotes from Genet's *Querelle de Brest:* "Querelle could not get used to the idea, an idea never formulated, of being a monster. He would consider, would regard his past with a smile that was ironic, frightened and tender at the same time, insofar as this past merged with himself. A young boy who had been metamorphosed into an alligator and whose soul appears in his eyes might in like manner—if he is not quite conscious of his maw, of his enormous jaw—consider his scaly body, his solemn tail that slaps the water or the beach or grazes other monsters. . . . He knows the horror of being alone, stricken by an immortal enchantment in the midst of the living world." *Saint Genet*, 11. "I would become aware of being suddenly naked in a crowd which sees my nakedness; or that my hands would become overgrown with leaves and I would have to live with them." *Saint Genet*, 11.

20. "He knows that he is drowning, but it seems to him natural to sink to the bottom of his phantasmagoria. And yet, on the other hand, his dreams are growing poorer, are becoming stereotyped, they bore him, at times frighten him: it is impossible for him to deliver himself without the help of an external event, but it is equally impossible for this event not to occur. Human reality oddly resembles the atoms or undulatory mechanics and seems to be likewise composed of a corpuscle that is linked to a train of waves: when it has

sunk down into its inveterate habits, into its anxieties, into its stereotyped ruminations, it is already outside, far ahead of itself." *Saint Genet*, 434. "As the hero or heroine enters the labyrinthine lower world, the prevailing moods are those of terror or uncritical awe. At a certain point, perhaps when the strain, as the storyteller doubtless hopes, is becoming unbearable, there may be a revolt of the mind, a recovered detachment the typical expression of which is laughter. The ambiguity of the oracle becomes the ambiguity of wit, something addressed to a verbal understanding that shakes the mind free. This point is also made by generic changes from the tragic and ironic to the comic and satiric. Thus in Rabelais the huge giants, the search for an oracle, and other lower-world themes that in different contexts would be frightening or awe-inspiring are presented as farce." Frye, *The Secular Scripture*, 129–30.

21. As a writer, Genet demythologizes the word *thief,* ending the narrative that was his fate. "He has now understood his error: he wanted to make himself what the others saw him to be, whereas he should have made the others see him as he wants to be. . . . The stroke of genius, the illumination that finds the way out, is the choice of writing." *Saint Genet*, 590. "He is only a faceless freedom that sets fascinating traps for other freedoms." *Saint Genet*, 596. In other words, the enchanted is the enchanter, the wordsmith.

22. *The Family Idiot,* trans. by Carol Cosman (Chicago, 1986), I, 387.

23. "He wills his destiny; he will try to love it. How did this solution occur to him? I do not know. It came from the heart, no doubt of that. Moreover, he had been preparing himself for it by the game of saintliness. As an abandoned child he wished to attain the inhuman out of resentment toward men. They are casting him into it. Perfect. It was certainly not *that kind of inhuman* that he desired. He wanted to transcend the human condition, and he was relegated to a level below humanity. But in any case he was ready for an exceptional destiny. He dreamt of ideals surmounted, of asceticism, of endless torments. Here they are, the ordeals and the torments! Perhaps the road to the heights and the road to the depths are one and the same. Perhaps they meet somewhere outside the world. Surely misfortune is a cipher, surely it *indicates* something." *Saint Genet*, 61.

24. See *The Family Idiot,* Vol. II, for the failure of the artist. The poet as prophet is followed by the *poète maudit* who is the Knight of Nothingness after the events of 1848.

25. "He [the decent man] will define himself narrowly by traditions, by obedience, by the automatism of Good, and will give the name *temptation* to the live, vague swarming which is still himself but a himself which is wild, free, outside the limits he has marked out for himself. His own negativity falls outside him, since he denies it with all his might. Substantified, separated from any positive intention, it becomes a pure negation that poses itself for its own sake, a pure rage to destroy that goes round in circles, namely Evil." *Saint Genet*, 35.

26. "The most powerful outside influence is Hegel." Douglas Collins, *Sartre as Biographer* (Cambridge, Mass., 1980), 84.

27. *On the Genealogy of Morals,* trans. by Walter Kaufman (New York, 1967), 36.

28. *The Will to Power,* trans. by Walter Kaufman and R. J. Hollingdale, ed. by Walter Kaufman (New York, 1968), 206, 382.

V

SARTRE
AND
OTHERS

15

SIMONE DE BEAUVOIR: TEACHING SARTRE ABOUT FREEDOM

Sonia Kruks

"Independent" professional women, Simone de Beauvoir observed,

> are not tranquilly installed in their new realm: as yet they are only
> halfway there. . . . For when she begins her adult life [the independent
> woman] does not have behind her the same past as does a boy; she is
> not viewed by society in the same way; the universe presents itself to her
> in a different perspective.[1]

Later, Beauvoir explained that she had begun her monumental
study of woman, *The Second Sex* (1949), at a time when she had wanted
to write about herself. For although her own femininity did not seem to
present any difficulties to her, she had—as Sartre pointed out—been
raised very differently from a boy; thus, self-understanding called for an
investigation of "the female condition."[2] But whatever her initial motivations for writing *The Second Sex,* in the completed work Beauvoir seems
to stand aloof from her subject: it is other women she is discussing and
not, it appears, herself. It is striking that nowhere in her volumes of
autobiography does she offer any acknowledgement that she personally
experienced her femininity as a handicap, or even that she recognized it
as a source of inner conflict in herself.

Even so, we still must see an autobiographical element, however unintended, in Beauvoir's comments on the "halfway" and untranquil character of the life of the independent woman. A careful reading of Beauvoir's autobiography suggests that characteristically feminine patterns of otherness and subordination, such as she had described in *The Second Sex,* were present in her relations with Sartre and others. This becomes a matter of importance if one attempts to examine her *philosophic* relationship to Sartre and to evaluate her own contributions to philosophy.[3] Repeatedly, and until the last years of her life, Beauvoir insisted that she lacked originality and was merely Sartre's disciple in matters philosophical. She attributed originality in the field of literature to herself; but in the more hallowed field of philosophy she could not compete but only follow. "[On] the philosophical level," she insisted, "I adhered completely to *Being and Nothingness* and later to *Critique of Dialectical Reason.*"[4]

Most scholars and commentators have taken Beauvoir at her word. While some have upbraided her for her intellectual dependence on Sartre,[5] few have asked whether her self-portrayal is justified. Most assume that, as one author has recently put it, she simply uses Sartre's concepts as "coat-hangers" on which to hang her own material, even to the point where it can be said that "Sartre's intellectual history becomes her own."[6] I will argue in this article that such a view, even though it is asserted by Beauvoir herself, is inaccurate. Although Beauvoir is clearly not of the same stature qua philosopher as Sartre, she is far from philosophically derivative. On the contrary, the case can be made that at certain points in Sartre's development it is Beauvoir's intellectual history that becomes his. This is particularly so with regard to Sartre's struggle, for a decade beginning in the late 1940s, to develop a social philosophy. In this struggle—first evidenced in his abandoned *Cahiers pour une morale* and reaching a certain fruition in the first volume of the *Critique*—Sartre can be seen to modify the absolute and radically individualistic notion of freedom he had elaborated in *Being and Nothingness.* In time he replaced it with a more nuanced notion of freedom as relative and as socially mediated—a notion which, however, Beauvoir had already developed by the late 1940s.

Sartre himself, while stressing Beauvoir's importance to him as a critic of his work,[7] did not attribute to her a significant role in the transformation his thought underwent between *Being and Nothingness* and the *Critique.* Rather, it was to Merleau-Ponty that he attributed the role of mentor and intellectual inspiration. It was, he said, Merleau-Ponty's collection of essays *Humanism and Terror* (1947) that forced him, in the face of events, to go beyond his individualism and taught him about the collective aspects of human existence, about history, and about politics.[8] But Beauvoir, it must be pointed out, had grasped the implication of Merleau-Ponty's work earlier than Sartre, and perhaps better. It was she, and not Sartre, who in 1945 wrote an extensive review of Merleau-Ponty's *Phenomenology of Perception* for *Les Temps Modernes*. In the review she both discussed the social aspects of Merleau-Ponty's thought and highlighted his divergences from Sartre. Merleau-Ponty, she pointed out, denied Sartre's notion of an "absolute freedom," elaborating in its place a notion of the "incarnate subject"—a subject in which history is incarnated through the generality of the body:

> While Sartre, in *Being and Nothingness,* emphasizes above all the opposition of the for-itself and in-itself, the nihilating power of consciousness in the face of being and its absolute freedom, Merleau-Ponty on the contrary applies himself to describing the concrete character of the subject who is never, according to him, a pure for-itself. . . . [For Merleau-Ponty] history is incarnated in a body which possesses a certain generality, a relation to the world anterior to myself; and this is why the body is opaque to reflection, and why my consciousness discovers itself to be "engorged with the sensible." It [that is, consciousness] is not a pure for-itself, or, to use Hegel's phrase which Sartre has taken up, a "hole in being"; but rather "a hollow, a fold, which has been made and which can be un-made."[9]

In this passage Beauvoir perceptively puts her finger on the main divergences between the two philosophies. But what is striking is that she also refrains from making any judgment between them. Although not prepared to criticize Sartre, her "superior" in matters philosophical, it would seem that she was also unwilling, at this time, to defend him. For, in fact, there is a notion of the subject, and of freedom, in her own work which is strikingly close to Merleau-Ponty's: a notion of the subject that is "never a pure for-itself" but an embodied consciousness, a socially situated and conditioned freedom.

Beauvoir's disagreement with Sartre over the notion of freedom predates the writing of *Being and Nothingness.* In the autobiographical volume *The Prime of Life,* published in 1960, Beauvoir describes a series of conversations she had with Sartre in the spring of 1940. Sartre, briefly in Paris on leave from the army, sketched out for her the main lines of the argument of what was to become *Being and Nothingness.* Their discussions, Beauvoir recalls, centered above all on the problem of "the relation of situation to freedom." On this point they disagreed:

I maintained that, from the point of view of freedom, as Sartre defined it—not as a stoical resignation but as an active transcendence of the given—not every situation is equal: what transcendence is possible for a woman locked up in a harem? Even such a cloistered existence could be lived in several different ways, Sartre said. I clung to my opinion for a long time and then made only a token submission. Basically [she comments in 1960] I was right. But to have been able to defend my position, I would have had to abandon the terrain of individualist, thus idealist, morality, where we stood.[10]

The "submission" Beauvoir made to Sartre in 1940 was indeed "token." Although she was never willing to challenge Sartre's conception of freedom head-on, she was quietly to subvert it—both in her ethical essays *Pyrrhus et Cinéas* (1944) and *The Ethics of Ambiguity* (1947) and, above all, in *The Second Sex* (1949). In these works, while ostensibly beginning from the central Sartrean premises of *Being and Nothingness,* her tenacious pursuit of her own agenda led her—doubtless in spite of herself—to some most un-Sartrean conclusions. This is particularly the case concerning the question of freedom and the related question of oppression.

Already in 1940 Beauvoir had insisted against Sartre that "not every situation is equal" from the point of view of freedom. In *Pyrrhus et Cinéas,* begun while *Being and Nothingness* was in press,[11] and again in 1947, in *The Ethics of Ambiguity,* she suggested that there might be situations of oppression in which freedom, such as Sartre describes it in *Being and Nothingness,* ceases to be possible. Freedoms, she suggested, are *not* self-sufficient but *interdependent.* For "[only] the freedom of the other is able to give necessity to my being."[12] But if my freedom depends on that of others, then it is vulnerable to their attack: "It is this interdependence [of freedoms] which explains why oppression is possible and why it is hateful."[13] If the life of the oppressed is reduced—as it can be—to no more than physically "perpetuating itself," then, she asserted, "living is only not dying, and human existence is indistinguishable from an absurd vegetation."[14] However, it was only in *The Second Sex* (begun in 1946 and completed in 1949) that she attempted systematically to analyze oppression. The attempt proved to be impossible within the confines of Sartreanism.

Beauvoir begins *The Second Sex* on firmly Sartrean ground. "What is a woman?" she asks, and she answers initially that woman is defined as that which is not man—as other: "She is determined and differentiated with reference to man and not he with reference to her; she is the inessential as opposed to the essential. He is the subject, he is the Absolute: she is the Other."[15] However, very early in the book, Beauvoir introduces a nuance into the notion of otherness that is not found in *Being and Nothingness*. For Sartre, at least in his early work, my "being-for-others" arises on the ground of the other's attempt to destroy my freedom. But since my freedom is an indestructible power of nihilation, the other can never finally touch it. Instead, the other must attempt to nihilate the visible *exterior* of my freedom: my "being-in-situation." It is thus when he or she *looks* at me that the other steals my "being-in-situation" from me and incorporates it, objectlike, within his or her own situation. But although the other objectifies what we might call the external manifestations of my freedom, I always remain a freedom. I remain free to choose my own action in response to the other's transcendence; and I always retain the possibility of turning the tables on the other. Conversely, if I objectify his or her "being-in-situation," I will always fail to reach the other's core freedom, and the other will thus remain for me always a potential threat, an "explosive instrument."[16]

In this account, Sartre assumes the freedoms in conflict to be not only autonomous but also *equal*. For in relations of looking per se there is no reason to assume that human beings are anything but equal. When he describes the torture victim turning the tables on his torturer by *looking* at him,[17] Sartre is asserting that two equal freedoms confront each other, irrespective of the fact that the torturer has the power of physical domination over his victim. Similarly, Sartre argues that "the slave in chains is as free as his master."[18] For, given Sartre's notion of the indestructible freedom of the "for-itself," the question of material or political inequality between master and slave is simply irrelevant to their relation *as two freedoms*. In the same vein, Sartre is able to write—in 1943!—that the Jew remains free in the face of the anti-Semite because he can choose his own attitude toward his persecutor.

It is this assumption—that relations of otherness are conflictual relations between two *equal* freedoms—that Beauvoir quietly challenges. Her challenge, as we will see, implies an account of human freedom that is much closer to Merleau-Ponty's than to Sartre's: it implies that there are degrees, or gradations, of freedom—and that social situations modify freedom itself and not merely its facticity or exteriority. Let us return now to *The Second Sex*. Having begun from the Sartrean notion that woman is other, Beauvoir immediately proceeds to qualify or nuance that notion. We can, she argues, distinguish two significantly different kinds of relations of otherness: those between social *equals* and those that involve social *inequality*. Where the relation is one of equality, she

289

suggests that otherness is "relativized" by a kind of "reciprocity": each recognizes that the other whom he or she objectifies is *also* an equal freedom.

Furthermore, for Beauvoir, such "reciprocity" is not essentially a relation of *looks*. It is expressed and mediated through *institutions*— institutions as diverse as war, trade, festivals. Where, however, otherness exists through relations of *inequality,* there "reciprocity" is to a greater or lesser extent abolished; relations of oppression and subjection (also mediated through institutions) take its place. When one of the two parties in a conflict is privileged, having some material or physical advantage, then "this one prevails over the other and undertakes to keep it in subjection."[19] In relations of subjection, or oppression, as we will see, Beauvoir argues that freedom *itself* undergoes modification. For Beauvoir, the slave is *not* "as free as his master," for the restrictions that operate on his situation come to operate *internally* on his freedom—so as to suppress *his very capacity to project.* In reply to her question of 1940, "What transcendence is possible for a woman locked up in a harem?" Beauvoir's answer is now, "sometimes none." It is not, then, woman's otherness per se but her subjection—the *non*reciprocal objectification of woman by man—that needs to be explained.

Woman is not only other; she is an unequal other. Why? Beauvoir begins by rejecting the most pervasive explanation: biological inferiority. There is no such thing as biological "destiny." In current feminist terms she is saying that the biological facts of sex do not determine gender; the latter is a social construct, to be explained in the realm of human social existence. Beauvoir here agrees with Sartre that only the realm of the "in-itself" is subject to causality. Thus we can never describe any human condition as inevitable, as inscribed in nature. What is often called the "internal feminine"—what today we would call gender—is not natural.[20] Moreover, and most importantly, since it is humanly created it is transmutable.

However, Beauvoir goes on to point out that although the "eternal feminine" is humanly created, it is created by *man* through the situation *he* imposes on woman. Moreover, this situation is not constituted only by woman's relations with the particular men who treat her as an inferior. For, subtending such direct, personal relations, woman also encounters as fundamental to her situation what we might call a set of social *institutions*. It is these institutions that function analogously to natural forces in perpetuating her inequality. If all that took place between an individual man and woman was a Hegelian—or Sartrean—struggle of consciousness between two human beings, one of whom happened to be male and one female, then we could not anticipate in advance which of them would objectify the other. If, however, we examine the relations of a *husband* and a *wife,* then it is very different. For the institution of marriage in all its aspects—legal, economic, sexual, cultural, and so on—has formed *in advance* for the protagonists their own relation of inequality. As Beauvoir points out in a strikingly un-Sartrean passage, "it is not as single individuals that human beings are to be defined in the first place; men and women have never stood opposed to each other in single combat; the couple is an original *Mitsein;* and as such it always appears as a permanent element in a larger collectivity."[21] Furthermore, although Beauvoir insists that biology is not a "destiny," the social constructions placed on the female *body* are very central in defining woman not only as other but as inferior other. There is, she argues, "a constant relation" between sexuality and other social and economic structures of a "collectivity," and she cites Merleau-Ponty's remark that "the body is generality" as part of the explanation for the ubiquity of woman's oppression. For Beauvoir, as for Merleau-Ponty, it is the *incarnate* nature of consciousness that accounts for its inherence in a world "anterior" to itself,[22] a world that is, for women, *already* structured as one of immanence. Expanding on Merleau-Ponty's remark, she discusses the generality of human existence in the following most un-Sartrean manner:

> Across the separation of existents, existence is all one: it makes itself manifest in analogous organisms; therefore there will be constants in the relation of the ontological to the sexual. At a given epoch, the techniques, the economic and social structure, of a collectivity will reveal an identical world to all its members: there will also be a constant relation of sexuality to social forms; analogous individuals, placed in analogous conditions, will take from what is given analogous significations. This analogy does not establish a rigorous universality, but it does enable us to rediscover general types within individual histories.[23]

In *Being and Nothingness,* Sartre cannot account adequately for the existence of "collectivities," of "general types," or of such a generality as "woman's situation." There is in his work a radical individualism which amounts to a kind of solipsism: each of us construes the meaning of both past and present only from the perspective of our own project. "There is," Sartre insists, "no absolute viewpoint which one can adopt so as to compare different situations, each person realizes only one situation— *his own.*"[24] Since situations are each uniquely brought into being by an individual free project, we cannot, for Sartre, conceive of a *general* situation. Nor, of course, could we judge one situation to be more free

291

than another. The central problem raised by Sartre's early work is what I will call the problem of *discontinuity,* and it is a problem with which he himself had to grapple as he became increasingly committed to a politics of radical social transformation in the 1940s. There is a discontinuity, a hiatus he could not bridge, between, on the one hand, discrete, individually constituted meanings and, on the other, the existence of social and historical wholes that appear to have a reality beyond that given to them by each unique individual project. How could one consistently participate in a collective struggle to create a different society unless one could show that there is social being and that individuals can freely act together to create and transform it? In the above passage, while eschewing an "absolute viewpoint," Beauvoir points a way beyond Sartre's dilemma.

For Beauvoir, there is a generality, a weight, to woman's situation— even, we could say, an objectivity. Thus, although her situation is humanly created, a woman may frequently experience it as a "destiny," an exterior conditioning. Moreover, such an experience is not necessarily a choice of "bad faith" on her part. For if a woman is oppressed to the point where transcendence is no longer possible, then her situation *is* effectively her "destiny"; it functions upon her analogously to a natural force. "Every subject," she writes,

> continually affirms himself through his projects as a transcendence; he realizes his freedom only through his continual transcendence toward other freedoms; there is no other justification for present existence than its expansion toward an endlessly open future. Each time that transcendence falls back into immanence there is a degradation of existence into the "in-itself," of freedom into facticity; this fall is a moral fault if the subject agrees to it; it takes the form of a frustration and an oppression if it is inflicted upon him.[25]

Woman is locked in immanence by the situation *man* inflicts upon her— and she is not necessarily responsible. A consistent Sartrean position would make woman responsible for herself, no matter how constrained her situation. But for Beauvoir, although there are some women who comply with their oppressors in "bad faith,"[26] they are not the primary source of the problem. For many there is no moral fault because there simply is no possibility of choice. In the notion that freedom can "fall back into the 'in-itself,' " that the "for-itself" can be turned, through the action of other (that is, male) freedoms, into its very opposite, Beauvoir has radically departed from the Sartrean notion of freedom. Not only does woman fail freely to choose her situation, she is in fact its product: "when . . . a group of individuals is kept in a situation of inferiority, the fact is they are inferior . . . yes, women on the whole *are* today inferior to men, which is to say that their situation gives them less possibilities."[27]

Beauvoir's notion of the falling back of "existence" into the "in-itself" is not to be dismissed as a mere metaphor. Yet, from a Sartrean perspective one could not take the statement as wholly literal either. Strictly speaking, within Sartre's usage of the terms, the "degradation of existence into the "in-itself' " would have to mean that oppressed woman has actually ceased to be human—which is not at all what Beauvoir wants to say. For Sartre, there is no middle ground. Either the "for-itself," the uncaused upsurge of freedom, exists *whatever* the facticities of its situation, or else it does not exist. In the latter case, one is dealing with the realm of inert being.

Insofar as Beauvoir's account of woman's situation as one of immanence involves the claim that freedom, the "for-itself," can be penetrated and modified by the "in-itself," it implies another ontology than Sartre's. Beauvoir is trying to describe human existence as a synthesis of freedom and constraint, of consciousness and materiality, which, finally, is impossible within the framework of Sartrean ontology. It is, however, possible—and indeed clarified—within the framework of Merleau-Ponty's ontology. It is possible that Beauvoir herself realized this. For, as we saw, not only was she very familiar with Merleau-Ponty's work, but she also quite explicitly drew on his notion that "the body is generality" in trying to establish the generality of woman's situation of oppression.[28] But if she did realize how close her own positions were to his, she was not prepared to say so. Moreover, even when, in 1955, Beauvoir tried to rebut Merleau-Ponty's critique of Sartre, she did not do so by arguing that Merleau-Ponty's philosophy was flawed. Instead she reversed her analysis of 1945, now claiming that Sartre's philosophy was, after all, like Merleau-Ponty's, a philosophy of embodied subjectivity and intersubjectivity.[29] It is, paradoxically, a Sartre refracted through Merleau-Ponty's lenses whom Beauvoir defends against Merleau-Ponty.

But, to return to 1945, a brief examination of Merleau-Ponty's account of human freedom in his *Phenomenology* will show how profound are the similarities between his ideas and Beauvoir's. As Beauvoir had observed in her review, Merleau-Ponty develops, as against Sartre's notion of consciousness as an "*absolute* freedom," an account of *embodied* consciousness. He describes, as she says, a consciousness "engorged

293

with the sensible," a consciousness that is not a "pure for-itself." There is, for Merleau-Ponty, unlike Sartre, an undifferentiated or "general" being, a "primordial layer at which both things and ideas come into being," which is "anterior to the ideas of subject and object"[30] and in which each of us participates as embodied existence. It is through this common participation that we escape the solipsism implied in the Cartesian *cogito*—a solipsism still lurking in *Being and Nothingness*. For our common inherence in being grants us, however ambiguously, an indubitable "primordial communication," an "interworld," an "intersubjectivity." For such embodied and intersubjective consciousness, freedom "is not distinct from my insertion in the world."[31] Rather, as Merleau-Ponty puts it, it "thrusts roots into the world,"[32] and thus it admits of degree. We will be more free or less free depending on how far our situation enables us to engage in free *actions*. By free actions, Merleau-Ponty means those actions that open onto and shape a future. From this perspective, it is clear that situations—particularly social situations—may qualitatively transform and even suppress freedom.

What Beauvoir described as "immanence," as the falling back of existence into the "in-itself," no longer presents itself as a philosophical problem if, with Merleau-Ponty, we accept that existence is embodied and intersubjective through and through. Against Sartre's claim that we are in principle free at any moment to choose fundamentally to change our lives, Merleau-Ponty insists that *generality* and *probability* are "real phenomena."[33] They exist as the real weight of human history, of institution, of circumstance upon us. Although Merleau-Ponty agrees with Sartre that we are not causally determined, he does not go on to conclude with Sartre that freedom is absolute. Our freedom "gears" itself to our situation, and it does not overturn it in an instant of choice. If women, or other oppressed groups, have "geared" their freedom to an oppressive situation—one that effectively denies them the possibility of action that opens onto the future—then there is no problem involved for Merleau-Ponty in saying that freedom has been suppressed. Since freedom involves *action* which is open, it can cease to be possible. The slave for Merleau-Ponty (like Beauvoir's woman in the harem) is not "as free as his master," because action that would bring a different future is closed to him.[34]

Indeed, in describing the situation of oppressed workers who lack class consciousness, Merleau-Ponty describes in other terms what Beauvoir had called "immanence." If such workers evaluate their situation at all, says Merleau-Ponty, their evaluation "represents the thrust of *a freedom devoid of any project* against unknown obstacles; one cannot in

294

any case talk about a choice."[35] For Sartre, a freedom "devoid of any project" is, of course, a contradiction in terms. Beauvoir *described* such a crippled freedom. But without a critique of the Sartrean notion of freedom and its ontological basis—a critique she did not fully develop—she was unable adequately to *explain* how it was possible. Merleau-Ponty, we can now see, offers us such an explanation.

Moreover, having recognized that situations of oppression may modify freedom itself, Beauvoir and Merleau-Ponty offer striking parallel accounts of what is required for oppression to be overcome: they both recognize—well before Sartre—that there can be no effective *individual* freedom in the face of oppression, that oppressive situations must be changed collectively for freedom to be possible. This insight, already present in *Pyrrhus et Cinéas,* is fleshed out in the discussion of the "independent woman" at the end of *The Second Sex.* Here, although Beauvoir applauds those who struggle in their individual lives against their oppression, she also points out that such a struggle is doomed to failure. For the "independent woman's existence is shaped not only by her own project but by the practices, institutions, and values of the world into which she is born. Oppression is socially instituted, and to overcome it requires a social as well as an individual transformation.

Similarly, for Merleau-Ponty, an oppressive situation cannot be lived as a freely chosen individual project; nor can it be overcome by individual initiative alone. Freedom comes into being in slow, tortuous movements born of "the concatenation of less and more remote ends." It cannot emerge until the point is reached where individuals cease to experience themselves as the isolated victims of an anonymous oppressive "fate" and experience oppression as collective. Such a transition from immanence can take place only because "my" situation is not, strictly speaking "mine," but part of a more general situation which transcends my immediate experiences. As such it can return to me (as in an emerging revolutionary situation) transformed into an opening toward a new project of which I had not previously dreamed. Freedom is a two-way relation, and it is, we have seen, "not distinct from our insertion in the world." On the contrary, "freedom is always a meeting of the inner and the outer."[36]

In 1960, looking back to 1940, Beauvoir had commented: "To defend my position, I would have had to abandon the terrain of individualist, thus idealist, morality where we stood." By 1949, in *The Second Sex,* she had already tacitly abandoned that terrain. The new terrain she had moved to, we can now see, was one that was not contiguous with that occupied by Sartre in *Being and Nothingness.* It was the terrain Merleau-

Ponty had mapped out more fully than she in the *Phenomenology.* But by the late 1940s Sartre was also beginning to shift his ground. When he did so, he was influenced philosophically not only (as he acknowledged) by Merleau-Ponty but also by Beauvoir.

Sartre's intellectual trajectory from *Being and Nothingness* to the *Critique* is complex. I sketch here only an outline of what I take to be his path, but the outline will allow us to see the ways in which his thought moved closer to Beauvoir's. What Sartre lacked in *Being and Nothingness* was a theory that would permit him simultaneously to encompass and link, on the one hand, individual subjectivity and freedom and, on the other, the general weight of institutions, social structures, and events—in short, of history—on individual existence. The radical disjuncture between being "in-itself" and "for-itself," central to his early ontology, precluded such a theory. It was not until the late 1950s, when he wrote the *Critique of Dialectical Reason,* that he fully came to grips with this problem. But already in his *Cahiers pour une morale,* written in the late 1940s but abandoned as a "failure,"[37] he can be seen struggling with it, albeit indecisively.

The material in the *Cahiers* was written in 1947 and 1948, a period in which Beauvoir wrote one of her own works on ethics, *The Ethics of Ambiguity,* and also worked on *The Second Sex.* A detailed comparison of the first of these with the *Cahiers* would certainly be worth undertaking. Here I can only observe that if one contrasts the *Cahiers* with Beauvoir's contemporary works, it is striking that Sartre, still clinging to his early philosophy, finds himself mired in difficulties that do not arise for Beauvoir. In *Being and Nothingness* he had written: "[The] meaning of the past is strictly dependent on my present project. . . . I alone can decide at each moment the bearing of the past."[38] In the *Cahiers* he still writes in a similar vein: "[The] nothingness which separates consciousness from each other makes each determination by these consciousness absolute. . . . Thus, in the midst of History, each historical being is at the same time an a-historical absolute."[39]

Yet, against such a radically individualistic and detotalized notion, we also see Sartre grappling in the *Cahiers* with the fact that History, with a capital H, appears to be a real and supra-individual process,[40] and suggesting that one can talk of the "human condition." Thus, he writes:

> *A* man is a totality and he is an absolute subject. But he cannot be totalized with *another* man. On the other hand the *human condition* is a totality but it does not totalize itself with the in-itself. This does not

mean there is no other kind of truth: it is rather that there is a truth of external relation. Triple external relation: between men, between man and nature, between natural phenomena themselves.[41]

But the relation of "the human condition," as a nontotalizing totality, to individual freedom is not explained in this passage. Nor is it clear how the different kinds of "external relations" Sartre lists here—between human beings, between human beings and nature, and within nature—are related either to each other or to "men" as "absolute subjects." While such questions are posed in the interior monologue that constitutes the *Cahiers*, no sustained replies are offered. Later Sartre was able to clarify such issues, first in *Search for a Method* and the *Critique*, then (at a biographical level) in *The Words* and *The Family Idiot*. But in these works he finally abandons the notion of the "absolute subject" (and its absolute freedom) for a notion closer to the embodied and "impure" subject of Merleau-Ponty and Beauvoir.

Sartre's reformulation is perhaps most clearly seen in the *Critique*. For here Sartre's investigation begins from an account of the subject as embodied, as an agent of *praxis*, who, in order to overcome organic need, transforms nature into those humanized forms of matter Sartre calls the *practico-inert*. Much of the work examines the dialectic through which forms of the practico-inert come to function as alienating forces against their human creators. Praxis might seem, at first glance, to be a new word Sartre has substituted, after his discovery of Marxism, for "being-for-itself." However, this is not the case. For, unlike "being-for-itself," praxis does not involve an absolute freedom. The practico-inert does not merely impose itself as a series of *external* constraints on praxis. It can, through the mediation of other men and in its most intensely alienating forms, effect a transformation of freedom *itself*. Sartre uses the term *destiny*—Beauvoir's term from *The Second Sex*—to describe such a praxis alienated from itself. Like Beauvoir, he now describes a "destiny" that is not natural but is the result of a human oppression so intense that no element of choice, no possibility of a freely chosen project, remains for its victim.

Moreover, Sartre's fullest discussion of "destiny" concerns, surely not by chance, a woman. His key example is of a low-paid woman worker on a production line in a shampoo factory. "Oppression," he now observes, "does not reach the oppressed in a particular sector of their life; *it constitutes this life in its totality*."[42] It constitutes this life such that, in Beauvoir's phrase, "living is only not dying" and no free project is possible. "The role and attitude imposed on her by her work

297

and consumption have never even been the object of an *intention,"*
Sartre says. Even her so-called inner life, her daydreams and fantasies,
are subordinated to the rhythm of the machine at which she must work.
While outside the factory her low wages preclude for her the "choice"
of motherhood:

> [When] the woman in the Dop Shampoo factory has an abortion in
> order to avoid having a child she would be unable to feed, she makes a
> free decision in order to escape a destiny that is made for her; but this
> decision is itself completely manipulated by the objective situation: she
> *realizes* through herself what she *is already;* she carries out the sentence,
> which has already been passed on her, which deprives her of mother-
> hood.[43]

Just as Beauvoir's woman, living her "destiny," is not guilty of "bad
faith," so Sartre's woman is not responsible for what she does since she
could not have done otherwise. There is no future she could choose
other than the one past praxis has decreed. In such a "destiny," and in its
moment of subjective comprehension which Sartre calls *necessity,* praxis
is reduced to making oneself the material force through which things
happen. Insofar as it still involves a moment of comprehension, such a
praxis remains a distinctly human force; but it no longer involves the
moment of absolute freedom that is "being-for-itself." For, Sartre now
concedes, socially mediated worked matter can limit freedom to the
point where no effective choice is possible, only a passive recognition of
what one has been made to do: "the man who looks at his work, who
recognizes himself in it completely, and who also does not recognize
himself at all; the man who can say both: "This is not what I wanted"
and "I understand that this is what I have done and that I could not do
anything else" . . . this man grasps, in an immediate dialectical movement, necessity as the *destiny in exteriority of freedom.*[44]

What Sartre is describing here is, finally, what Beauvoir had called
"immanence" and Merleau-Ponty "a freedom devoid of any project."

As this brief sketch indicates, Sartre has here traveled a long way
from his claims, in *Being and Nothingness,* regarding absolute and indestructible freedom of the subject. Clearly many diverse elements—
political, personal, philosophical—are present in the complex trajectory
that took Sartre from *Being and Nothingness* to the *Critique,* from "absolute freedom" to "destiny." In her public statements Beauvoir consistently cast herself, at least in matters philosophical, as Sartre's disciple—
even, one might suggest, as a mere other to Sartre's philosophical absolute. But we should cease accepting her too "feminine" self-deprecation

at face value. For, her own assessment notwithstanding, we have seen that Beauvoir's philosophical ideas of the 1940s anticipate in important ways those of Sartre in the late 1950s. And thus her work can be considered one of the significant influences on Sartre's intellectual trajectory.

Notes

1. *The Second Sex*, trans. by H. M. Parshley (New York, 1974), 758. French original: *Le deuxième sexe*, 2 vols. (Paris, 1949). Cited hereafter as *TSS*. Citations will be given to the English edition. However, translations will sometimes be altered, in which case this will be indicated and a French page reference given in parentheses.

2. "Wanting to talk about myself, I became aware that to do so I should first have to describe the condition of woman in general." *Force of Circumstance*, trans. by Richard Howard (New York, 1964), 185. French original: *La force des choses* (Paris, 1963).

3. Beauvoir's relationship to Sartre has, of course, also been scrutinized on the biographical and psychological planes, but these are not my concerns here.

4. "Interférences," interview of Simone de Beauvoir and Jean-Paul Sartre by Michel Sicard, *Obliques*, nos. 18–19 (1979), 325. In Alice Schwarzer, *After "The Second Sex": Conversations with Simone de Beauvoir*, trans. by M. Howarth, (New York, 1984), 109, Beauvoir makes a similar point: "In philosophical terms, he was creative and I am not. . . . I always recognized his superiority in that area. So where Sartre's philosophy is concerned, it is fair to say that I took my cue from him because I also embraced existentialism myself." See also Jessica Benjamin and Margaret A. Simons, "Simone de Beauvoir: An Interview," *Feminist Studies* 5 (Summer 1979), 330–45.

5. See, for example, Michèle le Doeuff, "Simone de Beauvoir and Existentialism," *Feminist Studies* 6 (Summer 1980), 277–89; Mary Evans, *Simone de Beauvoir: A Feminist Mandarin* (London, 1985).

6. Judith Okely, *Simone de Beauvoir* (London, 1986), 122. This standard view of the relation of Sartre and Beauvoir has so far been most forcefully challenged by Margaret A. Simons. In her papers "Beauvoir and Sartre: The Question of Influence," *Eros* 8, no. 1 (1981), 25–42; and "Beauvoir and Sartre: The Philosophical Relationship," *Yale French Studies*, no. 72 (1986), 165–79, Simons argues (via a somewhat different route from my own) that Beauvoir's work anticipates Sartre's at several important points.

7. "Interférences," 326.

8. "Merleau-Ponty," *Situations*, trans. by B. Eisler, (Greenwich, Conn., 1965), 174–76. Sartre's essay was originally published shortly after Merleau-Ponty's death as "Merleau-Ponty vivant," in a memorial issue of *Les Temps Modernes*, nos. 184–85, (October 1961).

9. "La Phénoménologie de la perception," *Les Temps Modernes*, no. 2 (November 1945), 366–67.

10. *The Prime of Life*, trans. by Peter Green (Cleveland, 1962), 346. Translation altered. French original: *La force de l'âge* (Paris, 1960), II, 498.

11. See ibid., 433–35, for Beauvoir's account of the circumstances surrounding the writing of this essay and her evaluation of its relation to Sartre's philosophy.

12. *Pyrrhus et Cinéas* (Paris, 1944), 95–96.

13. *The Ethics of Ambiguity*, trans. by B. Frechtman (New York, 1967), 82. French original: *Pour une morale de l'ambiguité* (Paris, 1947).

14. Ibid., 82–83.

15. *TSS*, xix. Translation altered; French I, 15.

16. Jean-Paul Sartre, *Being and Nothingness*, trans. by Hazel E. Barnes (New York, 1966), 364. French original: *L'Etre et le néant* (Paris, 1943). Cited hereafter as *BN*.

17. Ibid., 495 ff.

18. Ibid., 673.

19. *TSS*, 69.

20. For an intriguing discussion of some of the implications of this separation of gender and sex, see Judith Butler, "Sex and Gender in Simone de Beauvoir's *Second Sex,*" *Yale French Studies*, no. 72 (1986), 35–49.

21. *TSS*, 39. Translation altered; French I, 74. Compare with Sartre: "The essence of relations between consciousness is not the *Mitsein;* it is conflict"; *BN*, 525.

22. Maurice Merleau-Ponty, *Phenomenology of Perception*, trans. by Colin Smith (London, 1962), 219. French original: *La Phénoménologie de la perception* (Paris, 1945). Cited hereafter as *PP*. Beauvoir refers to this notion in her 1945 review of the *Phenomenology*.

23. *TSS*, 52. Translation altered; French I, 88.

24. *BN*, 673.

25. *TSS*, xxxiii. Translation altered; French I, 31.

26. Ibid., 802.

27. Ibid., xxviii. Translation altered; French I, 25.

28. See Ibid., 52; also 7 and 33n.

29. "Merleau-Ponty et le pseudo-Sartrisme," in *Privilèges* (Paris, 1955). The occasion for Merleau-Ponty's critique of Sartre and Beauvoir's attempt to rebut it was a political disagreement over the revolutionary potential of Marxism. However, in the course of the argument the major philosophical divergences also surfaced very clearly.

30. *PP*, 219.

31. Ibid., 360.

32. Ibid., 456.

33. Ibid., 442.

34. Ibid., 436 ff.

35. Ibid., 444; emphasis added.

36. Ibid., 454.

37. See, for example, interview with Sicard, *Obliques*, 9–29. See also his comments in Michel Contat and Alexandre Astruc, *Sartre by Himself* (New York, 1978), 77–78, 80–81. For my fuller evaluation of the *Cahiers*, see Sonia Kruks, "Sartre's *Cahiers pour une morale:* Failed Attempt or New Trajectory in Ethics?" *Social Text*, nos. 13–14 (Winter–Spring 1986), 184–94.

38. *BN*, 610.

39. Jean-Paul Sartre, *Cahiers pour une morale*, ed. by A. Elkaïm-Sartre (Paris, 1983), 32. Cited hereafter as *CPM*.

40. See, for example, the discussions of feudalism and of technological change in ibid., 81–86, 86–89.

41. Ibid., 477.

42. *Critique of Dialectical Reason*, trans. by Alan Sheridan-Smith, ed. by Jonathan Rée, (London, 1976), 232; emphasis added. French original: *Critique de la raison dialectique* (Paris, 1960).

43. Ibid., 235.

44. Ibid., 226–27.

16

BAD FAITH, GOOD FAITH, AND THE FAITH OF FAITH

Adrian Mirvish

To deal with any major topic in Sartre's work is almost to ensure difficulties. For he brings together the insights of both a perspicacious observer of human nature and a technically gifted philosopher, and he moves easily from discipline to discipline and from field to field. He does all of these things in the chapter of *Being and Nothingness*[1] dealing with the phenomenon of bad faith. Sartre's analysis is based on observation and predicated on nothing less than a functional interconnection between three major fields: psychoanalysis (construed in the broad sense of the term), Gestalt psychology, and studies of the notion of temporality. Not only is Sartre's treatment of bad faith understandably intricate, but the three topics are dealt with explicitly only after the chapter on bad faith itself. That is, the reader is confronted with Sartre's detailed analyses before he ever explicitly deals with these topics in the text.[2]

To add yet a further difficulty, temporality and psychoanalysis play a crucial role in Sartre's analysis, but the same is not true of Gestalt psychology. In fact, the core analysis which concerns the actual mechanism whereby a subject can act in bad faith—which depends on certain types of Gestalt delineations of experience—is never explicitly discussed anywhere in *Being and Nothingness*. Much of the material presented in the relevant chapter consists of descriptions as opposed to explanations of bad faith.

Another problem concerns Sartre's description of the phenomenon as one of "bad faith." Although this term is intuitively comprehensible, why does he not use instead the intuitively clearer term *self-deception*? Whereas in the literature "bad faith" has simply been taken as self-evident, we shall see that there are important historical reasons for its use. Also, the term *bad faith* can be misleading, because it is not a state in which one has a single faith but rather one in which one has a faith in this faith. Sartre, of course, talks about what is termed precisely "the faith of bad faith," but, given the above foundational problems and the fact that the analysis of this compound faith is complex, it is all too easy to misunderstand the author's true intent.

In spite of these difficulties, Sartre's psychological perspicacity is so palpable that one is easily persuaded, even at a first reading, that bad faith is a truly pervasive phenomenon of human experience. Providing a framework for understanding the above issue, however, means dealing with the respective issues of historical background and epistemology in a degree of detail all too often neglected in the literature.[3] Specifically, regarding the role played by the factor of psychoanalysis, I will show how Sartre is reacting not only to Freud but also to the intellectualism of his teacher Alain. Given the complexities outlined above, it can also be noted that even the best work dealing with bad faith can only provide piecemeal insights, because it lacks an overall and cohesive conceptual substratum.[4] By contrast, the analysis I offer will, I hope, be new as well as closer to Sartre's original intent.

Sartre starts his analysis by attacking Freud's view that there is a barrier between the conscious and unconscious levels of the mind. This criticism is well known, but given that we wish to present Sartre's own positive view of the phenomenon, we may note that, according to Sartre, Freud attempts to explain a host of complex patterns of human behavior on the basis of the notion of repression, which is in turn dependent on the existence of a rigid barrier between consciousness and the unconscious. Sartre shows that Freud's notion of the censor conflates these two levels of the mind into one psychic entity, thereby undermining the above dichotomy. In this way the problem is reduced to what is termed "bad faith." The notion of consciousness as opaque is reduced by Sartre to that of consciousness as translucent, and so we must now turn to Sartre's treatment of this latter notion.

The demise of the Freudian solution, however, leaves Sartre in what may appear a precarious position, because the dichotomy between consciousness and the unconscious seems to explain bad faith. By contrast, Sartre now has to explain this phenomenon while maintaining that consciousness is translucent. This problem is solved by Sartre's developing a notion of faith which is not at all blind. Rather, it allows humans to persevere in a particular mode of conduct without—at either a prereflexive or reflexive level—directly seeing the consequences of their actions or without seeing that in some sense they actively constitute the worlds they live in, or in spite of their holding contradictory values. In short, I shall analyze what Sartre means by the faith of bad faith. This type of faith depends on a selective mechanism of consciousness, understood in terms of what Sartre gleans from Gestalt principles.

Bearing in mind that, for Sartre, "bad faith is conscious of its structure,"[5] the problem is approached in terms of the question "How can we believe by bad faith in the concepts which we forge expressly to persuade ourselves?"[6] Belief, in turn, is spoken of as meaning "the adherence of being to its object when the object is not given or is given indistinctly."[7] This definition of belief is crucial to the analysis of the phenomenon of bad faith and can be consistently expanded on in terms of the following question: If I clearly set about to convince myself that a certain state of affairs exists where there is little or no evidence, that this is indeed the case, how can this conviction be maintained? Must I not be aware of the belief as *nothing more than* a belief?

To deal with this problem, let us consider the case of a waiter in a café:

> His movement is quick and forward, a little too precise, a little too rapid. He comes forward toward the patrons with a step a little too quick. He bends forward a little too eagerly. . . . All his behavior seems to us a game. He applies himself to chaining his movements as if they were mechanisms; the one regulating the other; he gives himself the quickness and pitiless rapidity of things.[8]

The description here is at once amusing and perspicacious. For who has not encountered just such a French café waiter, or his American equivalent serving nouvelle cuisine? What is strange about Sartre's description is that each member of the series of W's actions is performed as if it were distinct or discrete. So much attention is given by W to each act that the effect is marionettelike and artificial. This is why Sartre says that he "applies himself to chaining his movements as if they were mechanisms" and that "[all] his behavior seems to us a game." That is, we can sense the artificiality of his actions. Why is this so?

Sartre says that W would reflexively claim himself to be sincere

303

insofar as he is committed to being the quintessential waiter: "One must be what one is."[9] The key resides here in the term *is*. For W sees his role—with the concomitant actions it entails and engenders—as something fixed; he takes it as a given. Hence the intensity and deliberateness of his actions which, in some sense, allow him to convince himself that he has realized the "being-in-itself of the café waiter."[10] That is, one is dealing here with an individual who is totally identified with his role and with the actions it demands. For W to continue with his life-style, certain actions have to be performed of a different order and type from those described above. Thus Sartre writes that the waiter has "the obligation of getting up at five o'clock, of sweeping the floors of the shop before the restaurant opens . . . etc."[11] What the waiter proudly takes to be his waiterly actions only exist as a function of other actions which, were he asked about them, he would categorically reject as forming an essential part of his role.

The example shows that the waiter is in bad faith, to the extent that he avoids realizing the consequences of much of his own activity. The waiter acts as though his role is a given in spite of evidence to the contrary—getting up at five o'clock, sweeping the café floors. Admitting that these actions constituted an essential part of his waiter role would make it extremely difficult for him to act as though his role were a given.

As a preliminary to a more complete and exact analysis of the phenomenon of bad faith, we can therefore write:

$$xbp \tag{1}$$

where this must be taken to read, "x believes p." In the present example, x denotes the waiter, and p means "he is a waiter." However, the language involved in stating "x believes he is a waiter" can be very misleading. For "xbp" does not denote an isolated and/or monadic mental event. In this regard I have shown elsewhere how Sartre combats both intellectualism and idealism[12] and, moreover, how under the influence of Max Scheler and psychologist Kurt Lewin, a subject for him constitutes a world not in terms of mental acts but rather on the basis of its always being an embodied consciousness.[13] For present purposes, however, W's bad faith can be satisfactorily described entirely in terms of the various kinds of actions he performs, without referring to any mental acts or events. Thus, for x to have a belief is for x, as an embodied consciousness, to constitute a world of belief. Hence, W has to perform the series of actions described above which will allow him to behave as though his role is indeed a given, in spite of there also being evidence to the contrary. When it is said that "x believes he is a waiter," this must be taken as a shorthand for "x constitutes a world of belief of being a waiter."

This tells us why Sartre is concerned with explaining the phenomenon in question in terms of faith. For now it can be seen that the waiter has a faith, acting in accord with his constituting a mere world of belief. He has a faith in the sense that he has a commitment to constitute the world in question in spite of the fact that it is founded on what is nothing more than a belief or set of beliefs.

The formula xbp, however, only partially captures the phenomenon of bad faith. For simply to have faith does not entail that one is in bad faith. We can see that although (1) does effectively denote x's relevant constituting activity, it does not capture his dissimulation. We need a description that will not only capture the fact that x constitutes a world of belief but also shows us that x actually believes that he constitutes such a world. In order to capture this self-dissimulation, we can write:

$$xb(xbp) \qquad (2)$$

This means: "x believes that x believes p." This means that "x acts as though there is little or no evidence, or no contradictory evidence, that he is constituting nothing but a world of belief."

That (2) indeed captures what Sartre means by bad faith can be seen when applied to the case at hand. As we know from (1), x constitutes a world of belief; he acts as though he has—in Sartre's terms—attained the being-in-itself of the waiter in spite of some of his own constituting activity which provides evidence to the contrary. What (2) tells us is that x also acts as though there is little or no evidence, or no contradictory evidence, that he has not in effect attained the being-in-itself of the café waiter. Formula (2) thus surely characterizes the double or complex element of duplicity of self as manifested by the waiter's behavior. He not only creates an ultimately ill-founded world of fantasy that ignores a crucial aspect of his own activity, but he is also able to ignore his glaring ignorance.

This second element, or belief in (2), captures what Sartre calls "the faith of bad faith." For whereas (1) was seen to capture x's having a faith in constituting a world of belief, (2) now shows us that x has a faith in this faith; x is able to commit himself to having merely a belief in constituting his world of belief. But—and here misunderstanding could easily arise—this suggests that bad faith is not simply a faith but rather a phenomenon that necessarily involves a faith in this faith. We can thus conclude that (2) captures the phenomenon in question and gives us an understanding of Sartre's difficult locution.

We are now in a position to understand the historical genesis of the term *bad faith*. Sartre reacted to an idea of his teacher Alain, who exerted considerable positive and negative influence on his pupil.

In his work *Quatre-vingt-un chapitres sur l'esprit et les passions,*[14] in a chapter entitled "Free Will and Faith," Alain tells us that without the exercise of judgment there can be no freedom whatsoever for any given subject. Alain considers three cases. The first of these, (A), occurs when S acts on the basis of instinct and feeling. Alain notes here that instincts give rise to passions or feelings, and that these in turn motivate or cause S's action. The result is unfortunate insofar as S's behavior is uncontrolled and impulsive, a mere reflection of a basic affective state of affairs. Finding himself in such a state, S can respond by exercising rational judgment. This can result in undercutting or even abnegating the causes of the uncontrolled behavior, or in at least making clear to S the true source and motivation of his behavior.[15]

A second way in which judgment can be exercised—(B)—is by S refusing to allow incipient instincts and feelings to develop. In this way it is ensured, says Alain, that the above type of behavior is obviated from the start. That is, by virtue of exercising judgment I simply refuse to allow the affective cause of action to be realized. Alain goes on to note that such a refusal amounts to wisdom, "and that (for example) an honest man does not amuse himself by imagining how he could steal without being caught, still less how he might rape or seduce."[16] The operative principle in these, it is important to stress, is not anything like the Freudian notion of suppression, nor is it like the later Freud's view of repression resulting from anxiety, in which a type of *Gedankenexperiment* is performed so that repression is automatically activated insofar as the subject starts to foresee the socially unacceptable consequences of his affective drives or complexes.[17] In both of these the ontological assumption is that the unconscious is the dominant psychic faculty which consciousness, or the rational ego, manages to hold at bay. By contrast, Alain's point is that rationality, as manifest in the act of judgment, is primary, making it possible to obviate the continued growth of affective causes of behavior.

A third function of judgment—(C)—is to impose order upon the imagination, where "everything changes and is in a state of dissolution in the play of images."[18] This emphasizes that those using judgment in their actions will differ substantially from the subclass of individuals who by and large allow their actions to follow the dictates of their imaginations. In the former case an individual's behavior will exhibit a purpose and order as opposed to the latter case, where an individual can be characterized as one "who looks at himself living, curious to know where his desires will lead him."[19]

Given (A), (B), and (C) above, Alain then tells us: "By these descriptions, from which the man of good faith will recognize himself, we have gone well beyond those mechanical schemas . . . where causes only exist by virtue of the judge (i.e. the faculty of judgment)."[20]

Alain has clearly delineated criteria for an individual in good faith. But why call this faith? It is clear that S is exercising judgment and thereby behaving in a rational and ordered fashion, to the extent that (A), (B), and (C) are fulfilled, but why does this entail—as it does for Alain—that S is acting in good faith? The answer, which will be crucial for the nature of bad faith, needs to be presented in a number of stages.

Let us first note that, on the level of perception, judgment plays a crucial role in any individual's constitution of a world. Thus, for example, Alain writes: "I do not touch this cubic die. Rather I successively touch edges, points, smooth and hard surfaces, and reuniting all these appearances in a single object, I judge that this object is cubic."[21]

The senses do not present us with objects as such. Rather, localized sensations are synthesized via rational judgment to provide the experience of a total entity or entities. Moreover, the perceptual world which we experience as a totality is constituted on the basis of judgments.[22] But if judgments are the sine qua non for experiencing a delineated perceptual world, it does not follow that one can create a world of one's own choice. Quite to the contrary, this constitution encounters obstacles on both physical and psychological-moral levels. This implies that all humans use judgment in constituting a world of ordered perceptual experience. Those who also invoke rational judgment on moral as well as ("depth") psychological levels have a definite advantage. For they can create on a yet higher level an ordered and free world to the extent that they are not slaves to the obstacles or constraints of instincts, passions, and imagination. The issue of faith surfaces again for Alain. In conjunction with the discussion of constraints, let us note what Alain has to say regarding the topic of rational action:

> the execution assumes a set of acts that follow and a path that changes perspectives and clarifies causes . . . often deliberation assumes another try. Action is . . . like an enquiry. . . . A [rational] will followed through does not believe itself beaten when it has decided but been stopped by obstacles: then it is a matter of perseverance by seeking and deliberation from afresh. There are more than two paths and crossroads are everywhere. The [rational] will shows itself less by decrees than by a constant faith in itself, and an honest look at every step.[23]

307

Alain's point is that the rational subject must have faith in the sense of courage and determination that a rational and free world order can be created, strong constraints notwithstanding.

There is yet another reason why Alain stresses faith. It centers around the idea that a rational will does not operate or show itself in terms of decrees. The point is elaborated on in terms of Renouvier's statement affirming the existence of a free will, namely, "the principle is that it is necessary to make oneself free. One must will, when all is said and done."[24] Alain notes dramatically:

Here is faith in its purity; here one calls to mind the theological proofs long deflected from their true object, for it is faith itself that is God. It is necessary to believe because [a principle] is not. For example, in justice because it is not. Not to believe that it is loved or desired, since this does not add anything, but rather believe that I can create it.[25]

This vividly illustrates—even in terms of locution—how some of Sartre's conceptual roots find their basis in Alain's work, and gives us more insight into the nature of faith according to Alain. Specifically, faith "in its purity" is the product of a rational will creating in some sense de novo. Such an act requires faith insofar as there is no teleology to assure the subject that what is being created will ultimately be realized, although it is the product of a rational will. Thus there is no a priori assurance that justice will prevail, even as the product of a subject's rational act or volition. For, in Alain's view—as opposed, for example, to the idealism of Brunschvicg—no inevitable evolution of knowledge ensures the ultimate triumph of a just or rational world order.

Recall that Alain initially put forward three criteria for rational action—namely, (A), (B), and (C)—which would result in a subject's being in good faith. We can now fully understand why Alain talks about faith. For even if this subject acts in a rational fashion as specified by (A), (B), and (C), and is relatively free from impulse and passion, the appearance of an ordered, structured, or just world is still subject to a set of constraints or resistances and to there being a lack of teleology. So powerful are these conditions that they preclude any assurance that rational constitution will succeed. Hence, according to Alain, a faith is required. Not a blind faith, to be sure. For rational volition or action ensure the possibility of a structured and just world order, and hence the possibility in principle of good—which is to say rational—faith. However, faith is still required.

This provides the clue to why Sartre describes the phenomenon as bad faith. As just seen, good faith for Alain is predicated on the assumption that the rational faculty—the faculty of rational judgment as exercised in volition—is what is most fundamentally human. This faculty exhibits what can be called the transparency of mind insofar as it enables one to both know and control one's emotions, desires, or passions, and therefore Alain's talking about being able to trace emotions back to their source or imposing a rational order on the imagination. Thus the phenomenon Sartre describes as bad faith would in fact constitute a pseudo-problem for Alain's rational subject in good faith. For such a person would always in principle be able to overcome such a state by a determined and persistent use of rational judgment. For Sartre, on the other hand, bad faith is a pervasive human phenomenon which cannot be annulled or extirpated by the use of reason alone. Although the issues are complex, it will still be possible to indicate how for Sartre bad faith is a manifestation or symptom of neurosis, and one that is only able to be truly resolved by existential psychoanalysis. One is reminded of the portrayal in *Baudelaire* of Gide overcoming an initial bad faith engendered by his acceptance of the sexual status quo, as opposed to Baudelaire, who remains mired forever in just such an acceptance:

> look at the distance traveled by another Christian . . . André Gide. In the fundamental conflict between his sexual anomaly and accepted morality, he took sides with the former against the latter, and has gradually eaten away the rigorous principles which impeded him. . . . In spite of a thousand relapses, he has moved forward toward *his* morality. . . . In a similar situation [to that of Baudelaire] he made a different choice; he wanted his conscience to be clear, and he understood that he could only achieve liberation by a radical and gratuitous invention of Good and Evil.[26]

This demonstrates that for Sartre bad faith is not amenable to rational treatment alone, as it would be for Alain. Gide would not have initially possessed a completely perlucid self-identity—as would have been the case on Alain's model—which could then have served as guide for his constitution of a world.

Sartre's presentation of bad faith provides an alternative to two opposite and extreme views of the psyche. On the one hand, it stands as a counter to the opacity of mind with its concomitant determinism, as espoused by Freud. On the other hand, it offers a counter to the intellectualist transparency of mind as espoused by Alain. Sartre's "bad faith" can now be understood as reacting against Alain's notion of good faith. Existential psychoanalysis, and not purely intellectual or rational efforts at elucidation, will provide the basis for a viable world order characterized by minimal mendacity of self—one not overwhelmed by excessive influences of the so-called passions. In typical iconoclastic irony, Sartre names "bad faith" precisely what he takes to be his teacher's intellectualist apotheosis in the form of good faith.

Although a description of one of two types of bad faith was given above, the mechanism allowing this phenomenon to occur has yet to be explained. Given Sartre's refutation of the Freudian conscious/ unconscious dichotomy, any such explanation must take into account Sartre's own claim that consciousness is translucent. Yet nowhere in the chapter on bad faith, or for that matter anywhere else in *Being and Nothingness,* does Sartre explicitly deal with such a mechanism. This fact has promoted misunderstanding in the literature, in that we have been given descriptions and not explanations of the phenomenon at hand.[27]

In what follows, a notion of constitution will be presented which, although it goes beyond what is explicitly stated in the text, is accurate to the spirit of Sartre's epistemology and ontology at the time of *Being and Nothingness.* Two main topics will need to be addressed: the phenomenon of the prereflexive constitution of the subject's world and the relation of various figure/ground configurations to this world.

Let us consider a number of examples. In the first, a subject, S, is driving alone for a distance of twenty miles along an expressway in relatively heavy traffic. When S gets off the expressway he suddenly becomes reflexively aware that he has traveled the entire distance while imagining details of an upcoming hike in Nepal. He is not at all reflexively aware of, nor can he explicitly recall, any of the details of his half-hour trip either in terms of his driving or in terms of the external environment traversed. Now consider the same type of case except that this time S has been reading a report balanced on the steering wheel as he drives along. Again, when he gets on the expressway, S is not reflexively aware of any of the details of what he did as a driver during the course of the trip, nor can he recall many details of the report. Although during the trip he was reflexively unaware, this does not mean that S was a passive agent. On the contrary, especially given that traffic was relatively heavy, he had to make many maneuvers in order to arrive safely. In fact, when one thinks about the kind of maneuvers involved, one realizes how complex and coordinated they would have to be. Although instinct and habit are involved, they are simply not sufficient to give a complete account of the phenomenon.

Thus circumstances in the environment are constantly and rapidly changing. Indeed, given the number of cars and lanes, different speeds, and weather conditions, S's interactions with his environment are not going to be repeated. Concomitantly, in order to complete the trip safely, S will have to constantly exhibit a spontaneity which cannot be accounted for purely in terms of repetition of behavior, given the extreme complexity of actions required relative to constantly changing variables. Indeed an explanation in terms of habit would force one to a notion of generalization so broad as to undercut the very notion of habit. We can thus say that what S does during driving, among other things, is to calculate distances—not in Cartesian terms as an essentially disembodied spectator or third party, but instead as a center of instrumental activity. For S directs his automobile through a field of obstacles, and this via actions involving assessments of changing distances between these obstacles and himself as embodied agent, with the car as instrument.[28]

Another term for *calculation* is *judgment*. It can then be said that S performs a series of actions involving prereflexive judgments enabling him to successfully complete the trip. These judgments moreover entail that S was conscious; were he not, he would never have survived. We can thus state that at the level of prereflexive consciousness, S delineates and constitutes a world in which he performs extremely complex sets of actions enabling him to travel the distance. It should, however, be noted that S's risk of having an accident increases to the extent that he is not centrally occupied with the task of driving. This suggests a relation between the activities that S is focused on—imagining his trip or reading his report—on the one hand and the conditions in his environment and his response to them on the other hand.

To explain these examples we have to account for a subject exhibiting a functionally dichotomized consciousness with two series of functionally disparate actions, in spite of there being a clear interconnection between them. If we recall Sartre's Gestaltist affinities, the notion of figure/ground can be used to solve our problem. We have discussed two variations of the example in which S is reflexively aware during his trip and can expressly recall an imaginative series of events on the one hand and the contents of the report on his steering wheel, on the other. During the period in question, S has (a) an imaginative series of events as reflexive figure and the world delineated and constituted in the above sense as prereflexive ground; or (b) the perceived report as reflexive figure and the world delineated and constituted in the above sense as prereflexive ground.[29]

We can now return to the discussion of bad faith, and specifically the mechanism enabling it to occur in spite of the translucency of consciousness. The waiter, W, constitutes a world in which he acts as though his role is a given, in spite of other aspects of his constitutive activity which provide evidence to the contrary. Moreover, W somehow manages to avoid facing or becoming directly aware of this evidence.

Let us consider W's behavior from a number of points of view. First, suppose that even during his work hours W is called upon to perform any of those types of actions which provide clear evidence that his role is not a given. Suppose that there is a shortage of staff so that W is forcefully assigned to washing dishes in the café kitchen. Under these circumstances W could well daydream while performing his task efficiently. He could, for example, imagine that he was a waiter, or for that matter even *chef de cuisine* at a famous Parisian restaurant and do this while dextrously washing dishes without mishap. Moreover, suppose that after his stint of dishwashing is over W cannot explicitly recall how many or what kinds of dishes he had washed. For that matter let us suppose that he cannot even recall talking to anyone during this period, although he can, by contrast, explicitly recall his fantasy in detail. The case here is clearly analogous to the one in which S travels twenty miles unscathed on an expressway while imagining a hiking trip in Nepal. In fact, a comparison yields the following: (a) W holds or experiences as reflexive figure his imagining being *chef de cuisine* and so on, while his actions of washing the dishes form the prereflexive ground of his experiences;[30] (b) as was the case for S, for W prereflexive judgments enter into his actions so that a complex delineation and constitution of a world occurs at the level of prereflexive consciousness; (c) it is not at all surprising that W can prereflexively perform the task at hand without mishap. For if S can drive on an expressway without accident as a result of prereflexive actions that form the ground of his experience, then W, too, can wash dishes without mishap.

Instead of indulging in an imaginative fantasy, consider that W turns on a radio and becomes quite involved in listening to music during the course of his demeaning work. Were W asked after this period of dishwashing what had occurred during this time, he would be reflexively aware of having listened to the music. He would moreover be able to recall in detail what songs had been sung. W may have had no explicit recollection of what kinds of dishes he had washed or how he had done so. For that matter, one could reasonably suppose that he could not even recall talking to anyone or any other activity except for listening to the music. Then we can again draw a comparison, this time with S driving unscathed on the expressway while reading a report. The following can be noted: (a') W holds or experiences as reflexive and perceptual figure his listening to the music, while his actions of washing the dishes form the prereflexive ground of his experience; (b') and (c') correspond to (b) and (c) above.[31]

We can now understand the mechanism of bad faith, which explains how a subject is able to avoid what appears to be obvious evidence in spite of the translucency of consciousness. For a subject to focus attention on a specific (although possibly complex) object or phenomenon as figure is automatically going to result in the remainder of the field of experience becoming less differentiated relative to this figure. Thus, for W to hold as figure either his listening to the music or his imagining being *chef de cuisine* is to automatically ensure that the background activity of his washing dishes becomes less focused or more undifferentiated relative to the figure. But this is crucial. For those actions of W giving rise to the evidence he wishes to focus on are precisely those constituted as figure for the experiences in question. By contrast, those actions of W giving rise to the evidence he wishes to ignore are precisely those constituted as their ground. That is, it is by virtue of their forming part of the relatively undifferentiated ground of his experience that W avoids becoming directly aware of the import of those actions that provide clear evidence that his role is not a given. It is important to stress here that, in general, bad faith is a function of the subject's fixating on a particular figure and underscoring the degree of differentiation between figure and ground.

The notion of figure/ground is also able to account for Sartre's central claim that consciousness is translucent. It is not as though there is an absolute dichotomy between figure and ground; quite to the contrary, the very existence of the former always depends on its in some way being articulated with its ground. The fact that consciousness is not transparent follows directly from the discussion indicating that focusing on a figure automatically entails that its ground becomes less differentiated. On the other hand, consciousness is not opaque. If it was so, there would in some sense be an absolute barrier between figure and ground, and none of the tasks completed by S or W above could be possible. For if S and W would only have been able to focus their attention on actions associated with the figure, they would never have been able to travel or wash dishes without mishap. In other words, they would never have been able to simultaneously and successfully constitute a world, on a prereflexive level, as the ground of their experience. It can be seen that consciousness is neither transparent nor opaque. This implies an inherent connection between figure and ground which the subject must in some sense be aware of, which is to say that consciousness must be translucent. Thus, it can be concluded, the notion of figure/ground can account for the phenomenon of bad faith. It enables us to understand how a subject can avoid becoming directly aware of seemingly obvious evidence, in spite of the translucency of consciousness.

The artificiality inherent in bad faith is the result of a subject's fixating on a figure, thereby heightening the distinction in the degree of differentiation and awareness between figure and ground. This same analysis can now be applied to Sartre's description of W given earlier:

> His movement is quick and forward, a little too precise, a little too rapid. He comes forward toward the patrons with a step a little too quick. He bends forward a little too eagerly; his voice, his eyes express an interest a little too solicitous . . . he returns, trying to imitate in his walk the inflexible stiffness of some kind of automaton.

Sartre clearly intends there to be an aura of artificiality associated with W's actions. This is made apparent by the relatively high degree of self-consciousness or reflexivity W manifests. The actions described above constitute part of the complex and continuous figure of W's field of experience. W's behavior can be explained by asking what would occur were W not to reflexively fixate on the above-mentioned set of actions as figure but rather to act in a prereflexive and spontaneous fashion. The answer should now be unequivocal: this would not allow for an artificially heightened figure/ground dichotomy such as that induced by W above. Spontaneous, W would not be able to avoid having to face evidence (prereflexively) in the ground of his own experience which would show him that his role was not a given. Hence bad faith involves a subject's fixating on a particular figure and heightening the distinction between figure and ground.

This allows us to further clarify the phenomenon. Recalling the formulation

$$xb \ (xbp) \qquad\qquad (2)$$

it now becomes clear that x's fixation on a particular figure with its concomitant evidence is expressed in terms of the vested belief, xbp, whereas the ground of x's field of experience with its concomitant evidence which x wishes to avoid facing directly is expressed in terms of the second element of belief, xbp.

More needs to be said to fully analyze this phenomenon. For, according to Sartre, "the ontological characteristic of the world of bad faith with which the subject suddenly surrounds himself is this: that here being is what it is not, and is not what it is."[32]

Given this claim, the case of W can be seen to typify the class

314

characterized by the expression "being is what it is not." We read this in the sense that "being is what it is not (even yet)." The waiter believes that he is what he is and that he will exist in this same given fashion even in the future. This means that we still need to consider a case of bad faith characterized by the formulation "being is not what it is." As Sartre makes clear above, bad faith somehow involves both the fact that "being is what it is not" and the fact that "being is not what it is."[33]

Consider, then, an example in *Being and Nothingness* which involves the case of a woman going out with a certain man for the first time. From the start she is aware that he wants to have an affair with her, but she does not yet want to make a decision. She enjoys and is actually charmed by being sexually attractive to him, and indeed she requires his desire in order to keep their meeting romantic. And yet she also vacillates, for his sexual desire in and of itself is not what she wants; she also wants to be liked and respected as a total person. Moreover she does not want this desire to be so strong that it forces her at this early date to an explicit choice. She attempts to resolve this difficulty by refusing "to apprehend the desire for what it is; she does not even give it a name; she recognizes it only to the extent that it transcends itself toward admiration, esteem, respect and that it is wholly absorbed in the more refined forms which it produces."[34]

Thus "she concerns herself only with what is respectful and discreet in the attitude of her companion"[35] and refuses to see that in all his actions there is a strong overtone of sexual desire. For example, "[if] he says to her, 'I find you attractive!' she disarms the phrase of its sexual background."[36] That is, she abstracts the words from their context and concentrates artificially on their literal and present meaning, that she is "attractive as a total person."

The woman constitutes a world of fantasy in order to obviate what she wishes to ignore, although this world is as yet not highly developed. Suppose, however, that the man suddenly takes her hand in his warm hands. This is a much more manifestly sexual move, so much so that she can no longer maintain that the man likes her in the way she had construed. And since he has therefore forced the moment to a crisis, she must act. At first she may appear to have only two choices. She could leave her hand in his, which would mean that she has consented to become involved with him. She could, on the other hand, withdraw it, but this would "break the troubled and unstable harmony which gives the hour its charm."[37] What she wants, of course, is neither, but rather to maintain her belief in spite of evidence to the contrary. This she does by ignoring her hand and divorcing herself from the present. She creates a world of romantic and essentially asexual fantasy in which she waxes sentimentally about the nature of life, quite apart from the actual reality of the present. In fact, she becomes divorced from the present: "she contemplates [her body] as though from above, as a passive object to which events can happen but which can neither provoke them nor avoid them because all its possibilities are outside of it."[38]

Thus the young woman maintains her belief and ignores the man's intentions, at the price of no longer experiencing herself as a lived body. Her experience is primarily of a *Körper*, or a purely physiological and anatomical entity. This is why Sartre says that "during this time the divorce of the body and the soul is accomplished"[39] and "she realizes herself as not being her own body."[40]

Here we are surely presented with an instance of bad faith. For the subject—let us call her Q—identifies herself with a world of fantasy in the attempt to ignore what is the case. We can analyze the situation first in terms of the mechanism of bad faith and then in terms of Sartre's descriptive formulation of it. When the man says, "I find you attractive!" Q takes these words out of context. Q avoids paying direct attention to the look on his face, the tone in his voice, and a certain type of tension in his bodily posture, all of which would show her—were she to pay direct attention to it—that he is interested in her sexually. Instead Q romanticizes the phrase out of context by taking it to mean that he likes and admires her as a total person. How is all this possible? Recalling the cases of S and W above, it can now be seen that what Q does is to attend exclusively to the phrase so that it forms the figure for her experience; the man's looks, his tone of voice, his tension are certainly experienced but as forming part of the (relatively unfocused) ground of her experience.

By the time her hand is taken, Q can only maintain that the man likes her as a total person by constituting a world of fantasy. The mechanism that explains this phenomenon is the same as above. Q fixates on her imaginary world as figure, whereas the action of the man's taking her hand is experienced as forming part of the (relatively unfocused) ground of her experience.[41] It must be stressed that as part of the ground of her experience, Q is certainly inchoately aware of the sexual import of his action. This results in her objectivizing her own body.

Both when she takes the man's utterance out of context and when she constitutes an imaginary world, Q believes that the man likes her as a total person. She ignores the evidence that his interest in her is primarily sexual. Like W, Q can be said to have a faith, namely, to act in accordance with her constituting a mere world of belief. As in the case of

W, it can be written that xbp, meaning, in this case, "Q believes the man likes her as a total person."

It is not merely the case that Q holds this belief. It is also the case that she believes this belief. For to say xbp here would merely mean that Q constitutes an imaginary world. In fact, because this unwanted or contrary evidence is the partial ground of her experience, Q is able to persist with her imaginary activity. That is, Q acts in accordance with there being little or no evidence that the world she is constituting is only a world of belief. But, as with W, Q's bad faith consists not merely in her having a faith but in her having faith in this faith.

This instance of bad faith can thus be fully captured by writing, consistent with the case of W, that $xb(xbp)$ meaning, "x believes that x believes p."

The same formulation thus captures two very distinct examples of bad faith. Recall that the world constituted by someone in bad faith is such that "being is what it is not, and is not what it is." Regarding Q, this exemplifies that class of cases characterized by the second half of this quotation. For in her attempt to ignore the evidence that indicates the man's sexual interest in her, Q resorts to identifying herself with a world of fantasy. What she makes herself be is what she is literally not; or, in more general terms, it is the case for her that "being is not what it is."

The problem here is that Sartre clearly intends any case of bad faith to exemplify both characteristics, as can be seen by his saying that "being is what it is not, and is not what it is." What, therefore, is the connection between the two cases? This question now needs to be answered in order to complete the analysis of bad faith.

Sartre tells us that "[with] bad faith there appears . . . a type of being which is like that of objects."[42] And indeed, in the two cases of bad faith discussed, we saw that the agents involved, by virtue of fixation on a figure in their respective fields of experience, act as though they have an absolute or fixed and thinglike identity. Thus the waiter is totally identified with his role, while the young woman acts in accord with having the identity of being-someone-admired. It can thus be said that the structure of bad faith allows its agent to feign an essence.

But it is not as though in being identified with his role W would be satisfied with being the quintessential waiter for the present only; quite to the contrary, he is attempting to reify one fixed identity for the foreseeable future.[43] This suggests that W's actions can profitably be analyzed from two temporal points of view: his facticity and his transcendence. By the former is meant W's existence up to the present moment insofar as it involves his behaving as though his role is a given. By the latter is meant those actions that must be performed by W in order for his role to be maintained as such. Obviously W is going to attempt not only to emphasize but indeed to hypostatize the phenomenon of his facticity, while at the same time attempting to evade the phenomenon of his transcendence. For W wishes his identity to be, and to have been, a given. On the other hand, to accept his transcendence would be for W to undermine this false, absolute identity. What the waiter does is attempt to transcendentalize his facticity.

We can designate W's facticity as his dominant temporal mode and his transcendence as his subdominant temporal mode. The above case can be generalized by noting that, instead of acting in accord with the existence of the subdominant temporal mode as an independent variable—an act that would conflict with his belief as a function of the dominant temporal mode—the subject distorts this subdominant mode in the attempt to make it a function of the dominant one.

To fully capture the case of bad faith, with emphasis on the first half of the formulation "being is what it is not, and is not what it is," we need to write:

$$xb(xbp_{F_T}) \qquad (3)$$

where F_T represents the fact that x attempts to transcendentalize his facticity.

As will be recalled, Q takes her date's actions out of context. By the use of her imagination she construes them as evidence that he likes and respects her as a total person. But Q would not be prepared to admit that she is admired by virtue of her imagination only. Rather, she would want her imaginary experience to take on the characteristic of a given. She attempts to square many aspects of her given, actual life with her imaginary ideal. Equating Q's imaginary world with the temporal mode of transcendence and the actually obtaining situation with Q's facticity, we can say that Q attempts to make large areas of her facticity fit in with the world of imagination she has created. She attempts to facticitize her transcendence.

Designating Q's transcendence as her dominant temporal mode and her facticity as her subdominant temporal mode, we can then generalize by noting that, instead of acting in accord with the existence of the subdominant temporal mode as an independent variable—an act that would conflict with her belief as a function of the dominant imaginary mode—Q distorts this subdominant mode in the attempt to make it a function of the dominant one.[44]

318

To capture the case of bad faith where emphasis is placed on the second half of the formulation "being is what it is not, and is not what it is," we need to write:

$$xb(xbp_{T_F}) \qquad (4)$$

where T_F represents the fact that x attempts to facticitize her transcendence.

Thus, (3) and (4) capture in general form the two possible classes of bad faith, both of which have been analyzed by Sartre. The relation between them depends on the fact that an agent in bad faith distorts what was termed the subdominant temporal mode in the attempt to make it a function of the dominant one. In this way as homogeneous as possible a field of experience is created in which the distinctions between temporal modalities, or between imaginary and perceptual experiences, are minimized. It is important to stress that the subject cannot actually succeed in this task and thereby effectively eradicate what constitutes the background of the experience overall. Or rather, if this is really achieved, then bad faith no longer exists since the subject has effectively removed himself from true contact with his environment. Broadly speaking, Sartre's concern is with a neurotic and not a psychotic phenomenon, for to be in bad faith implies a state of tension. The agent both avoids reality and is still in contact with it, as opposed to psychotic cases where the agent's boundary with reality is far more tenuous.

Returning to the relation between (3) and (4), in the former case, although the subject overemphasizes or hypostatizes his facticity as the dominant temporal mode, he nevertheless takes cognizance of and in some sense recognizes his transcendence in the form of the subdominant temporal mode. In the latter case, although the subject overemphasizes or hypostatizes her transcendence as the dominant temporal mode, she still takes cognizance of and in some sense recognizes her facticity in the form of the subdominant temporal mode. This is the significance of the term *and* in Sartre's formulation that the world of the subject in bad faith is such that "here being is what it is not, and is not what it is." That is, the subject in bad faith—which is to say the subject who still has some contact with reality—in the very distortion of the subdominant temporal mode has to recognize and take account of just this mode. This, finally, is what (3) and (4) share on the basis of the mechanism of bad faith.

Obviously more can be said about bad faith. For example, the affective features involved in bad faith need to be treated in detail. In addition, Sartre tells us that this phenomenon is somehow wedged between that of cynicism on the one hand and good faith on the other,[45] so that these phenomena also need to be dealt with in detail. I hope, however, that my analysis has established a firm basis in terms of which these projects can be undertaken.

In conclusion, how prevalent is bad faith, according to Sartre? Recall that Sartre's bad faith can be seen as wedged between Freud's opacity of mind on the one hand and Alain's transparency of mind on the other. For both (via psychoanalysis or activities constituting good faith) it is possible to attain a degree of objectivity and to distance oneself from the world. These possibilities are foreign to the Sartrean point of view, because the subject is of necessity engaged in the world. In other words, the notions of facticity and situation in *Being and Nothingness* entail that the subject qua consciousness is partially but necessarily a function of a specific culture, and hence of a specific historical period or epoch. This implies that any cognitive or analytic activity, whether conducted on a prereflexive or on a reflexive level, is inevitably going to mirror or manifest attitudes, practices, and values of this period such that a truly dispassionate or so-called objective point of view is literally not possible. By contrast, although both Freud and Alain are profoundly aware of the reality of historical processes as they affect any particular subject, their influence is more contingent. Both members of the older generation see rationality as an objective and universal phenomenon, beyond the confines and constraints of a particular historical epoch. For Sartre, rational or intellectual endeavor is always, ultimately, manifested as a product of social and cultural—and therefore also historical—structures, and this feature of human experience can easily serve to promote bad faith.

Notes

1. Jean-Paul Sartre, *L'Etre et le néant: essai d'ontologie phénoménologique* (Paris, 1968); hereafter cited as *EN*. Also *Being and Nothingness: An Essay in Phenomenological Ontology*, trans. by Hazel F. Barnes (New York, 1956); hereafter cited as *BN*. I have kept to the English translation except where I felt that changes were necessary. In what follows the English version is cited first for convenience.

2. Regarding the issue of psychoanalysis, Sartre does obviously deal briefly with Freud's view early in the chapter in question, but this serves merely as a foil. His own positive view of the nature of this field is only dealt with much later in the text.

3. I have shown elsewhere how, on a number of topics, Sartre's detailed knowledge of psychology has helped him to forge a powerful epistemology. See "Sartre on Perception and the World," *Journal of the British Society for Phenomenology* 14, no. 2 (May 1983); and "Sartre, Hodological Space and the Existence of Others," *Research in Phenomenology* 14 (1984). This aspect of Sartre's work has unfortunately been largely

neglected in the literature. Such an oversight is especially strange in light of the fact that, as is well known, Sartre, as an advanced student, took courses in psychology at both the Sorbonne and the Ecole Normale Supérieure, so that then-current theories could well be expected to have influenced his work in some fashion. In addition, *L'Imaginaire* and *EN* both make explicit and, regarding the former, numerous references to then-current psychological material. On the basis of such oversights, however, misunderstandings of Sartre's position are bound to follow. For, among many other well-known works—both recent and older—that purport to deal with central themes in *EN* but yet themselves fail, minimally by making no reference to the material just mentioned, see, for example, Wilfred Desan, *The Tragic Finale* (New York, 1960); Anthony Manser, *Sartre* (New York, 1966); Joseph Fell, *Heidegger and Sartre: An Essay on Being and Place* (New York, 1979). A recent work in French which remedies this situation by dealing with Sartre's incorporation of psychological material into his own work is Anna Boschetti, *Sartre et Les Temps Modernes* (Paris, 1985). In this case, however, this psychological material is handled in too summary a fashion, and Sartre's own incorporation of the material is not dealt with in sufficient detail.

4. My purpose here clearly cannot be to give a comprehensive account of the literature dealing with bad faith, a task that would involve more than an article in itself. It would, however, in what follows, be useful to discuss a fundamental tenet of Herbert Fingarette's well-known account of self-deception insofar as it is indicative of certain general patterns of Sartrean criticism. In his book *Self-deception* (London, 1969), Fingarette notes that he is in some ways indebted to Sartre for his own viewpoint. In "Self-deception: Sartre's Resolution of the Paradox" (in *Jean-Paul Sartre: Contemporary Approaches to His Philosophy* ed. by Hugh Silverman and Frederick Elliston [Pittsburgh, 1980], Phyllis Morris shows that in fact Fingarette's degree of reliance on Sartre is far more profound than he himself actually claims. Our main concern with his account is to note a cardinal theme, that self-deception is said to depend on an agent's ability to refuse to reflect on a regular or standard pattern of his activity. Were this individual to reflect on such actions, however, says Fingarette, it would not be possible to avoid acknowledging that such a set of activities formed an integral part of his own essential self-activity. Although our concern here is not with Fingarette's analysis per se, a number of foibles inherent in this position should be elaborated on, precisely insofar as they exemplify well, by contrast, the Sartrean point of view.

(1) From a Sartrean point of view it would not, even for a set of limited cases, make any sense to talk about, for example, a possible world in which the subject was able to individuate and reflect upon every one of his prereflexive activities. For such activities are often inchoate, vague, transient in the extreme, incipient, or a combination of any of these factors, so that in some real sense of the term, they remain but poorly definable or even sometimes ineffable from a reflexive point of view. (In this regard, see below dealing with Sartre's rejection of Alain.)

(2) Fingarette—as do those adopting the above position—makes the untenable presupposition that reflexive activity is prelucid or transparent in the sense that it can perfectly mirror what is reflected upon. In fact, however, as Sartre makes apparent, it can sometimes be the case that reflection by its very nature distorts prereflexive activity. Thus, regarding bad faith, even if one could have unlimited reflection as above, this would by no means guarantee that all one's prereflexive activities were accurately and completely understood and delimited on a reflexive level, thereby obviating the possibility of bad faith.

(3) Given (1) and (2) above, it can be seen that Fingarette's type of explanation can in fact only account for a subclass of all possible cases of bad faith, and indeed one that can

only distinguish obvious but not the more numerous, subtle, and intricate cases of bad faith which involve the kind of inchoate, etc., prereflexive activity as outlined above.

5. *BN,* 68; *EN,* 109.

6. Ibid., 67, 108.

7. Ibid.

8. Ibid., 59; 98–99.

9. Ibid., 59; 98. Sartre is not literally referring to the waiter here, but from the context it is obvious that this quotation would apply to him, too.

10. Ibid., 60; 100.

11. Ibid., 60; 99.

12. I have discussed Sartre's relation to intellectualism in "Sartre on Perception and the World." For Sartre's reaction to idealism, see my "Sartre, Hodological Space and the Existence of Others."

13. For Scheler's influence on Sartre in this regard, see the first article mentioned in note 12. For Lewin's influence on Sartre, see the second article.

14. Alain, *Quatre-vingt-un chapitres sur l'esprit et les passions* (Paris, 1921).

15. Ibid., 164.

16. Ibid.

17. Sigmund Freud, *The Standard Edition of the Complete Psychological Works of Sigmund Freud,* Vol. XXII: *New Introductory Lectures on Psychoanalysis,* trans. by James Strachey (London, 1964), 89 ff.

18. Alain, *Quatre-vingt-un chapitres,* 164.

19. Ibid.

20. Ibid.

21. Ibid., 14. I have dealt with this aspect of Alain's work in more detail in "Sartre on Perception and the World."

22. See, for example, Alain, *Quatre-vingt-un chapitres,* 14 ff.

23. Ibid., 165.

24. Ibid., 166.

25. Ibid.

26. Jean-Paul Sartre, *Baudelaire,* trans. by Martin Turnell (New York, 1967), 50.

27. See my two articles mentioned in note 12 for Sartre's Gestaltist affinities plus the influence of Lewin and Scheler.

28. The full import of what is involved in S's constituting activity would necessitate an analysis given in hodological terms. The above, however, suffices for present purposes.

29. The notion of figure/ground is being used here in an extended or wider sense than is the case for more orthodox or standard types of Gestalt examples. It should, however, be noted immediately that some Gestalt experiments were conducted with reference to a much broader setting involving, for example, overall bodily response. See, e.g., D. Katz, *Gestalt Psychology* (New York, 1950), 71 ff. Katz mentions that the notion of a Gestalt is—in effect, operationally—very useful although it cannot as yet even be very exactly described, much less quantified. He goes on, however, to note that the difficulty of having to deal with Gestalt notions in a very much more generalized, and hence realistic, setting should not deter researchers from proceeding apace and using these notions. A similar point can be made for the cases that follow in the text.

30. It should not be thought that there is here an absolute dichotomy between figure and ground in that the former is highly differentiated while the latter remains completely undifferentiated. Rather, there is a gradation of degrees of differentiation in the ground.

31. The same point can be made *mutatis mutandis* for the issue of figure/ground here as was made for the case cited in note 30.

32. *BN,* 68; *EN,* 109.

33. Thus, in fact, the full analysis of the mechanism of bad faith will show how the other part of Sartre's formulation—that "being is not what it is"—will enter into the waiter-type case as well.

34. *BN,* 55; *EN,* 94.

35. Ibid.

36. Ibid.

37. Ibid. 55; 95.

38. Ibid., 56; 95.

39. Ibid.

40. Ibid.

41. In both this and the case in which Q takes the man's words out of context, it is for present purposes irrelevant whether the figure in question is experienced reflexively or prereflexively by Q.

42. *BN,* 68; *EN,* 109.

43. Strictly speaking, it is, under normal circumstances, not likely that W believes that he will live as a quintessential waiter literally forever, or that he believes that he was born a waiter. He may even expect, for example, to retire relatively young. Nevertheless, the phrase *for all time* is perfectly adequate to use in the present context.

44. It may initially seem as though there is a category mistake in this formulation. Note, however, that the subject's imagination—which involves what transcends the given—is what primarily determines Q's behavior in the case under consideration, and that Q attempts to mold her actual given situation, her facticity, to what is dictated by her imagination. Thus her facticity is a subdominant temporal mode relative to the subject's dominant and transcendent mode, her imagination.

45. *BN,* 68; *EN,* 108.

17

A NOTHING ABOUT WHICH
SOMETHING CAN BE SAID:
SARTRE AND WITTGENSTEIN ON THE SELF

Kathleen Wider

It is usual to see Sartre and Wittgenstein as belonging to two very different movements in twenthieth-century philosophy. They are the superstars of two rival camps, and both their methodologies and their philosophical views are thought to be as disparate as possible. It is my contention that this standard position is both inaccurate and unfruitful with regard to the early philosophy of the two writers. A comparative analysis of certain central points in Sartre's *Being and Nothingness* and Wittgenstein's *Tractatus Logico-Philosophicus* illuminates both philosophers' positions and gives the lie to the standard view. It is also common to see both Sartre's and Wittgenstein's analyses of the self in their early work dismissed as a simple replay, albeit in much greater detail, of Hume's criticism of the Cartesian notion of selfhood. But although both Sartre in *Being and Nothingness* and Wittgenstein in *Tractatus Logico-Philosophicus* agree with Hume in his rejection of the Cartesian ego, yet neither is truly Humean in his view of the self because, although each denies in a sense the existence of the metaphysical self, yet it lives on in Sartre as a nothingness that exists and in Wittgenstein as a boundary or limit of the world. There is no such ghost for Hume. This essay examines Sartre's claim that human consciousness is nothingness and Wittgenstein's claim that the metaphysical self is not in the world but is, rather, a limit to the world. My aims, although interrelated, are multiple. I intend to at least partially unravel the meaning of these two claims and in so doing to show their striking similarity to each other. In addition, I intend to show that although these positions can be read as a Humean denial of the self, in a very important way they go beyond this denial, because they are both concerned with consciousness, with the experience of the world. This concern is exhibited in Sartre's distinction between the for-itself and the in-itself and in Wittgenstein's distinction, which parallels Sartre's, between the metaphysical self and the world. For both Sartre and Wittgenstein, however, the self in a sense comes to nothing; therefore, they are both able to argue that the solipsism that appears to flow from their positions is, in the end, only apparent and dissolves upon closer inspection. Although both deny the existence of a transcendental ego, they both agree that even if science could describe all there is in the world, there would still be something unaccounted for. This something is consciousness or subjectivity, a something that for Sartre is nothing and for Wittgenstein is a limit about which we cannot speak.[1] In what follows I examine in detail each philosopher's analysis of the self. It is only by seeing each one's position in the context of his broader philosophical views that the similarities can be shown clearly and most forcefully.

I

The whole of *Being and Nothingness* is an attempt to discover the origin of nothingness in the world and its relation to being. Sartre begins in the introduction to draw a picture of consciousness as nothingness. He says that "the first procedure of a philosophy ought to be to expel things from consciousness and to reestablish its true connection with the world."[2] He develops this point into his intentionality-of-consciousness thesis. Husserl, he thinks, took the first step in the right direction but misinterpreted the nature of the intentionality of consciousness. To say that consciousness is intentional, that it must be *of* something, cannot mean, as Husserl thought it did, that consciousness is constitutive of the *being* of its objects, because if *being* belonged to consciousness, as it does for Husserl in Sartre's view, then to distinguish consciousness from its objects, we would have to say the objects are *nonbeing:* "If being beongs to consciousness, the object is not consciousness, not to the extent that it is another being, but that it is nonbeing" (*BN,* 22). In Husserl's view, according to Sartre, appearances only exist relative to consciousness; they have no being in themselves but only receive it from consciousness. For Sartre there is only one other meaning that can be given to the intentionality-of-consciousness thesis, and that is that consciousness is a relation to a transcendent being, a being that exists independently of consciousness.

Given his argument above that if consciousness is being, then its objects must be nonbeing, it would now seem to be the case that if its objects are being, then consciousness must be nonbeing. This is exactly what Sartre argues in *Being and Nothingness*. He begins in the introduction to draw the distinction between being-in-itself (the objects of consciousness) and being-for-itself (consciousness). Consciousness both is empty of contents (*BN*, 11) and has no Cartesian ego as owner. It is not a substance but is rather "total emptiness (since the entire world is outside it)" (*BN*, 17). Although consciousness exists as body for Sartre, as the body's relation to the world,[3] as a presence and point of view on the world and in that sense exists, it is, however, *in itself* nothing.[4] Unless consciousness is perceiving consciousness or believing consciousness or thirsting consciousness, for example, it is nonexistent. It is not *something* (over and above the body) that perceives or believes or thirsts. He denies, as Hume did, that there is a transcendental ego. Consciousness requires objects for its existence. It "is born supported by a being which is not itself" (*BN*, 23). This being is the in-itself which exists independently of consciousness. Although in one sense the dependency relation between the in-itself and the for-itself is one way, there is another sense in which it goes both ways. Just as consciousness requires being-in-itself for its existence, the in-itself requires consciousness for its existence *as a world*. Consciousness is not responsible for being, but it is responsible for organizing being into a world, a meaningful complex of instrumentalities in Sartre's language: "Without the world there is no selfness, no person; without selfness, without the person, there is no world" (*BN*, 157). Yet the two kinds of being remain distinct since one has being-in-itself and the other does not.

Sartre, explicating what he means by his claim that human consciousness is nothingness, that it does not have being-in-itself, argues that the for-itself "must *necessarily* be what it is not and not be what it is" (*BN*, 120). Consciousness is not identical to anything. It *is* no *thing*. It is nothing. Unlike being-in-itself, to which the law of identity applies, it does not apply to consciousness. The in-itself is identical to itself; in Sartrean terminology it coincides with itself. This is not the case with consciousness, for if it were to *be* itself, it would collapse into an in-itself and no longer be consciousness (*BN*, 147). There are several ways Sartre explicates this strange and striking thesis: that there is something (albeit a something that is nothing) that escapes Leibniz's law. The following are some of the major claims he makes in unraveling this thesis: (1) consciousness is the body, and yet it is not the body; (2) consciousness, the for-itself, is its past and future and yet is identical to neither; (3) consciousness is its acts and objects, and yet it is not. This last claim is the most basic and underlies all his other ways of explaining why consciousness must be nothingness.

There are really two parts to this claim. First of all, consciousness is presence to the world. As such, consciousness must exist at a distance from the world. Although consciousness is dependent on its objects for its existence, yet it cannot be any of its objects or it would lose the character that makes it consciousness—distance, that is, not being what one is conscious of. That is why Sartre says that the for-itself is a nihilated in-itself. The for-itself must make itself not be what it is conscious of. "Nonbeing is an essential structure of presence. Presence encloses a radical negation as presence to that which one is not. What is present to me is what is not me" (*BN*, 241). Consciousness requires an object to exist (the intentionality-of-consciousness thesis), and in a sense consciousness is just consciousness of the table or consciousness of the chair. That is, there is no Cartesian ego that is conscious of the table or chair. In this sense consciousness *is* what it is conscious of. "Consciousness of being is the being of consciousness," according to Sartre (*BN*, 68). Yet consciousness cannot be identical to its object or it would lose the distance required to be conscious of that object. Since consciousness must not be what it is conscious of, then consciousness must not be being, that is, the world. Consciousness must therefore be nonbeing, nothing:

> Of course the very apprehension of the world as totality causes the appearance *alongside the world* of a nothingness which sustains and encompasses this totality. In fact this nothingness as the absolute nothing which is left outside the totality even determines the totality. That is why totalization adds nothing to being, for it is only the result of the appearance of nothingness as the limit of being. But this totalization *is not* anything except human reality apprehending itself as excluded from being and perpetually beyond being, in commerce with nothing. (*BN*, 251)

Consciousness arises for Sartre (*BN*, 786) from within being as that which is not being but causes being to appear as a world.

But consciousness is not just presence to the world. For Sartre all consciousness must also be self-consciousness. Consciousness as such must be present to itself as well as to the world. But for consciousness to be present to something, for Sartre, it cannot be that to which it is present. But then consciousness cannot be identical even to itself as consciousness. To understand what Sartre means by this, we must look more closely at his claim that all consciousness is self-consciousness. For Sartre humans exist as consciousness in two ways: we exist for ourselves, and we exist for others. Within our existence for ourselves there are two modes of consciousness: the prereflective and the reflective. Every level of consciousness for Sartre must involve self-consciousness, although the degree and fullness of self-consciousness increase at each level. But what does this mean at the most basic level, that of prereflective consciousness? It is because self-consciousness is present as a feature of even the most basic level of consciousness that nothingness is an essential part of consciousness. Prereflective consciousness does not reflect upon or know itself (*BN,* 12). Consciousness at this level is directed outward, toward the world. Yet even at this level there must be at least minimal self-consciousness. This consciousness of an object must somehow be consciousness of itself (as consciousness of an object). But this consciousness of itself is not explicit yet. Sartre calls it nonpositional self-consciousness. What he seems to be claiming is that whenever consciousness is explicitly aware of *x*, it is implicitly aware of being conscious of *x*. Sartre gives the example of his counting cigarettes. He is explicitly aware of the cigarettes and how many there are but only implicitly aware of the activity of counting. That is, he has not reflected upon what he is doing, although if someone were to ask him what he was doing, he could answer such a question. What I think is at work here is a notion of a latent awareness. It only becomes activated, if at all, at the level of reflective consciousness. This awareness (whether latent or activated) is the reflexivity of consciousness. Sartre argues that all consciousness of necessity must have this reflexivity, because if consciousness were closed off to itself in such a way that it could be conscious of *x* without being able through reflection to become aware that it was conscious of *x,* then consciousness would be unconscious: "If my consciousness [of the table] were not consciousness of being consciousness of the table, it would then be consciousness of that table without consciousness of being so. In other words, it would be a consciousness ignorant of itself—an unconscious—which is absurd" (*BN,* 11).[5] But how does this claim that all consciousness is self-consciousness even at the prereflective level introduce nothingness into consciousness and cause consciousness to fail to coincide with itself?

The law of the being of the for-itself, Sartre says, is to exist as a presence to itself. But such presence requires that consciousness exist "at a distance from itself" (*BN,* 25). So "if being [for-itself] is present to itself, it is because it is not wholly itself" (*BN,* 124). But what separates it from itself is itself, its reflexivity. And since consciousness is nothingness, nothing separates it from itself. He illustrates this with examples of consciousness as belief, as thirst, as anger. His longest discussion is of belief. Belief as a mode of consciousness is self-aware. That is, belief is implicit consciousness of belief. And yet, because belief as a mode of consciousness is self-conscious, it is no longer identical to itself. Once "my belief is apprehended as belief, it is no longer only belief . . . it is troubled belief" (*BN,* 121). Somehow because consciousness is always implicitly self-aware, a subtle division occurs within it like a barely visible crack in the foundation of a building after an almost imperceptible earthquake. But the cause of the split is nothing, because self-consciousness at the prereflective level is "one with the consciousness of which it is consciousness" (*BN,* 14). That is why implicit consciousness of belief is belief. But since it alters belief it is somehow not belief. Implicit self-awareness troubles the waters of translucent consciousness and divides it from itself.

Sartre worries that a consciousness that is not conscious of itself would be unconscious. But he does not want to claim that in prereflective consciousness there are two acts of consciousness: one that takes as its object something in the world for instance, and another that takes the first as its object. That would lead to an infinite regress. So he has to argue that the act of consciousness and the awareness of that act are one and the same. Yet for consciousness to be conscious of something, it must exist at a distance from what it is conscious of; therefore, for consciousness to be conscious of itself it must exist at a distance from itself. So on the one hand it must be itself, and on the other it must not be identical to itself. It is this position Sartre is trying to defend in his discussion of belief as a mode of prereflective consciousness. Belief and implicit consciousness of belief are not identical, but nothing separates them from each other. Perhaps Wittgenstein's duck/rabbit phenomenon will clarify what Sartre is after here. The possibility of shifting one's attention in such a way that what appeared to be one thing now appears to be another (in this case, belief and implicit consciousness of belief) makes it seem as though something new is revealed, and yet nothing has been added. Nothing separates the duck from the rabbit. But a subtle disturbance infects the placid lines of the drawing, and what is one seems always on the verge of splitting. It is through this crack that nothingness seeps.[6]

From this analysis of consciousness as nothingness, a certain kind of epistemological solipsism seems to follow. Sartre acknowledges this. I cannot know the other as subject, as a conscious being. But this solipsism dissolves when it becomes evident that it also follows from his view of consciousness that I cannot know myself as subject either. Subjectivity cannot be objectified. Consciousness as such is not in the world. "That *other* consciousness and *that other* freedom are never *given* to me; for if they were, they would be *known* and would therefore be an object" (*BN,* 363) rather than a subject. Although I can be certain of the Other's existence as another subject through my experience of myself as an object in the look of the Other, I can never *know* the Other as subject. The Other as subject including his look which transforms me into an object are not in the world. "By the Other's look I effect the concrete proof that there is a 'beyond the world' " (*BN,* 361). Because the Other as subject is not in the world, he cannot, as subject, be an *object* of experience. The same is true for myself as subject, as consciousness. Since consciousness in itself is nothing, it cannot be experienced. And since consciousness is the body, it follows for Sartre that the body as consciousness, as subject, as it is for me does not appear in the world in the sense that it cannot be an object of experience. It is inapprehensible and cannot be known; it is, instead, lived. Subjectivity (my own or another's) is not experienced as part of the world. It is the center that the world (the objects of experience) indicates. It is like the eye that is in the center of the perceptive field: we do not see this center because "*we are the center*" (*BN,* 419). The same is true for the body-as-it-is-for-me. It cannot be an object for me, because it is the orientation of the objects I experience. My body-for-me is indicated by the world as the center or reference point around which the world as a system of instrumentalities is organized (*BN,* 429). My body as subject is inapprehensible because it does not belong to the objects in the world. It is rather a point of view on the world but "the point of view on which I can no longer take a point of view" (*BN,* 433). He gives as examples of other points of view the hill I stand on and from which I observe the scene below or my glasses through which I view the world. But these points of view although close to the body can nonetheless be seen even though the distance between them and the body is minimal. But with the body itself as a point of view all distance disappears. It is impossible to step back and take a new point of view on this point of view. It is this that characterizes the body as subject.

Although Sartre follows Hume in denying that there is a mental subject of experience, a Cartesian ego, he does argue that the for-itself while nothing still exists. It exists as something that does not appear in the world. It is not therefore a nonworldly substance. But it is something that cannot be apprehended in the world since it is the necessary condi-

330

tion for the world's existence, the center of the world and its limit. This view of consciousness goes beyond a simple Humean denial of a Cartesian self. This is evident as well in the sections on the self and solipsism in Wittgenstein's *Tractatus*.

II

Wittgenstein makes claims about the self in the latter sections of the *Tractatus* which are as strange as the Sartrean claim that human consciousness is nothing. Indeed there are some interesting parallels between Sartre's claim and the remarks Wittgenstein makes in 5.6–5.641. Just as Sartre argues that consciousness is nonbeing, so too, Wittgenstein argues, if we are to take him at his word, the metaphysical self is not in the world: "The subject does not belong to the world: rather, it is a limit of the world."[7] There has been, however, a great deal of disagreement among commentators over how to interpret Wittgenstein's remarks on the metaphysical self. Max Black contends in his companion to the *Tractatus* that Wittgenstein only raised the idea of a transcendental ego in order to reject it.[8] Others have agreed that Wittgenstein is not espousing a solipsistic self transcendent to the world. There are just as many, perhaps more, commentators, however, who take Wittgenstein to be defending a solipsistic position and claiming that there is a metaphysical self that does not exist in the world. Robert Fogelin notes the tension in Wittgenstein which is illustrated by remarks in the *Tractatus* that seem incompatible with each other.[9] At 5.631 he says, "There is no such thing as the subject that thinks or entertains ideas," yet in the remark immediately following he says, "The subject does not belong to the world: rather, it is a limit of the world" (*TLP*, 5.632). At 5.62 he tells us that "what the solipsist means is quite correct," but he later claims that "solipsism, when its implications are followed out strictly, coincides with pure realism" (*TLP*, 5.64). Those commentators who think Wittgenstein does not defend solipsism in the *Tractatus*—that he raised the possibility of a transcendental ego and dismissed it—see Wittgenstein as simply a Humean with regard to the existence of a Cartesian ego. But they fail to see what more is at work in his position which shows up in his discussion of the willing self in the section on ethics and values in the *Tractatus* and again in the solipsistic positions he articulates and argues against in his later work. Elizabeth Anscombe warns:

> It is very much a popular notion of Wittgenstein that he was a latter-day Hume; but any connections between them are indirect, and he never read more than a few pages of Hume. If we look for Wittgenstein's

philosophical ancestry, we should rather look to Schopenhauer; specifically, his "solipsism," his conception of "the limit" and his ideas on value will be better understood in the light of Schopenhauer than of any other philosopher.[10]

I will argue that Wittgenstein is serious when he claims that what the solipsist means is correct but that he also thinks that solipsism collapses into realism. The solipsistic self, the transcendental ego, vanishes into nothing for Wittgenstein, but nonetheless that nothing has significance. In this way he is very close to the Sartrean position that consciousness is nothingness. Several versions of solipsism have been attributed to Wittgenstein; I will examine only one, although another flows quite easily from it. The version I will focus on is traditional solipsism, the view that all experience is my experience, and connected to this the view that there is no world independent of a self's experience. I will argue that Wittgenstein is exploring this position when he says that what the solipsist means is that the world is my world. Given Wittgenstein's theory of meaning, it is easy to derive a linguistic version of solipsism from this more traditional statement of the position. If language mirrors the world and the world is my world, then language pictures only my world. If I am correct that what Wittgenstein's analysis finally brings us to is a self that does not exist in the world and so in a sense is nothing, but is at the same time a nothing with significance, that might explain the apparent confusion in Wittgenstein's position and the inability of critics to agree about what Wittgenstein's position actually is. Wittgenstein at least acknowledges that such a position cannot be stated. The attempt in the *Tractatus* leads to some extremely obscure and dense remarks. Likewise Sartre's attempt to expound what I take to be a similar position leads to very obscure and often tortured prose. Whether this is because the position is one that cannot be spoken about but only manifests itself or because the position is incoherent I leave open. To set the stage for an examination of the relevant sections in the *Tractatus* on the self, let me offer a crude account of the metaphysical and semantic theories Wittgenstein sets forth in the first three-fourths of the book. I shall ignore for the most part the many problems of interpretation associated with the text.

The task of philosophy and hence of the *Tractatus*, according to Wittgenstein, is to "set limits to what can be thought; and, in so doing, to what cannot be thought. It must set limits to what cannot be thought by working outwards through what can be thought. It will signify what cannot be said, by presenting clearly what can be said" (*TLP*, 4.114–4.115). Consequently, it is only after Wittgenstein has dealt with what can be said that he tackles what cannot. What the solipsist means falls into the latter category. Just as Sartre begins *Being and Nothingness* with an analysis of being and the relation of being for-itself with the world, so Wittgenstein begins with an analysis of language and the relation of language to the world. Both are interested in intentionality, how we can think about and speak about or be conscious of the world.

The world for Wittgenstein (*TLP,* 2.04) is the totality of all existing states of affairs. A state of affairs is a combination of objects, and these objects are simple and unalterable (*TLP,* 2.0272).[11] A thought is a logical picture of a state of affairs (*TLP,* 3), and so, "The totality of true thoughts is a picture of the world" (*TLP,* 3.01). A proposition, for Wittgenstein (*TLP,* 3.1), expresses a thought in sensible form. A proposition, therefore, is a picture of reality (*TLP,* 4.01). There are two kinds of propositions: elementary and molecular. Elementary propositions are made up of names (*TLP,* 4.22), and every name refers to an object that gives the name its meaning (*TLP,* 3.203). An elementary proposition pictures a state of affairs and is true if there is such a state and false otherwise (*TLP,* 4.25). A molecular proposition is made up of two or more elementary propositions and is a truth function of those elementary propositions. "The totality of true propositions is the whole of natural science" (*TLP,* 4.11); that is, the totality of all true propositions is a complete description of the world (*TLP,* 4.26). The reason why thoughts and their expression in propositions can picture reality is that they all share the same logical form (*TLP,* 4.12). But this logical form which thought, propositions, and reality share cannot be stated or described but only shown (*TLP,* 4.121–4.1212). It is the scaffolding of the world, and the propositions of logic represent this scaffolding (*TLP,* 6.124). Language can only speak about the world, about possible states of affairs. That is why tautologies and contradictions are senseless; they do not speak about the world but about the form of the world (*TLP,* 4.462). Logic is a mirror image of the world and so, for Wittgenstein (*TLP,* 6.13), is transcendental.

Against the background of his general analysis of the intentional nature of language and how it is that language can speak about the world, Wittgenstein makes several remarks about the self. The first remark comes before the section on solipsism and arises in the context of his discussion of propositional attitudes. Wittgenstein considers propositions that express propositional attitudes as possible counterexamples to his claim that all molecular propositions are truth functions of the elementary propositions of which they consist. If a proposition such as "*A* believes that *p*" is taken to express a relation between an object *A* and a proposition *p,* then the truth or falsity of the molecular proposition is independent of the truth or falsity of *p* itself. The molecular proposition would be true just in case a relation of belief held between the person *A* and the proposition *p* and false otherwise. To avoid this consequence, Wittgenstein offers an alternative analysis of such propositions. In presenting his analysis he rivals Sartre for obscurity of exposition. He claims that "it is clear" that such propositions are of the form " '*p*' says that *p*" (*TLP,* 5.542). At first glance, this appears to remove *A* altogether from an analysis of propositions expressing propositional attitudes, and that seems a strange way to handle things. On the most plausible and frequent reading of this section, *A* does disappear in a way; that is, *A* construed as a thinking substance disappears and is replaced by what P. M. S. Hacker calls a "neo-Humean analysis of the empirical self."[12] The analysis of "*A* believes that *p*" that Wittgenstein appears to be offering no longer involves a relationship between a thinker and a proposition but rather a relation between a collection of psychical elements (a thought) or its expression in a proposition on the one hand and a combination of objects, a state of affairs, on the other. Consider the truth conditions for propositions of the form " '*p*' says that *p.*" Take as an example " 'It is raining' says it is raining." This proposition will be true just in case the collection of names in the proposition pictures the combination of objects that would constitute the state of affairs "it is raining." Likewise, for the proposition "*A* believes that it is raining": it will be true just in case there is a collection of psychical elements or a proposition *A* utters or consents to which mirrors the combination of objects constituting the state of affairs "it is raining." It will be false otherwise. This analysis entails that, in order to fit propositions expressing propositional attitudes into a truth-functional analysis of language, the notion of a Cartesian ego must be abandoned. Wittgenstein indicates as much in the remark following his analysis of such propositions: "This shows too that there is no such thing as the soul—the subject, etc.—as it is conceived in the superficial psychology of the present day. Indeed a composite soul would no longer be a soul" (*TLP,* 5.5421). The only way to make sense of propositions expressing propositional attitudes is to posit a Humean self. If these propositions are thought of as mirroring a relation between a thinker and a proposition, Wittgenstein's semantic theory cannot account for them. But if *A* is construed not as a subject that has thoughts but simply as a collection of thoughts and other psychic elements, then such propositions can be accommodated by the theory. A remark Wittgenstein makes later in the *Tractatus* supports this interpretation. At 5.631 he says, "There is no such thing as the subject that thinks or entertains ideas." He follows this remark up with what Hacker refers to as "the Humean argument of non-encounterability of a Cartesian self."[13] Wittgenstein says that if he were to write a book entitled *The World as I Found It*, the subject could not be mentioned in it (*TLP*, 5.631). Bernard Williams thinks that Hacker's interpretation of this remark and of Wittgenstein's Humean denial of a Cartesian self mistakenly transfers Hume's emphasis onto Wittgenstein. Hume's stance is of someone who looks for something and finds that *in fact* it is not in the world. Wittgenstein, however, claims that what is being looked for *could* not be found in the world.[14] Why it *could* not be found requires that we look more carefully at his remarks in the 5.6 sections to see how he goes beyond a simple Humean denial of the existence of the Cartesian self.

Wittgenstein's discussion of the metaphysical subject rests on all kinds of equivalences that need to be spelled out. He begins 5.6 with the first of them. He identifies the limits of my language with the limits of my world, because the limits of each turn out to be the same. Logic determines the limits of both. Logic determines the range of possibilities. It does not, of course, determine which possibilities will be actualized, so it cannot say what will be found in the world. Rather, it specifies the necessary conditions for anything to be a possibility. It sets the limits within which the possibilities are realized, and the realization of possibilities *is* the world, so it sets the limits of the world (*TLP*, 5.61). Language, for Wittgenstein, is meaningful only if it mirrors the world. So the limits of language are identical to the limits of the world, and since the world's limits are determined by logic, so too are language's. Logic determines what can *be* and what can *be said*. But it cannot say a priori what is in the world or what elementary propositions there are (*TLP*, 5.5571).

But why does Wittgenstein speak not just of language and the world but of *my* language and *my* world? At 5.62 Wittgenstein, in referring to the limits of language, qualifies his use of the term *language* by adding "that language which alone I understand." That is what apparently makes it *my* language. But why so? He does not say (as an early translation had him saying) "that language which I alone understand." It is the only language I understand. Why does that fact make it mine? It is mine in the obvious sense that it is the only language I have, but it is also mine because language pictures the world and because, according to Wittgenstein (*TLP*, 5.62), "the world is *my* world." So "the limits of language . . . mean the limits of *my* world." But what does the claim that the world is *my* world come to? It appears that the solipsist intends something like this, since the remark immediately follows his comment

335

that "what the solipsist *means* is quite correct; only it cannot be said, but makes itself manifest" (*TLP,* 5.62).

Hacker illuminates this view most clearly by appealing to the influence of Schopenhauer on Wittgenstein.[15] For Schopenhauer the world is my idea; it is an appearance to a subject. A necessary condition for there being a world is that there be a subject whose world it is. Against this background some of Wittgenstein's remarks in the *Notebooks, 1914–1916* begin to make some sense. For example, his remark that "my idea is the world"[16] echoes Schopenhauer's view; and his remark that "There are two godheads: the world and my independent I" (*NB,* 74) reflects the relationship Schopenhauer argues holds between the self and the world. It is his acceptance of Schopenhauer's view, perhaps, that leads him to say such seemingly outrageous things as "What has history to do with me? Mine is the first and only world!" (*NB,* 82). It might also explain his enigmatic remark that "So too at death the world does not alter, but comes to an end" (*TLP,* 6.431). It follows from the fact that the world is my world that "The world and life are one" (*TLP,* 5.621) and that "I am my world (the microcosm)" (*TLP,* 5.63). The world and consciousness of the world are one in Schopenhauer's view, and, as Hacker points out, Wittgenstein identifies life, consciousness, and the world in presenting the solipsist's position in "Notes for Lectures on 'Private Experience' and 'Sense Data.' "[17] What the solipsist thinks his opponent neglects is life, "but not life physiologically understood but life as consciousness. And consciousness not physiologically understood, or understood from the outside, but consciousness as the very essence of the experience, the appearance of the world, the world."[18] This echoes a remark of his in the *Notebooks:* "Physiological life is of course not 'Life.' And neither is psychological life. Life is the world" (*NB,* 77). It is precisely because life as consciousness and the world are one—that is, that the world just is the world as an appearance to consciousness—that I am my world. This is what lies behind the remark in the *Notebooks* that "if I was contemplating the stove *it* was my world" (*NB,* 83). This is very close to the Sartrean notion of the intentionality of consciousness. Because of this coincidence between myself and the world, there is no such thing as a metaphysical self in the world. The self is the limit of the world. Just as logic functions as the limit of the world and language by setting the conditions for the possibility of states of affairs and meaningful propositions, so too the metaphysical self as a necessary condition for the world as appearance to a subject is a limit, and consequently it cannot be found in the world.

To explain what he means by this, he appeals, as Sartre does, to the

336

analogy of the eye in the visual field (*TLP,* 5.633–5.6331). Although the eye is a necessary condition for there being a visual field and sets the limits of the visual field, it does not appear in the visual field and in fact cannot so appear given its function. Likewise, the self is not an object (*NB,* 80) and cannot be so: "The subject is not a part of the world but a presupposition of its existence" (*NB,* 79). Of course, the metaphysical subject, the self philosophy is interested in, is "not the human being, or the human body, or the human soul, with which psychology deals" (*TLP,* 5.641), because those are all in the world and the metaphysical self is not. What falls within the limits of the world and experience are all contingent facts (*TLP,* 5.634), but it is a necessary feature of experience that it belongs to someone. The metaphysical self is the formal possibility of the world as experience. As such it cannot exist in the world, but it also does not exist outside of it. It is the form of the world and as such is identical to it. That is why solipsism coincides with pure realism. That is why "the self of solipsism shrinks to a point without extension" (*TLP,* 5.64) and all that is left is the world. This harks back, as Derek Bolton notes, to the first proposition of the *Tractatus:* "The world is all that is the case." The self is nothing in the sense that it is not in the world and is nothing more than the world seen from its formal side. Bolton sees Wittgenstein as swinging between three incompatible theses about the self: (1) there is no self, just the world; (2) the self is the world; and (3) the self is the limit of the world.[19] But these three really come to the same. The self as a necessary condition for the world is its limit, and as its limit it is identified with the world as a totality. I am my world, and the world is my world, so I am the world. But as a limit, as a formal condition for its possibility, I am *nothing* but the world: "On the one side *nothing* is left over, and on the other side, as unique, *the world*" (*NB,* 85).

Wittgenstein's point here is very similar to Sartre's in *Being and Nothingness,* and both use it to avoid or dissolve solipsism or collapse solipsism into realism. For Sartre the for-itself is a necessary condition for there being a world, since the world just is a set of appearances to a subject, but as such the self is not in the world and consequently the for-itself is nothing. All that is left is the world. For Wittgenstein you can describe the world completely, give all the propositions of natural science, state all the meaningful propositions, and still there is something left over—a something that is nothing and so cannot be spoken of but can be shown. What is left over is the metaphysical self, life as consciousness, the fact that I occupy a point of view, that the world is my world. For Sartre, too, you can describe all of being and there is still something

337

left over—again a something that is nothing and yet functions like Wittgenstein's metaphysical self as a condition for the possibility of a world and as a point of view on the world. There is nothing left over for Hume. And that is why both Sartre and Wittgenstein go beyond the Humean denial of the Cartesian ego. This something, for both Sartre and Wittgenstein, is consciousness, subjectivity—a something that, when one tries to capture it and characterize it, turns into nothing. It is this nothing that causes so much trouble both for those who would reject it and for those who cling to it as though it were themselves.

Notes

1. The first draft of this essay was written at an NEH summer seminar in 1985 at Cornell University, given by Sydney Shoemaker. I am grateful for comments from Shoemaker and seminar participants, especially Natika Newton.

2. Jean-Paul Sartre, *Being and Nothingness,* trans. by Hazel E. Barnes (New York, 1966), 11. Hereafter cited as *BN.* Sartre had already maintained in *The Transcendence of the Ego,* trans. by Forrest Williams and Robert Kirkpatrick (New York, 1957), 42, that consciousness was nonexistent. He rejected Husserl's notion of a transcendental ego and argued that the ego was not the owner of consciousness but an object of consciousness. That is, at the prereflective level consciousness is impersonal; there is no consciousness of self. It is only on the reflective level that consciousness constructs the ego as an ideal object (see especially 44–58). These earlier notions are greatly expanded in *BN.*

3. I am grateful to Phyllis Morris for making the nature and importance of this point clear to me both in her book *Sartre's Concept of a Person: An Analytic Approach* (Amherst, Mass., 1976) and in conversations.

4. This helps to explain why Sartre sometimes speaks of the being of consciousness and at other times of the fact that consciousness is nonbeing, nothingness.

5. Marjorie Grene, in *Sartre* (New York, 1973), 119–20, argues that Sartre is mistaken in requiring all consciousness to be self-consciousness, and she thinks that mistake mars his entire work. But she misreads his view that consciousness is always reflexive. She takes him to mean that whenever consciousness is explicitly conscious of an object, it is also explicitly conscious of itself being conscious of an object. She argues that if this were the case consciousness would be unable to be conscious of anything. It is consciousness's "lack of consciousness itself, its "ignorance" of itself if you will, that *makes* it conscious." But for Sartre the consciousness that must accompany every act of consciousness is an implicit act of consciousness. He makes this quite clear in the cigarette-counting case, although he does, later in *Being and Nothingness,* sometimes slip into taking this reflexivity requirement as involving an explicit act of consciousness.

6. Sartre fails to show that belief does not coincide with itself at the prereflective level because he makes an unacknowledged and illegitimate shift from the latent reflexivity of consciousness that exists at the prereflective level to an activated form of such reflexivity (which exists only at the reflective level). If reflexivity is latent, belief will not be troubled and consequently will not fail to be itself. To show in detail how his argument fails would take us too far afield.

7. Ludwig Wittgenstein, *Tractatus Logico-Philosophicus*, 2nd ed., trans. by D. F. Pears and B. F. McGuiness (New York, 1971), 5.632. Hereafter cited as *TLP*.

8. Max Black, *A Companion to Wittgenstein's "Tractatus"* (Ithaca, N.Y., 1964), 308.

9. See Jaakko Hintikka, "On Wittgenstein's Solipsism," *Mind* 68 (1958), 88–91; and H. O. Mounce, *Wittgenstein's Tractatus* (Chicago, 1981), 87–92, for commentators who argue that Wittgenstein is not really a solipsist. See Bernard Williams, "Wittgenstein and Idealism," in *Understanding Wittgenstein*, ed. by Godfrey Vesey (Ithaca, N.Y., 1974), 76–95; P. M. S. Hacker, *Insight and Illusion: Themes in the Philosophy of Wittgenstein* (Ithaca, N.Y., 1960), 220–22; and Richard W. Miller, 'Solipsism in the *Tractatus*," *Journal of the History of Philosophy* 18 (January 1980), 57–74, for commentators who think he is defending solipsism. Robert J. Fogelin, *Wittgenstein* (Boston, 1976), 84–86, stands in the middle.

10. G. E. M. Anscombe, *An Introduction to Wittgenstein's Tractatus* (London, 1963), 12.

11. There is a great deal of debate over what these simple objects are and whether they are empirically accessible. Wittgenstein himself left conflicting clues. Miller argues that these simple objects are mental entities and that, construed that way, solipsism follows from the *Tractatus*'s metaphysics.

12. Hacker, *Insight and Illusion*, 62.

13. Ibid. It is Hacker's analysis that I am following most closely, although Irving M. Copi, " 'Tractatus' 5.542," in *Essays on Wittgenstein's "Tractatus"*, ed. by Irving M. Copi and Robert Beard (London, 1966); Fogelin; Mounce; and Derek Bolton, *An Approach to Wittgenstein's Philosophy* (London, 1979), all offer similar interpretations.

14. Williams, "Wittgenstein and Idealism," 77–78.

15. Hacker, *Insight and Illusion*, especially 64–75.

16. Ludwig Wittgenstein, *Notebooks, 1914–1916*, trans. and ed. by G. E. M. Anscombe (New York, 1969), 85. Hereafter cited as *NB*.

17. Hacker, *Insight and Illusion*, 69.

18. Ludwig Wittgenstein, "Wittgenstein's Notes for Lectures on 'Private Experience' and 'Sense Data,' " ed. by Rush Rhees in *Philosophical Review* 77(July 1968), 297. Although Black (*A Companion*) thinks Wittgenstein did not follow Schopenhauer in positing a transcendental ego, it is almost impossible to make sense of many remarks in this section of the *Tractatus* as well as in the *Notebooks, 1914–1916* and in the sections on ethics and the willing subject if one follows Black's interpretation.

19. Bolton, *An Approach*, 33–34.

VI

A
FAREWELL
HOMAGE

18

SARTRE BY HIMSELF:
AN ACCOUNT, AN EXPLANATION, A DEFENSE

Michel Contat

Another title, "Patricidal Sentiments of an Optative Son," inspired by Proust's "Filial Sentiments of a Patricide," might have been equally appropriate for this film. After all, the film's creation is intimately bound up with co-director Alexandre Astruc's and my relationship with Sartre; it remains more or less unfinished because of the circumstances of Sartre's life and the historical period. How to explain and justify this rough, flawed work, which bears our signatures but ended up being so far from either of our original conceptions? Perhaps it is best to present a simple eyewitness account of how the film was conceived and produced. After all, I have a real stake in the outcome, but I can now also look back critically at the film, which was shot in 1972, edited in 1975–76, and shown in 1976.

As a literary critic I have specialized, in terms of the categories established by Gérard Genette, in the "pre-text."[2] This includes all the material, from the preparatory files to the corrected proofs, that precedes the text proper and functions as the trace of the creative process. According to the same categories, the film *Sartre by Himself* belongs to the "epitext" of *The Words* whenever it provides information that throws new light on Sartre's childhood autobiography and some of his other works.

343

But it is not a filmed autobiography. Neither is it, strictly speaking, a filmed biography. The latter is an established genre with its own rules, similar to cinematic narrative fiction (the film biography differs only in that its main character is based on a real and famous personality and the story focuses on a long period of his life). A glance at the title, *Sartre by Himself*, indicates how totally ambiguous it is. In the credits, *Sartre by Himself* is followed by "Directors: Alexandre Astruc, Michel Contat." Obviously, had the film been a genuine autobiography, it might have been entitled something like "My Life Story and My Writings" and been signed by Jean-Paul Sartre. In truth, no film corresponds exactly to the definition Philippe Lejeune gives of the "autobiographical pact." The latter supposes the identity of the writer, the narrator, and the signatory of the work. To meet Lejeune's definition, one would have to imagine a filmmaker filming himself in his own life story (which, of course, can only be done in the present), and then he would have to do the editing, he would recognize himself in the self-portrait he presents to the public. One of the most autobiographical films I know is *Mes petites amoureuses* by Jean Eustache.[3] In it an offstage voice narrates the story of a summer during his adolescence when Eustache discovered girls and work, but of course an actor is playing him at the age of fifteen or sixteen. To be sure, there are many autobiographically inspired films. To take a recent example, the entire pre-text of *Platoon* underlines its autobiographical nature: it stresses the fact that Oliver Stone lived this story in Vietnam and hence that the film is true—therefore, what it says is indisputable.[4]

The purpose of these preliminary remarks is to stress the ambiguous status of our film, and I have invoked Philippe Lejeune intentionally. A remark by Fellini fits my attitude toward *Sartre by Himself:* I am also "sufficiently masochistic to agree immediately with anyone who criticizes anything I have done." At its first showing in Paris in 1976, *Sartre by Himself* was well received by the entire Paris press. It was also well received at the Cannes festival, where it was an official selection in the section "Un certain regard." This provided Lejeune with the opportunity for a searching and remarkable analysis entitled "Sartre and Narrated Autobiography." There he states that "two types of errors have been committed: one when the film was shot—and one when the film was edited. And these errors are of the same kind: both recreate about Sartre, in the most serious manner possible, the legend of the famous man, a legend which Sartre himself had parodied [in *The Words*]. What is most amazing is that Sartre has authorized this type of hagiography. . . . [The] ideas that illustrate it are so simplistic and conventional and so badly produced that the relieved spectator ends up concluding that he is dealing with a parody of a movie about a famous man. In fact, this is a parody but not an intentional one. The movie is hopelessly serious."[5]

This judgment was obviously formulated in polemical form in response to the—somewhat suspect—unanimously positive press. Lejeune explains its attitude as follows: at a funeral you do not create a scandal. He experienced the film as a first-class burial of Sartre. In fact, only Jean-Marie Domenach had dared write in *Esprit*, "Sartre deserves better than this."[6] In spite of his criticisms Lejeune believes that the film will remain an essential archival document because of the abundance of information it provides about Sartre, who is seen talking very spontaneously for three hours about the most varied subjects.

Why did Sartre accept our making a film about him in 1972, when he had not entertained the idea before? It is Gide's fault: without Marc Allégret's film *Avec André Gide*,[7] made just before Gide's death and shown in 1950, the film about Sartre might never have seen the light of day. I found the Gide film striking. The author of *The Notebooks* and *The Counterfeiters* gives a music lesson to his niece and comments in a simple manner on Montaigne. To see a great writer in an intimate setting was a totally new experience. From the moment in 1957 when I saw the film in Switzerland, I wanted to make a film about Sartre. Our generation of intellectual movie buffs saw literary, critical, political, and movie projects as part and parcel of the same overall project: to give a shape to one's age. Somewhat later, around 1960, I became familiar with cinema verité, especially thanks to Jean Rouch's *Moi, un noir (I, a Black)* and his *Chronique d'un été (Summer Chronicle)*.[8] The latter deals with a whole series of intellectuals, some of them already well known, such as Edgar Morin, others totally unknown but who would become famous later, such as Régis Debray. I told myself, that is what we should do on Sartre, a documentary in the rough; it will have a lasting impact. My plan was to call at his apartment on the rue Bonaparte, camera in hand, and tell him out of the blue, "Sartre, we are here to do a film about you for the following reasons. What do you think?" And we would have filmed his spontaneous reaction. Personally, I think this kind of youthful fantasy about filmmaking deserves being taken seriously.

Critics have demonstrated convincingly that the autobiographical element is a permanent vein in Sartre's works.[9] His first writings are a transposition of his adolescent experiences, and his novels, including *Roads to Freedom,* have a solid basis in autobiography. This can also be illustrated by the stories, such as "Erostratus," that can be seen as the pathological inversion of his wish for literary fame. ("Erostratus" is an

345

illustration of the mania for "instant fame" at the heart of many notorious murders in the United States, such as the murder of John Lennon.) "The Childhood of a Leader" can be viewed as a kind of musing about what Sartre would have become had he really been Mancy's son rather than his stepson. In other words, the autobiographical origins of Sartre's literary work are clearly visible and also exist, although Sartre denies it, in his philosophy.[10] Sartre's works can be seen to move from a disguised to an openly stated autobiography. In the early 1950s, he intended to write a book about Italy to be called *Queen Albemarle or the Last Tourist.* It was never finished. Sartre's difficulty was that he tried to let the first-person narrator assume his identity of the famous writer, while at the same time he sought to portray himself as being just anybody. Like Roquentin in *Nausea,* the peripatetic observer, he was to be an anonymous tourist who meanders through Italy's cities and has a kind of phenomenological intuition about Italy which he attempts to shape by means of his knowledge and reflections about its sociohistorical structures.[11] Elsewhere I have tried to show that the text's failure is precisely the result of the indecisive nature of its first-person narrator (since it does not make clear whether it is Sartre who is speaking or someone who is like Sartre in all respects except that no one knows that he is the famous writer).[12] This failure leads Sartre to write the autobiography that will become *The Words.* At least that is the hypothesis we are using in our analysis of the pre-texts of *The Words,* and it seems chronologically probable.

Sartre laid out his first plan for *The Words* in interviews. He would narrate not just his childhood and the origins of his vocation as a writer but his whole life, and he would present it as representative of that of the intellectuals of his age and even, beyond that, of his entire generation— its childhood experience of World War I, the distant impact of the Russian Revolution, its adolescent and youthful experiences between the wars, reaching maturity at the time of France's defeat and the raised hopes of the Liberation period. But as Lejeune shows, *The Words* is, from a literary point of view, a parody of the memoirs of the famous man.[13] The text reflects different styles within a general framework of self-contestation, and the autobiographical narration covers only the first thirteen years of Sartre's life. Indeed, in terms of the meaning, he really covers his entire life up to 1963, the year of the final version which ends, as do so many of Sartre's books, promising a sequel.

The next installment never appeared and, as far as we know, was never even begun. Sartre explained later that he felt the essential had been said in *The Words.* Also, it was hard to write the next part while his mother was still alive because she would have been hurt by his account of her second marriage, to Joseph Mancy. It provoked Sartre's inner break with her and led to his years of affective withdrawal in La Rochelle. Above all, it would have been the story of his troubled years and would have compelled him to come face to face with his neurosis.[14] The fact is that Sartre seemed "blocked" in his autobiography at the stage of his break with his mother, as Lejeune indicates, because the break did not really take place but was only a neurotic repression of his exclusive attachment to his mother.[15]

At the beginning of the 1970s Sartre has interrupted his planned autobiography and is working on his "Flaubert," fragments of which he published in *Les Temps Modernes* in 1966 and left him dissatisfied. Since *The Words* he has published nothing of importance. His last work for the theater was an excellent adaptation of Euripedes' *Trojan Women,* but it had no great impact. He is barely in the news anymore except for his links with the left-wing agitators of the post–May 1968 movement. Suddenly, in October 1970, he makes worldwide headlines with a photograph that shows him standing on a barrel haranguing the workers in front of the Renault factories in Billancourt.

The picture (there are several, but the reporters present all used the same one) shows Sartre surrounded by a multitude of microphones and journalists, but there are no workers to be seen. Either they were really absent or they were not even the subject of the picture or of the story, no more than they were the subject of history. The captions say nothing about what Sartre might have been saying to them. In fact, the titles, the framing, and the captions, without daring to state it explicitly, all suggest that we have here a philosopher who is losing his popularity and is using eccentric means to gain publicity. One could do a complete analysis of this photograph à la Barthes's *Mythologies.*[16] Sartre's fame came back to haunt him, to the point where it completely obscured his message. In its place was an image he simply could not control, even as he thought he was exploiting it to further a cause (not his own but that of the newspaper *La Cause du Peuple*). Although I did not yet suspect it, deep down Sartre had decided to climb on the barrel at Billancourt precisely to fight off his own despair about the workers at this symbolic home of the working class.

This media treatment shocked me. But also I did not really understand the meaning of this act, or rather of this gesture, for Sartre himself. I thought then (and I still do) that he was allowing himself to be manipulated by his Maoist friends. I mistrusted them and their emphatic dramatizing of militancy. I considered them thoughtless for having dragged him into a kind of action that backfired on him, and generally on all intellectuals, without anyone benefiting by it. I do not really know why, but the Maoist intimidation of "democratic intellectuals" (they used the term condescendingly) has never impressed me. It struck me that Sartre would never have decided on such an action on his own, but, good or bad, he had done it. I had too much affection and esteem for him to skip over it lightly without discussing it with him, if only to know his reasons. In short, I was tempted to hide this incongruous behavior behind a mantle of meaning. Father had behaved in an unacceptable manner, and I, as a good son, was going to help him make good.

Hence I went to see him in the spring of 1971 at La Coupole on a Sunday morning and told him, "Sartre, this picture is everywhere. Nobody knows what to make of it and why you are doing it. Don't you think the time has come to return to your old project for an autobiography, but this time on film? Since the media are making you look ridiculous and are distorting the meaning of your actions, you must respond by using the media to reach a large public and explain the trajectory that has led someone of a bourgeois background to break with that culture and try to contact the masses directly. We will start with the picture of you on the barrel and retrace your steps to your childhood. The film will illustrate how it all happened, and finally we will come back to the barrel, but this time we will hear what you said to the workers and understand its meaning. Nobody will snicker anymore."

Sartre laughed; he liked the idea and said, "Write a screenplay and we'll talk about it." I intended to write it during the summer holidays at the Lausanne high school where I taught. But problems came up—there was an expulsion from the school for political reasons. My involvement increased Sartre's esteem for me, but by fall the screenplay was still not written. In the meantime *The Family Idiot* came out. It rekindled interest in Sartre in the literary magazines. The filmmaker Alexandre Astruc proposed doing a film on Sartre.[17] Astruc had known Sartre since 1944; he wrote one of the first reviews of *Being and Nothingness*,[18] and he had been a member of the group of young Sartre admirers after the war, when he thought of adapting *Nausea* to the screen. He now proposed a film that, in accordance with his own theory of the camera as writing pen, would trace Sartre's thought and the evolution of his work. Sartre told him, too, that he liked the idea. Then he remembered that he had already given me permission and proposed that we work out an agreement and make one common project out of two.

In fact, the idea of a film about Sartre was in the air, and the moment for putting it into practice was ripe. Guy Seligmann and Pierre-

André Boutang, both television directors, also had the idea but needed a contact with Sartre. They called on their friend Alexandre Astruc, and they decided to be the producers. Before I saw Sartre, I had been contacted by André Harris and Alain de Sédouy, who had just successfully brought out *Le Chagrin et la Pitié* (*The Sorrow and The Pity*).[19] They had agreed to do an extensive film and television series on famous contemporaries for a production company being set up by the publishing house Rencontre in Lausanne; they wanted to start with Sartre. They wanted to be the directors and producers and do at least some of the interviews, hoping to have a dialogue with Sartre. They offered to collaborate with me and asked me to present the project to Sartre. I told them that I wanted Claude Goretta to direct it, because some time ago we had written the screenplay of a movie for television, *Le Jour des noces* (*The Wedding Day*).[20] He and I got along well and had decided to collaborate on a Sartre film.

Sartre's reaction to the Harris and Sédouy proposal was clear: he did not like *The Sorrow and the Pity,* and he thought we would make a better film with Claude Goretta. At that time Swiss movies were very popular in Paris with movie buffs and even others; Sartre had liked Alain Tanner's *Charles, mort ou vif* (*Charles Dead or Alive*)[21] or at least had heard it praised warmly by Simone de Beauvoir (I am not sure he had seen it himself). The film also had the support of the Left because it expressed forcefully, emotionally, and humorously the deep desire for freedom at the heart of the May 1968 movement. He also really liked *The Wedding Day* on television, which was warmly received by Maurice Clavel in *Le Nouvel Observateur.*[22] The notion of a Swiss film about himself did not displease Sartre either; it even seemed to guarantee a kind of independence.

When he called me to talk about Astruc's project, he told me, "Go see him; it would be great if you two came to an agreement, but the decision is up to you." Those remarks showed his great kindness but also brought out his wily side, because I am nearly sure that he told Astruc the same thing. For Sartre the trio corresponded more or less deliberately to the basic pattern of his life. One always says "Sartre-Beauvoir," but in reality and quite early in the couple's evolution a triangular relationship was formed: Sartre, Beauvoir, and someone else. This undoubtedly reproduces Sartre's original childhood relationship: Poulou–Anne-Marie Schweitzer–Karlémami (Grandfather Schweitzer absorbs his spouse as if the grandparents were one and the same person). In a sense this also characterizes *No Exit,* this time negatively. It reproduces the hellish adolescent relationship: Poulou–Mme. Mancy–M. Mancy. Sartre recreates it

349

spontaneously, or at least tries to improve upon it in all his personal relationships, which are never dual but always triangular. It is as if occupying the apex of the triangle permitted Sartre, through clever affective manipulations of the two other partners, to maintain control. He is at the center of their relationship even in his absence and hence remains the trio's principal character. This trio is not always made up of one man and two women, as is the case in *No Exit*. All three variations are possible. For example (and, for once, I deliberately am not choosing examples from his love life), Sartre cleverly promoted collaboration on his bibliography between Michel Rybalka and myself. Rybalka was a friend of Michelle Vian, I was a friend of Arlette Elkaïm, Sartre's adopted daughter. This also happened with Astruc: I was Elkaïm's protégé, and Astruc was Bost's and Beauvoir's. In short, it fit in with Sartre's affective logic that two parts of his parallel lives join up to make a biographical film.

Astruc and I have never stopped arguing, amicably but vigorously, over the film. He would probably disagree even with my account of events, perhaps along the lines of *Rashomon* (where the same incident is narrated from three different points of view, yielding three incompatible stories). In his memoirs Astruc states that he was going through a bad period at the time. To me he remained the respected moviemaker Alexandre Astruc. The originality of his ideas continually surprised me, and he possessed a childlike charm and a kindness I found irresistible. We hit it off more because of a shared existential style than a similarity of ideas. His ideas about the movie were at once abstract and ambitious. He spoke of a cinematographic essay on Sartre's thought and invoked Rossellini. Personally I had no model to go by; Allégret's film about Gide was much more of a precedent than an example to follow, even if I also hoped to capture on film what I knew and loved about Sartre's private existence. But with the little experience I had of screenwriting I could not consider myself a moviemaker in comparison to Astruc. This explains why Goretta and I had planned the movie as a co-production. He would handle the properly filmic aspects and I the intellectual conception of the film. Both would require reciprocal agreement.

My goal, in appearance much more modest than that of Astruc, was to place ourselves at Sartre's service to help him produce an autobiographical piece of work—for which we would function as cinematographic intermediaries. Astruc pretended to accept my idea, and I his. I now believe that we were both afraid of Sartre, that is to say, of the amplitude and difficulty of the subject matter. We also knew that the film's completion depended on both of us and that if we did not work together there would be no film at all about Sartre. It meant a great deal more to Simone de Beauvoir than to him, and she thought that bringing in Astruc was a good idea. To Sartre this collaboration between Sartreans of two different generations must have seemed potentially fruitful. One was an experienced moviemaker whose aesthetic inventiveness he counted on to make the movie more than a documentary; the other knew his work well and could be trusted to make sure that it was not unfaithful to his thought. In sum, we represented the marriage of the artist and the intellectual: an intelligent moviemaker and an intellectual movie buff. It should work, Sartre must have thought. After all, his principle was to not discourage budding projects about him. Besides, he would only have to commit himself when he had seen the screenplay.

The production was to be a Franco-Swiss co-production. Harris and Sédouy withdrew from the Sartre project, but they remained involved in the "Great Contemporaries" project of which "Sartre" could be a part. For France, only commercial distribution along the lines of *The Sorrow and the Pity* was planned. State television, still an ORTF monopoly,[23] refused to show the Ophüls film because of its political content. Sartre refused in principle to have the film shown on television, even if the government had tried to win him over by offering to show it in spite of its political content. The producers knew this, and they also knew that the film could not pay for itself in France and would have to be sold to foreign television outlets.

Astruc and I started to work. The results were mediocre. In the wrestling match that each of us had unwittingly engaged in to make the film conform to our own preconceptions, I had won the first round. My victory was more physical than intellectual or aesthetic. It was a result of my youthful energy; Astruc was not really at his best during the period when we wrote the first screenplay together. Initially, the screenplay was the typical product of a schoolteacher and was strikingly academic. I think that when Sartre and Beauvoir read it they were flabbergasted. Those friends of Sartre who liked me laughed a lot about an idea that I was crazy about. I proposed to zero in on a glass of beer to explain the theory of eidetic reduction and intentionality as Sartre had adapted it from Husserl. Afterward, during shooting, each time someone had a glass of beer, they would say, "This one is for Contat," and everyone would laugh.

In short, this screenplay would not do at all. I knew that perfectly well; we had worked hastily and knew it had to be redone. However, production could not continue without a screenplay. People who invest in a film project panic easily, so you have to give them something that looks serious: a bound volume with a title. Besides, if you want to work

351

with professionals you have to deposit a screenplay at the Centre National de la Cinématographie. Regardless of its quality, that is the rule. Why was everyone in such a hurry? I will come back to the other reasons later, but the first if not the principal reason was economic: money had been invested in the preparation. Seligmann and Boutang had run out of money, and for the production to start, Sartre had to sign a contract so that we could show some scenes to the backers. Sartre was kind enough, or perhaps whimsical enough, to sign the contract (however, he was well protected: it stipulated that he had to approve the final version). Therefore, we decided to shoot a first series of interviews with Sartre and to revise the screenplay afterward. The main cameraman was Renato Berta, who was already known for his work on *Charles Dead or Alive.* He also had the advantage of being Swiss, since the co-production agreement imposed a quota of Swiss technicians.

We shot for two weekends in February and March 1972, for about four hours a day. First we did one session at Beauvoir's, then three in Sartre's little apartment on the Boulevard Raspail. We used two cameras so that Sartre would not be interrupted when a camera was being reloaded, thus allowing the conversation to develop freely. The technicians were told to stay out of the action as they worked. As a result, when the sound engineer had a problem with Sartre's tie microphone, he did not dare interrupt. This explains why the sound is bad in a large part of the rushes we had to use when editing for continuity in the storyline and the ideas. The participants were chosen in a straightforward manner, especially since we had planned interviews at other times, notably with the absent Claude Lanzmann on the question of Israel. Therefore, except for him, we shot with all the members of *Les Temps Modernes,* Jean Pouillon, André Gorz, Jacques-Laurent Bost, and, of course, Simone de Beauvoir. Astruc was behind one of the cameras, but he was free to enter into the debate, and I was in front of the cameras in the midst of the discussants. The conversation used the question-and-answer format and followed a straightforward chronological pattern. My role was to maintain continuity using a questionnaire inspired by the one Jean-José Marchand had used for the television series "Archives du XXᵉ siècle." ("The Archives of the 20th Century" interviewed intellectuals without planning to show them immediately on television. Pierre-André Boutang had, among others, taped a discussion with Emmanuel Berl).[24]

Sartre was cheerful, eloquent, and amusing, and the technicians were completely charmed by his simplicity and the faith he showed in them. He left his apartment to them for hours to set up the lights. He was interested in everything and extremely patient, and in front of the camera he acted as if he was as used to it as Marlon Brando. He seemed not at all worried about how he looked. I believe that during those days he gave everyone a concrete idea of authenticity, which is composed of many complex and difficult elements but first and foremost requires the total absence of playacting.

He had had his first stroke the previous year. It had affected him, according to friends who knew him in his glory years as a tremendous conversationalist. Between two sessions, Jean Pouillon, pleasantly surprised by Sartre's good condition, told me sadly, "He should have been filmed in 1950. Now you only have a pale notion of how brilliant he could be." I suspect that Sartre took corydrane or benzedrine to dope himself up, but I am not sure. The previous year, Rybalka and I had interviewed him for *Le Monde*. We thought he was in very good shape, and we did not suspect the slightest problem. Some time later Arlette Elkaïm told me he had admitted to her that he had taken corydrane for the occasion even though it was strictly forbidden. One morning of the shooting, he arrived rather tired (at the start of the film's second half he suddenly seems affected by his age), and then he progressively came around again. The dialogue setting favored him, of course; he was surrounded by friends, he talked about himself, and if there were disagreements, they were handled graciously.

The resulting movie is a truthful portrait of him as he behaved in private with his intellectual friends. Certainly this was different from the way he behaved privately with the women he loved or seduced. The *Herald Tribune* has criticized the film because it surrounds Sartre with "yes men."[25] I fear that we indeed let one of Sartre's statements pass unchallenged. He claimed that de Gaulle had legitimized his power by using referendums, comparable to the way Napoleon III used plebiscites. In fact, de Gaulle gave up power after he lost a referendum. None of us had the reflex to raise a single finger and object. Lejeune criticizes us also for letting Sartre tell stories already familiar to us, the way one lets a child or an old man endlessly repeat his favorite stories.[26]

In fact, these first interviews were above all meant to be friendly and casual and, in our minds, to lay the biographical foundation on which were to be built a series of diverse interviews involving different kinds of dialogue. Sartre was supposed to debate Michel Foucault; we had also proposed Raymond Aron, but he objected: "No, I don't want to debate him. It will lead nowhere." On the other hand, he was eager to debate with the young philosopher François George, and he liked the idea of discussing politics with Alain Krivine, the leader of the Trotskyists of the Revolutionary Communist League. The idea of debating with his Maoist

353

friends was also suggested, especially with Benny Lévy, who then called himself Pierre Victor. The latter lived a more or less clandestine existence, which made his appearance on the screen somewhat problematic.

But before the start of the second series of interviews, the venture collapsed. The Swiss backers became afraid that the increasingly radical and extremist positions Sartre began to assume, which were publicized regularly in the newspapers, would be found objectionable and scare off the other "great contemporaries" of the series such as Fangio,[27] John XXIII, and even Fidel Castro (whom they hoped to convince). They concluded that a pilot film on Sartre was not the best idea, and they withdrew. (The series itself was never produced because the Swiss production company was dissolved.)

However, in September 1972 Astruc took the time to write an entirely new screenplay. It was based on the first one as well as on the interviews already done. He took great liberties with the narration and invented several sequences dealing with Sartrean themes (something remains of it in very simplified form in the final version, for example, the sequence based on *Nausea* filmed in the public park in Rouen). He had reverted to his initial idea of doing a cinematographic essay on Sartre the writer and philosopher. Neither Sartre nor I agreed entirely with that screenplay, but we both felt it to be superior to the first. It moved more quickly, it was more inventive and freewheeling, and it was felt that we could rework it together.[28] Sadly, after the production was abandoned, this never happened.

The project was only resurrected when the ORTF was broken up. Seligmann and Boutang still wanted to finish the film, but each time they found a potential backer they ran into the same problem. Sartre's categorical refusal to let the film be shown on television meant that it could not pay for itself. In addition, Astruc's version of the screenplay was costly. Then Giscard d'Estaing's election as president in 1974 created a new situation. The ORTF television monopoly was broken up and replaced by ostensibly politically independent stations as well as the National Audiovisual Institute (INA), whose task was to create and preserve archives. The INA promptly proposed to underwrite the completion of the film by offering to co-produce it with Seligmann and Boutang's company. However, it did not offer the standard facilities for a film production but only the much more limited facilities of a television production. Then followed the proposal made in public by Marcel Jullian, president of Antenne 2. He offered Sartre a television program free of any interference. The intent was to display the new liberalism of public service television (supposedly different from state monopoly television) by showing that even Sartre could express himself freely on it. Marcel Jullian had in mind a film portrait of a star.

Sartre planned a political piece, and he made Jullian a counterproposal, offering to do historical broadcasts on the twentieth century seen from the perspective of a concrete subjectivity: Sartre's. It would be a monthly show with a total of twelve segments. It would receive the same backing as a regular series and therefore enjoy the biggest budget available. The telecasts would be conceived by a collective directed by Sartre and produced by a moviemaker of his choice, and each telecast would end with a live sequence focusing on contemporary political struggles. It was clearly a political and historical program, and on this basis negotiations for a contract began. Even before it was signed, a team made up of Sartre, Simone de Beauvoir, Pierre Victor (Benny Lévy), and Philippe Gavi set to work and rapidly decided to create activist research groups to gather documentation and eyewitness reports and to reflect upon historical questions dealing specifically with the labor movement and feminist struggles.

Of course, when Sartre announced that he had accepted Jullian's proposal, our producers felt there could not be two different standards. If Sartre accepted being shown on television, he should also accept our film being shown on television. I impressed this argument on Sartre, but he was not very enthusiastic about finishing the film. First, he was spontaneously attracted to new projects, and what he had said three years ago he would no longer say in the same way today. Also, at the time of the presidential election Alexandre Astruc had called for a vote for Giscard and adopted a publicly embarrassing position. (It embarrassed me more than it displeased me. I had never taken Astruc's political posturing very seriously. During the shooting of the film he out-Maoed the Maoists and had made Sartre and the people from *Les Temps Modernes* laugh; they all liked Astruc but did not credit him with much political sense.) Lastly and specifically, our film was initially conceived as a political tool and ran the danger of conflicting with the planned television broadcasts. But, all the same, Sartre understood perfectly well that we wanted to finish it, and he felt himself bound not just by a legal contract but also, if I may say so, by friendship. Therefore we proposed an amendment to the contract specifying that the film could be shown on television but on a date and with conditions laid down by him, that is to say, when he felt like it. Now the INA could participate in the production.

This raised the question of whether we were going to bring the film up to date by doing new interviews. A lot had happened in three years.

355

The Maoists had ceased operations and had dissolved their organization. Sartre had abandoned Marxism, or at least the kind of dialogue with Marxism in which he claimed to be more authentically Marxist than they were. The war in Vietnam was over, the first oil crisis had taken place, and Pompidou's authoritarianism had been replaced by Giscard's economic liberalism. The concept of revolution had to be rethought outside the framework of Marxist-Leninism and Maoism. Libertarian socialism had become the watchword on the radical side, and the "new philosophy" (which, according to Sartre, was neither one nor the other) offered itself up as the philosophy of democracy and human rights. Sartre wanted to deal with all these subjects in his historical broadcasts.

But something had also happened to him personally: he was partially paralyzed. He had nearly lost his eyesight and could no longer exercise his profession as a writer. His condition had affected his diction, the rhythm of his speech, and occasionally his thought. Those who have seen the film on Simone de Beauvoir,[29] in which he appears and which was shot at about this period, will understand why we were hesitant to provide two such dramatically different images of the same man in one film—all the more since Sartre had not yet publicly acknowledged his loss of sight (he did this only in 1975, during the editing of the film, and I may have helped push him into it by proposing to do his "self-portrait at age seventy," an interview I completed later).[30] Therefore we decided very deliberately to edit the film not exactly as a posthumous film but by dating its making explicitly in 1972. We brought it up to date only in the commentary and by the use of certain shots to evoke the changes that had taken place.

The funeral rite to which Lejeune had alluded becomes pertinent here. We were not sure about how to end the film. For a concluding shot the idea of Sartre on a barrel no longer worked. It stressed a militant Sartre, and he was no longer that. Emotionally, Sartre's illness and physical deterioration may have affected me worse in a certain way than it had him; it struck me as a death in life. Therefore I wanted to end the film on a serious note. During Sartre's absence, Astruc had panned his empty room with a single long shot which swept the manuscript-laden table. It showed Sartre's Flaubert manuscript open where he was working on it, and then the camera moved to his narrow student bed and framed the alarm clock which showed the time, and, in a sense, the camera stopped it. Astruc thought he could use that shot somewhere. When we neared the end of the editing, this shot, beautiful in itself, struck us as providing a possible ending because it was a visual commentary that revealed what Sartre was currently doing. I discussed it in detail with Sartre, read him the commentary, and together we chose the music: two movements of Beethoven's last quartet. *Quartet no. 16* corresponded exactly to his state of mind: a kind of serene resignation in face of the inevitable. But indeed that final sequence was somewhat solemn, no doubt because of its stentorious commentary and its tone of voice. Sometimes it moved us and then again it seemed incongruous.

It struck Lejeune as producing the "Simonnot" effect. As you will recall in *The Words,* Simonnot, a colleague of Grandfather Schweitzer, is the professor who is absent at a party given at the Living Language Institute. It provokes the grandfather into stating, "There is someone missing here, and it is Simonnot." This remark makes Poulou dream of being necessary to the entire world. The empty office also seemed to say, "There is someone missing here, and it is Sartre." Of course, we had not intended this, but we had probably experienced it in this way.

We showed Sartre the edited version before we mixed the sound. I awaited his reaction with curiosity. I have already indicated that Sartre's contract allowed him to make changes to this version if he did not like it. We invited him and Simone de Beauvoir. He showed up with Benny Lévy, and neither one made the slightest remark about the ending. Sartre stated that on the whole he was satisfied. "I think that I did not come off too badly," he said at the end of the showing.

Just before the Cannes Film Festival, we had another screening for Sartre, Beauvoir, and their friends, and no one criticized the ending. It was this "approved" version that was shown in Cannes, and since then it has never been touched. Even so, I was struck by a remark Claude Mauriac made after a press showing: "If you decide to show the film on television after Sartre's death, all you'll have to do is change the commentary of the final sequence." This remark was not intended to be critical; it was simply an observation. Even so it upset me. Especially after the Cannes showing, which was attended by Liliane Siegel (one of Sartre's girlfriends of Maoist tendencies with whom I did not get along at all). Sartre let me know that her Maoist friends found the film "a little funereal," but he assured me that he did not agree. I was not too surprised that Sartre's activist friends did not like this film. To them its completion was even more of a bitter pill since in the meantime their historical television broadcasts had been scrapped. Marcel Jullian had not known how, or had not wanted, to resist Gaullist pressures to drop it. And if Jullian procrastinated to the point of wearing out Sartre's patience and provoking him to a break, this was also because he felt that Sartre had become a hostage of his Maoist friends. (Someday this story needs to be told in detail, but it requires a historian's rigor.)

I was surprised to read one morning the following lines in *Libéra-tion,* in an interview of Sartre by Pierre Victor (Benny Lévy) about their work in progress (they were planning a two-person essay on "Power and Freedom"):

> PIERRE VICTOR: Lately the press talks again a lot about you. And that seems surprising. People thought you were dead.
> SARTRE: An impression created by Contat himself who finished his film with a shot of my empty apartment. Completely empty. It followed upon some very lively statements and arguments and then you are shown the man as dead. That is to say, absent from his apartment; no doubt they had already buried me in the Montparnasse graveyard.[31]

Thus Sartre ended up by sharing the judgment of the ex-Maoists. But Beauvoir certainly did not share it. She always defended the film after it came out. She had been very reticent and even hostile to it after we had carelessly shown her a first edited section (made up of extracts taped end to end and cut from the rushes). Notice that Sartre speaks of "Contat" and not of Astruc and Contat. Astruc had fallen somewhat out of favor when he became right-wing. But Sartre had also been forced to choose when Astruc and I began to disagree completely about how to edit the film. Astruc, no longer very happy with the way we had filmed the interviews, wanted to take very short extracts and arrange them freely in a musical way. He wanted to proceed by associating images and ideas and placing them into opposition. It seemed attractive, but it turned out to be impractical. I wanted to edit the film in a discursive manner and highlight the coherence of Sartre's thought; to do this I proposed to follow a chronological line as much as possible. Sartre agreed with me and delegated to me the right of the "final cut," his right of ultimate judgment on the film.

Therefore I am responsible for the film; I took the responsibility for editing it and directed it on a daily basis. Astruc and I finally agreed upon this: I did the editing; he came around now and then and suggested an idea or an opinion. If at the end he did not agree with the editing he would withdraw his signature. He did not do that even though he always considered my conception of the film as "academic." Annie Chevallay, the editor, was my real collaborator on the film. She had a great feeling for music, and I believe that the cinematographic quality of the film consists mainly in the rhythm of her editing. It allows one to follow the three-hour narrative without tiring or getting bored, and it creates a Mozartian impression of relaxed and spontaneous naturalness. That was the feeling the rushes gave; to reproduce it in the editing, which breaks up the natural duration, required eight months of work. Only profession-als can appreciate the difficulty and the skill needed to achieve this result. If the film strikes one as academic, the choice of documents makes it so (many of them are used again and again as part of television broadcasts). So does the biographical point of view we adopted in order to talk about the great writer.

I have said that I felt responsible for the film and that it contained an element of patricide. This is because any biography has to adopt a posthumous perspective on a living person. The mistake in the film, which Lejeune notices, was to load a typically biographical film narra-tive on the shoulders of the biography's subject, and not having the authors assume it. The film lacked a perspective on Sartre. I produced, with Sartre, a written interview for the press dossier. To the question "Is it a film by Sartre or about Sartre?" I made him answer, "Both at the same time." He called after he had these remarks read to him and asked me to correct them: "It is a film about Sartre . . . a film about Sartre in 1972." He was right, but I was not wrong. It is at once a film by Sartre, to the extent that he talks about his life, and a film about Sartre, to the extent that what he says is situated in the framework of a biography. The film characteristically vacillates between the biographical and the auto-biographical discourse, and that makes it a document rather than a work of art.

But I do not agree that it is a hagiography, in terms of the very definitions that Lejeune provides of *autobiography* and *biography*. A *hagiography* presupposes a narrator distinct from the saint (St. Teresa does not write her hagiography but memoirs); thus Lejeune can use the word only metaphorically. To his polemic term I will oppose an apolo-getic one and state that this film is a *patrigraphy*—a filial tribute. Astruc and I were placed in a filial position in relation to Sartre, because we loved him a great deal and we did not feel we were his equals or his collaborators but beholden to him. Making us work together was a poor idea. The struggle among the sons for the father's recognition neutral-ized our specific creative audacity. The result was a film without an author. Neither Sartre nor Astruc nor I was able to recognize ourselves in it completely because it was a neutered, academic film. Even so, Sartre's relationship to the cinema was such that at that moment no other film about him but this one was possible. He would not have accepted working with Godard, for example.

When I later saw *Nick's Movie* by Wim Wenders,[32] I understood what I had wanted to do with Sartre: a film made by a young man about an old and enfeebled man whom he admires and loves and helps to live through his old age and his sickness (and ultimately, if necessary, to face his death). Why is this beautiful story about old, cancer-ridden Nicolas Ray, who dies during its making, a work of art and not simply a document? Because, unlike ourselves, someone says "I" and assumes authorship—even if it is about Nick. This is the kind of film that could have been made "about Sartre."

But, imperfect as it is, the document exists, and this is not insignificant, especially given its length. The ten hours of film done in 1972 can be edited again someday or the rushes taped end to end, to be shown to a specialized audience, such as scholars. As it stands, it bears witness to an era—as do all documents. One might say that at that time it was still possible, even if it was difficult, to shoot a film about a writer and show it commercially. It was possible with Sartre because in French literature, and hence on the world scene, Sartre had assumed the status of Zola and Gide. In 1975 the film was seen in Paris by fifty thousand people. There were fifty thousand people at Sartre's funeral in 1980. These were probably the same people, people to whom Sartre meant a good deal. They had read him and loved him for the values they collectively shared. No French writer today has a public of this size; the very function of the writer has changed as French society has changed and its importance in the world declined. It is impossible to make a commercial film about a provincial writer.

Notes

This essay is an edited translation of a transcription, revised and footnoted by the author, of two improvised lectures. The first was given to the Sartre Society of North America at Wayne State University and the University of Windsor in April 1987; the second was given at the colloquium "Sartre e Beauvoir al cinema," organized by Sandra Teroni and Andrea Vanini at the Bottega del Cinema and the French Institute in Florence, May 1987.

Sartre par lui-même (1976), film directed by Alexandre Astruc and Michel Contat, produced by Guy Seligmann and Pierre-André Boutang. Sodaperaga, Institut National de l'Audiovisuel; 180 minutes, in two parts of 90 minutes each; Eastmancolor. The film is distributed in the United States in 16mm with subtitles by Citadel Films Ltd., Chicago; it is also available in videocassette. The text of the film was published as *Sartre: Un film réalisé par A. Astruc et M. Contat. Avec la participation de Simone de Beauvoir, Jacques-Laurent Bost, André Gorz, Jean Pouillon. Texte intégral* (Paris, 1977); trans. by Richard Seaver, *Sartre by Himself* (New York, 1978).

1. See Marcel Proust, "Sentiments filiaux d'un parricide," *Le Figaro*, February 15, 1907; reprinted in *Contre Sainte-Beuve* (Paris, 1978), 150.

2. The notion of *avant-texte* has been put forward by Jean Bellemin-Noël, *Le Texte*

et l'avant-texte (Paris, 1972). Gérard Genette uses this notion as part of his categorization of the "paratext" in *Seuils* (Paris, 1987).

3. *Mes petites amoureuses* (1974), screenplay, dialogue, and direction by Jean Eustache, produced by Elite Films (Pierre Cottrell). The title is taken from Arthur Rimbaud.

4. *Platoon* (1987). This film, written and directed by Oliver Stone, tells the story of an American platoon in Vietnam formed mostly of black draftees and one middle-class white soldier who has enlisted (representing the author-director himself). Even so, I do not think it is appropriate to invoke Lejeune's "autobiographical pact" for this film, not only, of course, because author and actor are not the same person but because the film is filled with *inverted* Hollywood stereotypes (which makes them stereotypes nevertheless) instead of being a singular, individual voice.

5. Phillipe Lejeune, "Sartre et l'autobiographie parlée," in *Je est un autre* (Paris, 1980), 192–93. An earlier version of this article was published under the title "L'Autobiographie parlée," *Obliques*, nos. 18–19 (1979), 97–116 (this was read to Sartre).

6. *Esprit*, December 1976, 861–62.

7. *Avec André Gide* (1950), film by Marc Allégret. Gide died February 19, 1951.

8. See the polemical article attacking *Chronique d'un été* by Claude Tarare (pseudonym of Jacques-Laurent Bost), "Faussaires et truqueurs," *Les Temps Modernes*, no. 187 (December 1961), 769–75. This article also reflects some of Sartre's ideas on cinema verité.

9. See especially Phillippe Lejeune, "L'Ordre du récit dans *Les Mots* de Sartre," in *Le Pacte autobiographique* (Paris, 1975), 197–243; François George, *Deux études sur Sartre* (Paris, 1976); Douglas Collins, *Sartre as Biographer* (Cambridge, 1980); Josette Pacaly, *Sartre au miroir* (Paris, 1980); Geneviève Idt, "Préhistoire de Sartre biographe d'apres *Les Carnets de la drôle de guerre*," in *Literarische Diskurse des Existentialismus*, ed. by H. Harth and V. Roloff. (Tubingen, 1986), 57–73; and also the prefaces and reviews of Sartre's *Oeuvres romanesques*, ed. by M. Contat and M. Rybalka, with the collaboration of G. Idt and G. Bauer (Paris, 1981).

10. See Serge Doubrovsky, "Sartre: retouches à un autoportrait," *Autobiographiques: de Corneille à Sartre* (Paris, 1988), 123–67.

11. See M. Contat, "Enquête en cours sur un livre inexistant. Genèse d'un inédit de Sartre: *La Reine Albemarle ou le dernier touriste*," in *Leçons d'écriture. Ce que disent les manuscrits*, ed. by A. Grésillon and M. Werner (Paris, 1985), 217–40.

12. Ibid.

13. See Lejeune, "L'Ordre du récit."

14. See Pacaly, *Sartre au miroir.*

15. See Phillippe Lejeune, "Ça s'est fait comme ça," *Poétique*, no. 35 (September 1978), 269–304. This article analyzes three minutes of the film *Sartre by Himself* from different methodological and theoretical angles and with extreme precision.

16. See Roland Barthes, *Mythologies* (New York, 1972).

17. Alexandre Astruc (born in 1923) is the director of *Le Rideau cramoisi* (1952), *Les Mauvaises rencontres* (1955), *Une vie* (1957, his masterpiece, adapted from Guy de Maupassant's novel of the same title), *La Proie pour l'ombre* (1960), *Education sentimentale 61* (1961, a modernization of Gustave Flaubert's novel), and later a few other films for television. He is the theoretician of the "camera as writing pen," a conception of the film as a means to express ideas as well as emotions (see "Naissance d'une nouvelle avant-garde, la caméra-stylo," *L'Ecran Français*, no. 144 [March 1948]). He has written numer-

ous articles and is also the author of several novels, including *Les Vacances* (Paris, 1945) and a volume of memoirs.

18. See *Poésie 44,* no. 17 (1944), 87–92.

19. *Le Chagrin et la pitié* (1971), film directed by Marcel Ophüls, produced by André Harris and Alain de Sédouy. The film, well known in North America, is a documentary about German occupation in wartime France and consists mostly of interviews of people from all political horizons about their attitude toward the Germans and the Resistance. It caused a scandal both in Gaullist circles and on the Left, because it attacked the myth of France rising up as one against the Occupation.

20. *Le Jour des noces* (1971), television film by Claude Goretta, screenplay and dialogue by C. Goretta and M. Contat, freely inspired by the story "A Country Party" by Guy de Maupassant.

21. *Charles, mort ou vif* (1969), film produced, written, and directed by Alain Tanner. Released in Paris, January 15, 1970.

22. See Maurice Clavel, "Noces de rêve," *Le Nouvel Observateur,* June 12, 1972.

23. The Office of French Radio-Television (ORTF) was directly controlled by the state, and network directors were named by the state, which thus exercised an indirect but absolute authority over programming. Sartre's position, after the signatories of the Manifesto of 121 against the Algerian War were not allowed to appear on television in 1960, was to reject any involvement with ORTF as well as other institutions controlled by the state (private channels were only authorized in France in 1985).

24. Emmanuel Berl (1892–1976) was one of the influential intellectuals of the 1930s. He was chief editor of the left-wing cultural magazine *Marianne* (supported by Gaston Gallimard), and he wrote numerous books, ranging from novels to political essays. He was known as one of the most independent minds of his time.

25. See Thomas Quinn Curtiss, "Portrait of Sartre Reveals More Than Was Intended," *International Herald Tribune* (Paris ed.), November 10, 1976.

26. See Lejeune, "Sartre et l'autobiographie parlée," 193.

27. Juane Manuel Fangio, champion racing driver, so well known worldwide in the 1950s that Fidel Castro kidnapped him for forty-eight hours in Havana in February 1958 in order to gain worldwide publicity for the guerrilla war against the Batista dictatorship.

28. Both screenplays can be consulted in the collection of Sartreana at the Institut des Textes et Manuscrits Modernes (ITEM), Centre National de la Recherche Scientifique (CNRS) in Paris.

29. *Simone de Beauvoir* (1978), film by Josée Dayan and Malka Ribowska, directed by Josée Dayan.

30. Sartre, "Autoportrait à 70 ans," *Situations* X (Paris, 1976); trans. by Paul Auster and Lydia Davis, "Self-Portrait at Seventy," *Life/Situations: Essays Written and Spoken* (New York, 1977). This interview was originally published in 1975 by *Le Nouvel Observateur* and in the United States by the *New York Review of Books.*

31. "Pouvoir et liberté: actualité de Sartre," *Libération,* January 6, 1977, 10–11.

32. *Nick's Movie (Slow Boat to China)* (1980), film by Nicolas Ray and Wim Wenders. Begun under co-direction, the film was finished by Wenders after Nick Ray's death.

19

SIMONE DE BEAUVOIR'S *ADIEUX:*
A FUNERAL RITE AND
A LITERARY CHALLENGE

Geneviève Idt

I have buried myself in
the funeral monuments which
mark my career.
— Simone de Beauvoir,
Old Age

"Adieux: A Farewell to Sartre, a fine title, but one which immediately gives off the scent of parody."[1] This long-awaited account of the death of a great man by his privileged witness, herself a professional writer, is incongruous, on the fringe of propriety and good style, and, in some people's opinion, devoid of benevolence, beneficence, and even truth; it is out of place because of its ambiguous status, ambivalent motivations, and trivial style.

This "American-style trampling underfoot"[2] of the literary and social proprieties gave rise in Europe to extreme and contradictory opinions regarding the timeliness of its publication, the purity of its author's intentions, and the value of its style. Simone de Beauvoir, rightly or wrongly, according to each reader's morality and taste, artlessly wrote unspeakable things. "A painful exhibition" (*L'Echo du Centre*) or a testimony "of great modesty in its frankness" (*Etudes*), this book "is one

363

of the most beautiful love stories we can read today" (*V.S.D.*), "terse and bare, extraordinarily tender" (*Le Matin*). Or else Beauvoir, "an English nurse with mechanical gestures" (*Magazine Littéraire*), is "settling an obscure account with her lifelong companion" (*Le Point*), for "how could so much venom enter the soul of a devotee?" (*L'Echo du Centre*). As for her style, seen by all as "neutral" and "transparent," either she's a "tireless writing machine, who hammers everything flat, who leaves *nothing* between the lists of petitions and the medical crises" (*Commentaires*), or else she attains "the somber, deeply moving greatness of works in the modern literary style of a Blanchot" (*Franc-Tireur*).

No doubt one can always find such contradictions in a press file. But this ambiguous text lends itself more than most to tendentious interpretations, prejudices, and projections of fantasms. Thus "Esculape," in *Médicine et Hygiène,* sees in this account "the model of what you're not allowed to do when you're a doctor."[3] *Le Nouveau F. Magazine* considers the book exemplary because it describes "what so many couples live through and nobody ever talks about: the descent of the husband toward death and the burden this imposes on his companion."[4] According to Michel Crouzet in *Commentaires,* the book betrays "the exhaustion of the existentialist age and school" and "the decline of intelligence in France," and the image of an absent, empty, disembodied, indifferent Sartre hides, for the edification of the masses, "the alarming idol of totalitarianism, the Moloch of the cold monster of the deified state."[5]

There is only one constant note in this cacophony: almost all the critics express unease and uncertainty about the meaning and value of a work that is both ordinary and unexpected. "Embarrassing but moving" (*Le Journal de Genève*), "this strange book" (*Magazine Littéraire*) "embarrasses and does not convince" (*Commentaires*). "This book filled with tenderness and horror leaves us highly embarrassed. . . . We read it uneasily, but a certain fascination is at work, adding further to our unease" (*Bulletin Critique du Livre Français*); "unease takes a permanent hold of us and provokes a vague uncertainty about what genre the book belongs to" (*Construire*), for it is "a book that is situated beyond any literary or moral judgment" (*Figaro-Magazine*). "The ambiguity regarding Simone de Beauvoir's real intentions and the unease we feel when reading her book . . . spring from a lack of art which is almost derisory. This zero degree of writing . . . authorizes the most discrediting interpretations" (*L'Echo du Centre*), "a misunderstanding threatens this book" (*Le Monde*), "this meticulous report on the end of a dear friend is in danger of being misused" (*La Croix*).

Why this unease, this uncertainty, this vague, unexpected scandal?

The book is exceptional for the notoriety of its author and the fame of its hero, for the circumstances of its publication (eighteen months after Sartre's death, in the middle of the quarrel over a great man's intellectual estate, and in the middle of all the rumors about the star's supposedly mysterious end), and yet it obeys the rule governing even the plainest accounts of the most obscure lives: don't tell us about your life; answer the way we tell you to. If questioned by several different authorities at once, one gives only misplaced answers. This text is at the same time the expected solemn funeral oration for a national celebrity and the latest work by an author who debunks myths. However, the literary challenge of speaking the unspeakable, of lifting the modern taboo on old age and death, is allowed these days in diaries, sociological surveys, novels of love or hatred, and short stories of the fantastic; in a funeral oration it creates a scandal. Conversely, the recapitulation of information, the soothing commonplaces, and the edifying scenes imposed by the style of funeral orations nowadays devalue a literary work. We have here both a gesture of language subject to the rules of polite society and a literary text regulated by an aesthetic code; a bizarre and even kitschy thing, constructed at every level of its elaboration—enunciation, referential content, rhetorical code—according to the incompatible models of the funeral rite and the literary achievement.

A Tomb for Jean-Paul Sartre

"Nothing obliged Simone de Beauvoir to tell in one of her ordinary books something which, for her, is intimate and serious. Unfortunately she took that risk."[6] Why did she, when she has so often been blamed for it? Out of "vengeance" according to Pascal Brüchner,[7] out of "resentment" according to Yves Laplance.[8] Perhaps, but nothing in the text itself confirms these projective judgments. Because "Simone and Jean-Paul were always relentless to debunk," says *Le Journal de Genève*.[9] Because "she always defended an extremist idea of truth," according to Cella Minart.[10] Perhaps, but Beauvoir never swore to tell everything. According to the autobiographical pact which is reaffirmed in her narratives, she has always reserved the right to omit things, and she does.[11]

Besides a liking for risk, *The Prime of Life* suggests two more likely motivations. One has to do with why Beauvoir writes—"there are times that are so dark that the only hope left is the cry one would like to utter"[12]—and the use of language in mourning rites, whether personal or public. "How convenient a good traditional funeral is! The dead person disappears into the grave and his death goes with him; you throw earth on it, you turn around, you're quits," Beauvoir wrote twenty years before.[13] No doubt, every "good traditional funeral" has to have a funeral oration; for Beauvoir, in any case, the work of mourning is completed in and by writing, and her work is studded with accounts of deaths[14] which arm the survivor against the return of the ghosts. Against the most worrying ghost of all, one poorly buried, with no speeches or music,[15] dread had to be warded off by an especially solemn rite, the fantastic had to be repressed by a pronounced degree of hieraticism, a life had to be finished off and reconstructed into a success story.

The other motivation has to do with the declared aim of all her autobiographical work, founded as this is on the drawbacks of notoriety: she wished to nip rumors in the bud, to be a witness in the full sense of the word, in an ongoing trial before public opinion: "one of my intentions is to dissipate misunderstandings";[16] "I wrote these memoirs largely to restore the truth."[17] Since Sartre's death, Olivier Todd and Georges Michel had published their testimony, and the public was wondering about the meaning of Sartre's interviews with Benny Lévy in *Le Nouvel Observateur,* which were sometimes interpreted as a recantation and a conversion to a sort of mysticism. *Adieux* is a written reply to these rumors; it was logical, given her work, that Beauvoir would give her version of the facts.

Funeral Rites

This book, which the publisher has not yet classified in any genre, contains the verbal apparatus of a funeral ceremony. Performative and narrative at the same time, it accomplishes a rite and recapitulates in memoriam a series of celebrations.

The title, dedication, preface, and dust jacket—whose density is in marked contrast with the free-flowing style of the narrative—are enough to perform the ritual office, to utter the sacramental words, to call on posterity as a witness. The title, universally admired, takes on a large part of this task, even if it shows in its polysemy the ambiguity of a text with two authors and several functions. As the spokesperson of the deceased, the narrator has borrowed the expression from a joke made by her character, reporting it twice, in the novelistic mode in her story and in the symbolic mode on the dust jacket. The novelistic version hides the meaning under insignificance. It locates the episode in a sequence of events dated June 1971: "He was going to spend three weeks with Arlette and two with Wanda, while I would be traveling with Sylvie." A brief allusive décor is provided: "I had lunch with him at La Coupole, where Sylvie was to pick me up at four o'clock." A behaviorist-style scene unfolds, with no authorial comment, in which the characters communicate by mimicry or gesture, and which at the end is left hanging in silence, with a remark put off until the publication of the account: "I stood up three minutes early. He gave an undefinable smile and said, 'So, it's the farewell ceremony!' I touched him on the shoulder without answering." The retrospective analysis that follows leaves the hero with all his mystery, outlining the novelistic structure of the misunderstanding and the missed opportunity: "The smile, the remark, haunted me for a long time. I gave the word *farewell* the ultimate meaning it took on a few years later, when I was the only one who said it."

The dust jacket omits this novelistic scene setting and brings out the symbolic meaning of the episode, and of the title and the whole story: " 'So, it's the farewell ceremony?' Sartre said to me, as we were saying good-bye for a month, early one summer. I felt the meaning those words would take on one day. The ceremony lasted ten years: these are the ten years I tell about in this book."

That sums up the narrative content of the book: Sartre's successive farewells to sight, to writing, to drinking and smoking, to walking and independence, the character's farewells to the narrator, with the steady distancing of the couple from each other that the text suggests. But the converse, the narrator's farewell to her character, takes place in the preface, in a surprising metalinguistic commentary. The author stresses the transformation of her addressee into an object, an in-itself. "[This book] is completely for you and doesn't concern you. . . . This 'you' I use is an illusion, a rhetorical artifice. Nobody hears it; I'm not talking to anybody."

It is a death certificate based on the analyses of *Being and Nothingness*. In fact, it is an even more solemn document than that. The first sentence, which few people read literally, uses a euphemism but presupposes a terrible commitment for a writer and a feminist: "This is the first of my books—*and no doubt the only one*—that you won't have read before it's printed."[18] This solemn remark, although uttered in passing, at the speed of Beauvoirian speech, is a farewell to writing.[19] It opens a new career free of the need for an imprimatur and immediately closes it, it refuses to literarily survive the privileged addressee, it is a symbolic suicide like that of an Indian widow. After *A Very Easy Death*, the author had already felt disgusted with writing: "literature seemed useless to me; I had switched over to the side of death and its silence."[20] But she hadn't solemnly sworn a vow of silence. For whom are the flowers

367

on the tombs? The dedication and the preface, which are redundant on this point, develop this commonplace of philosophical reflection.[21] "In fact I'm talking to Sartre's friends," the preface declares. The dedication, set out like an epitaph—

> To those who loved Sartre
> who love him
> who will love him

—has the brief poetic form[22] of occasional writing, it designates an anonymous collective public which may grow to universality in time and space.

It is a *captatio benevolentiae* addressed to posterity, perhaps justifying, insofar as the text and Beauvoir's whole work confirm it, the doubt expressed by Arlette Elkaïm-Sartre in her open letter to the author: "Does your fierce concern for posterity agree with what Sartre saw in it?"[23]

It doesn't, of course. Beauvoir points this out herself in *Adieux,* when she analyzes Sartre's attachment for Pierre Victor (Benny Lévy):

> Sartre had always lived with his eyes fixed on the future; he couldn't live any other way. Limited to the present, he felt he was dead. . . . He fell back on an artificial substitute: Victor, a militant and a philosopher, would create the "new intellectual" that Sartre dreamed of and would have helped bring into existence. To have doubts about Victor was to give up that living extension of himself, which was more important for him than the votes of posterity. (151)

This baroque intuition of change, of the rebirth of ideas and beings in a new form,[24] is opposed in Beauvoir by a classical liking for traces and monuments. One believed in the virtue of forgetting, the other in the virtue of faithfulness, of Kierkegaardian "repetition."[25] For Sartre the past does not exist,[26] whereas it "inhabits," "besieges," and "delights" Beauvoir.[27] Among the primitive beliefs from which fantasms sometimes take their shape, one preferred the myth of the Zârs and the Loas, of the reincarnation of the ancestor in the newborn baby; the other believed in the eternal survival of an essential image: "Certain primitive peoples imagine that after their death they will forever remain as they were at the moment they died. . . . I act as if my existence were to continue beyond the grave as I succeeded in my last years in *reconquering* it."[28]

Hence Beauvoir's constant concern to "recuperate" a life, hers or another's, to achieve a "totalization" for posterity, to balance the books:

"To revive forgotten memories, reread, review, to complete incomplete knowledge, fill in gaps, cast light on obscure points, gather together what is scattered"; in other words, to *complete,* in every sense of the word, to end the work and finish the dying person off—such, for the author, was the purpose of her last work that had an unambiguously autobiographical title, *Force of Circumstance.*[29] It is likewise what she wanted to do for Sartre in her conversations with him in 1974[30] and in *Adieux:* to recapitulate, to dress the dead man.

This is certainly not a Sartrean thing to do, for Sartre, like his favorite authors, hated to conclude and only liked mornings. *Recapitulation*—in the premonitory short story "The Room," this "long whitish" word, slipping out of the hero's mouth against his will, warns his wife of the onset of dementia praecox.[31] Yet *Adieux,* the annals of an illustrious old age, contains, although in a fragmentary way, a brief but thorough retrospective of a public life, a chronology. The author summarizes well-known commemorative works by Sartre's friends: the film *Sartre by Himself* and the interview with Michel Contat on Sartre's seventieth birthday. It tells of the success of his lectures and the revivals of his plays, it lists the receptions in his honor, the reissue of his works in prestigious editions, the books and magazine issues and the photo album put out in homage to him, everything that constitutes the comeback of a forgotten star—"A funeral comeback," said the party concerned, laughing. Even the listing of manifestos and appeals that Sartre signed, which his political adversaries have made fun of (an easy target),[32] serves the twin purposes of an obituary: to inform and to honor. Simply by their accumulation, these solicited signatures seem less like deliberate policy than acts of politeness and further proofs of fame.

A "Good Death" for an Atheist

To finish the deceased off properly but also to edify and console the survivors—such is the role of the funeral oration, which always tends toward hagiography. *Adieux,* likewise, contains a success story, memorable and imitable, the exemplary happy end of a man, of a couple, and of an autobiography. In a society where a man's last moments still decide his eternal fate,[33] the public was waiting for Sartre to reach old age and death, watching for or fearing a recantation or a weakness, or dreaming of a pathos-laden cliché-ridden romantic end.[34] *Adieux* responds partially to that expectation by presenting Sartre's death as logical, serene, and reassuring.

Sartre's illness is logically presented here as the necessary outcome of

369

a freely chosen conduct: "The drama of his last years is the consequence of his whole life. . . . Sartre experienced the decline and death that his life called for" (133). What is affirmed here is the identity of a man and his thought until the last moments: "he had grown old, to be sure, but he was really himself" (136). The last chapter of the 1974 interviews that follow *Adieux* indeed confirms Sartre's fidelity to his previous choices and invalidates the recantation that some people, including Beauvoir herself, thought they saw in his interviews with Benny Lévy. The book ends with a selection of his 1974 remarks which constitute a profession of atheism[35] on the lines of *All Said and Done*. On several occasions the narrator recalls Sartre's adherence to his life and work: "he was sufficiently satisfied with his past to accept the present serenely" (110); "he had done what he had to do and he was pleased with it" (138). An end that is in accordance with the life is thus a "happy ending." Playing for Sartre the part that Joinville played for Saint Louis, Beauvoir gives manifold proofs of Sartrean wisdom or sainthood, composed of virtues as much Christian as Socratic—modesty, patience, discretion:

> I was astounded by his good humor, his patience, his concern not to seem a burden; he never complained about his loss of sight. (76)

> He had always modestly put up with whatever happened to him. He didn't want to bore others with his worries . . . the idea of death was familiar to him. He accepted its coming without fuss. (156)

And as if this testimony could be suspected of bias, the narrator quotes others: "Courchay was amazed by Sartre's good humor and cheerfulness" (147); "he was resigned, Housset [the doctor] said to me; or, rather, he corrected himself, confident" (156). Under these commonplace and almost naïve expressions, the aging Sartre appears as the hero of a conventional novel.

Conventional images, *des images d'Epinal*,[36] also illustrate the couple's happy end. "There is one definite success in my life: my relationship with Sartre," says the first sentence of the epilogue to *Force of Circumstance*. Eighteen years later, the last sentence of *Adieux* confirms this success, but in a more ambiguous and less triumphal form: "His death separates us. My death won't reunite us. That's how it is; but it's wonderful enough that our lives were in harmony so long." The body of the narration, however, contains an attenuation of anything that could tarnish that success; it acquits the narrator on two counts. The first fault is confessed at the end of the book—"Shouldn't I have warned Sartre that he was about to die?"—and immediately forgiven—"His case was

370

unclear . . . like him, I was hovering between hope and despair. By keeping silent I kept us together" (159). The second fault is only presupposed. After the dissension caused by the publication in *Le Nouvel Observateur* of the interviews with Benny Lévy, a medical authority had to clear Sartre's entourage of responsibility in his illness: "Housset assured me that the upset he had suffered had in no way affected his health" (156). Finally, the author tells of the conflict caused by the quarrel with Pierre Victor (Benny Lévy): "I was sorry that a part of Sartre's life was henceforth closed to me" (141).

But by way of compensation she publishes an intimate anthology of affectionate remarks: proofs of good feelings (33), memories of their first meetings (34), compliments (81), signs that he preferred her (91). One of them has a more precise social function. It's a "funny remark" that slipped past the ideological control of its utterer and legitimates the narrator's testimony: "One morning, as I was giving him his medicine, he told me 'You're a good wife' " (86).

At the end of the book, these little unpretentious acts, these "little flowers" of Sartre's, give way to two short hieratic scenes, figurative and highly stereotyped like funeral emblems and bas-reliefs. Twenty years before, it had been the author's most heartfelt desire that "people will repeat in silence certain words that I had linked together."[37] Since then Beauvoir has worked on other modes of expression. She took part in the two biographical films about Sartre and herself and in the TV shows about contemporary France, and she wrote the commentary for the photo album put together by Liliane Siegel. It is as if she had traded words in for simple "beautiful images." The last of these is surprisingly romantic and has struck some people as affected. Yet it picks up a motif present in the work of both writers, although the text does not point out this connection of the work with the life or with its staging. For Hilda says to Göetz in *The Devil and the Good Lord*, "If you die, I will lie down beside you . . . you will rot in my arms and I will love you as rotten meat." And Beauvoir writes in *The Prime of Life*, "Even if we were to lie corpse beside corpse, it was only an illusion: between nothing and nothing there is no link." The transformation of this cultural and personal stereotype in *Adieux* is striking in the terseness of its style and the polysemy of the action. It happens during the wake: "At one point I asked to be left alone with Sartre, and I wanted to lie beside him under the sheet. A nurse stopped me: 'No. Be careful. Gangrene.' Then I understood what his bedsores really were. I lay down on top of the sheet and I slept for a while" (157).

The best commentary on this text could be found in *Nausea*, in the

371

description of the "privileged situations" that Anny is looking for and that she describes as "those they used to show in engravings": "The drawing was crude [*fruste*]. . . . But it was full of grandeur. . . . They were situations that had a really rare and precious quality, they had style. . . . You had only to be in a dead person's room; since death was a privileged situation, something emanated from it and was communicated to all the people present. A kind of grandeur."[38]

Fruste means more than crude; it is used of a medallion or a faulty sculpture worn away by time. The scene in *Adieux,* barely sketched out in a few simple sentences, owes its particular "style" and its "kind of grandeur" to its terseness and to the cultural references one can see in it; in the words of Camus's *The Stranger,* it is an image of recumbent statues on tombs, turned to stone while still alive, where the thickness of a sheet separates Tristan from Isolde and sleep from death. Much earlier in Beauvoir's text, another image, very different in tone but similar in technique, illustrates the other great moment of Sartre's decline, namely, the beginning of his years of blindness in 1973. It happens in Venice. Sartre is leaving for the airport: "Standing in the boat, he waved to us, smiling with that kindly smile which rarely left his lips" (73). Reduced to a direction in a movie script, this scene from a "Death in Venice" derives its meaning from its allusions to literature and movies. But the ceremony has moved from the movies to sculpture; it ends as a tomb figure.

A Literary Challenge

Tombs are empty, they bear traces only of their sculptor. *Adieux,* therefore, disappointed those who were looking for Sartre and found only Beauvoir. And yet the preface could have warned them, for it draws the attention back to the narrator: "I have told [his last years] as I lived them. I have talked a bit about myself, since the witness is part of the testimony, but I have done so as little as possible."

This wish to be discreet merely stresses the presence in the text of its signatory, the dominant role she plays in the action, the fact that we have only her narrative perspective, the autobiographical aim of an account intended, like the previous ones, to suggest "the flavor of a life,"[39] hers, without actually revealing it: "As I noted in reply to some friends who asked me how I was taking things: 'You can't say it, you can't write it, you can't think it; you live it, that's all.' "

To quote this cliché of private correspondence in a preface is to program a reading between the lines in search of what is suggested, to publicly issue oneself the literary challenge of saying the unsayable. The attempt may have failed, but it was made. This book is an extension of the work of an essayist, novelist, and autobiographer. It has the aim and manner of that work: to lift the taboos on old age and death, to convey the sense of being abandoned, to refuse the consolation of a beautiful style. It is a scandalous breach of the rules of ritual.

"Pathography" of an Ordinary Old Age

The customary law of surrounding old age and death with family secrecy was formulated most clearly—ironically enough—by the weekly magazine *Minute,* which condemned Beauvoir's breach of it:

> In ordinary French families which respect tradition, out of modesty and love, people keep quiet about the suffering of those who die. The children, the women, the husband maintain the cover. They see no point in telling the details of the death agony, however long and painful it was. Madame de Beauvoir is not of that race. She is an intellectual, on the fringe of society, and the French heritage nauseates her.[40]

This text of exemplary clarity defines the ritual of the death agony, imposes silence about the reality of such a moment, and shows that behaving differently has a subversive meaning. The medical press formulated the accusation even more precisely, blaming the wife for usurping the doctor's exclusive right to speak of the body and its decay, for violating professional secrecy by stripping away the anonymity of the case study: "We are interested in pathographies, but we do not think that, to understand the actions of a politician, the works of a writer or the reactions of an artist, it is necessary to reveal one by one all the most intimate details."[41]

The literary reviews are of the same opinion. They recall the separation of genres, depict the narrator as an "intern on duty" or an "English nurse with mechanical gestures,"[42] reject her account as nonliterary, as "the horrible report of a decline, recorded with the detachment of a clinician though the eyes of a table companion."[43] At best her work is accepted as a naturalistic imitation of medical discourse, "a slice of death,"[44] an outdated recipe for creating a scandal, or the "proof of a Cathar horror of the body."[45]

Other critics interpret the dominant objectivity of the narrative, and the abundant information of a physiological nature, from a Sartrean philosophical perspective. Although based on notes made day by day during Sartre's lifetime, the whole account was written entirely after his death. In conformity with the analyses of *Being and Nothingness,* it can only adopt an exterior point of view vis-à-vis its object; laying no claim to empathy, it consecrates death, that is to say, "the triumph of the other's point of view over the point of view that *I am myself*."[46] The ontological status of a posthumous account of a life hands over its object to an all-powerful survivor, to an "abuse of the dominant position," to "an ultimate possession,"[47] to a form of "cannibalism," which is exactly what Beauvoir herself blamed in some of her readers who were eager for details about her own old age. In fact the narrator indirectly satisfies this curiosity, turning it aside from her own case toward the loved-and-hated other. Among the symptoms of old age, she gives pride of place to those that reduce the subject to the dependency and passivity of a newborn baby:

> The other is stripped bare and exposed to the public in all his weaknesses and physical wretchedness. . . . Simone de Beauvoir offers us the portrait of a man in his second childhood, an account of a humiliating relationship in which the old man is treated exactly like a child or an idiot, supervised, scrutinized, cajoled, humiliated, reduced to the status of an object looked at by the victorious Other.[48]

The model underlying these criticisms is the fabulous image of Madame Flaubert in *The Family Idiot:* "a hardworking unemotional mother," unloving but efficiently caring, "an excellent mother but not a delightful one: punctual, bustling, skillful, no more than that," spying every minute on the organism of a *moriturus*, observing without tenderness.

A different light, however, is shed on the medical communiqués and naturalistic episodes of *Adieux* by Beauvoir's other works. In this continuation of her autobiographical corpus, the chronicler of the couple continues to carry out her duty of informing us about two twentieth-century celebrities. Nothing in this text modifies the autobiographical pact proposed in *The Prime of Life* and its oath of truth: "In this book I have agreed to omit things, but never to lie. My memory has probably let me down on little details, but the slight errors the reader may notice certainly don't compromise the truth of the whole."[49]

"I have told [Sartre's last years] as I lived them"—we have here the declaration of a witness hiding behind the inevitable subjectivity of her testimony. It is for future historians to concern themselves with objectivity, comparing this testimony with others so as to rectify errors and omissions, working on this document.

It is from this perspective that the diagnoses of Sartre's doctors are summarized or cited; they don't shed light on the work of the writer, but the narrator waited for them and heard them with anguish. They answer the questions presumably asked by the unknown faithful and the ordinary curiosity of the public about the health of those who rule them or impress them, and they put an end to gossip. As for the concrete signs of "the irreversible degradation of old age"—a stain on an armchair, lips soiled with food, a little plastic bag full of urine—they have the same purpose as the essay on *Old Age,* namely, "to describe *truthfully* the condition of these pariahs" called old people, "to break the conspiracy of silence" around them, "to reveal the shameful secret" of old age and the death agony.[50]

It doesn't matter if this information, pushing back the borders of private life,[51] desacralizes the writer—in fact, so much the better. Already in *The Prime of Life* Beauvoir had analyzed the debunking of myths achieved by her autobiographical writings: "The public consecrates [writers] even though it knows very well that they are ordinary people, and it resents them for this contradiction; it uses every sign of their humanity as evidence against them. . . . If it discovers that you're not superhuman, it classifies you as subhuman, a monster."[52]

To continue this debunking in *Adieux* is to knowingly run the risk of an even worse sacrilege; it is a provocation. To show, in the middle of a funeral oration, the great man's undocile body slobbering and losing control of itself like a child's is to solemnly reject all official portraits and to claim to belong to the common human condition—which is not to contradict the image of the "good death," for there is no sainthood without humanity: "The life, coma, and death of Sartre. In other words, the life, coma, and death of anybody."[53]

Sartre's singular case also serves as experimental verification of the hypotheses of the essay on *Old Age.* It verifies the constants determined in the second and most phenomenological part, on "being-in-the-world": the confusion between old age and illness, indifference, resignation, old people's lack of curiosity, their taking refuge in habit, their moroseness, their incapability of invention, their harrowing feeling of physical, financial, and emotional insecurity:

> He had kept his intelligence, he commented on our reading and discussed it. But he dropped conversations pretty quickly, he asked no questions, he offered no ideas. He was not interested in much, on any level. By way of compensation, he stuck to routines and habits, faithful to them on principle, replacing true taste by obstinate fidelity. (92)

Such descriptions, which simulate the scientific objectivity respected in *Old Age* and reduce the case observed to the rule of degradation, are

375

found here side by side with the opposite, with the lyrical evocation of the vitality of an individual who is privileged by his social class, his intellectual activity, and his literary and political vocation: "He liked to keep moving and informed. . . . If, as some people say, old age is loss of curiosity, he wasn't old at all" (139).[54]

These apparent contradictions are resolved in the reformist and voluntarist conclusion of *Old Age:* "If old age is not to be a derisory parody of our existence hitherto, there is only one solution, namely, to go on pursuing the goals which give our life a meaning: devotion to individuals, collectivities and causes, and social, political, intellectual, creative work."[55]

Sartre's end thus appears as the latest of "some examples of old age," all famous ones, collected in Chapter VIII of this historical and sociological study, in a brief moralizing imitation of Plutarch. Parallel with the "childhood of a famous man" told in *The Words*, Beauvoir realizes one last time one of the oldest Sartrean fantasies, recalled in the *Interviews:*[56] the transformation of his own life into an intelligible, memorable, imitable model, its integration into the pantheon of a biographical series.[57]

More secretly, *Adieux* keeps another kind of faith with Sartre, one that the narrator doesn't talk about. And yet in the 1974 *Interviews* she seems to have been asking for guidelines on how to narrate her companion's old age:

> BEAUVOIR: In the course of sixty years, do you think there has been a widening as well as a narrowing? How do you see these two movements in detail?
> SARTRE: I would describe my life, toward the end, as a series of parallel straight lines; they would be my knowledge, my actions, the movements I have belonged to . . . and below that I would draw as a dotted line my real life moment by moment, the illnesses that can rot my guts. . . . It's my death, but I draw that as a dotted line.
>
> (537–39)

No doubt, one can blame the narrator for having drawn the continuous line of life too lightly and the dotted line of death too heavily. But by describing in turn the hero's activities, his reading, his travels, his meetings, his intellectual undertakings, his political actions, his openness to the universal and the future, and on the other hand his passivity, his abandonment to the degradation and reduction of his self—by integrating pathography into biography—she drew the portrait as suggested by the late Sartre.

Posthumous Annals

"If we approach him in his subjectivity, the old man is not a good hero for a novel; he's done with, fixed, expecting nothing, hoping for nothing; for him the die is cast, death lives in him already."[58] This is why, according to Beauvoir, literature gives old men only a minor role and draws only thumbnail sketches of them. In 1967 her *Age of Discretion* already tried to fill in this gap. That short story ended with the heroine questioning her future: "Don't look too far ahead. In the distance were the horrors of death and the *farewells* [*les adieux*]. . . . Will I manage not to look toward those horizons? Or will I learn to see them *without dread?*"[59]

Adieux is the novel of the final overcoming of this dread, and it has the narrative structures, themes, and rhythm suitable for that genre. The novelistic dread is born of the sight of an inevitable but skillfully postponed transformation.

This type of narrative shows us a fascination: the subject of enunciation contemplates the horror being experienced by somebody else, without yet experiencing it herself. To put this structure into *Adieux,* the narrator has only to draw in her feelings as a dotted line, to scatter the paradigm of fear throughout the text, in a brief stereotyped form: "At the end of September fear suddenly gripped me" (21); "I was distraught" (59); "I was torn apart, it's awful to watch a hope die" (88); "my vague anguish gave way to total despair" (131). Then toward the end she displays the usual paradoxical remission of fear—"I was a bit worried for the future"—before concretely describing a vision of horror (for its own sake, for she didn't see it): "these 'bedsores' were frightening to see, big violet and red blotches" (155). But the ultimate horror, the sight of the consciousness of the suffering subject, is avoided.

The fear of other people's fear, which dominates the text, implies that the hero's subjectivity remains problematic nearly until the end. The narrator interprets it through her behavior and her words, modifying it with numerous modal verbs: "I didn't really know what he thought of the state he was in" (77); "he seemed almost resigned to his half-blindness" (95); "he said he was completely *happy*. . . . But what he felt inwardly nobody could have said, not even him" (97–98). When the account reaches 1975, however, the modal verbs become less frequent: "in fact he was quite joyful," "Sartre was delighted," "very happy with this visit." And she disappears behind the usual reassuring account of a death agony: "I understood that he knew he was dying and wasn't upset by it" (155); "he certainly felt death coming, but without anguish" (156).

377

In this respect the text conforms first to one of the two incompatible narrative models and then to the other one. It begins in the novelistic mode of doubt and anguish and the mystery of the other person, and it ends in the serenity of the funeral oration.

The sight that fascinates the narrator is the gradual transformation of the familiar into something radically different. In 1971, at sixty-six, "he already seemed to be on the other side of life" (34). Portraits of Sartre as something unrecognizable stud the narration at each reunion: "as always when I saw him after an absence, he looked bad to me: his face was puffy, there was something numb and clumsy in his gestures" (68); "when I saw Sartre again, one morning in the hallway of his hotel, I hardly recognized him because . . . of a thick white foam all over his chin" (96). Such images are fantastic in the Sartrean sense of the word. They are so, first, because in them the mind seems to have "fallen into slavery and matter impregnates and coarsens it."[60] In a very Sartrean metaphor, death congeals him: "hunched up, dull, dozing . . . distant, a bit sleepy, almost gloomy, with a smile of kindliness toward everybody congealed on his lips" (69). She reifies him alive: "he felt he was an object unrelated to people" (64). Second, "one doesn't just leave room for the fantastic," according to Sartre; "either it doesn't exist, or it covers the whole universe."[61] Changed into stone, the hero "freezes the bones" of his entourage, "petrifies" it (32, 87), contaminating the whole universe: "it seemed to me that the world was toppling, toppling over forever into death" (62). To be sure, these are clichés, but their relation to the Sartrean themes of petrification reactualizes them. The traditional fantastic theme of the living dead is broached by the hero himself first, in a "joking" mode—"I don't know if you're kissing *a bit of tomb* or a live man" (87); "have you entered the house of the dead?" (97)—or in a delirious mode, still marked with a most Sartrean black humor: "you're dead too, my dear. How did it feel to be incinerated?" (153).

The whole narration leads to this delirium at the speed of dread; "a dark foreboding" (21) comes true. In *All Said and Done*, Beauvoir had given up chronological order to "embrace as a whole that strange object called a life," especially because she had lost the feeling of progressing toward a goal and profoundly changing.[62] In *Adieux*, however, living is again "an undertaking with a clear direction," albeit directed toward unhappiness. The narrator rediscovers the rapture of irreversibility: "What counts above all in my life is that time passes; I grow old, the world changes, my relationship with it varies; to show the transformations, the maturing, the irreversible degradations of others and myself, nothing is more important to me."[63]

Even if the kind of narration she adopts no longer satisfies her because it breaks time up into "strings of congealed moments,"[64] life recovers its intensity in the alternation of hope and anguish. A future becomes visible in the form of a reprieve, whose duration is the subject of frequent, almost playful conversations: "As I was speaking of Picasso, who had died at ninety-one, I said, 'It's a good age; that would give you another twenty-four years to live—twenty-four years isn't long' " (68). The game only stops toward the end, in her account of 1977, when a doctor's "death sentence" reveals its cruelty: "a few more years to live; the expression suddenly took on a tragic meaning for me" (131, 134). The certainty of the outcome and the uncertainty of the length of the wait define the period of dread and tragedy.

"Destroy All These Lying Beauties"

In *All Said and Done,* Beauvoir tried to spell out her relationship with literary writing; she didn't claim to be creating a work of art, yet she did not give up all aesthetic concerns: "why should the intention of giving testimony rule out happy turns of phrase?"[65] The misunderstanding she was trying to dispel recurs in the critical reviews of *Adieux.* Some say the text is "grave and beautiful like its title";[66] "its icy, tense, transparent, clinical style" has a "somber and overwhelming grandeur."[67] For others it is a "report," "a crazy clumsy document" written "with a lack of art which is almost derisory,"[68] and it doesn't belong to literature but to journalism: "Simone is certainly one of our best journalists, but she's no writer."[69] The range of possible tastes and aesthetic values is not enough to explain this divergence among critics. Beauvoir's writing in *Adieux* conforms to two different stylistic models, unequally represented: the classical rhetoric of the formal speech and the hyperrealism of nonsignificance.

Sporadically, but at the key points of the text—in the title, the preface, the conclusion, and the synthesizing commentaries which bring out the meaning of events—"happy turns of phrase" draw on the poetic function of language and, with austere moderation, use its rhetorical resources. For example, there is the chiasmus and the emphatic repetition of the negative in the preface—"nobody hears it; I'm not talking to anybody"—and the line that symmetrically corresponds to this in the conclusion: "his death separates us. My death won't reunite us." And there is the expressive repetition of the emotion contained in the scene of the last kiss: "Then he pursed his lips toward me. I kissed his lips, his cheek" (155). These are but slight traces of aestheticism and funeral service eloquence, reduced to the bare essential signs of ceremony, censored down to their simplest expression. The writer in mourning blue-pencils the "lying beauties" of style.[70]

On the other hand, a straitjacket of almost raw, stereotyped, direct, hyperrealist style wraps around the narration as a guarantee of authenticity. "I was never a virtuoso of style,"[71]Beauvoir readily admits. Not that this is a raw document, for her notes have been rewritten, and she has not done a slapdash job. But her efforts have been devoted not to games with signifiers and cultural connotations but to referential transparency, to the insatiable multiplication of "reality effects."

The first issue of Les Temps Modernes, in its column called "Vies" ("Lives"), which was intended to show "the mutual involvement of the collective and the individual" and to let people speak who don't get to, contained the "Life of a Disaster Victim." A straightforward third-person account whose heroine, author, and transcriber are unknown, in a naïve, stilted, dull historian's style, factual and pathetic, it bears surprising resemblances to Adieux. Like an ordinary person, making no attempt to ward off banality, Beauvoir transcribes the congealed syntagms of everyday speech, though not marking them as being oral: "he had his ups and downs"; "he learned to live with his illness"; "he was not getting better, but he was not getting worse either"; "we spent some very lively evenings together"; "he enjoyed the delicious dinner"; "the weather was fine, Sartre was happy to be back in the south of France, he was reading detective novels"—and one could continue this list of platitudes, as indeed Michel Crouzet unkindly does.[72] But the list would read less like Delly, Zénaïde Fleuriot, and Max du Veuzit than like postcards or conversations among acquaintances, everybody's language, in its raw state. Adieux is a hagiography in a popular style. Nothing sets this text apart from many other accounts of anonymous lives, except the fact that the hero and the author are famous. But, after all, neither of them laid claim to elitism.

Simple, clear, and didactic, Beauvoir's style in Adieux reveals her two trades. But, unlike Sartre, she cuts out any signs of cultural complicity. The Words and Adieux are two opposed farewells to literature, one "written as well as possible," "stylish," ignoring the body, "trimmed down," polysemic, a closely woven fabric of structural relations in the text and allusions to the context; the other as little "stylized" as possible, with no marks of brilliance, literariness, or culture, ensuring the primacy of the corporeal, as a sign of mourning and universality.

"We will let the facts speak for themselves," said the introductory note to the "Life of a Disaster Victim." Beauvoir subsequently discovered that "the facts don't dictate anything," but in Adieux she gives a wealth of "the sort of details people call trivial" and which constitute the raw material of existence: "Not only is it thanks to them that we feel an age and a person in flesh and blood; but also, by their nonsignificance, they are the touchstone of truth in a true story. They point to nothing but themselves, and the only reason for mentioning them is that they are there."[73]

Thus she justifies the place taken up in the narrative by the tools of daily life—taxis, planes, radios, TV; the hotel rooms, menus, whiskies consumed in the Auberge du Vieux Moulin or the Oustau de Bavière, that entire "personalized Gault-Millau food and travel guide" that Michel Crouzet makes fun of. And one can also see in this the clumsy figure of happiness, the memorandum of privileged moments, and the sign of their fragility: "I have not, like Virginia Woolf, Proust, or Joyce, revived the subtle play of sensations and captured the external world in words. I wasn't trying to."[74]

More austere and Jansenist than ever in its apparent intermittent frivolity, *Adieux,* a social act, a literary text that refuses literature, expresses bareness and denounces the lie of beauty: "All beautiful works were created for privileged people by privileged people . . . they disguise the scandal of naked misery."[75]

Notes

This essay was originally published in French in *Récits de vie: Revue des sciences humaines,* vol. 63, no. 192 (October–December 1983), 15–33.

1. *La Cérémonie des adieux* (Paris, 1981); trans. by Patrick O'Brian, *Adieux: A Farewell to Sartre* (New York, 1984). All references are to the French edition. Quote from *L'Est républicain,* November 28, 1981. Readers should keep in mind the important word *cérémonie,* which has been lost in the published translation of Beauvoir's book.—Trans.]

2. Pierre Daix, in *Le Quotidien de Paris,* December 8, 1981. It is true that, whereas Sartre's work anchors its effects in a classical and strictly French culture, Beauvoir's seem rootless, cultureless, with a (perhaps affected) form of naïveté, brutality, and frankness which stereotypes attribute to the New World.

3. *Médicine et Hygiène* (Geneva), January 20, 1982.

4. *Le Nouveau F. Magazine,* no. 1 (February 1982).

5. Michel Crouzet, "*La Cérémonie des Adieux,* Simone de Beauvoir, mémorialiste," *Commentaires,* no. 16 (Spring 1982). This long study is accurate, insightful, and brilliant, but surprisingly biased. Even as a joke or in a polemic, one cannot without bad faith and excessive honor or simplicity equate Sartre with "the French Left," nor without misusing language identify the leveling effect of a colorless style with social egalitarianism, nor without misreading the texts see Sartrean anarchism as state totalitarianism.

6. Ibid., 93.

7. *Le Point.*

8. *Construire,* February 24, 1982.

9. *Le Journal de Genève,* February 3, 1982.

10. *La Croix,* January 15, 1982.

11. *La Force de l'âge (The Prime of Life),* (Paris, 1960 [folio]), I, 10: "I must warn readers that I don't intend to tell them *everything.*" [All quotations are translated from the original French. The titles used in the text are from the published English versions. The pagination in the citations is that of the French version used by G. Idt.—Trans.]

12. *La Force des choses (The Force of Circumstances)* (Paris, 1963 [Folio]), II, p. 498.

13. *La Force de l'âge.*

14. A whole list of them is given in *Tout compte fait:* the shattering deaths of Zaza, Dullin, and her mother; of Evelyne, the only one Beauvoir didn't want to talk about; of Camille, Lise, Mme Mancy, and Mme Lemaire, which did not affect her but which she does talk about; and of famous people in *Old Age.*

15. "I told myself that it was exactly the funeral Sartre wanted and that he wouldn't know," writes Beauvoir about that ceremony. Such a banal remark becomes specific and laden with emotion if it refers to Sartre's unpublished prayer "Epiméthée" or "I Will Have a Fine Funeral," whose hero is invisibly present at his own funeral; it was one of Sartre's fantasies and recurs in *Saint Genet.* But that doesn't mean that this ceremony was as the survivor would have wished. In any case, she hardly experienced the event, being semiconscious and passive. A book was therefore needed to restore the verbal dimension of the missing ritual.

16. *La Force des choses* I, 8.

17. Ibid. II, 496.

18. [Author's italics.—Trans.]

19. This doesn't prejudge the future of Beauvoir as a writer; one can break a promise. The adverb *no doubt* attenuates the firmness of the commitment and leaves open the possibility of a return to writing.

20. *Tout compte fait (All Said and Done),* (Paris, 1972 [folio]), 187.

21. This famous dissertation subject is popularly believed to have been assigned by Alain.

22. It lays out the paradigm of tense in the syntagm, repeats in an incantatory redundancy the same verb of feeling, is symmetrically laid out, and leaves pauses for reading sotto voce.

23. *Libération,* December 3, 1981. The disagreement between Arlette Elkaïm-Sartre and Beauvoir can be interpreted as the rivalry of two sorts of legitimacy: daughterhood by belated but legal adoption, authorizing the daughter to bear the father's name, and a half-century-old relationship, famous but with no variety, and not simply love or friendship. But beyond this apparent rivalry of situation and emotional interest, which the media played up, the misunderstanding springs, if we judge solely by the work of the one person and the published statements of the other, from two opposite perceptions of time, finiteness, and death, which cannot be explained by their difference in age alone.

24. It is a feeling close to a certain conception of fatherhood. But Sartre would not recognize that, since he sees fatherhood as a matter of authority and inheritance, that is, of possessions.

25. This is the intentional theme of *The Mandarins:* "to really possess something, you have to have lost it and found it again." *La Force des choses* I, 369.

26. See the 1974 interviews, *Cérémonie des adieux,* 518.

27. *Tout compte fait,* 49–50.

28. Ibid., 60.

29. As early as 1963 she wrote: "I have lived poised toward the future and now I *recapitulate myself,* in the past." *La Force des choses* II, 504.

30. Sartre was not always obviously eager to join in this activity. See the beginning of the interviews in *Cérémonie des adieux,* which may be taken either as a proof that old men become indifferent or else as a flat refusal on Sartre's part to live in the past and work on his monument:

> BEAUVOIR: Let's talk about the literary and philosophical side of your work.
> SARTRE: If you like.
> BEAUVOIR: But are you interested in it?
> SARTRE: Yes. Well, not exactly. These days nothing interests me. But I was interested in it enough, for many years, that I'm willing to talk about it now. (165)

31. An artist's work often seems premonitory. In Sartre's and Beauvoir's parallel lives, "The Room" announces *Adieux,* although the latter text doesn't say so. The heroine of the short story struggles alone against her companion's irreversible madness, like a "good wife" or an "Agathe"; and she promises herself she will kill him.

32. These allusive lists are useful for those who have followed this sort of political action closely, but they are meaningless to anybody else. Hence the contrasting opinions of Robert Maggiori in *Libération,* December 2, 1981: "we feel . . . that we are watching old newsreels, again rereading headlines in the papers, so intimately was Sartre's life interwoven with the course of events"; and of Michel Crouzet in *Commentaires:* "The real *actions* . . . of these militant chronicles, which are just press clippings, are the lists of signatures, like figures on a balance sheet, which the author smugly adds up."

33. "My religious education was very extensive," Beauvoir wrote in *Tout compte fait* (629). This education left a secularized trace, the tendency to "lock up the absolute in the last moments of a dying person." (*Une Mort très douce* [*A Very East Death*], (Paris, 1964), 95.

34. Sartre's death has long been a literary cliché, in Boris Vian's *L'Ecume des jours,* in Jean-Pierre Enard's *Le Dernier dimanche de Sartre,* but also in *The Words,* whose child hero imagined that he would pass away in his little room "abandoned by everybody, but serene," or be killed by a woman admirer kissing his hand.

35. The construction of this interview reveals Beauvoir's insistence on this point. "Death has never weighed on my life. I want to end this chapter with that fact," Sartre declared (544). But Beauvoir drags the interview out for another fifteen pages: "has the thought of an afterlife never crossed your mind . . . the Christian idea, for example?"

36. Annie Cohen-Solal uses this term in the title of her article on *Adieux* in *Le Matin* November 27, 1981, "Notre image d'Epinal."

37. *La Force des choses* II, 499.

38. *La Nausée* (Paris, 1976 [folio]), 207.

39. This strongly stressed metaphor is used by Sartre to designate the singular aim of achieving a totality (*Situations* VIII, 450), and by Beauvoir to designate the purpose of autobiography. (*Tout Compte fait,* 634).

40. François Brigneau, *Minute,* December 7, 1981.

41. Esculape, *Médicine et Hygiène* (Geneva), January 20, 1982.

42. J. Didier Wolfromm, *Magazine Littéraire,* no. 180 (January 1982).

43. *Le Soir* (Brussels), December 15, 1981.

44. François Nourrissier, *Figaro-Magazine,* December 5, 1981.

45. Crouzet in *Commentaires.*

46. *L'Etre et le néant* (Paris, 1976), 598.

47. Jean Vigneaux, *Pourquoi Pas?* (Brussels), December 17, 1981.

48. Translated from Sandra Menzella-Teroni: "Gli ultimi dieci anni di Sartre espositi al publico: *La Ceremonia dei addii* di Simone de Beauvoir," *Manifesto,* February 28, 1982. This is the only unfavorable article by a woman. The feminine solidarity seen in every other case was overridden here by piety toward Sartre.

49. *La Force des choses* I, 11, n. 1.

50. These diagnoses cannot be taken as certificates of mental incompetence supporting Beauvoir's thesis that Pierre Victor (Benny Lévy) "corrupted" an old man. Until the very end the symptoms of decline alternate with proofs of "indomitable vitality." Beauvoir argues that Sartre was unduly influenced by Victor, yet not because of mental senility but because of a personal emotional and philosophical inability to live without any future other than the approval of an anonymous posterity.

51. Both Sartre and Beauvoir criticize this notion, even if on this point Sartre doesn't match theory to practice.

52. *La Force des choses* II, 493.

53. Yves Laplace, *Construire,* February 24, 1982.

54. "Some people" includes Beauvoir herself.

55. *La Vieillesse (Old Age)* (Paris, 1970), 567.

56. "The lives of Victor Hugo, Zola, and Chateaubriand were important. . . . Those lives ran together to form a life which was going to be mine" (209). A letter to Simone Jollivet, written in 1926 and published in November 1982 in *Les Temps Modernes,* already revealed the modeling function of accounts of other people's lives in Sartre's imagination: "I can get interested in almost nothing except accounts of the lives of great men. I want to try to find in them a prophecy about *my* life."

57. There is only one woman in this pantheon: Lou Andreas-Salome, whose image seems identified with that of Beauvoir herself. And this is the only case where "adult life is prolonged without a break and old age is not spoken of" (544). In this perspective, Sartre's old age, like other people's, is used as a foil.

58. *La Vieillesse,* 224.

59. *La Femme rompue (The Woman Destroyed)* (Paris, 1967), 84. [Author's italics.—Trans.]

60. *Situations* I, (Paris, 1967), 124.

61. Ibid.

62. *Tout compte fait,* 10.

63. *La Force des choses* I, 502.

64. *Tout compte fait,* 162–63.

65. *Tout compte fait,* 162–63.

66. Jean Mambrino, *Etudes* (April 1982).

67. J. P. Salgas, *Franc-Tireur* (January 1982).

68. Pol Vandromme, *L'Echo du Centre,* December 27, 1981.

69. Jean Chalon, *Figaro-Aurore,* December 4, 1981.

70. The title of this section, "Destroy All These Lying Beauties," is from *La Force des choses* I, 502.

71. *Tout compte fait,* 636.

72. Crouzet in *Commentaires,* 96.

73. *La Force des choses* I, 9.

74. *Tout compte fait,* 634.

75. *La Force des choses* II, 502.

INDEX

Index

386

Index

This collection of essays on and by Jean-Paul Sartre reflects the conviction that his thought and career remain vitally important today, especially in the realms of politics, philosophy, literary studies, and psychology.

The book contains major pieces of Sartre's corpus unknown by the public at large. They show a sophisticated Sartre who is more sensitive to the close interaction of history and ethics than has usually been thought. One such piece is an account of Sartre's notes for lectures that he planned for Cornell University in 1965 but cancelled to protest the American bombing of North Vietnam. The book also includes the first English translation of an interview with philosopher Pierre Verstraeten that originally appeared in a short-lived Belgian journal.

An international assembly of scholars have contributed essays that demonstrate Sartre's contemporary political relevance on such issues as the nuclear menace, the Israeli-Palestinian hostility, and the dynamics of labor conflicts. Other essays discuss Sartre's relationship to Flaubert, de Beauvoir, Gestalt psychology, and his conceptions of the ego and of evil. The collection concludes with a ringing defense of Sartre and Simone de Beauvoir's unsentimental appraisal of life in an essay that celebrates de Beauvoir's unsettling account of Sartre's final years.

Sartre Alive aptly substantiates the conclusion that, more than a decade after his death, Jean-Paul Sartre remains one of the freshest, most contemporary thinkers of the twentieth century.